D0082795

BUDDHISM IN HAWAII

Louise H. Hunter

Buddhism in

UNIVERSITY OF HAWAII PRESS

Hawaii

ITS IMPACT ON A YANKEE COMMUNITY

HONOLULU   1971

Library of Congress Catalog Card Number 76-116878
ISBN 0-87022-355-0
Copyright © 1971 by University of Hawaii Press
Manufactured in the United States of America

To the memory of
Bishop Yemyō Imamura and the
Venerable Ernest Shinkaku Hunt

Contents

Illustrations

Preface

ALL THE RELIGIONS OF MANKIND ARE
ENTITLED TO A RESPECTFUL HEARING, AND
at this critical juncture in East-West relations when an understanding of the major religions of the Orient, especially Buddhism,
commands the urgent attention and consideration of the Occident,
it is sincerely hoped that this study will serve to deepen the layman's
appreciation of the great philosophy-religion bequeathed to the
world by the Wise Man of the Śākyas. Hopefully, too, it will
provide additional insight into the ethnic and socio-economic
roots of religious conflicts and expose the folly of bigotry and
cultural arrogance. In tracing the origin of Buddhism and its
growth and transformation at the crossroads of the Pacific, and in
dealing at length with the reaction of the American-Christian
community to the propagation of Buddhist thought, I have
recorded, unavoidably, a legacy of animosity and intolerance
built upon much misunderstanding and ignorance of the teachings
of Gautama. I have tried along the way to clarify those misconceptions of Buddhism which, though by no means peculiar
to the Hawaiian scene, made it virtually impossible, until just
recently, for Buddhists and Christians to meet on friendly terms
and benefit from the wisdom of their respective traditions. It
is hoped that these and other misconceptions of a similar nature,
springing inevitably from callous indifference or complacent
ignorance, will in the future (in keeping with the new ecumenical
spirit) be minimized by uncompromisingly honest and open-

minded appraisals of the religious aspirations of all men, without which an understanding of the peoples and cultures of the world cannot be achieved.

This book is based on articles from English and Japanese newspapers; numerous personal interviews; documentary materials from the Archives of the State of Hawaii; the correspondence of Christian missionaries and the official reports of the Hawaiian Evangelical Association on file at the Hawaiian Mission Children's Society Library; and various collections of private papers, including those of the late and controversial Reverend Takie Okumura. Most of the Japanese sources consulted are in the East-West Center Library, East Asian Collection, of the University of Hawaii.

I wish to acknowledge my deepest appreciation to the late Venerable Ernest Shinkaku Hunt for allowing me the courtesy of perusing his private correspondence and for sharing with me on many pleasant occasions his personal reminiscences of a half century of missionary work in the Islands. My sincerest aloha goes to Mrs. Yukiko Niiro, my patient and good-natured translator and interpreter, without whose assistance a vital part of this study could not have been completed. Much of the excitement involved in preparing the manuscript involved my late husband, Professor Charles H. Hunter, and I am particularly indebted to him for his many constructive suggestions and professional assistance. Mr. Roy Shinsato deserves special thanks for making the Okumura Papers available to me, and my deepest appreciation is extended to the Reverend Yoshiaki Fujitani of the Honpa Hongwanji for his enthusiastic support of this study.

BUDDHISM IN HAWAII

I have recognized the deepest truth, which is sublime and peace-giving, but difficult to understand; for most men move in a sphere of worldly interests and find their delight in worldly desires. The worldling will not understand the doctrine, for him there is happiness in selfhood only, and the bliss that lies in a complete surrender to truth is unintelligible to him. He will call resignation what to the enlightened mind is the purest joy. He will see annihilation where the perfected one finds immortality. He will regard as death what the conqueror of self knows to be life everlasting. The truth remains hidden from him who is in the bondage of hate and desire. Nirvana remains incomprehensible to the vulgar whose minds are beclouded with worldly interests.

—GAUTAMA THE BUDDHA
Sayings of the Buddha

CHAPTER I

The Buddha and
Buddhism in Japan

THE CONTROVERSY OVER BUDDHISM
WHICH RAGED IN HAWAII FOR HALF A CENTURY
sprang from busy intolerance and willful ignorance of Buddhist
beliefs and values. In order to grasp the full import of the long
and bitter conflict in Hawaii between Japanese Buddhists and
those stern, unrelenting zealots who, while espousing Christianity
in the 'Paradise of the Pacific,' preached without respite that
Buddhism was antidemocratic and an enemy to American ideals,
one must at least be familiar with the teachings of Gautama and
know something of the development of Buddhist thought in
Japan. For persons unacquainted with the Buddhist tradition,
the following pages offer a brief account of what the Buddha
taught and provide a summary of the vital role Buddhism played
in the evolution of Japanese culture.

GAUTAMA THE BUDDHA

The founder of Buddhism was born about 563 B.C. in Lumbini
Grove on the outskirts of the city of Kapilavastu in the valley
of the Ganges.* He was the son of Queen Māyā and King
Suddhodana, a rāja of the Śākya clan of warriors. His parents

*Unless otherwise indicated, materials in this chapter concerning the life and
teachings of Gautama the Buddha are based on Henry Clarke Warren, *Buddhism
In Translations* (New York: Atheneum Press, 1963); the writings of Walpola
Rahula, an eminently qualified and enlightened Indian scholar; the basic works

named him Siddhārtha, which means the All-Successful One, and his contemporaries called him Gautama, a name borne also by others of his clan. The millions who later followed his Path of Wisdom and Compassion called him Śākyamuni, which means the Wise Man of the Śākyas.

Gautama's mother died a few days after giving birth to him, and he was reared by his aunt in a sheltered environment of ease and luxury consonant with his father's rank and wealth. He grew up, the scriptures say, to be a remarkably handsome lad and at the age of sixteen in a contest of arms he won his beautiful wife, the Princess Yasodhara, who bore him one son, Rāhula.

Riding out of the palace courtyard one day into the streets of Kapilavastu, Siddhārtha saw for the first time and in rapid succession, an old man, a sick man, and a dead man. The spectacle of human suffering, of the tragic in the commonplace, profoundly affected him, and he rode back to the palace in deep distress. The frivolities of court life soon became intolerable; its sensual delights, insipid. Outside the walls of his father's palace there were other old men perishing in loneliness, other sick men languishing in despair. There were other dead men: the living dead, bound to the Wheel of Rebirth by their avarice and lusts, and the departed dead, doomed by selfish cravings to endless rebirths in a world of fleeting pleasures and manifold sorrows.

Reflecting on the vicissitudes of life and the foolish abandon with which men pursue the paltry and insubstantial, Siddhārtha was completely overcome, and the tides of natural affection that swelled in his breast for Yasodhara and his child overflowed suddenly in a mighty surge of universal compassion. So it came to pass, the scriptures say, that one evening he bade a silent farewell to his sleeping wife and infant son, stole out of the palace, and rode out on his stallion to the edge of the city. There he dismounted, cut off his long black hair, donned the robes of a mendicant, and disappeared into the night. This was the Great Renunciation. A young man, who had everything, had renounced everything, to go in search of a truth that could rescue not only himself but all men from the fetters of egoism and rebirth in a world of suffering.

In his search for wisdom, Gautama wandered in and about Benares for several years looking into the minds and hearts of many men. He consulted with the proud and sanctimonious who mistook arrogant erudition for wisdom, and he encountered the smug brahmans (priests) who appeased vengeful gods and atoned for their moral indigence by slaughtering animals. Following the advice of other so-called wise men, he practiced the severest

of Christmas Humphreys, the renowned and distinguished English Buddhist; the authoritative commentaries of the late Daisetz T. Suzuki, Japan's foremost Buddhist philosopher.

mortifications until his haggard, emaciated appearance showed that he, even more than they, was ready to die for a truth that could satisfy the mind and pacify the heart. But after six years of ascetic practices, which left him broken in body and on the brink of death, Gautama was no closer to his goal. Then he began to realize that those who thought themselves wise were in ignorance; that no gods are worthy of homage if they do not touch the hearts of men and set them afire with compassion for suffering humanity; that spiritual riches do not come from physical deprivation; and that wisdom does not emanate from holy books if it is not first mirrored in the minds of men.

Gautama then went south of the Ganges into the town of Uruvelā. On the banks of the river Nerañjara, he sat at the foot of a gigantic fig tree and vowed not to move until he attained Enlightenment or Perfect Wisdom. Then, say the scriptures, hosts of Māra, the Evil One, besieged him with many vile temptations. But Siddhārtha persevered in his meditations, and one day in May, when the moon was full and the earth stood still in joyful expectation, the thirty-five-year-old erstwhile heir to Indian royalty plumbed the deepest secrets of the universe, fathomed the mystery of life and death, and beheld a way to transcend the anxieties and griefs of human existence. At that moment of extraordinary insight, Siddhārtha Gautama became the Buddha, which means the All-Enlightened One.

The vision of Reality that flashed through the Buddha's mind and illumined the lives of the numberless men and women who later trod his Noble Eightfold Path had set his countenance aglow with a serenity that bore witness to all who saw him that he had found what he was looking for. Yet he was not content. The potential for Enlightenment and the realization of Nirvana was latent in all men from the noblest to the most venal. So Siddhārtha arose from his 'state of exalted calm' and transfigured by a truth which had truly set him free, aflame with compassion for those still bound to the Wheel of Rebirth, he went out to teach those of lesser minds and fainter hearts who through many karmic existences had anxiously awaited the birth and awakening of this Blessed One. To those who hungered for a fuller life and the certainty of moral justice, Śākyamuni bequeathed his holy Dharma, or Teaching.

Siddhārtha thought first of the hermits and ascetics who dwelt in desolate haunts of self-mortification and whose agony of spirit he had known so well. At the Deer Park near Benares, five ascetics listened to him as he spoke gently to them of the futility of ascetic excesses and of his better Middle Way to spiritual maturity, which avoided both the folly of the sensualist, who tried to compensate for deep-seated inadequacies by exploiting nature, and the vanity of the ascetic, who isolated himself from nature to practice mortifications ignoble and useless. The audience of five, who heard the Enlightened One's first sermon and experienced at last the peace of mind they had so earnestly sought, embraced the Dharma and became the first members of the Buddhist Sangha, or brotherhood of monks. The Buddha then went among the rich and the poor, the well-born and the lowly, among queens and prostitutes, brahmans and untouchables, teaching them tactfully by parables and by personal example, and considering always the different dispositions of their minds.

During his ministry of some forty-five years, Gautama was asked many questions which 'tended not to edification.' There were those who wanted to know about the will and the ways of the gods; Māluṅkyāputta, a vain and querulous philosopher, demanded to know whether the world was eternal; and Vaccha, a wandering ascetic, wanted to know if the saints existed after death. But the Buddha dismissed such inquiries, because they would not, he said, lead to the cessation of suffering and peace of mind.[1] Human anguish cannot be alleviated by postulating the existence of inscrutable or capricious deities, and the man who escapes the Wheel of Rebirth and attains Nirvana is superior to whatever gods that be, for even they are subject to the cycle of births and deaths. Nor can the evil that men do be nullified by presumptuous and misleading hopes of an undeserved happier future. He who believes that the consequences of his acts will be erased by divine fiat lives in ignorance, for the gods will not erase the only means whereby men may learn to distinguish between good and evil, light and darkness, and ignorance and wisdom.[2]

When Gautama left unelucidated all such things which tended not to edification, Māluṅkyāputta angrily protested. Until he could get satisfactory answers to his questions, he would not, he said, make any effort to lead the religious life. The Blessed One then likened the philosopher to a man who had been wounded with a poisonous arrow yet refused to have it removed until he had learned the caste, the name, the class, and the place of origin of the man who had wounded him. The endless speculations and disputes of philosophers concerning That Reality which transcends all human conceptions of it will not lead to the cessation of suffering, but only to confusion and emotional turmoil, to bitterness and animosity among men. The metaphysical preoccupations of priests and philosophers will never, the Buddha admonished, help men to bear their sorrows and shortcomings with fortitude and serenity; these preoccupations are, rather, a jungle, a wilderness, a puppet-show, and when added to man's already sufficient burdens, they further impede his realization of Nirvana. He who is truly wise, said Śākyamuni, will maintain a

Noble Silence about matters which disquiet men's minds and trouble their hearts.

Thus Gautama did not satisfy the curious or complacent who harassed him with questions which could add nothing to man's moral or spiritual stature. There were those, too, who rejected the Dharma outright—those who were too irresponsible to accept the Enlightened One's teaching that one can never get more out of life than one puts into it—and those who were too morally indolent to take seriously Gautama's faith that tomorrow and the future could be better than today only if men chose and struggled to make it so. But there were many among the humane and strong in spirit and among the weak and humble, too, who, inspired by Gautama's conviction that all men could attain Enlightenment through a selfless love of others, found solace, new strength, and a deeper purpose in life in the Buddha's message. And to those who understood that the measure of a man lies not in the thought he gives to his own soul or the inscrutable ways of the gods, but in the treatment he gives to his fellow men and his efforts to better the lot of mankind, Gautama bequeathed his sacred Dharma. To those who trod his Noble Eightfold Path toward the realization of the Oneness of Life and the brotherhood of man, he promised the consummate bliss of Nirvana, where selfishness and sorrow are no more.

In the course of a long and fruitful ministry, Gautama gathered together some sixty disciples and bade them go forth to preach the Dharma. At the age of eighty, when death was near, he called to his side those whom he loved. Asking them not to grieve for him, reminding them that all component things are impermanent, he said: 'And now, O priests, I take my leave of you; all the constituents of being are transitory; work out your own salvation with diligence.' Then the All-Enlightened One passed into *Parinirvana*, that everlasting ecstasy of highest consciousness for which all men are destined but which none can describe.

THE DHARMA: THE FOUR NOBLE TRUTHS AND THE NOBLE EIGHTFOLD PATH

Buddhism teaches that most men are born in a state of ignorance that blinds them to the facts of existence and binds them to the Wheel of Rebirth in the ever-flowing, ever-changing stream of life. Everything is incessant metamorphoses, and every person remains a *samsārin*, or wanderer on the road of life, until, by bursting the barriers of egoism, he attains Enlightenment and experiences Nirvana, in which the divine element within, 'having completely detached itself—by the force of its own natural expansion—from what is individual, impermanent, and phenomenal, embraces and becomes one with the Universal, the Eternal, and the Real.'[3]

The First Noble Truth affirms that since all that exists is *anitya*, or impermanent, all temporal existence is *dukkha*, or misery-ridden, fraught on every side with grief and anxiety. Lasting happiness can be found nowhere in samsāra (the temporal world of change and impermanence) for nothing endures. Joy gives way to sorrow, hope to despair, love to hate—or to indifference, and peace to war. Man, too, for all his incommunicable uniqueness, is subject to ceaseless change and to old age, sickness, and death; his nature is restless, inconstant, and ever-changing for he possesses no separate soul which sets him apart from the rest of nature. That which 'pertains to any one human being is not immortal; and that which is immortal and unchanging is not the possession of any one human being.'[4] Thus the nature of man is *anātman*, or non-separate-soul. Human personality is the result of a particular combination of the five *skandhas*, or causally conditioned elements of existence inherent, actually or potentially, in all forms of life: physical form (*rūpa*); feeling or sensation (*vedanā*); perception and the assimilation of sensations (*saññā*); impressions resulting from *vedanā* and emotional reactions (*sankhāra*); and self-consciousness (*viññāna*). Gautama did not deny the existence of an integrating consciousness or temporal ego which could perceive, interpret, and react to experience. What he *did* reject was the doctrine of transmigration of souls. There could be, he said, no bodily transportation of a spiritual essence from one place to another because man is a temporal being made up of a series of conjoined phenomena, and thus has no more reality apart from such phenomena than does a chariot devoid of the body, wheels, and pole of which it is composed. The self or ego in the Buddha's thought is thus simply a growing, evolving bundle of attributes or changing series of mental and emotional states, and there is no unique entity in man which survives death in a permanently unchanged and glorified (or unregenerate) state. At death the *skandhas* which made up a 'human becoming' disperse to form the initial composite of another temporal existence; thus death is 'transition from one perishable form to another.'[5] It is the cumulative effects of a person's thoughts and actions which are reborn, not some ghostly entity or soul. In the case of the saint who attains Nirvana and withdraws from samsāra, the *skandhas* disappear for good.

At no time did the Buddha say that the saint who is not reborn lives no more. Some scholars therefore have concluded that while Gautama assuredly did not believe that man possesses an immutable, separative inner soul, neither did he deny the existence of that divine spark or spirit in man which is equated in the Upanishads with the Brahman or spiritual Absolute.* Be that as it may, the law of all temporal reality, according to the Dharma, is one of continual transformation.

Enlightenment and Nirvana, furthermore, cannot be attained in a single lifetime. Each new life is the effect of previous earthly sojourns and the cause of subsequent rebirths. This is the Law of Karma. The circumstances of man's pilgrimages depend on the energy force of volitional actions (karma) which is carried over from one existence to the next. As a man sows, so shall he reap.

> We suffer from ourselves alone,
> For we must reap what we have sown
> The Karma of each deed
> Till we have learned the self to slay
> And live the Teaching day by day
> From sorrow's fetters freed.[6]

As long as a man imagines that he is sufficient unto himself and strives to preserve a mean and egocentric pattern of life, rebirth in samsāra, with all its attendant ills, is inescapable. The Second Noble Truth states therefore that the cause of suffering is *trishnā*, the frantic desire to pursue and perpetuate a self-centered and vacuous existence. Man is lured back to earth by his insatiable appetite for ephemeral pleasures.

The Third Noble Truth heralds the eventual liberation of all mankind from the Wheel of Rebirth. Since all that exists is the manifestation of one indivisible Life, and dependent on the same karmic law of cause and effect, men are truly brothers, reflecting the same divine element and possessing, one and all, the potential for Enlightenment. There is thus a Way to the extinction of *trishnā*, of release from the karmic cycle of births and deaths, and to the realization of Nirvana.

The Fourth Noble Truth, the Way itself, is the Noble Eightfold Path, a gradational course in character development through straight thinking and generous living within the Law of Karma.[7] The Path distinguishes between reality and illusion, and knowledge and self-deception; it leads gradually from insatiable cravings (the folly of *trishnā*) and the egoism of asceticism to an inner peace and contentment born of humility and moral integrity. The steps of the Path are Right Viewpoint, Right Mindedness, Right Speech, Right Action, Right Living, Right Effort, Right Attentiveness, and Right Concentration. The Path forbids idle talk, all unconscionable lying, and any use of language which creates bitterness or divisions among men; it counsels against sexual behavior which attempts to compensate for inner inadequacies

---

*See Christmas Humphreys, *Buddhism* (Great Britain, 1954), pp. 20–21 and 85–88; and Edmund Holmes, *The Creed of Buddha* (London, 1957), esp. pp. 99–135.

by extracting pleasure from others; it prohibits cruelty, violence, and the destruction of life; it encourages the practice of *mettā*, that active goodwill and selfless concern for others which is the first of the *Brahma Vihāras*, or Sublime States of Consciousness, through which one attains buddhahood and the bliss of Nirvana.

SUBSEQUENT BUDDHIST THOUGHT: THERAVĀDA AND MAHĀYĀNA BUDDHISM

After the death of the Enlightened One, Gautama's disciples, in deference to their master's command to work out their own salvation with diligence, strove assiduously to achieve the arhat ideal of personal sanctity. Arhats were 'worthy ones,' serene and self-possessed, who had tread the Noble Eightfold Path and attained the Goal.[8] Those who later sought to join their venerable ranks and rest content in the peace of Nirvana were said to subscribe to the Theravāda, or Doctrine of the Elders.

As the centuries rolled on, a growing number of Buddhists thought and spoke more often of another ideal which they believed to be closer to the heart of Gautama's teaching than the vocation of the arhats. These schismatics within the Sangha believed that selfless love was a more potent force than was wisdom in effecting transformation of character. They exalted, therefore, not those who had merely attained Enlightenment, but rather the magnanimous bodhisattvas, or buddhas of compassion, who, remaining acutely attuned to the suffering and hopes of mankind, had taken pity on the unenlightened, yearned for their emancipation, and vowed not to enter Nirvana until the Goal had been reached by all. These bodhisattvas, embodiments of boundless compassion, had lived holy lives through many rebirths and had accumulated thereby a 'Treasury of Merit,' or vast storehouse of karmic energy, which was diffused in 'rays of light and love' among men whose inner defilements had rendered them all but helpless to save themselves.[9] Before the selfless benevolence of the bodhisattvas, it was said, the whole of Nature bowed, for theirs was the 'Power in the Universe that makes for good,'[10] the love that makes the world go round, overflowing and permeating the stream of saṃsāra and altering even the unbending course of karma by overcoming evil with good.[11]

The bodhisattva ideal of world compassion, an outgrowth of the seeds of compassion sown and nurtured by Gautama, became the single most distinguishing feature of Mahāyāna Buddhism, *mahā* meaning great, and *yāna* meaning vehicle or career. In addition, the Mahāyāna schools of Buddhism shared with the Theravāda the following basic tenets of Gautama's Dharma: (1) all component things are *anitya*, or impermanent, including man, whose nature is anātman, or non-separate-soul; (2) all existence is governed by, and rebirth occurs in accordance with, the law of cause and effect, karma; (3) man is therefore the architect of his fate, fashioning his future with the karma of his thoughts and deeds, good and bad; (4) Life in all its impermanent forms is indivisible and immortal; (5) death is thus a transitional state from one form of That Life to another; and (6) the cessation of suffering and attainment of Nirvana come with an intuitive realization of the Oneness of Life and the brotherhood of man. The Mahāyāna sects envisioned, too, the existence of many buddha-realms, infinite in number and splendor,* each with its corresponding buddhas and bodhisattvas who invite men to tread the Eightfold Path and to enjoy, as a reward or stepping stone to Nirvana, radiant 'heavens of joy and blessedness.'[12] Mahāyāna Buddhists believed, also, that all buddhas, past, present, and future, including Siddhārtha Gautama, were but temporal manifestations of the Eternal Buddha, or Dharmakāya, Infinite Source of all Life, and Fountainhead of Love and Wisdom.[13] Mahāyāna Buddhism predominates to this day in Tibet, Mongolia, China, Korea, and Japan.†

BUDDHISM IN JAPAN

From India, Buddhism spread to Ceylon, Burma, Thailand, and Cambodia, then northward to China. From China it reached Korea about A.D. 372 and became the state religion by the sixth century.[14] Buddhism was introduced into Japan in 552 when the ruler of the Korean kingdom of Paekche, desiring military aid, sent the Japanese emperor a Buddhist image and some sūtras (scriptures).[15] Later the eminent scholar Prince Shōtoku (574–622) saw to it that Buddhism took root and flourished in Japanese soil, and in 749 the Emperor Shōmu declared himself the humble servant of the Three Treasures—the Buddha, the Dharma, and the Sangha.[16]

As Buddhism entered the mainstream of the life of Asian countries, it was readily adapted to local conditions and amalgamated with crude indigenous beliefs. In China, monks taught that Buddhism was no different from Taoism or Confucianism, that truth was 'like the wild goose that receives different names when it flies to different regions.'[17] Taoist deities were enshrined in Buddhist temples and bodhisattvas took on the characteristics

---

*Buddhism has never denied the possibility of life in a glorious hereafter. It does, however, deny that any kind of life experience apart from Nirvana, or oneness with the Absolute (Dharmakāya) is *permanent*.

†Some scholars are still in doubt as to which school of thought is the older, so neither the Theravāda nor the Mahāyāna may be considered more 'orthodox' than the other. Ancient scriptures depict Gautama approving Mahāyāna ideas, and some of the Mahāyāna texts are at least as old as any surviving portion of the Theravāda Canon.

of native deities. As early as A.D. 166, a shrine was built in the imperial palace honoring Huang Ti (the Yellow Emperor), Lao Tze (the founder of Taoism), and the Buddha. In its own homeland, by the sixth century, Buddhism became infected with perversive Tantrism, a system of magic spells and charms devised to ward off evil spirits; and by the seventh century, the Emperor Harsha was celebrating sacred rites in honor of the Buddha, Śiva (a Hindu goddess), and the Sun.[18]

In Japan, too, exponents of the Dharma compromised with indigenous beliefs. The native religion was Shinto, or *Kami-no-Michi*, the Way of the Gods, and its objects of reverence were called *kami*, meaning superior or above.[19] Most kami were supernatural forces, good or evil, whose *mi-tama* (spirits) were believed to reside in Shinto shrines. Other kami were good and bad ghosts of the dead. There were also the kami of nature—of the earth and sky, and of the wind and sea. The kamikaze were the divine winds that long ago destroyed foreign vessels which threatened to invade the land of the gods.* The most venerated of the living kami was the emperor, who was believed to be descended from the most venerated member of the Shinto pantheon, the august Sun Goddess, Amaterasu-Ō-Mikami. From the point of view of the common people, the emperor was far-separated, majestic, and worthy of reverence; thus he was called the distant kami.[20]

Gradually Buddhist and Shinto beliefs were merged in various forms. The most important of these was called Ryōbu Shintō, and in keeping with the Ryōbu notion of *honji suijaku* (original substance manifests traces),[21] Shinto gods were in time identified with the buddhas, and even minor native deities were declared to be manifestations of the Eternal Buddha. At the same time, into the buddha-realms of joy and blessedness, the Shinto pantheon was admitted with its '800 myriads of *kami*.'[22]

Despite such curious intermixtures of Buddhist and Shinto beliefs, the best elements of Japanese culture had their roots in authentic Buddhist tradition. Buddhism introduced painting, sculpture, and some of the oldest types of Chinese architecture.[23] During the eighth century, the capital at Nara, situated amid wooded hills and timbered mountains, became a Buddhist paradise of exquisitely carved three- and five-storied pagodas. Majestic temples raised in later centuries depicted the enlightened ones in gorgeous, larger-than-life iconography. Buddhist monks introduced the arts of flower arrangement, landscape gardening,

*In 1281, Japan was invaded by 150,000 Mongols, but before they could deploy their forces ashore, a typhoon wiped out the fleet. The Japanese divined that the typhoon was a kamikaze sent by the gods to protect Japan from the foreign invaders. This incident was glorified in the historical tradition of the country and bolstered Japanese delusions that Nippon was invulnerable.

and the tea ceremony; the greatest and most revered works of Japanese thought came from the pens of monks who, meditating in isolated mountain retreats, wrote from the heights of mysticism on the Oneness of Life, the compassion of the buddhas, and the bliss of Nirvana.[24]

Buddhism also intensified the Japanese love of life and nature. *Yūgen*, an old aesthetic ideal savoring the sweetness and mystery of the fleeting moment, was reflected in the classical noh dramas, symbolizing the eternal in the temporal.[25] Japanese literature was permeated with *aware*, a nostalgic love for the innocent pleasures of life evoked in poets by a poignant awareness 'of a sight or sound, of its beauty and . . . perishability.'[26]

The first decade of the ninth century in Japan witnessed the introduction from China of two great schools of the Mahāyāna. In 805 Saichō, a monk of Chinese descent, who exemplified 'the highest ideals of the Buddhist priesthood,'[27] brought to Japan the intellectual Tendai sect (in Chinese, *T'ien-t'ai*) and later built a monastic center on Mt. Hiei, northeast of Kyoto, which became the most venerated seat of learning in Japan.*[28] The esoteric Shingon (True Word) sect (considered the most 'superstitious' of Buddhist sects by those who know little about it) was introduced to Japan by the social reformer and religious genius Kūkai, who became best known to the Japanese people by his posthumous name, Kōbō Daishi, meaning Propagator of the Law.

THE POPULARIZATION OF BUDDHISM

During the tenth and eleventh centuries, capital aristocrats in Kyoto lost control over the political life of Japan to provincial lords who managed large estates and defended them with armies of sword-fighting retainers called samurai. In the twelfth century one of the daimyō, or great names, among the military clans settled down in Kamakura, set up the *bakufu*, or military government, and obtained from the imperial court the title of Sei-i-tai-Shōgun, Barbarian-Subduing-General and defender of the empire.[29] During the next four centuries, great clans waged intermittent and violent warfare against one another for control of Japan. The emperor, meanwhile, reigned in impotent splendor and at times in great penury.

During these years of feudal warfare and social turmoil, Buddhism became a mass movement. Popularized by itinerant preachers, it found its way into the humblest household. But the Buddhism embraced by the common people was not the Buddhism which had appealed to court intellectuals in the earlier centuries. The idea of attaining buddhahood and Nirvana by meditation and self-discipline was often bypassed in favor of other facets of

*The capital was transferred from Nara to Kyoto in 794.

the religion which could more readily be made intelligible to the masses.[30] Several sects sprang into prominence in the twelfth and thirteenth centuries, and the Pure Land sects became, by far, the most popular.

The Pure Land school of Mahāyāna Buddhism originated in China about A.D. 400 and was popularized in Japan by Hōnen (1133–1211) and his protégé Shinran (1173–1262), respective founders of the Jōdo-shū (Pure Land sect) and the Jōdo-Shin-shū (True Pure Land sect). Central to the teaching of Hōnen and Shinran was a grateful recognition of the compassion of *Hōzō Bosatsu* (Bodhisattva Hōzō) who long ago, like Siddhārtha Gautama, had renounced a throne to bring light to the ignorant and love to the hopeless. Eons ago, it was said, Hōzō took an 'Original Vow' to become a universal savior, promising to rescue from their bad karma all those who called upon him in humility and good faith.[31] Through the course of numerous rebirths, Hōzō accumulated much merit, turned over the karma of his good deeds for the emancipation of other people, and finally, through his perfect and selfless compassion, became the Buddha Amida, that is, the Buddha of Infinite Light and Love.[32] The energy force of Amida's love would in time, it was said, overcome the bad karma of all men who with grateful hearts and perfect faith devotedly recited the nembutsu (invocation) 'Namu Amida Butsu,' Hail to the Buddha of Infinite Light and Love.*

Hōnen and Shinran did not believe that most men were capable of following Gautama's *shōdo-mon,* or path of good works.[33] Yet at the heart of the universe they could see nothing but light and love. They reasoned, therefore, that a man is enlightened and eventually experiences Nirvana through a gradual purification of the emotions and a transformation of character effected in the human heart by the wonderful, omnipotent love of Amida Buddha. This was *Jōdo-mon,* the path of perfect trust; it was *tariki-kyō,* the doctrine of liberation by faith, as opposed to *jiriki-kyō,* the doctrine of self-help, or attainment of Enlightenment by one's own efforts.[34]

At the heart of the Pure Land teaching lay Gautama's own assurance that there is no reaching the Goal without self-forgetfulness, that as long as men are preoccupied with egocentric desires or obsessed by their own wickedness and vile inclinations, they will find no peace. So Hōnen and Shinran focused attention on the Other-Power, the Power of Love, and to those who argued that *Jōdo-mon* implicitly condoned wrongdoing by an over-reliance on the Vow, the followers of Shinran replied

*Nembutsu, meaning 'to think of the Buddha,' is a Japanese reading of the Sanskrit phrase, 'namo amitābhabuddhāya,' meaning Adoration of the Buddha of Infinite Light. See Daisetz T. Suzuki, *Mysticism: Christian and Buddhist, The Eastern and Western Way* (New York, 1962), pp. 123, 128.

that the evil that men do is the result of past karmic defilements, not of reliance on Amida Buddha, and that no man was ever made worse by putting his faith in a Higher Power.[35]

Devotees of the Pure Land sects who left the world with trust in Amida Buddha and goodwill toward their fellow men looked forward to a joyous afterlife in the Western Paradise or buddha-realm over which Amida presided, where Enlightenment was finally attained and Nirvana ensured. To some, the Pure Land of Amida was literally a place of incomparable beauty; to other less ordinary-minded persons, it symbolized, as it does today, 'union with the Eternal Buddha.'[36]

Hōnen himself founded the great Chion-in, mother temple of the Jōdo sect in Kyoto. In the same city, ten years after the death of her father, Shinran's daughter supervised the construction of a small Jōdo-Shin temple upon which the Emperor Kameyama later conferred the title Kuon Jitsujō Amida Hongwanji, Temple of the Original Vow of Amida Who Achieved Enlightenment in Eons Long Past.[37] Hongwanji means Temple of the Original Vow, and the Kyoto Hongwanji became the official headquarters of the Jōdo-Shin (True Pure Land) sect which centuries later became the most predominant Buddhist sect in the Hawaiian Islands.

Two other sects (*shū*) became extremely popular during the feudal era—the Nichiren-shū and the Zen-shū. Nichiren Buddhism was founded in the thirteenth century by a fisherman's son whose name was synonymous with the faith. After years of study in the Tendai monastery of Mt. Hiei, Nichiren 'discovered' that the *Hokkekyō*, or *Lotus Sūtra*, contained the whole teaching of Sākyamuni and was thus, he asserted, the sole key to Enlightenment and the attainment of Nirvana.[38] Nichiren even affirmed that the very name *Hokkekyō* was worthy of worship—hence, the prayer to be heard ever since on the lips of his followers: 'Namu Myōhō-renge-kyō,' Hail to the Lotus Sūtra of the Wonderful Law.[39]

Much of what the fisherman's son taught, especially his emphasis on moral perseverance and self-sacrifice, was in the finest tradition of Mahāyāna Buddhism. But he was intolerant of views other than his own, a trait denounced by his beloved Sākyamuni yet common, then as now, among persons who imagine they have discovered the whole Truth and the only Truth. Nichiren vilified the teachings of Hōnen as a perversion of Buddhism. Hōnen, he ranted, was the enemy of all Buddhas, all scriptures, all sages, and all people, a contemptible traitor who had enchanted and led astray thousands of Buddhists by his infernal *tariki-kyō*. Official recognition of Pure Land teachings had enabled the evil kami, he said, to wreak terrible havoc on Nippon.[40] Nichiren attributed the earthquake of 1257 and the hurricane of the following year to patronage of heresy by persons in high places.[41] Japan would never, Nichiren insisted, enjoy lasting peace and prosperity until she embraced his, and *only* his, interpretation of Buddhism.

The Way of Zen or Ch'an, as it was known in China, was very different from the Way of the Pure Land sects or the doctrines of the Nichiren-shū. Zen, which came from the Sanskrit word *dhyāna*, meaning intuitive vision or simple meditation, had nothing to do with the veneration of sūtras or the doctrine of deliverance through some Other-Power. Gautama had taught that the Buddha-nature was innate in all men; Enlightenment and Nirvana therefore could be realized, Zen masters said, by the practice of intense concentration which would lead to a direct seeing into the nature of Reality. The instrument of Enlightenment, or the light which illumines, was thus the intuitive faculty of mind. Zen scholars also laid much stress on the practice of *za-zen*, sitting in quiet meditation; and a great deal of attention was given to the importance of self-discipline, a virtue which appealed enormously to the samurai, whose warriors' code of bushidō (selfless loyalty and fearlessness in the face of death) owed much to the ethics of Zen.[42]

Zen reached China in the fifth century through the efforts of the renowned Indian missionary Bodhidharma.* Later it was introduced to Japan by two eminent scholars, Eisai and Dōgen. In the twelfth century, Eisai, confident that the propagation of Zen would protect the prosperity of the Empire, founded the Rinzai-shū in Kyoto and Kamakura. Dōgen founded the Sōtō-shū in 1227.[43]

With all the diverse means (*upāya*) they embraced to bring the Dharma into the hearts and lives of the people, the Mahāyāna sects of Buddhism (focusing attention on the Buddha-nature latent in all) summoned all men, the rich and the poor, the weak and the strong, the virtuous and the ignorant, to persevere in the quest for Enlightenment by meditating on the Four Noble Truths and emulating the selfless compassion of Śākyamuni. They exalted, above all, the ideal of the bodhisattva, or savior-buddha, who embodied in this and all other worlds the boundless mercy of the *Muga-no-Taiga*, or Great Selfless Self, from which, it was said, there continually flowed 'a never-drying stream of sympathy and love.'[44]

THE DECLINE OF BUDDHISM

As far back as the twelfth century, a distant kami (emperor) admitted that there were three things which not even he could control—the fall of the dice, the waters of the River Kamo, and the monks of Hieizan.[45] And during the centuries of feudal

*Recent scholarship places Bodhidharma in China as early as A.D. 470–480.

warfare which followed, the temporal power of Buddhism mounted alarmingly.[46] Temples and monasteries acquired huge areas of tax-exempt land, and Buddhist monks fiercely defended their interests with the help of hired mercenaries who descended on the capital whenever those interests were threatened. In 1568 Oda Nobunaga, an eccentric and impetuous feudal baron who ruled over three provinces east of Kyoto, seized the capital and became virtual ruler of Japan.[47] To consolidate his power and to bring the whole country under one sword, he boldly set out to crush the Buddhist strongholds which menaced his rule. In 1571 Nobunaga stormed the holy mountain-fortress of Mt. Hiei, burned its three thousand buildings and massacred its twenty thousand inhabitants.[48] Inflamed but not satiated, intent on spilling more Buddhist blood, he met his nemesis, finally, against the determined forces of the Jōdo-Shinshū. In vain Nobunaga laid siege for ten years to the Hongwanji in Osaka; foot soldiers of the faith marched from all over the country to battle 'to save their beloved Order from the enemy of the law.'[49]

But Buddhism never fully recovered from the persecutions of Nobunaga, and with the establishment of the Tokugawa shogunate (1600–1868) and the military unification of the empire, it ceased to nourish the intellectual life of the country. There was nothing in Gautama's Dharma to buttress the military dictatorship of the Tokugawas. It was the Confucian ethic, with its rigid, hierarchical classification of society and its idealization of unflinching loyalty to rulers, which supplied the rationale of the new feudal order.[50] Tokugawa administrators meanwhile kept a watchful eye on all centers of Buddhist activity. Registered membership in Buddhist temples was made compulsory; all branch temples were placed under the strict jurisdiction of the headquarters of their respective sects; teachers in the *terakoya*, or temple schools, were compelled to teach loyalty to the shōgun; and monks were shrewdly distracted from political matters by generous shogunate 'grants' for scriptural studies and exegeses. Ieyasu, the first and most famous of the Tokugawa potentates, had capitalized early on an opportunity to weaken the power of the Hongwanji. When a quarrel arose over hereditary succession to abbotship of the Kyoto temple, he gave one of the disputants a tract of land for a separate temple, thereby splitting the Order by setting the *Higashi*, or East, Hongwanji apart from the *Nishi* (*Honpa*), or West, Hongwanji.[51] The power and prestige of Buddhism were thus steadily undermined, and its intellectual life and spiritual vitality effectively strangled.

The decline of Buddhism was also reflected in a transformation of Japanese society which submerged Buddhist ideals in a wave of secular concerns. Ukiyo, the sorrowful world of dust and grief, became an alluring 'floating world' of sensuous delights.[52]

Great art was eclipsed by fashionable art glorifying brute power and the pleasures of wine, women, and song;[53] popular *kabuki* plays, depicting violence and vulgar themes with bizarre make-up and exaggerated gestures, displaced the sedate noh dramas inspired by Buddhist mysticism.

During the eighteenth and nineteenth centuries, moreover, the Dharma was trampled underfoot by a militant Shinto revival which culminated in deification of the imperial head of state.[54] Native scholars had spent much of the leisure time afforded by the long peace of the Tokugawa regime in the study of Japanese history and mythology. Led by the famous Shinto apologist Motoori Norinaga, scholars of the *kokugaku*, or national classics school, spearheaded a movement in the eighteenth century to restore the emperor to actual sovereignty. Amaterasu-Ō-Mikami, they declared, had bequeathed to the distant kami, and to him alone, the right to rule the country. Later the Mito school of historians, emphasizing the eternity of the imperial succession, focused similar attention on the person of the emperor and enjoined the worship of the reigning Mikado—a practice which became, by the middle of the nineteenth century, 'the most widely accepted and compelling belief among the people.'[55] All duties and obligations to the feudal daimyō and even to the shōgun, said the Shintoists, should be transferred to the god-emperor. *Sonnō*, reverence for and exclusive loyalty to His Imperial Majesty, became the sole basis of morality.[56] Meanwhile Buddhism was castigated as a foreign heresy; its ceremonies and funeral rites were scorned; and its priesthood was censured as unfit to administer to the needs of the Japanese people.[57]

In addition to the increasing popularity of these new religio-political dogmas, seeds sown during the Tokugawa period had germinated into widespread social unrest. Peasants, hard put to survive droughts and famines, had long resented high taxes and exploitation by the samurai. Meanwhile, the latter, who continued to measure wealth in bushels of rice and depended on a roused peasantry for their subsistence, soon found themselves heavily in debt to a new and powerful merchant class.[58] Even before the ships of Commodore Perry cruised into Uraga Bay, important segments of Japanese society thus were ready and even clamoring for a change. When the great Sei-i-tai-Shōgun was forced to submit to the demands of the Western 'barbarian,' malcontents quickly rallied round the popular Mito slogan, 'Sonnō Jōi,' Revere the Emperor, Repel the Barbarians![59] Discontented samurai transferred their allegiance from shōgun to emperor and joined the forces of the Kyoto court to restore imperial rule.[60] Civil war broke out, and by April 1868, imperial sovereignty was restored. The following month, in an armed clash between imperialist and former shogunate combatants, forces of the new regime seized control of Yokohama—a minor incident, actually, but one which caused the greatest annoyance to one Eugene Van Reed, an American businessman in nearby Kanagawa, who had just concluded negotiations with ousted shogunate officials on a matter of the greatest importance to the government of the Hawaiian Kingdom.[61]

CHAPTER 2

Japanese Immigration to Hawaii

THE ANTAGONISM WHICH YEARLY
WAXED MORE INTENSE BETWEEN AMERICANS
and the Japanese in Hawaii during the first four decades of
the twentieth century was provoked by the animosity of religious
difference and mutual distrust of race. At the same time the
recurrence of economic disputes of long standing frequently
reignited smoldering racial and religious antipathies which during
these years shattered all hopes for amity between East and West. To
view in the widest perspective possible the clashes between Orient
and Occident at the crossroads of the Pacific, it is necessary to recall
the economic situation as well as the social and religious conditions
which prevailed in the Islands when Oriental immigrants were
first imported to work on sugar plantations.

Throughout the long and prosperous reign of Kamehameha III
(1825–1854), whaling ships that plowed the North Pacific and
flocked to Hawaiian ports to replenish supplies became symbolic
of Hawaii's economic prosperity. But in the late 1860s, whales
became scarce and the new petroleum industry replaced whale oil
as a cheap lubricant. During the Civil War, too, Confederate
commerce destroyers seized forty-six of the whaling vessels, and
a few years later the Arctic ice destroyed thirty-three more. By
the early 1870s, the 'Golden Age' of whaling was no more.[1]

Before the familiar ships disappeared altogether from Hawaiian
ports, businessmen, fortunately, had found another and more stable
basis for the Islands' economy. During the 1850s, small sugar
plantations had combined to form larger ones; better fertilizers and

methods of irrigation were introduced; planters had experimented successfully with centrifugal machines which separated sugar from molasses; steam engines and agricultural implements were brought into the kingdom duty-free.[2] The quality of Hawaiian sugar was thus greatly improved, and the crop was successfully adapted to local conditions. Agencies like C. Brewer & Co. and Walker, Allen & Co. supplied the planters with capital; the Civil War boosted the price of sugar; and the growth of urban communities on the West Coast, especially in Oregon and California, provided ready markets for the Hawaiian crop. By 1865 sugar had superseded whaling as the foundation of Hawaii's economy.[3]

With the expansion of the sugar industry, the labor problem became chronic. Between 1852 and 1866, over one thousand Chinese coolies were brought to Hawaii from Hong Kong, Macao, and San Francisco to meet the need for plantation hands.[4] But the Chinese were painfully ambitious. As their contracts expired, they swarmed into urban areas, opened up independent retail shops, and competed with native and white businessmen. When the five-year contracts of the first coolies expired, seventy Caucasian residents of Honolulu beseeched Kamehameha IV to protect his royal domain from the pestiferous Chinese who were seen 'prowling about, at all hours of the night, without limit, or restraint.'[5] The keener the competition became, the more undesirable and 'depraved' the 'heathen Mongolians' appeared. They were accused of, among other things, petty theft, burglary, gambling, opium smuggling, and plotting to do away with the king.[6]

The labor shortage was aggravated by a related crisis. Epidemics of smallpox, measles, and other diseases had wiped out the major part of the native population. The census of 1860 reported a decrease of more than fifteen thousand Hawaiians in a single decade. Three years later, Hawaiian Foreign Minister Robert Wyllie warned, 'Unless we get more population, we are a doomed nation,' and since the Chinese were considered undesirable, it became, in the words of Kamehameha IV, a question 'of some moment whether a class of persons more nearly assimilated with the Hawaiian race could not be induced to settle on our shores.'[7] In 1864 the Planters' Society was organized to devise a solution to the labor shortage. Later the same year, to relieve the population crisis, a Bureau of Immigration was formed to import foreign laborers and to encourage the introduction of free immigrants.[8]

THE INTRODUCTION OF JAPANESE LABOR

The idea of introducing Japanese laborers to the Islands evidently first occurred to Foreign Minister Wyllie, who had reasoned that with several hundred Japanese at work on his sugar farm on Kauai his retirement years as a gentleman planter would be profitable as well as pleasant ones. In 1865 Wyllie wrote Eugene

Van Reed a letter in which he freely discussed his thoughts about importing Japanese to meet the labor deficiency. A short time later, Van Reed was appointed Hawaiian consul general for the Empire of Japan.[9]

Wyllie died before the year was out, but his successor, Charles de Varigny, approved the scheme of introducing Japanese to the Islands. At a meeting of the Board of Immigration in March 1868, Foreign Minister de Varigny spoke persuasively about the project, even convincing board members that the Japanese so 'resembled our native race [that] there was not the slightest doubt that they would most readily amalgamate.'[10] The board then converted available funds into a draft in the amount of $1,925, which de Varigny forwarded to Van Reed.

Meanwhile Van Reed had obtained permission from the tottering shogunate to dispatch a shipload of immigrants to Hawaii, and a man named Hanbei had recruited a group of persons who were willing to work three years in Hawaiian fields or sugar mills for four dollars per month. The 800-ton British ship *Scioto* was chartered for the voyage to Honolulu, and Hanbei's recruits, who had congregated at Fukui's Inn in Yokohama, began boarding ship in the first week of May, 1868.[11] But on May 9, the day before the *Scioto* was scheduled to sail, forces of the new imperial government took over the administration of Kanagawa and Yokohama, making it necessary for Van Reed to renegotiate for new passports. His efforts to do so failed. Imperial officials insisted that the American obtain a guarantee from one of the treaty powers that the Japanese would be returned when their three-year contracts expired.[12] Van Reed construed the demand as a subterfuge to revoke the favorable decision of shogunate officials, and when the Emperor Meiji's* government not only declined to issue new passports but also refused to reimburse the businessman for the money spent on chartering the *Scioto* and recruiting the prospective immigrants, Van Reed retaliated by ignoring the demands of the imperial bureaucracy. On the afternoon of May 17, 1868, against the express wishes of the Japanese government, the *Scioto* sailed out of Yokohama Bay.[13]

THE GANNEN MONO

The first lot of Japanese immigrants who came to the Islands were called the 'Gannen Mono,' or First-year People, because they sailed for Hawaii in *Meiji Gannen*, the first year of the long and benevolent rule of the Emperor Meiji.[14] Most of them were city ruffians who claimed to be barbers, wood workers, tailors, and blacksmiths. Few, if any, were tillers of the soil. Some of them thought they were going to India; some thought China; others referred to their destination as *Tenjiku*, the resting place

*Emperor Mutsuhito is better known by his reign name, Emperor Meiji.

of the Buddha. A few expected to ply back and forth from and to Yokohama with ease. All of them expected to get rich quick and return to the homeland.[15]

Most of the Gannen Mono were young. The youngest was Ichigorō Ishimura, a rowdy thirteen-year-old who drank and gambled with gusto and mercilessly taunted his shipmates who dubbed him 'Mamushi-no-Ichi,' Ichi the Viper.[16] Another member of the crew was thirty-four-year-old Sentarō Ishii, a samurai from Okayama. Foreseeing a bleak future for samurai in a time of decadent feudalism, Ishii had hurled his sword into the river, deserted his lord, and fled to Tokyo, where news reached him of a ship in Yokohama Bay which had been chartered to take men to the Hawaiian Islands.[17]

The Gannen Mono passed the time aboard ship by gambling, fighting, and infuriating the Chinese cook by pouring rubbish into his brew. Early in the voyage a storm arose and filled the Japanese with unspeakable fear and consternation. When it subsided, all but Sentarō Ishii and Ichi the Viper cut off their topknots as thank offerings to the benevolent buddhas and the great god Kompira, dragon king of the sea, who rescued from peril all those who went down to the deep.[18]

On June 19, the *Scioto* docked at the port of Honolulu, a busy haven for merchant vessels, a few whalers with weather-stained canvasses, and one or two schooners that scuttled back and forth between island ports. One of the Gannen Mono had died after a brief illness and was thrown overboard. The others—141 men, 6 women, and 1 child—arrived in excellent condition.[19] King Kamehameha V, a man of 'immense proportions' who had been ailing for several weeks, came in a carriage from his seaside cottage in Waikiki and greeted the immigrants with a barrel of salted fish.[20]

The Gannen Mono Arrive

The new arrivals, given a few days off, eagerly welcomed an opportunity to see the capital and the inhabitants of Kamehameha's Kingdom. Slipping into comfortable kimonos and *zōri* (slippers), they made an exhaustive tour of the town. The people of Honolulu, for the most part, were not an attractive lot. A few fashionably dressed haoles (Caucasians) rode about in private hacks, but all too frequently unclean and disfigured lepers who lived in hidden caves and valleys behind the village ventured into town and walked the streets.* Noisy Chinese chattered with rowdy and shabbily clad vagrants in coffeehouses along the waterfront, and,

---

*Measures had been taken in the early 1860s to eradicate and prevent the spread of leprosy, which evidently had been brought to the Islands by the Chinese. Eventually hundreds of lepers were sent to an isolation settlement on the north side of Molokai, but as late as 1873 it was evident that many were still living scattered among the healthy members of the kingdom.

on street corners near the wharf, fat and barefooted Hawaiian women in long muumuus peddled their rose and ilima leis.[21] The Gannen Mono, shuffling along on narrow horse trails and under coconut and algaroba trees, were sorely disappointed.[22] Those who expected to see a castle town were even more disillusioned. Honolulu was a town of unsightly frame structures with dilapidated shutters and awnings. A few grass huts were scattered here and there among a few buildings of brick or stone and four adobe houses with shingle roofs. The 'palace' of His Royal Majesty, a bungalow built of coral as were all 'pretentious' houses, must have been a shock in comparison with the Imperial Palace of Japan with its massive walls and ramparts.[23] The Honolulu Theater, where divas traveling to and from Australia performed the romantic operas of Verdi and Donizetti, was described by a countryman of the Gannen Mono as 'a barn with the paint worn off.'[24]

The steepled churches of Jehovah and His Christ, situated in the busiest sections of the town, were finished with a most rigid economy and bore no semblance to the gorgeously carved Japanese pagodas nestled in shaded groves far from the noisy distractions and frivolous pleasures of city life. In downtown Honolulu, near the saloons and houses-of-ill-repute which had done a thriving business in bygone whaling days, stood the two-story Seamen's Bethel, a quaint New England landmark erected in 1833 as a refuge and moral lighthouse for sailors off whaling and trading vessels. Atop its small, white bell tower, a blue flag with the word 'Bethel' fluttered in the trade winds, and in the vestry the Temperance Legion held meetings every Thursday evening. On Sabbath morns, with walking stick and silk Puritan hat in hand, the Reverend 'Father' Samuel C. Damon, the 'seamen's chaplain,' climbed its high pulpit to deliver the Gospel.[25] The natives worshipped in their own Kaumakapili Church, and from within the walls of Kawaiahao, the Old Stone Church, in marked contrast to the clash of gongs and drums heard in Buddhist temples of Japan, a newly installed pipe organ pealed out the strains of "The Earth is Jehovah's.'[26] Behind the town, mountains heavily laden with ohia and breadfruit trees were divided by verdant Nuuanu Valley, which rose in a gradual ascent to the famous Nuuanu Pali (precipice) where long ago the half-naked warriors of Kamehameha the Great, armed with spears and javelins, defeated another native chief to set the stage for the unification of the Hawaiian Kingdom.

The ancient Hawaiians were descendants of a branch of the Polynesian race which settled in the Islands hundreds of years ago. Before the coming of the missionaries, they worshipped wooden idols and stone images in great open-air temples called heiaus. Outside the fitted stone walls of the heiaus, which were situated near sacred burial places or on promontories overlooking the sea, kahunas (priests) bedecked in the red feather capes of their calling, practiced sorcery and divination or offered up animal and human sacrifices to protect their people against disease, crop failure, and defeat in warfare. In his private 'house of the gods' built upon a mole jutting into the sea, Kamehameha the Great once worshipped the gruesome war god, Kukailimoku, a small wooden image with sharp dog's teeth and a hideous grin. Adorned with a headdress of yellow feathers, Kukailimoku accompanied the mighty alii (chief) into every crucial battle and was said to utter shrill and terrifying cries that could be heard above the clash of arms.

The Hawaiian kapu system of religious laws consisted of numerous tabus and of penalties for violating them. A kapu breaker, having ignored the command to 'obey or die,' usually fell under the penalty of death; some offenders were punished by the gods with loathsome and lingering diseases curable only by the kahuna lapaau, a priest or medicine man who restored health with magic spells and mixtures of drugs and herbs. Priests wielded a good deal of power in old Hawaii, and the most feared among them was the kahuna anaana who, it was said, specialized in praying people to death.

Ancient beliefs and superstitions die hard, and even as Sentarō Ishii and his comrades walked the streets of Honolulu, the 'infernal sorcerers' were still 'prowling about the islands' praying natives to death with their fearsome anaana spells. The kahuna lapaau also survived. One of them, a certain 'Dr. Levi,' infuriated the Puritan clergy by quoting Holy Writ and commanding entire chapters of the New Testament to be read aloud as he concocted his 'sacred panacea of sea-slugs and sunfish galls.'[27]

Although some of the kamaainas, or old-timers, clung tenaciously to the old customs and beliefs, Hawaii was a Christian kingdom when the Gannen Mono went ashore. The American Board of Commissioners for Foreign Missions in Boston had dispatched missionaries to the Islands since 1820, and not until 1863 did it withdraw its support of the Hawaiian field to leave the propagation of the faith in the hands of the Hawaiian Evangelical Association, the 'home mission' which was organized in 1853.[28]

The missionaries who had come from Puritan New England 'for no private end, for no earthly object,' but solely for 'the glory of God our Saviour' had done their work well. Impressed with the sincerity and self-sacrifice of the 'Lord's anointed,' high-ranking and influential alii had accepted the Ten Commandments as a basis for the laws of their kingdom. Thus the New England kapu system replaced the native one. In 1829 Kamehameha III declared, 'The laws of my country prohibit murder, theft, adultery, fornication, retailing ardent spirits at houses for selling spirits, amusements on the Sabbath day, gambling and betting on the Sabbath day and at all times.' In the missionary-inspired Constitution of 1840, the same sovereign guaranteed that 'no law shall be enacted which is at variance with the word of the Lord Jehovah.'[29]

But the grim and unyielding Puritan ethic seemed just as absurd then as it does now to persons unfamiliar with the terrors and scrupulosity of men who acted in the belief that they had barely escaped the wrath of an angry God. A Japanese newspaperman who visited Hawaii shortly after the arrival of the Gannen Mono was shocked by the 'unjustifiable restraints . . . restrictions and prohibitions . . . inflicted by the Missionary Ring.'[30] Yet whatever their shortcomings, however narrow their beliefs, the missionaries who entered and dominated the public life of Hawaii made immeasurable contributions to the political and cultural life of the kingdom. With the cooperation of the Hawaiian monarch and his council of alii, they brought about a legislative form of government and a reliable judiciary; through their efforts the common people for the first time gained a voice in the government. Missionaries also worked to abolish the old feudal landholding system and instituted a reform program which gave the natives and foreign residents the right to purchase land in fee simple and at low prices. One missionary, Dr. Gerrit P. Judd, was an administrative and diplomatic genius who organized the public treasury and managed to keep the little kingdom out of the clutches of foreign powers. Missionaries gave the Hawaiians their first printed literature, too, and were pioneers in secular education, establishing an excellent system of common schools throughout the Islands. They also encouraged the natives to be thrifty and industrious, to 'have more business on their hands, and increase their temporal comforts.'[31] When all was said and done, they bequeathed to the Polynesian inhabitants of the Sandwich Islands some of the noblest moral and spiritual ideals of Western civilization.

The Gannen Mono Go to Work

Within two weeks after their arrival, the Gannen Mono went to work. A few were employed as domestic servants in Honolulu, but most of them were assigned to planters. Sentarō Ishii and seventy others went to the island of Maui, twenty-two to Kauai, and four to Lanai. Fifty-one remained on Oahu.[32] Adjusting to an exhausting routine of plantation work under the blazing Hawaiian sun did not come easily, and complaints from employers and employees alike soon reached the Board of Immigration. Several of the Japanese became ill and refused to work; others were lazy;

and many were homesick. One of Sentarō Ishii's co-workers on Maui, aching to go back to his country, hanged himself from a tree on the slopes of Mount Haleakala. Twenty-nine of the group that had gone to work for Wilder Plantation on Oahu marched down Honolulu's Nuuanu Avenue in February 1869 to protest not being given time off to celebrate their New Year's Day, a privilege which, they noisily pointed out, had been granted to the Chinese laborers.[33]

Rumors soon drifted back to Japan that the Gannen Mono were being mistreated, and the Tokyo government promptly sent a special two-man committee, headed by 'Wooyeno-no-kami,' to investigate. Both men made a cursory examination of conditions on Oahu and Maui and, finding no evidence of abusive treatment, returned to Japan after concluding an agreement with Hawaiian officials that forty of the most dissatisfied Gannen Mono would be returned to the homeland.[34]

The men who returned to Japan went to work as patrolmen in the foreign settlement in Kanagawa to pay back the cost of their transportation. On the backs of their *happi* jackets they wore the symbol 'ha' for Hawaii. But their memories of the Islands were bitter. Upon returning to Japan, they had written to Kanagawa officials expressing their ineffable joy upon setting foot once more in the land of the gods and their equally ineffable disgust with the humiliations they had endured in Hawaii.[35]

The Gannen Mono who remained in Hawaii continued to quarrel with lunas (plantation overseers) and to protest the assessment of fines and unsatisfactory payment of wages. But most of them gradually adapted to the new environment and eventually received from the Japanese government passports granting them permission to remain in Hawaii. Thirty-six of them expressed a wish to go to the United States to learn 'some Arts but by Degrees,' and thirty-seven others were content to 'Sojourn in this Richest and Beautiful Kingdom.'[36] In time some heard the 'tidings of salvation' and were won to Christ by the zealous missionaries who had already 'wrought such wonders in the islands.' Ichi the Viper foreswore his 'heathen ways' and became a devout Protestant 'whose earnestness and kindness attracted many a man.' Sentarō Ishii gave up Nichiren Buddhism and was baptized a Roman Catholic.[37]

RECIPROCITY AND LARGE-SCALE JAPANESE IMMIGRATION

Prior to the departure of the Gannen Mono, Eugene Van Reed had foreseen that a treaty of commerce and friendship with Japan would facilitate immigration to Hawaii. But relations between him and the Tokyo government rapidly deteriorated after the *Scioto* incident, and Ambassador 'Wooyeno-no-kami' had made it unmistakably clear to Hawaiian officials that Van Reed would be unacceptable as the negotiator of such a treaty. Later Van Reed resigned as Hawaiian consul general, and in 1871 a Treaty of Friendship and Commerce was signed in Tokyo by representatives of the Japanese government and the American minister resident.[38] Article V of the treaty removed all restrictions against the employment of Japanese subjects in Hawaii. The Meiji government continued to frown on emigration, however, and no more Japanese came to Hawaii for fourteen years.

Meanwhile Kamehameha V, 'the last great chief of the olden type,' had grown 'excessively corpulent, eating enormously and taking little or no exercise.'[39] He died in 1872 leaving the throne vacant and the crucial problems of repopulation and labor supply still unsolved. His successor was William Charles Lunalilo, Mark Twain's 'Whiskey Bill,' charming, witty, and beloved as no other monarch by his own people. Lunalilo was the grand-nephew of Kamehameha the Great. His mother, believing him destined for great things, named him 'Lunalilo,' meaning so high up as to be out of sight. But Lunalilo's health was poor, and he fraternized too often with 'those who sought conviviality and dissipation.'[40] After a reign of little more than a year, 'the people's king' died of tuberculosis and related illnesses. As his body was moved to its tomb in the Kawaiahao churchyard, a thunderstorm struck—a heavenly sign to grief-stricken natives that their departed alii had indeed been 'highest of them all.'[41]

The Hawaiian legislature then elected to the throne David Kalakaua, an ambitious, conceited, and often irresponsible descendant of the alii, who was destined to be the last male monarch of the Hawaiian Kingdom. Kalakaua was barely in office when sugar factors and businessmen urged him to take steps to obtain a vitally needed reciprocity treaty with the United States. In November 1874, the king left Honolulu with a party of officials and for three months was a guest of the American people and government. Effusing an abundance of native charm, and as the first monarch ever to visit the United States, Kalakaua made a surprisingly good impression on the American people who let it be known that they favored reciprocity. President Grant made the treaty an administrative measure, and ratifications were exchanged in June 1875. The next Congress passed ancilliary legislation, and reciprocity became a reality in September 1876.

The treaty of 1876 provided that unrefined sugar, rice, and minor Hawaiian products be admitted to the United States free of customs duties and that most American products and manufactured goods be admitted free to Hawaii. The effects of reciprocity were phenomenal. In the next two decades, invested capital increased fourfold; sugar acreage jumped from 22,455 in 1879 to 125,000 in 1898; and the tonnage of shipped raw sugar rose from 12,500 tons in 1875 to 250,000 tons in 1897. At the same time, the need for more labor again became critical. The native population, continuing to decrease, seemed destined to extinction, and the Board of Immigration, under constant pressure from the planters, searched frantically for outside sources of labor. British India, Dutch Malaysia, and Japan were investigated— but only the Chinese continued to come in great numbers. Twenty-five hundred Pacific Islanders were imported, but they were too few and too costly, and the source was not dependable. Approximately twelve thousand Portuguese as well as 613 Norwegians and 1,337 Germans were brought to Hawaii, but the cost of white labor was prohibitive. The planters wanted *cheap* labor. So despite the repeated protests of a few anti-coolie humanitarians and businessmen who resented competition from the enterprising Chinese, more 'celestials' arrived from Hong Kong and California. But even these were not sufficient.

Meanwhile Kalakaua had decided to make the rest of the world aware of his kingdom and its king. In January 1881, he departed on a global tour, accompanied by Attorney General William Armstrong, to whom he suggested, in all seriousness, the introduction of Buddhism to Hawaii.* Upon his arrival in the Bay of Yedo, and as the first sovereign of a Christian country ever to set foot in Japan, Kalakaua was invited to be a guest of the Emperor Meiji. Mindful of Hawaii's need for labor and 'cognate' people to replenish the dwindling population, he took the opportunity to propose the resumption of Japanese emigration to Hawaii.[42] Nothing happened as a direct result of this historic meeting, but soon thereafter, economic conditions in Japan changed to warrant approval of emigration to the Islands. Robert W. Irwin, an American businessman who was named acting Hawaiian consul general in 1880 and later became minister to Japan, was appointed to handle the negotiations. Unlike Van Reed, Irwin was very popular with Japanese officials. He had long been a resident of Japan, spoke the language, was married to a Japanese, and was a business associate of Count Inouye, Japan's foreign minister from 1879 to 1887. He had also made a good impression on Kalakaua during the latter's sojourn in the empire. As agent for the Board of Immigration, Irwin counseled patience and persistence.[43]

On Sunday morning, February 8, 1885, the old Pacific steamer *City of Tokyo*, which drew too much water to enter port, dropped anchor outside Honolulu Harbor after a thirteen-day voyage from Yokohama. Aboard were 943 Japanese who, by special agreement between Irwin and Japanese officials, had come to work on Hawaiian plantations. Unlike the Gannen Mono, these people

*Kalakaua had been a nominal Episcopalian, but after his trip he 'lapsed' and 'reverted to paganism.' See Rt. Rev. Henry B. Restarick, *Hawaii from the Viewpoint of a Bishop* (Honolulu, 1924), p. 142.

were not city drifters. They were healthy, robust, tenant farmers, 'as strong a body of men as ever came to the country.'[44] Like the thousands who followed them, these immigrants came in the hope of escaping a desperate economic plight. The Meiji government had inaugurated a vast deflationary program which had plunged small businessmen into bankruptcy and had made it next to impossible for small farmers to pay their taxes.

King Kalakaua visited the immigration compound with a troupe of hula dancers and greeted the newcomers in a few words of Japanese remembered from his visit with the distant kami four years before.[45] On the third day after their arrival, the immigrants put on a kendō (fencing) match and a sumō (wrestling) exhibition at the depot. Practiced for centuries by the masters of Zen, kendō requires consummate skill with the sword. Sentarō Ishii would have been proud of the two combatants who, in the presence of the Hawaiian king, performed with wooden swords, wire masks, helmets, and padded gloves. Kalakaua himself was most impressed and awarded a silver dollar to each participant in the tournament. The first sumō match staged in Hawaii followed the kendō contest. Forty men, twenty on each team, tried to throw their opponents out of a grassy court encircled with sandbags. The winners of the match stomped through a slow, stately victory dance which appeared to a baffled newspaper reporter like something 'after the manner of the Gilbert Islanders, or the Mount Lebanon Quakers perhaps.'[46]

Some of the Japanese wrote home a few days after their arrival, and one wonders what they found of interest to pass on. Honolulu had grown since the Gannen Mono made their disappointing tour. During the reigns of the last two sovereigns with Kamehameha blood, about a million dollars had gone into public works projects, and the face of the town showed evidence of money well spent. Honolulu had broader streets, and the Hawaiian Hotel, a first-class, forty-two-room edifice, had been built to accommodate the numerous tourists who flocked to Hawaii after the establishment of trans-oceanic steamship communications. Iolani, the new two-story royal palace, was a marked improvement over the bungalow of the Kamehamehas.

Most of the Japanese were soon assigned to plantations on Oahu and outlying islands. A few stayed in Honolulu to make 'a fernery, rockery and pond combined' (Japanese garden) for the queen's house.[47]

About a year later, in January 1886, a convention was signed in Tokyo by which the Japanese government sanctioned free and voluntary emigration to Hawaii. Its provisions stipulated that all emigration must originate from Yokohama and that all contracts must be signed in Japan by the prospective immigrants and the special agent of the Hawaiian government, namely, Robert

Irwin.[48] It guaranteed free steerage passage to Hawaii and required that the Hawaiian government employ physicians to attend ailing Japanese. A sufficient number of inspectors and interpreters were called for to act as liaison between the immigrants and Hawaiian authorities. On paper the provisions looked good, and nearly twenty-nine thousand Japanese whose economic distress made even meager wages and long, hot hours of cutting and hauling sugar cane look attractive emigrated to Hawaii from 1886 to 1894.[49]

The Japanese who came to Hawaii were simple folk who had been uprooted from rural communities where familiar, time-honored rituals gave meaning to life, solace in death, and consolation in time of misfortune or affliction. The Irwin Convention had made provision for adequate burial grounds, but the all-important funeral service (in the absence of priests) was usually bypassed. This gave rise to acute psychological 'stress situations'* among devout Buddhists, who attached profound significance and deep sentiment to traditional burial and *hōji* (memorial rites). An ancient legend had it that Buddhist priests knew immediately of the death of their parishioners because the *shin-botoke* (newly dead) rapped heavily on the doors of their family temples.[50] But in the Hawaiian Islands there were no temples over which the *shin-botoke* might hover; there was no one to chant the sūtras, burn incense, and throw open the gates of Amida's Pure Land for the forgotten dead who had been buried ignominiously in shallow, unhallowed graves.[51] In Japan, meanwhile, a young priest of the True Pure Land sect, deeply concerned about the spiritual plight of his countrymen in Hawaii, had resolved to discuss the matter with his religious superiors at the Nishi (Honpa) Hongwanji in Kyoto.

*For a discussion of this type of psychological phenomenon, see Elizabeth K. Nottingham, *Religion and Society* (New York, 1954), p. 32ff.

CHAPTER 3

A Priestly Visit to a Tottering Kingdom

NO ONE KNOWS FOR SURE WHEN A BUDDHIST PRIEST OR LAYMAN FIRST SET FOOT IN America, but years ago the British anthropologist Sir Henry Howorth noted that an entry in the Chinese state annals recorded a journey made to America as early as the fifth century by Buddhist priests who called the country 'Fusang.' In an article written for a professional journal in 1921, the same scholar ascribed the origin of ancient Hawaiian artifacts to itinerant Yellow Lamas whose travels antedated European voyages. The Hawaiian yellow cloak of royalty and feathered warrior-helmet, unique in shape and color, were patterned, Howorth theorized, after the patched monastic robes and headdress of the Gelugpa, or 'Yellow Sect,' of Tibetan Buddhism.[1]

Such speculations aside, it is a fact that years before the arrival of the Gannen Mono, the Hawaiian Islands were reached sporadically by shipwrecked Japanese, some of whom were 'remarkably religious.'[2] In June 1839, seven Japanese from 'Iko,' about one hundred miles from 'Jedo,' or Tokyo, were rescued from the shipwrecked *Chōja Maru* and brought to Lahaina, Maui, aboard an American whaleship.[3] The eldest of the crew was fifty-year-old Heshero, a man 'most punctual in his devotion to a little gilded idol which, with a string of beads, was enclosed in a wooden box.'[4] The idol was probably an image of Amida Buddha; the string of beads was undoubtedly a *juzu* (Buddhist rosary), and the wooden box was very likely a portable *butsudan* (private shrine). Dr. Dwight Baldwin, the missionary doctor at Lahaina, tried to persuade the Japanese to embrace Christianity, but they politely declined. The god of Americans is good for Americans, they explained, and our gods are good for us. When asked to surrender his idol, a terrified Heshero, clasping his hands upon his breast, shook his head vigorously and exclaimed, 'By by, me die!'[5] Eventually Heshero did die and was given a Christian burial. Reverend Hiram Bingham, leader of the first Christian mission to the Islands and the 'enemy [of] every form and species of wickedness,' presided at the funeral, and one of Heshero's countrymen later recalled that Bingham had read from a big black book about three inches thick which looked rather like the *o-kyō,* or Buddhist sūtras.[6]

THE ARRIVAL OF SŌRYŪ KAGAHI

The history of Buddhism in Hawaii as a matter of written record begins with the arrival of Sōryū Kagahi, a priest of the True Pure Land sect and a native of Oita Prefecture, which is famous for the stone images of the buddhas that dot the slopes of the Usuki hills. Kagahi had been worried for some time about his countrymen in Hawaii, and in what appears to have been a characteristic burst of youthful zeal, he journeyed to Kyoto in the early months of 1889 to discuss the Hawaiian situation with Abbot Myōnyo of the Honpa Hongwanji. Reminding his religious superior that thousands of Japanese were toiling (and that many had already died) in a foreign land without the consolations of their religion, Kagahi pleaded with Myōnyo to dispatch missionaries to the Islands immediately. Abbot Myōnyo listened sympathetically to Kagahi, but considered the priest's proposal premature. Missionary efforts at that moment were concentrated in Manchuria, South China, and Korea,[7] and virtually nothing was known by Hongwanji officials about social and religious conditions in Hawaii. Nevertheless, with the encouragement of the abbot and personal friends, Kagahi decided to survey the Hawaiian scene and report back to Kyoto.[8] So in February 1889,* with the blessing of Abbot Myōnyo, he boarded the new steel steamer, *Ōmi Maru,* bound for the capital of the Hawaiian Kingdom.[9]

On Saturday, March 2, 1889, after a pleasant twelve-and-a-half-day voyage from Yokohama, the *Ōmi Maru* cruised into Honolulu Harbor, where vessels with sharp bows and towering masts lay anchored.[10] The small seaport town had become a vacation

*One Japanese source states that Kagahi arrived in 1887; another says 'about 1887.' Hongwanji sources and a third lay source give 1889 as the date of arrival. It is certain that the priest arrived in March 1889, but I am unable to confirm any previous visit. The passenger list of the *Ōmi Maru* (AH) registers Kagahi's name as 'Kagahi, Gorro.' His age is given as thirty-three, and his profession as 'merchant.'

paradise for writers, poets, painters, and diplomats from around the world; and along Nuuanu Avenue, in mansions brightly illuminated by the new electric lights, members of the Hawaiian diplomatic and consular corps feted visiting dignitaries at official receptions and dinners. At Iolani Palace, King Kalakaua, the urbane and pleasure-loving 'Merry Monarch,' and his queen, Kapiolani, in her 'magnificent peacock robe and train,' presided at extravagant grand balls staged in honor of Her Britannic Majesty's Navy.[11] Tourists frequently took horseback jaunts up lush Nuuanu valley to the scenic Pali or basked in the sun on Waikiki Beach, Honolulu's 'fashionable bathing place.'[12] On the afternoon of Kagahi's arrival, visitors and residents alike rode out in new, brightly colored tram-cars to Kapiolani Park in the shadow of the brown bluff of Diamond Head, where one Professor Emil L. Melville was scheduled to perform an unprecedented 'Grand Balloon Ascension.' By 4 P.M. a large crowd had arrived at the park on horseback or in hacks and private carriages. The king and queen, with government officials in dapper duck suits and straw hats, had come to 'witness the details of an operation never before seen in this country' and which had been 'the talk of the town for days.'[13] To the great disappointment of the curious spectators, Professor Melville was unable to get off the ground.

Tourists returning from such special events or sight-seeing excursions rendezvoused in the early evenings at the popular Hawaiian Hotel where the uniformed and spirited Royal Hawaiian Band gave weekly concerts on the wide hotel lawn.[14] On Sabbath morns tourists worshipped at the Fort Street Church or in St. Andrew's Episcopal Cathedral at Emma Square near the Hawaiian Hotel. A few malihinis (newcomers) even took time to inspect the new Kaumakapili Church, a modern brick structure on the edge of Chinatown which replaced the old native place of worship destroyed by the fire of 1886. The new two-story Kaumakapili had dome-shaped windows, the best organ in the town, and two spires instead of one—an architectural innovation inspired by King Kalakaua, who had reasoned that 'as a human being has two eyes, two ears, two hands and two limbs, so the new church must have two towers.'[15]

While malihinis and Hawaiians worshipped in their respective churches, Sōryū Kagahi sipped sake (an alcoholic beverage) and chatted with his countrymen who had found employment in Honolulu. He told his comrades of his visit with Abbot Myōnyo and expressed the hope that Hongwanji headquarters would soon extend its mission field to the Hawaiian Islands. With the assistance of a few devout Buddhists, he went from door to door among Japanese in the town, soliciting money to purchase a piece of land on Beretania Street for the construction of a mission hall. Within a week after his arrival, two hundred Japanese laborers, before returning to the homeland, gave Kagahi one hundred sixty dollars

SŌRYŪ KAGAHI

of their hard-earned savings, and plans were then promptly drawn up for the construction of a Buddhist temple in the heart of Honolulu.[16]

As the Buddhist priest walked the streets of the Puritan village, members of the Blue Ribbon Temperance League, which held weekly meetings at YMCA headquarters on the corner of Beretania Street, evidently noticed the activities of Kagahi and his companions. The Hawaiian Evangelical Association (hereafter referred to as the Hawaiian Board) commented disparagingly on the appearance of 'a Buddhist organization among us, which encourages drinking habits,' and the *Daily Bulletin* reported that a Buddhist priest had come in the interests of 'that old Asiatic system of belief and worship.'[17] Most members of the wider community, however, paid little attention to Kagahi. For the moment they had other and far more urgent matters to ponder, the most serious of which was the character and shenanigans of his majesty the king.

THE 'MERRY MONARCH'

The reign of David Kalakaua reeked with scandal and corruption. Sale of public offices was common, and land was leased illegally. The legislature of 1882 had repealed a law prohibiting the sale of liquor to natives; and the legislature of 1886 had passed a bill giving the government a monopoly on the sale of opium—a transaction in which the king had become shamefully involved. Frivolous and unprincipled, Kalakaua, the grandson of a chief who was tried and hanged for murder in 1840, was a disgrace to the noble heritage of the Kamehamehas. With few of the talents befitting his office, he had nevertheless resolved to rule as well as reign, and with 'malice aforethought,' he defrauded others 'for his own profit.'[18] He was 'tricky' and 'shifty,' recalled Judge Alfred S. Hartwell, associate justice under Kamehameha V, and cloyingly polite in his ways, 'fond of making himself agreeable.'[19] Kalakaua had no sense of right and wrong, and his colossal ego made him an easy prey to men who sought their own ends by feeding the flames of his outrageous vanity. He gave no thought to the consequences of his arbitrary whims, and from 1878 to 1887, with impetuous displays of despotic irresponsibility, he appointed and dismissed cabinet ministers at will. In 1880 he appointed as prime minister, Celso Caesar Moreno, an Italian soldier of fortune who expected the Hawaiian government to subsidize a private steamship line between Honolulu and China. In 1882 he appointed as cabinet minister, Walter Murray Gibson, a crafty opportunist who had been ousted by the Mormon Church. Gibson stirred up native hatred of the whites while pampering Kalakaua's delusions of grandeur, and with Gibson's active approval, the king devised grandiose projects to satisfy an insatiable appetite for adulation. Kalakaua envisioned (among other things) a 'Polynesian League' or empire of Pacific islanders over which he would reign in resplendent, unrivaled sovereignty; and, as a first step toward the realization of this preposterous dream, he dispatched to Samoa a rotting guano and copra carrier as evidence of his naval strength. The crew of the vessel consisted largely of reform school boys, who (once in Samoan waters) wallowed in debauchery, mutinied, and reduced the ship to 'a scene of disaster and dilapidation.'[20] Then there was the king's coronation in 1883 which, conceived and staged to attract the attention of the world, took place in the presence of eight thousand persons on palace grounds in an atmosphere of theatrical grandeur. Participating dignitaries came from the United States, Great Britain, Japan, Sweden, Mexico, Russia, and elsewhere. The king's regalia

LORRIN A. THURSTON

included a 'jeweled crown, a scepter, and a sword of state, all made in Europe.'[21] The exorbitant cost of this extravaganza merely served to further provoke the already disenchanted tax-paying residents of Honolulu. By 1885 disgust with Kalakaua was widespread and contagious. A tourist who spent six months in the town ridiculed the monarch as 'a great big softhead' who lived in ease at his royal palace and 'rove[d] about the islands scaling cocoanut trees.'[22]

On the day after Christmas in 1886, as prominent attorney Lorrin A. Thurston stood at the front gate of his Judd Street home, Dr. S. G. Tucker drew up in his buggy and asked, 'Thurston, how long are we going to stand this kind of thing?' Thurston replied, 'What kind of thing?' The 'running away with the community by Kalakaua,' Tucker answered, and the king's 'interference with elections, [his] running the Legislature for his own benefit, and all that.' When Thurston asked what could be done about the situation, the homeopathic physician suggested that an organization be formed 'including all nationalities, which shall force him [Kalakaua] to be decent, and reign, not rule, or take the consequences.'[23] Thurston then promptly took up the matter with influential members of the Caucasian community, and six months later, in June 1887, a mass meeting was called in the armory on Beretania Street. People of all classes, creeds, and nationalities overflowed the hall and passed unanimous resolutions 'denouncing the government and demanding that the king dismiss his cabinet [and] make a pledge that he would never again interfere with politics.' During the state of emergency which followed, local representatives of foreign powers declined to come to Kalakaua's assistance, and the king was compelled to sign the 'Bayonet Constitution' of 1887 which badly crippled his power by requiring cabinet approval for every official act and abrogating the sovereign's right to dismiss cabinet ministers or to appoint favorite alii to the legislature.[24] Though, by the spring of 1889, when Sōryū Kagahi arrived in Honolulu, the Merry Monarch had regained some of his former powers and prestige because of dissension within opposition ranks, still there was unrest in all segments of the community. In addition, the king's health was not good, and he was often fearful for his personal safety. He even stole off in his royal carriage to solicit advice and moral support from his friend Robert Louis Stevenson, who was convalescing in a rented cottage by the seashore in Waikiki.[25]

THE 'HEATHEN CHINEE'

Members of the haole, or foreign, community who fretted over the evils of the Kalakaua-Gibson regime were also irked by another, and to them, equally unsavory development. By the 1880s many Chinese, who now made up some two-fifths of the entire male population of the kingdom, had moved off sugar plantations and opened up retail stores in urban areas. Soon they monopolized the restaurant business, controlled the fishing industry, and obtained a major interest in the wholesale liquor trade.[26] Small businessmen thus once again noisily complained of the economic competition afforded by the Chinese. At the same time, Puritan clerics, struggling to combat a resurgence of kahunaism which 'densely enshrouded the kingdom from Hawaii to Kauai,' loudly deprecated the 'rampant immorality' of the Orientals and their 'transplanted heathenism' which enjoyed such 'a vigorous life in the heart of a Christian land.'[27]

In 1887 the Reform Cabinet attempted to enforce a practical limitation on Chinese immigration, and the following year prominent business interests organized the Hawaiian Anti-Asiatic

League in a futile effort to keep the Chinese on the plantations. The Chinese, of course, would have found no favor with the American community even if they had been perfectly content to remain on the plantations. Lay and religious leaders alike resented their flagrant vices—their habits of gambling and opium smuggling, their 'wanton disregard for human life, their concealment and assistance of criminals, their reckless perjury in courts of justice, and the despicable practice of polygamy among those who could afford it.'[28] Their religion, too, was an abomination to the entire community. Shrines in great numbers, the missionaries lamented, adorned private quarters and the stores of Chinatown as necessary pieces of furniture. On altars in the houses of merchants and storekeepers, wine and fruits, sweetmeats and rice, were offered daily to tutelary deities.[29] Demons were placated, too, especially those who, on the slightest pretext, might afflict the negligent with bad luck or a loathsome disease; and every New Year was celebrated with the crashing of gongs and cymbals, the screeching of fiddles, and the explosion of firecrackers to frighten off devils and evil spirits.[30] Probably the most venerated of the friendly deities were the gods of good health, wealth, and longevity.[31] The ancient custom of ancestor worship was a revered and seldom neglected filial duty. Devout Chinese arose early every morning to burn incense before ancestral tablets of their beloved dead who dwelt with the immortals 'in the ages of unending spring.'[32] Some Chinese religious customs and beliefs observed at this time, especially the custom of ancestor worship, were so strikingly similar to Japanese Buddhist practices observed at a later date that at this point it would be well to review the background of the early Christian encounter with the 'curious and inflexible' beliefs and practices of the immigrants from the Asian continent who remained 'remarkably tenacious'[33] to the customs of their homeland.*

From the moment the Chinese arrived in the Islands, the American community set out to Christianize them. In 1864 a group of stockholders of the Kohala Sugar Company met to discuss 'the expediency of requiring the Manager to institute more vigorous measures to compel' the Chinese to attend church, and they seriously pondered 'the advisability of inserting into labor contracts a clause enforcing Sabbath church attendance' at the risk of dismissal from service.[34] No such drastic measures were taken, but a systematic program of evangelization was begun four years later when Father Damon, the seamen's chaplain, opened a Sunday school for the Chinese at the Old Bethel Church. The following year the Hawaiian Board hired the eloquent and well-educated S. P. Aheong to preach the Gospel among his countrymen in the Islands.[35] Aheong belonged to a literati family in China and spoke

*Many Westerners were unable to distinguish one Oriental race from another, let alone to distinguish their religious customs and beliefs.

several Chinese dialects. He had been lured to the Islands by rumors of fabulously high wages on Hawaiian plantations, but after working only briefly as a plantation clerk on Maui, he was 'won to Christ' and became known as 'the converted Chinaman.' Thereafter he held frequent prayer meetings in the vestry of the Old Bethel in Honolulu and distributed religious tracts and copies of the New Testament among the Chinese on the outside islands.[36]

Other colporteurs soon followed in Aheong's footsteps. Foremost among them was the colorful Sit Moon, a one-time member of the Presbyterian Mission in San Francisco, who came to Honolulu in 1875 under the auspices of the YMCA.[37] Tourists found Sit Moon an engaging figure as he vigorously led favorite hymns in the Old Bethel with the aid of huge posters on which were printed in large Chinese characters the words to 'There Is a Happy Home' and 'Rock of Ages.'[38]

In 1878 a group of Christian families from Hong Kong arrived to strengthen the 'not deep rooted' faith of the nucleus group, and the following year, the Chinese Church, a twelve-thousand-dollar wooden structure with a 'spire pointing heavenward,' was erected on Fort Street and dedicated in 1881 in the presence of the Merry Monarch.[39] Sit Moon became its first pastor, and every Sabbath morn its bell summoned a small congregation to worship. Over its doorway, in large gilt characters, were the words 'Fuk Yam Tong,' Hall of Glad Tidings.[40]

By the 1880s, then, every effort had been made to convert the Chinese. Nothing deterred the pious zeal of Gospel workers, and Father Damon had even been privileged to officiate at a few Chinese marriages and funerals.[41] Yet, after some fifteen years of proselytizing, the Chinese Christian was still a rarity. In 1881 Sit Moon lamented that only 248 Chinese throughout the kingdom had been converted. Too many of his countrymen, alas, had remained 'firmly settled in their habits [of] gambling, opium smoking and joss house worship.'[42]

Eight years later things were no different. In three joss houses, located several blocks south of Emma Street where Sōryū Kagahi and his group of Japanese Buddhists gathered at sundown, offerings of rice, fruit, and fowl were laid before altars 'decked with hideous idols.'[43] One of the joss houses was dedicated to a ferocious-looking deity called Kwan-Ti, a military hero who was executed in 220 B.C. and canonized centuries later by the Sung Dynasty.[44] In scores of houses, in meeting rooms of secret societies, on makeshift altars in the rear of stores and merchant houses throughout Chinatown, this livid, scowling god of war stood 'frowning over all.'[45] In rice fields and on plantations through the length and breadth of the land, joss sticks flickered nightly before brazen idols of the heathen god.[46] At twilight in a private residence near Ewa on Oahu, laborers returning from work in a nearby rice mill burned incense before a painted image of their favorite deity as tireless mission workers recounted the parables of Jesus. In a private residence in Kealia, Kauai, Francis W. Damon, son of the seamen's chaplain, supped with celestials beneath a 'disagreeable picture' of Kwan-Ti, and a light before the idol was kept well-trimmed and burning all night as Damon unfolded the 'great truths of the Gospel.'[47] Missionaries in Kaneohe on Oahu found another image of Kwan-Ti enshrined in a house that belonged to members of the secret Triad Society. The goal of the society, which numbered about eight thousand Chinese in Hawaii, was *chieh-pai*, or unity through worship; and its members in the Islands had been very effectively united in organizing plantation strikes and protecting gamblers, runaway laborers, and opium smugglers.[48] During the Triad initiation ritual, candidates kowtowed to Heaven, burned incense, and invoked Kwan-Ti as the divine overseer of fraternal rites to bless their spirit of mutual cooperation and fidelity.[49]

For all Kwan-Ti's widespread popularity, it was Kwan-Yin, the feminine counterpart of the bodhisattva Avalokitesvara, who inspired the noblest sentiments of the immigrants from China.[50] Through the centuries this magnanimous 'Buddha of Compassion' had been worshipped by the Chinese as the harbinger of peace, the protectress of children, and the compassionate Queen of Mercy 'who watches for the Cry of the world.'[51] Kwan-Yin was popular in Japan, too, where she was known as Kwannon-sama and the 'Lovely One whose eyes are full of pity and sweetness.'[52] Saint Shinran, founder of Sōryū Kagahi's True Pure Land sect, was deeply devoted to Kwannon-sama. A vision of her, it was said, had persuaded him to renounce celibacy for marriage.[53]

In the course of his fund-raising campaign in Honolulu, Sōryū Kagahi probably passed the large wooden joss house on Vineyard Street dedicated to Kwan-Yin. The first temple built in honor of the bodhisattva had been destroyed by the fire of 1886, and a new temple was erected the following year. Kagahi perchance entered the new joss house. If so, he saw in the central shrine a large image of the maternal goddess seated on the opened petals of a lotus flower.[54] Chinese women dressed in their traditional *cheong-ma* and adorned with the jade bracelets that bring good luck moved in and out of the temple to gossip and to kowtow before favorite idols. In one corner of the joss house, a lay priest rattled a jar of bamboo sticks until one fell to the floor. The inscription on the fallen stick was then matched with characters in a sacred text to determine the will of the gods and the fate of an anxious devotee.[55] Before leaving the temple some worshippers burned red paper in an outdoor crematory to honor the dead, and others offered thanks to Omito-fu, the Chinese equivalent for Amida Buddha.

Meanwhile the Japanese devotees of the Buddha Amida (most of whom were working on cane fields in the Hilo and Hamakua districts along the east coast of the island of Hawaii) had no temple at all in which to pay homage to the Buddha of Infinite Light and Love. But Sōryū Kagahi was soon to remedy that.

KAGAHI ON THE BIG ISLAND

By April 1889, a few weeks after his arrival, Kagahi had boarded an interisland steamer for the island of Hawaii and was 'maintaining Buddhist rites at Hilo.'[56] Rainy, tropical Hilo, with its gentle trade breezes and natural harbor, was the principal port town of the island of Hawaii and lies on the east coast of the 'Big Island' in the lap of two snowcapped volcanoes.[57] Northwest of the town proper stretched the Hilo and Hamakua districts, extensive tracts of fertile land where thousands of Kagahi's countrymen were planting and hauling cane on large plantations.[58]

One of the first persons Kagahi came across in Hilo was Saiji Kimura, a native of Nagasaki who had traveled and studied in Paris.[59] Kimura arrived in Hawaii in 1885 and was soon employed by the Hawaiian government as an inspector of immigrants on plantations of the Hilo district.[60] In time he was to amass a small fortune as the owner of a general merchandise shop in Hilo and a sake store on Nuuanu Street in Honolulu, and occasionally he pocketed a profit from wife-selling ventures.[61] Kimura's mother had been a devout Buddhist and fond memories of her, it was said, prompted him to assist Kagahi in making plans for the construction of a Buddhist temple.[62]

Kimura and Kagahi canvassed Hilo and outlying plantations, and soon collected enough money to lay the foundations in Hilo proper of the first Japanese Buddhist temple in the Hawaiian Islands.[63] Construction of the sanctuary was completed by the end of April 1889. The temple was of modest dimensions—twenty-four by thirty *shaku* or about 728 square feet—and was situated on approximately 1,029 square feet of land on the corner of Ponahawai Avenue and the seaside of Front Street. Nearby were 'shanties and shops,' a few Christian edifices including the Old Mission Chapel built in 1825, and the Foreign Church erected just a week before the arrival of the Gannen Mono.[64] There was a Roman Catholic church in the town, too, under the pastorage of Father Charles Pouzat.[65]

In May 1889, as torrents of rain filled the streams and springs of the Hilo district, Kagahi traveled on foot and on horseback along muddy roads and treacherous footpaths on the east coast of Hawaii.[66] He went from plantation to plantation comforting his countrymen who were under 'heavy burdens both in the physical and spiritual [and who were] distressing and wandering, as sheep not having a shepherd.'[67] To his great dismay, the Buddhist priest discovered that the Japanese, who had expected to accumulate

HILO HONPA HONGWANJI

money fast and return to Japan, had in fact accumulated very little money and a great deal of bad karma. Gambling had become such a prevailing vice among the Japanese that many would have 'no funds at the expiration of their contracts, to return to their homes, if they [paid] their gambling debts.'[68] To make matters worse, plantation managers in the Hilo and Hamakua districts had inflicted on their field hands an unjust 'docking' system whereby wages were allotted in accordance with the number of tasks performed rather than by the number of hours worked as labor contracts had specified.[69]

On a few plantations Kagahi was abruptly turned away as a troublesome busybody. Late one evening, weary and finding no shelter, he fell asleep in the rain and awoke soaked and shivering in a brisk morning wind.[70] But most of the priest's compatriots, with all their burdens of body and spirit, gladly welcomed the itinerant sensei* who had come with news of the homeland.

Little is known about Kagahi's activities between June and October 1889. On June 8 he sailed from Hilo back to Honolulu aboard the *Kinau*, permitting himself the luxury of traveling first class on the steamship. Also aboard was the sister of the Merry Monarch, Her Royal Highness Princess Liliuokalani who was destined to be the future queen.[71] A month later Kagahi was back on the Big Island—to the great annoyance of one Jirō Okabe, a hard-working Hilo evangelist, who complained bitterly to his

---

*Sensei, usually translated teacher, is a general term applicable to a learned person.

religious superiors that the Japanese in his district had hardened their hearts against 'the sweet name of Jesus Christ' because 'the Buddhist preast [who] came here of late . . . is preaching round the plantations to collect mony for the building of their worship.' Okabe noted further that Kagahi was 'very popular among the Japanese, for most of them are strong believers on that religion.'[72]

The Buddhist priest remained in the Islands a total of seven months. Japanese sources state that during that time he also visited the islands of Kauai and Maui.[73] In October when his 'reconnaissance' work was completed and when he had brought as much consolation to his countrymen as any one priest could bring, Kagahi decided to return to Japan and request material support from Abbot Myōnyo for his new Hawaiian mission. On October 5, 1889, he returned to his homeland aboard the *Yamashiro Maru*.[74]

KAGAHI BACK IN JAPAN

In Japan, Kagahi recounted to friends and interested persons the details of his sojourn in Hawaii. He reported to Hongwanji authorities the plight of the Japanese in Hawaii—their moral indolence, impotent faith, and slough of despair. Members of an independent missionary association in Kyoto listened sympathetically and promised Kagahi financial help should he return to the Islands. Hongwanji leaders, too, began to view conditions in Hawaii with more concern.[75] But in his overwhelming desire to promote Buddhist mission work in the Hawaiian Islands, Kagahi unwittingly dropped a bomb in the troubled waters of the Japanese religious scene. He wrote for a popular journal an essay which urged Buddhist missionaries in Western countries to identify the Christian God with the Eternal Buddha. Kagahi had reasoned that devotion to the Supreme Reality was what really mattered, not the different and culturally contingent names given to That Reality. But the priest's proposal was immediately submerged in a deluge of abuses.[76]

Kagahi had returned to Japan just as Buddhists were struggling to regain some of their long-lost power and prestige and at a time when Christianity had become an aggressive and detested rival. Following the collapse of the feudal regime in 1868, the new Meiji government, in its determination to forge a nation founded on unconditional fealty to the throne, had made Shinto the state religion. The distant kami, the Emperor Meiji, was deified and became the focus of all loyalties. The light of the Dharma, meanwhile, burned low. Establishment of the Imperial Cult led to the 'violent disestablishment of Buddhism.'[77] 'Haibutsu Kishaku'— Expel the Buddha, Destroy the Teaching—became the motto of Meiji officials. Buddhist priests, threatened with military force, were compelled to wear Shinto ceremonial hats and to make offerings to the sacred kami. Shinto priests took over important Buddhist institutions, Buddhist shrines and art treasures were destroyed, and sūtras were burned. On the surface, at least, Buddhism had disappeared.[78]

By 1876, due in no small measure to the tactful intercession of Abbot Myōnyo of the Nishi or Honpa Hongwanji and Abbot Gennyō of the Higashi Hongwanji, the Meiji government relaxed its oppressive measures and adopted a policy of religious sufferance.[79] But Buddhists had been hit hard by 'Haibutsu Kishaku,' and a conservative reaction had set in among intellectuals of the faith. No sooner had Buddhists survived Shinto persecution than they found themselves in a life-and-death struggle against Christianity, an inevitable consequence of opening the country to Western influences.

So when Sōryū Kagahi returned to Japan, Buddhist leaders were wholeheartedly committed to *haja kensei*, purging the country of 'heresy,' or Christianity, and restoring the true religion, or Buddhism.[80] Kagahi's notion of equating Jehovah with the Eternal Buddha was accordingly rejected as an outrageous perversion of the Dharma.* Following publication of Kagahi's expedient propagandist proposal, members of the missionary association in Kyoto promptly withdrew their promise of financial support, and Hongwanji officials lost all interest in the priest's Hawaiian adventure. Kagahi himself vanished and was never heard from again.[81]

In the meantime, students at Dōshisha University, a Christian institution, had held a meeting in a Kyoto theater near the college campus, and in the presence of several hundred indignant Buddhist priests, they made a foreboding prophecy. Buddhism, they declared, was a standing corpse. It had failed miserably in China and India and was on the downgrade in Japan. Nothing remained for it, they sneered, but 'a watery grave in the Pacific.'[82]

---

*Ironically enough, only a few years later, syncretic ideas similar to those proposed by Kagahi became very popular, especially in Jōdo-Shin-shū circles. See G. B. Sansom, *The Western World and Japan: A Study in the Interaction of European and Asiatic Cultures* (New York, 1950), p. 477ff.

CHAPTER 4

The 'Dark Ages' and the 'Emissaries of the Foreign God'

BETWEEN THE RETURN OF SŌRYŪ
KAGAHI TO JAPAN AND THE ESTABLISHMENT
of institutional Buddhism in 1899, religious and political events in
Hawaii did not augur well for the Japanese. The hundred-year-old
monarchy came to an end, and with the creation of the Republic of
Hawaii pending annexation, the Japanese became increasingly unpopular. Politicians deplored congressional suspicion of Hawaii's
growing Japanese population and grew ever more determined to
restrict any further influx of the 'additional heathen element.' Missionaries, still repelled and thwarted by the 'superstitious' beliefs of
the Chinese, detested with mounting vehemence the equally
abominable heathenism of the immigrants from Japan. Wayward
in religion and aliens withal, the Japanese were considered a blight
on a community committed to the propagation of Christianity and
to the growth of American ideals. During the last decade of the
century, moreover, imposters masquerading as Buddhist priests
embezzled money from poor cane field workers while Japanese
Christian evangelists swarmed over the Islands entreating their
'benighted' countrymen to forsake 'heathen idolatry' (Buddhism)
for the 'pure light of the Gospel.' Japanese Buddhists, therefore,
with good reason dubbed the early 1890s the 'Dark Ages.'[1]

THE INFANT BUDDHIST MISSION AT HILO

No Buddhist priest followed Sōryū Kagahi to Honolulu to build a
mission hall on Beretania Street. In Hilo, however, prospects for

the extension of Buddhist propaganda appeared more promising, at least for a time. On October 1, 1889, four days before Kagahi returned to Japan aboard the *Yamashiro Maru*, a young priest, Dōrin Nishizawa, arrived on the same steamer and went straightaway to Hilo. In April 1890, another priest, Gyōya Gama, arrived on the scene, and for several years both men officiated at temple rites and befriended the Japanese on the Big Island.[2]

The presence of Nishizawa and Gama, of course, did not go unnoticed. In May 1890, Jirō Okabe, the Christian evangelist who had taken exception to Kagahi's presence, wrote to O. P. Emerson, corresponding secretary of the Hawaiian Board: 'Those who came to Christ already are shining their Christian lamps upon their fellow labourers who are still wandering in darkness.' But he conceded that, alas 'the children of darkness' were sometimes 'smarter than those of Light.' The Buddhists in Hilo, he lamented, had 'built a "mighty temple," and [had] established a hospital by the name of benevolence, finding those poor Japanese need greatly such a place.' Evangelist Okabe wrote that his countrymen in the district had even been obliged 'to be the memberships of the heathen hospital, persuaded by the official power and pretended kindness.'[3] Curiously enough, the Hawaiian Board interpreted the evangelist's letter to mean that Christian work in Hilo had 'aroused opposition from the Buddhist and pagan elements among the Japanese.'[4]

About a year later, in April 1891, two opportunists, Norio Himeji and Gyōun Ogino, arrived in Honolulu and took an interisland steamer to Hilo. Posing as bona fide priests from True Pure Land temples in Japan, they persuaded Gama that by touring the east coast of Hawaii enough money could be collected to meet the deficit incurred by construction costs of the Hilo temple. They toured a number of the larger plantations along the Hamakua coast, pocketed money from credulous Japanese, and then, without a word to Nishizawa or Gama, hastily returned to Japan.[5]

Rumors of the Himeji-Ogino hoax disillusioned and embittered some Japanese on the Big Island, and for quite a while thereafter, they refused to have anything to do with priests of the True Pure Land sect. Nevertheless, most of the Japanese who came to Hawaii remained faithful and practicing Buddhists. On the eve of their departure from Japan, many of the immigrants had visited national shrines and family temples to beseech the kami and merciful buddhas to protect them from the perils of the deep. Even those who had 'cared little or nothing for Buddhism in their homeland,' upon arriving safely in the Islands, became 'devoted idolaters,' worshipping 'every day and night' idols brought from Japan.[6] Before leaving their homeland, prospective immigrants were strictly admonished by friends and relatives not to deliver themselves or their sacred talismans into the hands of 'the emissaries of the foreign God.'[7] Few of them did.

Efforts to Christianize the Japanese had begun in earnest in 1885. Accompanying the immigrants who arrived that year aboard the *City of Tokyo* was a young divinity student, S. Aoki, who acted as an interpreter at special services held for the new arrivals in the old YMCA building on Hotel Street.[8] These very immigrants, who had performed their kendō and wrestling exhibitions so expertly for King Kalakaua and his entourage, became the immediate concern of Puritan clerics who resolved to give them whatever 'opportunities of Christian instruction and education as may be in our power to give.'[9]

In 1887, two years before the arrival of Sōryū Kagahi, the YMCA obtained a lease on the Queen Emma premises on the corner of Nuuanu and Beretania streets, and when the new Queen Emma Hall was opened in March of that year, Japanese in the village were invited to hear Dr. C. M. Hyde hold forth on 'The Life and Claims of Jesus Christ as the Divine Redeemer from Sin.'[10] Ten years earlier Hyde had resigned a successful pastorate in Massachusetts to take charge of the training of a native pastorate in Hawaii. As appointed Superintendent of the Japanese Mission of the Hawaiian Board, he was 'willing and ... indefatigable in carrying on ... work for the Japanese.'[11] Mrs. Hyde busied herself on Friday evenings at Queen Emma Hall with teaching the Japanese to sing Gospel hymns, and Francis W. Damon found time between skirmishes with Kwan-Ti to organize and to become vice-president of a Japanese YMCA.[12] As the year 1887 drew to a close, the *Friend* sounded a naively optimistic note. Christian institutions, it commented, seemed to have made a favorable impression on the Asiatic immigration to these islands.

At this precise moment, Kanichi Miyama, a tireless, magnetic evangelist of the Methodist-Episcopal Church, arrived in Hawaii. Following his conversion to Christianity in the 1870s, Miyama had been placed in charge of a small Japanese congregation in the San Francisco Bay area. His devoted parishioners, confident that their pastor was a real 'John the Baptist,' persistently urged him to go and look after the religious welfare of their 'destitute' countrymen in Hawaii. Shortly after his arrival in the Islands, Miyama became tremendously popular. Japanese flocked to hear him preach, showed a remarkable readiness to receive the Gospel, and 'turned from their idols to serve the living God.'[13] Following a series of evangelical meetings in Honolulu, Miyama toured the Big Island with Francis Damon and conducted revivalist meetings in Hilo and on outlying plantations, where he received much assistance from, of all people, Saiji Kimura who, a year and a half later, was to help Sōryū Kagahi build a Buddhist temple in Hilo.[14]

At the end of the year, Miyama returned to California. In his absence, Japanese Consul General Tarō Andō, Francis Damon, and Robert W. Irwin wrote to the Methodist Mission in San Francisco requesting Miyama's prompt return for a period of at least six months (with all expenses to be met by Irwin).[15] So in March 1888, Miyama returned and organized the Japanese Methodist Church on the outskirts of Chinatown, not far from Fuk Yam Tong, the Hall of Glad Tidings. A colporteur, Takeshi Ukai, came as his assistant and enjoyed remarkable success on a preaching tour of the Big Island. By this time, the Hawaiian Board had engaged the services of Taizō Shimizu, another 'licensed exhorter of the Methodist Church.' Shimizu made a highly successful tour of the island of Kauai and, like Ukai, was heartily welcomed by the Japanese in country districts on the outside islands.[16]

But no evangelist enjoyed as much popularity with the unlettered immigrants from Japan as did Miyama. His influence was paramount, and it was he who brought about the much talked about 'blessed revival.'[17] The *Friend* described him as a man of sweetness, spiritual fervor, and cultivated intelligence; and Dr. Hyde, rejoicing over the rapid culmination of personal interest in the spirit and aims of Christian life since the arrival of Miyama, praised the evangelist as a man of rare abilities and intense personal devotion. The *Pacific Commercial Advertiser*, reporting on a baptismal service for twelve Japanese in Honolulu, also noted that since Miyama's arrival a marked interest in the Gospel was evident among those who had formerly been indifferent or opposed to Christianity.[18]

In addition to directly working among the Japanese in the city proper, Christian evangelists dispatched thousands of lithographed letters to rural districts inviting plantation laborers to come to special Sabbath services at the Honolulu YMCA; and between the spring of 1888 and February 1889, eighty-four Japanese throughout the kingdom were baptized. Among the new converts was Ichigorō ('Ichi the Viper') Ishimura, youngest of the Gannen Mono, who had long since lost his venom.[19]

By far the most important convert made by Kanichi Miyama was Tarō Andō, the Japanese consular and diplomatic agent, 'an educated atheist' who had long ago given up 'the old views' and ceased to believe in any religion.[20] Miyama's pious exhortations planted the seeds of faith in the consul general's mind, and before long he and Mrs. Andō became devout Christians.[21] Other officers of the consulate soon 'began to feel the Christian influence,' and Andō discovered that the Gospel 'could accomplish great results where his political influence failed.'[22] On Sunday, July 15, 1888, Consul General and Mrs. Andō, along with two domestic servants and four attaches, were baptized by Miyama.[23]

In the fervor of new-found faith, the consul general set out to 'judiciously support' all schemes for the 'moral and religious uplifting' of his people. In the process, he exemplified the 'peculiar features' of Christianity's effects upon the Japanese: a 'marked degree of emotional excitement' over the claims of Christianity; and an 'intense national feeling' which was 'something deeper and more far-reaching than patriotism, the sense of personal obligation to do what only Japanese can do in carrying the knowledge of the Gospel to all the Japanese.'[24] At one time a nearly hopeless victim of 'demon alcohol,' Andō signed a temperance pledge and founded the Rising Sun Temperance Society. He also sponsored fairs to raise money for the Japanese hospital in Honolulu and, with Miyama's assistance, organized a Mutual Benefit Union for the relief of his destitute countrymen. By the end of 1888, some three thousand Japanese had become members of the Mutual Benefit Union, but only one-third as many had shown any interest in the Rising Sun Temperance Society. So Miyama and Andō quickly organized a successful temperance crusade, and on the eve of Sōryū Kagahi's arrival, the Friend proclaimed that drunkenness had 'nearly ceased among the Japanese in Honolulu.'[25]

Andō's zeal, like Miyama's, was boundless. In December 1888, a newspaperman exiled by the Meiji government arrived in Honolulu and quickly made it known that he was very bitter against Christianity. Andō nevertheless vigorously preached Christ to the newcomer who was deeply impressed. Indeed, so convincing were Andō's pleas on behalf of the Crucified One that the new arrival renounced Buddhism and 'broke into weeping, confessing his sins.'[26]

In their pursuit of souls, Miyama and Andō also spent a good deal of time 'fishing' at the immigration depot. On March 3, 1889, with Dr. and Mrs. Hyde, they conducted special worship services at the depot for the benefit of the Japanese, including Sōryū Kagahi, who had arrived the day before aboard the *Omi Maru*. Mrs. Hyde played a portable organ while a 'select choir' sang favorite hymns, and Miyama spoke 'earnestly and effectively' on the subject of temperance and urged the new arrivals 'to honor womanhood as the Bible has taught us.'[27]

In a very short time, primarily due to the influence of Miyama and Andō, the Japanese initially responded to Christianity with such enthusiasm that the Friend confidently declared that missionary efforts on behalf of the immigrants from Japan were 'the most immediately and largely fruitful of any Christian work' conducted in the Islands.[28] On October 5, 1889, Consul General and Mrs. Tarō Andō returned to their homeland aboard the same steamer that took Sōryū Kagahi back to Japan. Miyama, too, went to Japan, made a stirring series of evangelistic tours, and created a glowing and unforgettable impression. In September 1890, he became pastor of the Japanese Methodist Church in historic Nagoya, for centuries a stronghold of Buddhism; and in 'carrying the Gospel Message all over Japan,' he gained national renown as the most famous temperance evangelist of Japan.[29]

Meanwhile Miyama's Christian brethren in Hawaii were losing ground. Between 1891 and 1894, with the termination of numerous labor contracts, many of the hard-won converts had returned to Japan and to Buddhism. At the same time, the Methodist-Episcopal Church had temporarily withdrawn from the Hawaiian field, leaving propagation of the Gospel exclusively in the hands of the Hawaiian Board. Meanwhile thousands more of the 'additional heathen element' poured into the Islands, and most of them, the Japanese Christian evangelist in Kohala complained, had come 'from a place where the "Shin Shu" ("true sect") prevails . . . [a] most stubborn and superstitious sect, in which the greatest ignorance exists.'[30]

Christianity, nevertheless, continued to be preached with unabated fervor among the Japanese. By the end of 1891, mission stations had been established at key points on several islands— at Ewa on Oahu, Koloa on Kauai, Paia on Maui, and elsewhere.[31] And a new crop of evangelists was brought to the Islands to sow the seeds of faith in the Lord's ever expanding vineyard. Most of the newcomers, like Shirō Sokabe (who became pastor of the Honomu Church on the Big Island), resembled 'a cross between a New England Puritan of the olden days, a loyal devotee of Bushido and a Christlike lover of children.'[32] A few, like Jenichiro Oyabe, came to the Islands on their own. In 1895 Oyabe came from the West Coast to single-handedly deliver the Islands 'of heathen idolaters'—only to find, not without a tinge of disappointment, that the Christian cause was making headway slowly but surely 'without any assistance,' as he put it, 'from a Japanese-blooded little Yankee like myself.'[33] Oyabe was hired by the Hawaiian Board to work for two years in Paia, Maui; and during that time he took great pains never to look after his own pleasures, lest his flock look upon him as 'a chicken-hearted missionary.'[34]

In planting the seeds of Christian doctrine throughout the Islands, some clerics came to expect that Kohala on the island of Hawaii would prove their most fruitful vineyard—and Reverend Shigehide Kanda, one of the most zealous evangelists, faithfully held evening Bible classes in that district, presiding at each of five plantations alternately.[35] But as it turned out, the work sponsored by the Hawaiian Board 'scored its highest success' in Hilo, under Jirō Okabe, who had come from Oakland in 1888 at the invitation of Dr. Hyde.[36] Shortly after Sōryū Kagahi returned to Japan in 1889, forty-three Japanese to whom Okabe had preached Christianity (despite Kagahi's distracting presence) were baptized by Reverend

Baker of the Hilo Foreign Church. On every plantation many others who were eager 'to leave this miserable Earth any time to be with the lord forever' embraced the Gospel.[37] Okabe's work gained further momentum after his ordination in July 1890. Early the following year, he organized in Hilo a Japanese church with seventy-two members, and in 1892 he supervised the construction of a six-hundred-dollar place of worship in Hilo which was paid for in full by the Japanese of the district.[38]

The Buddhist priests, Nishizawa and Gama, by their very presence, continued to dampen the efforts of the Hilo evangelists. Writing once again to O. P. Emerson of the Hawaiian Board, Jirō Okabe complained: 'Two Buddhist priests, the Japanese inspector [Saiji Kimura] and the doctor are the leaders' of the devil's work. These antagonists, he wanted Emerson to appreciate, constituted 'no small opposition and we suffer [a] great deal from them in our Master's Couse.' Six months later he wrote with greater anxiety: 'The Buddhists in our town are [now] trying to convert not only the Japanese but even the native to their faith which they call truth, with a great zeal and power (earthly power); yet I am rejoicing to see our poor Christians, taking up Cross in hand marching cheerfully . . . to fight against the power of darkness.'[39] By this time, too, the 'Devil' had become so alarmingly 'jealous' of the success of these evangelists that he had spread a snare to entangle and destroy them by placing in their midst, of all things, 'a Catholic priest, who talks Japanese language' and who was trying to convert them to his faith.[40]

About a year later, hoping to glean some insight into the workings of the 'power of darkness,' the Reverend Baker paid a call on the Buddhist priests in Hilo. About this singularly unenlightening encounter, one Ken'ichirō Hoshina, contract laborer turned evangelist, wrote: 'I called Buddhist Chapel twice as an interpreter of Mr. Baker to here about the doctrine earnestry. But it will not satisfied him with those priests who are now at here.'[41] Not until some thirty years later did a Buddhist priest succeed, albeit meagerly, in clarifying the essentials of the Dharma for members of the non-Buddhist community.

THE REPUBLIC OF HAWAII AND THE JAPANESE SCARE OF THE 1890S

In November 1890, the Merry Monarch, his morale low and his health poor, took a trip to the West Coast and died two months later in the Palace Hotel in San Francisco. He was brought back to Hawaii aboard the cruiser *Charleston*, given an elaborate state funeral, and buried in grand style in the royal mausoleum in Nuuanu Valley. Succeeding him to the throne was his sister

Liliuokalani. Unlike her brother, Liliuokalani was of sound mind and good moral character. But like Kalakaua she was haughtily proud of the heritage of the alii and intensely resented the 'Bayonet Constitution,' which had so drastically crippled monarchial power. Once on the throne, without the slightest hesitation, Queen Liliuokalani inaugurated her own program of arrogating personal powers as ruler. Dissatisfaction with the queen's decision to rule spread quickly, and one day a newly arrived American, Henry E. Cooper, approached fellow attorney Lorrin A. Thurston and asked: ' . . . if Liliuokalani attempts to subvert the constitution of 1887, what do you intend to do about it?'[42] Cooper then proceeded to outline his own plan of action in the event of any such emergency. Shortly thereafter, the first and secret Annexation Club was organized by a handful of haoles who were committed, not to annexation especially, but to the formation of a group ready to act quickly and intelligently should the queen make such action mandatory 'by some move against the constitution, tending to revert to absolutism or anything of the nature.'[43] Liliuokalani, meanwhile, had drawn up her own constitution. When she made arrangements for its promulgation, a 'Committee of Safety,' composed primarily of members of the Annexation Club, was quickly organized under the leadership of Henry Cooper. The time had come, the committee resolved, to do away with the monarchy.

The leading light and guiding spirit of the Annexation Club and the Committee of Safety was Lorrin Thurston, grandson of Asa Thurston, one of the first two missionaries to set foot in Hawaii in 1820. Possessed of a resolute will and the keenest intellect among the missionary descendants, Thurston had little difficulty in persuading influential persons that the queen's government was a menace to the lives and properties of Americans and that abolition of the monarchy was the only remedy for an intolerable condition ever growing more intolerable. That the monarchy in fact came to an end under Liliuokalani was, however, purely incidental. The trouble, as Thurston later made clear, had 'gone beyond repair' during the 'iniquitous reign' of Kalakaua, under whose spendthrift policy the public debt had risen from $388,900 to $2,600,000.[44]

On Monday afternoon, January 16, 1893, U.S. Minister and pro-annexationist John L. Stevens arranged for troops to be landed from the American cruiser *Boston* anchored in Honolulu Harbor. The following afternoon, the Committee of Safety took possession of the government building, and Henry E. Cooper read from its steps a proclamation abrogating the monarchy and setting up the Provisional Government to exist until terms of union with the United States of America could be negotiated and agreed upon. A military arm for the new government was organized, and Queen

Dōshisha University, he pictured in a glowing manner the conditions and opportunities in Hawaii.[51] Among the seminarians who heard and later responded to Okabe's pleas was Takie Okumura, a devious and strong-willed fanatic who became and remained, up to the time of his death in 1951, the archenemy of Buddhism and Buddhist institutions in Hawaii.

TAKIE OKUMURA—EMISSARY EXTRAORDINARY OF THE FOREIGN GOD

Takie Okumura was born in 1864 on the island of Shikoku in the hot and rainy province of Tosa, now Kochi Prefecture. His mother came from a long and distinguished line of physicians, and his father, who died early in life because of an excessive fondness for liquor, was a proud descendant of the samurai. If one accepts Okumura's estimate of his own worth in the eyes of others, he was an exemplary child who lived up to every parental expectation and was much beloved by friends and neighbors, who spoke very highly of him.[52]

In the fall of 1884, young Takie attended in Tosa a series of night lectures conducted by two Dutch Reformed ministers—Messrs. Verbeck and Thompson—and devoured their message which, he surmised, was 'Bushido refined into a world religion.'[53] Later, Okumura digested Verbeck's *Evidences of Christianity* and two other works, *Introduction to Ways of Heaven* and *One View of Truth*. Then he 'glanced through the Bible once.'[54] Four years later, he and his bride of twenty months were baptized and admitted into the Japanese Christian church at Osaka. In September 1890, he entered Dōshisha University where two years later, as an impressionable sophomore, he heard Jirō Okabe's impassioned call for volunteer workers. In July 1894, under a three-year contract with the Hawaiian Board, he boarded the *Beldic* for Honolulu.[55]

In his youthful zeal, Okumura feared nothing and braved all. Shortly after his arrival, he became 'really indignant' at the sight of the Japanese harlots along Pauahi and Nuuanu streets who shamelessly poured themselves into tight-fitting holokus to lure weak souls to certain perdition. Setting out straightaway to clean up the evil and wipe out his country's disgrace, he dropped in on one of the prostitutes and called her, among other things, unpatriotic. The whore, properly incensed, bluntly informed the meddlesome moralist that she dutifully, and without fail, sent back to their homeland a large chunk of her monthly earnings. She, not he, was the patriot.[56]

After this encounter, which left him dumbfounded and speechless, Okumura was inclined more toward conservative programs of reform. In 1896 he founded the first parochial Japanese language school in Hawaii and the Okumura Home for Boys, which was run

TAKIE OKUMURA

in accordance with strict Christian principles. He also edited the first Japanese magazine in the Islands and organized the Excelsior baseball team. Remembering what alcohol had done to his father, he enthusiastically revived Tarō Andō's Rising Sun Temperance Society. His most important work, however, lay some twenty years in the future.[57]

About the time that Takie Okumura arrived in Honolulu, Reverend Orramel H. Gulick replaced the then controversial C. M. Hyde as Superintendent of the Japanese Mission.* The eldest son of pioneer missionaries who came to Hawaii in 1828, Gulick

*In 1889 Hyde had incurred the chastisement of Robert Louis Stevenson for what the latter considered a groundless and contemptible attack on the moral integrity of Father Damien De Veuster, the leper-saint of Molokai. For the Catholic view of Hyde's alleged scurrility against the memory of the deceased priest, see Father Reginald Yzendoorn, *History of the Catholic Mission in the Hawaiian Islands* (Honolulu, 1927), pp. 212–221.

was himself a veteran in the Lord's service and had preached the Gospel for more than two decades in Japan. Seeing fit to continue Hyde's policy of enticing young Japanese evangelists to Hawaii, Gulick stationed these 'emissaries of the foreign God' throughout the Islands in 'practically every strategic point.'[58] In time, the most zealous of them enjoyed a modicum of success, especially on plantations where their countrymen had been fleeced by frauds posing as envoys from Buddhist temples in Japan. Without doubt, some of the evangelists raised the morale and moral standards of many plantation hands. Consul General Hisashi Shimamura pointed out that Japanese working on plantations where 'the Lord's messengers' were posted fared much better spiritually than did the men employed on sugar farms where 'no such aid to right living' was profferred.[59]

The evangelists themselves were of no little faith and expected that in due course their efforts would be abundantly rewarded. But their hopes were destined to disappointment. Most of the Japanese who came to Hawaii remained firm adherents of their ancestral faith, and in the later years of the decade, institutional Buddhism came to Hawaii. As Takie Okumura put it, the 'formidable foe loomed up.'[60]

CHAPTER 5

Amida in Paradise

SHORTLY AFTER HIS ARRIVAL IN
HONOLULU IN 1894, TAKIE OKUMURA PAID A
call on 'a jolly Buddhist priest, a certain Mr. Matsuo.' In the course
of what appears to have been a protracted conversation, Okumura
'jokingly' asked the priest how many Japanese in the Islands were
Buddhists. Matsuo in turn asked how many were Christians. When
Okumura estimated that four hundred had 'come to Christ,'
Matsuo replied that if, as reported, some twenty-five thousand
Japanese had immigrated to the Islands and only four hundred were
Christians, there were—as a matter of simple deduction—24,600
Japanese Buddhists in Hawaii.[1] Okumura's new acquaintance was
a priest of the Jōdo-shū, or Pure Land sect, who had come to the
Islands on official business for the Zōjyō-ji, a temple in Shiba,
Tokyo.

THE JŌDO-SHŪ AND JŌDO-SHIN-SHŪ
COME TO HAWAII

Upon returning to their homeland, irate Japanese who had been
duped by clerical frauds promptly advised priestly authorities at
their home temples of the urgent need for bona fide mission work
in Hawaii. Abbot Michishige of the Zōjyō-ji and a priest from
Yamaguchi named Gyōkai Shiraishi decided to look into the
matter. After conferring with other concerned Buddhists in

Tokyo, they organized an overseas missionary society and collected enough money to send two priests to the Islands. One of them was the 'jolly priest,' Jōtei Matsuo, who had come on a reconnaissance mission; the other was Gakuō Okabe, who was sent to preach the Dharma.

Okabe tramped for months from plantation to plantation along the damp Hamakua coast of the Big Island, carrying a statue of Amida Buddha on his back and soliciting money to build a temple. He eventually collected about three thousand dollars and in 1896 the first Jōdo-shū temple in the Islands was erected in the center of five large sugar plantations in Paauhau on the east coast of Hawaii.[2]

In the meantime, the Kyoto Honpa Hongwanji had also received numerous complaints, directly and indirectly, about imposters who had come to the Islands, swindled the Japanese, and 'disgraced the name of the Blessed One with unspeakable deeds and drunken revelries.'[3] Between 1890 and 1896, an additional 16,807 Japanese had immigrated to Hawaii, and the census report for 1896 showed that of the actual 22,299 Japanese in the Islands, 711 were Protestants, 49 were Roman Catholics, 4 were Mormons, and 21,535 were non-Christian.[4] The time had come, Hongwanji officials decided, to reevaluate the Hawaiian situation. In the spring of 1897, the Honorable Right Reverend Kōson Ōtani sent a scout, Ejun Miyamoto, to investigate conditions in the Islands.[5]

Upon his arrival in Honolulu, the Hongwanji priest discovered that a Mr. Yukai Takibuchi and a Mr. Takizawa, both frauds, had collected money from Japanese in and about the city and were 'officiating' twice a week at Buddhist rites in a 'preaching hall' on Fort Street.[6] With Miyamoto's approval and probably at his suggestion, the Buddhists of Honolulu addressed a petition to Honpa Hongwanji headquarters in Japan. Dated June 5, 1897, it read as follows:

We, the undersigned Buddhists, have acquired some property and established positions in Honolulu, the capital of Hawaii, since we immigrated after traveling thousands of miles from Japan.

Although we have no worry in our living, we feel as if we were treading on thin ice when we come close to the burial of dead fellow workers, which happens almost every day.

In spite of this situation, the religion here is dominated by Christianity. Towns bristle with Christian churches and sermons, and the prayers of the missionaries shake through the cities with the church bells. To strong Buddhists like ourselves, these pressures mean nothing. However, we sometimes get reports of frivolous Japanese who surrender themselves to accept the heresy—as a hungry man does not have much choice but to eat what he is offered.

While strong Buddhists eagerly wished and waited for missionary work here in Hawaii, few priests, introducing themselves as special envoys from headquarters, came to Hawaii. They deceived honest believers by indescribable actions such as fraud and trickery, and then disappeared from the Islands. We, twenty thousand immigrants in the Hawaiian Islands, experienced this disappointment and grief again and again because of ignorance on our part about the relationship between headquarters and priests. We have no intention whatsoever to complain about the situation but eagerly wish to have real priests to be sent here.

In the middle of January, a certain 'priest' came to Honolulu and claimed to be a special commissioner sent by order of headquarters in Japan for the purpose of observation and missionary work among the immigrants. He tried to pretend that he was headquarters' appointee. Having learned from our past experience, we could hardly believe him. Nevertheless, he made an assertion firmly and he showed us a written appointment. We finally acknowledged him as special messenger from headquarters for whom we had waited for a long time. You have no idea how glad and thankful we were. . . . We all thanked the benevolence of the headquarters for saving us from chaotic situation, and this even encouraged many Buddhists.

After overcoming many difficulties, we managed to establish a Teaching Hall on Fort Street through campaigns and donations. We even hung our sign which said 'Shinshū Honpa Hongwanji Branch.' Knowing the weak position of the Shinshū religion here, we made every effort to support the priest, who was alone and unfamiliar with the conditions of this land. We raised Buddha's flag and did everything to serve Buddhists in Honolulu and the Hawaiian Islands to show our gratitude to the headquarters.

Quite unexpectedly, when Master Miyamoto came from headquarters, we discovered that the priest was an impostor. We were not only thrown into consternation but 'lost our faces' to many people—the Christians and other religious people who are cruel to Buddhists. . . . We were so shamed that we could not walk streets in daytime. In addition, the Teaching Hall, where we tried so hard to keep the faith, had to be closed. We fear now that the missionary work of the Shin-shū cannot be carried out because of this disgrace.

We realize our mistake but we are very disappointed for having been trapped again by intrigue like this.

Since we cannot cry endlessly over spilled milk, we asked Master Miyamoto to ignore the past and make use of the Teaching Hall . . . for missionaries, observers, or bishops from headquarters. We hoped that the place would be used, in the future, as branch sermon hall of the headquarters. In reply, Master Miyamoto said that nothing can be approved without headquarters' directions. Although mistakes were made on the part of our believers, they are resulted from enthusiasm of Buddhists who eagerly wished to have missionary work done in this land. It is, therefore, necessary for the representatives of the Buddhists here to report everything that has happened to the headquarters and to ask for leadership.

We hereby report the whole matter to you and ask for assistance. We request that special consideration be given the matter and a suitable priest be sent to reside in the Teaching Hall so we can be healed from this thirst for the Buddha's teaching.

Upon acceptance of this petition, we Buddhists will be responsible for any expense that the operation may incur, and we are willing to make every effort to campaign for the construction of appropriate temples.

[Signed]

Yasuhei Suga	Ichijirō Watanabe
Yasukichi Hirose	Kametarō Morimoto
Sukeji Shinhara	Tokujiro Murakami
Unosuke Kobayashi	Kikumatsu Ōdō
Yonekichi Hashimoto	Kazo Dokata
Tokusaburō Kobayashi	Naotaro Nishikida
Yūkichi Fukushima	Shizuo Yoshimi
Tomotarō Nakao	Jintarō Izukata[7]

On August 5, 1897, eight Buddhists in Hilo composed a similar letter, and Miyamoto took both petitions back to Kyoto.[8]

The pathos and urgency of these requests brought immediate action. In October 1897, Hawaii was officially incorporated into the Honpa Hongwanji foreign missions program, and two priests were dispatched to Hawaii. Sanju Kanayasu went to Hilo, and Shōi Yamada was assigned to Honolulu.[9] On the corner of Fort and Kukui streets, in an old wooden cottage owned by Archibald S. Cleghorn, father of Princess Kaiulani, Yamada began holding regular services for Buddhists in Honolulu. The 'Dark Ages' of rampant fraud and deceit were over, the Buddhists hoped, and Yamada's arrival was heralded as 'the true dawning of the light of the Blessed One.'[10]

Early in 1898, Hōji Satomi, a veteran missionary who had preached the Dharma in Vladivostok, Formosa, and elsewhere, was appointed by Hongwanji headquarters as superior general of the new Hawaiian 'diocese.' Satomi worked briefly with Shōi Yamada in Honolulu and then preached among the Japanese on Maui, Kauai, and the Big Island. By the sheer virtue of his amiable personality, he won the gratitude and enduring aloha of his countrymen; but in a few months his health failed, and in September 1898, he reluctantly returned to Japan. He left in an optimistic mood, however, and before long more priests were assigned to the new mission field. Chishō Uchida was sent to Honomu on the Big Island, and Hōjun Kunizaki was assigned to Wailuku, Maui.[11]

Before his departure from the Islands, Satomi had laid plans with Sanju Kanayasu in Hilo for a new and larger temple to replace the structure that was built on Front Street nine years earlier under the aegis of Sōryū Kagahi and Saiji Kimura.[12] After Satomi returned to Japan, a reporter for the *Hilo Tribune,* commenting on the 'fine work of the Buddhists,' composed this curious 'progress report' on the construction of the new temple:

With the passing of the car of progress, the Japanese adjacent to Hilo and themselves, have put their graft on one of the wheel spokes, and the

HŌJI SATOMI

horn of the prophet Buddha will shortly toot the wondrous reward in store for such as are really good, or reasonably virtuous. The architecture is to be a harmonious blending of the original Buddhist style with the modern haole idea, finished in North West and foreign roofing iron. The carving of the verandah pilasters has been under way for some time past, and designs of such cunning and peculiar forms have been evolved from redwood posts as will make the habitual wine bibber see things, while the drinker of real hard liquors will not frequent the place by night. . . . That a new church was needed by the Japanese has for a long time been a matter for general conversation and the construction of this temple is but another example of the vast possibilities of faith when accompanied by contributions in the shape of coin of the realm.[13]

On February 21, 1899, Hōji Satomi, his health restored, returned to Honolulu aboard the British steamer *Gaelic*. With him was Yemyō Imamura, a thirty-three-year-old priest of boundless energy and practical idealism.[14] Shōi Yamada was immediately transferred to Kealia on Kauai, and Imamura assumed jurisdiction over affairs of the sect as bishop of the Honpa Hongwanji of Hawaii, a position he was to fill for the rest of his life with a rare distinction that earned him a permanent place among Hawaii's most outstanding religious leaders.[15]

CONSTRUCTION OF THE HONOLULU HONGWANJI

During Satomi's absence, Shōi Yamada had collected enough money to purchase a temple site, and in December 1898, 12,550 square feet of land on the corner of Fort Lane was acquired from the estate of William C. and Mary Achi for the sum of $2,750.[16] Satomi and Imamura went promptly to work on plans for the proposed temple, interrupting the project just long enough to attend the royal funeral of the young and beautiful Princess Kaiulani at Kawaiahao, the Old Stone Church. In September 1899, actual construction of the Hongwanji was begun on the chief business street of the city. It was said that $15,725 was collected to meet building costs, and within two months the two-story temple was completed. Kagahi's old friend Saiji Kimura donated 240 chairs and furnished much of the building equipment.[17]

A few days later, before dedication ceremonies could be celebrated, an epidemic of bubonic plague hit Chinatown. The Board of Health ordered the burning of infected buildings to purge the area of the disease, but flames of the fire got out of control; and by nightfall on January 20, 1900, some thirty-eight acres of slum tenements from Kukui Street to the waterfront were reduced to ashes, leaving more than four thousand persons homeless and crazed with grief and horror.[18] Christian and Buddhist leaders rushed to the assistance of their stricken countrymen. Takie Okumura distributed shirts and trousers to clothe them and cooked sixteen hundred pounds of rice to feed them. Satomi and Imamura organized a *kyoaikai,* or relief association, to provide financial and medical aid for them.[19]

Finally, on April 1, 1900, the plague and fire victims were released from detention camps, and Shin-shū services were held for the first time in Honolulu's new Temple of the Original Vow. Buddhists hustled up the temple's broad flight of stairs, left their sandals on its wide verandah, knelt before Amida's shrine to meditate, and prayed with Bishop Imamura and four priests from the outside islands who had come to Honolulu for the occasion. Hōji Satomi was not present. He had returned to Japan in March, leaving the future of the Honpa Hongwanji in the capable hands of Yemyō Imamura.[20]

A formal *nyūbutsu-shiki* (dedication ceremony) for the two-story

Hongwanji was celebrated on November 20, 1900, and an *Advertiser* reporter, on hand for the occasion, bequeathed to posterity a quaint description of how the temple and a Buddhist service looked to an American who apparently had never witnessed a Buddhist religious ceremony. He wrote that the altar was installed in a room large enough to hold several hundred people, and suspended from the ceiling, casting a soft glow on the altar, was a pair of lamps designed 'in much the same style as Aladdin's famous lamps.' Incense from an urn on the altar 'drifted lazily upward . . . permeating the interior of the temple with a sweer odor, typifying the boundless mercy of Buddha.' Bishop Imamura, attired in the rich green and purple vestments of his office, opened the sacred service with a 'monotonous yet melodious chant,' while the faithful, with their circlets of coral or black beads (the *juzu*, or Buddhist rosary), reverently recited the nembutsu. Later in the service, kimono–clad children, 'with powdered faces and tinseled tiaras,' listened attentively to an address, delivered in English on the brotherhood of man, by Mrs. J. Barber, former librarian of the Golden Gate Lodge in San Francisco.[21] Among the non–Oriental spectators on hand for the ceremony were Dr. Auguste Baptiste Marques, secretary of the Australian division of the Theosophical Society who later became French consul, and Mrs. Mary E. Foster,* a wealthy Hawaiian lady who, a few years earlier, had been converted to the Theravāda, or Doctrine of the Elders,[22] by a visiting Indian Buddhist.

Bishop Imamura lost no time organizing and coordinating the activities of the new mission. With the help of ten enterprising men, including four young Japanese physicians, he organized the Young Men's Buddhist Association (YMBA) in July 1900, in order to provide religious education and solace for immigrants in and about the city. Before long, the YMBA opened a night school to teach English to the Japanese and began publishing its own organ, the *Dōbō* (Brotherhood). A year later, a capacity crowd of Japanese and haoles congregated on the Hongwanji grounds to participate in special services commemorating the first anniversary of the fast-growing youth organization. Fluttering in the trade winds at the entrance of the temple were the flag of the Rising Sun, the Stars and Stripes, and the multicolored emblem of Gautama the Buddha. In May 1901, the mission held its first services in honor of the birth of Shinran, founder of the Jōdo-Shin-shū. Several hundred persons attended that ceremony, too. Dr. Marques and Mrs. Barber were there, and so was the deposed and aging Liliuokalani,

---

*Mary E. Foster, one of the Ward sisters of Honolulu, was converted to the Theravāda in 1893 as the result of an acquaintance with the Ceylonese Buddhist propagandist, Anāgārika Dharmāpala. Later she became a friend of the Buddhists in Ceylon and contributed thousands of dollars for the endowment and upkeep of orphanages and hospitals in Ceylon and Calcutta.

who had not yet given up her long and apparently futile search for religious solace.[23]

By this time, Jōdo-shū officials had also taken a greater interest in the Hawaiian scene. Two priests of this sect, Mashien Tanaka from Yamaguchi and Daijō Yasuda from Shiga Prefecture, were sent to the Big Island in 1898 to assist Gakuō Okabe. Yasuda collected a few thousand dollars and built a temple in Laupahoehoe in 1899. At the same time, as the result of a conference of Pure Land leaders in Japan, Hawaii was incorporated into the Jōdo-shū mission field along with Korea and Formosa.[24]

The Christian community, of course, was not oblivious to these alien encroachments. Puritan missionaries, who continued to bewail the raucous festivals of the 'heathen Chinee' (which brought the celestials in ever closer touch with their own numerous gods and idols), soon began to complain even more bitterly about the competition and opposition of the Buddhists. Orramel Gulick reported that Buddhist priests or 'reputed priests' had confronted his evangelists many times, and Takie Okumura was very much perturbed about the 'recent great activity' of the heathen clerics. The *Friend*, philosophizing on the merits and demerits of Buddhism, asserted that Buddhism had totally failed to elevate the Japanese people anywhere near to the morality and decency of Christian peoples. Only those who loved what was murky and dim could find any satisfaction in Buddhism, for Jesus, the paper concluded, 'was the Sun of Righteousness [and] Buddha was but a dim star.'[25]

ANNEXATION AND ADDITIONAL JAPANESE IMMIGRATION

Meanwhile a treaty of annexation had failed to pass the United States Senate. A joint resolution, however, was subsequently passed by the House of Representatives almost as a formality, and on July 6, 1898, the Senate accepted it after a symposium of negative views and nothing else. Transfer of the sovereignty of the Republic of Hawaii took place in Honolulu on August 12, 1898, in a moving ceremony. The harbor and city were gay with bunting, and a large crowd gathered in front of Iolani Palace to witness the historic event. A remnant of the Royal Hawaiian Band played 'Hawaii Ponoi,' the Hawaiian national anthem, as old-time Hawaiians with heavy hearts watched their native flag lowered and the Stars and Stripes hoisted in its place. Then for nearly two years, Hawaii continued under the old regime while Congress settled the problems of empire. Not until April 30, 1900, did the Congress pass the Organic Act, under which the incorporated Territory of Hawaii would be governed for nearly sixty years. Citizens of the Territory became citizens of the United States, and voting privileges were extended to all male citizens who were at least twenty-one years old. On June 14, 1900, at Iolani Palace, on a platform decorated with the

YEMYŌ IMAMURA

American and the Hawaiian colors, Sanford B. Dole, president of
the former Republic of Hawaii, took the oath of office as the first
governor of the Territory.[26]

The capital of the new Territory, 'on the eve of the greatest
improvement in her history,' had taken on the appearance of a
busy, modern metropolis.[27] The streets of Honolulu had been
widened, pipes had been laid for a sewer system, and real estate
was enjoying an unprecedented boom as the city took a sudden
surge skyward. Two- and three-story brick and terra cotta buildings had gone up, and massive foundations for the six-story, 'up-to-
date, fireproof' Stangenwald Building had been laid on Merchant
Street near the law offices of Lorrin A. Thurston. Along Fort Street,
near Honolulu's new Temple of the Original Vow, a variety of
professional and business men plied their trade—doctors, dentists,
restaurant owners, druggists, retail grocers, hardware dealers,

novelty retailers, a baker, a jeweler, and H. H. Williams, undertaker and embalmer. Tourists continued to patronize the old Hawaiian Hotel and to visit Kapiolani Park in tramcars, which now ran every half hour to and from different sections of the city. Trains of the Oahu Railway and Land Company commuted on weekends between Honolulu and outlying rural areas of Oahu where Japanese field hands continued to work for a pittance on flourishing sugar plantations.[28]

Along with the growth of the city, a spectacular boom in the sugar industry followed annexation. The need for more labor thus again became critical. For the time being, the Japanese continued to be available;* but when Hawaii became an integral part of the United States, the contract labor system came to an end, and all outstanding contracts were cancelled. In November 1899, E. D. Tenney of the Hawaiian Sugar Planters' Association (hereafter referred to as HSPA) pointed out that the labor problem would be the most important one confronting the planters and urged that a large additional labor force, over ordinary requirements, be brought right away to the country.[29] Thus, in anticipation of possible federal proscription of Oriental immigration, an unprecedented number of twenty-six thousand Japanese immigrants was brought to the Islands before the end of 1899. Between annexation and the passage of the Organic Act, a total of forty-one thousand Japanese arrived in the Islands, and the census of 1900 showed that the Japanese alone comprised 40 percent of the entire population of the Territory.†

Bishop Imamura thus had ample reason to anticipate the 'rebirth' of Buddhism in a new civilization.[30]

---

*The only U.S. statute which applied to Hawaii prior to the passage of the Organic Act was the Chinese Exclusion Act of 1882.

†Hawaiians (30,000) and part-Hawaiians (10,000) made up only 26 percent of the population, as compared with 89.2 percent in 1876. Portuguese (18,000) and other Caucasians (9,000) accounted for a mere 17.5 percent. The actual number of Orientals had catapulted from a total of 2,500 in 1876 to 87,000 (26,000 Chinese; 61,000 Japanese), or 56.5 percent of the total population.

CHAPTER 6

'Abodes of Light and Love'

ANNEXATION LED TO MUCH REST-
LESSNESS AND DISORDER ON HAWAIIAN
plantations. Laborers who were freed from contracts drawn up
subsequent to August 12, 1898, fled from plantation to plantation or
wandered into the towns, penniless and hungry, in search of better
jobs. The desertion of field hands caused a drastic scarcity of labor
on several of the large cane fields—especially along the Kona and
Hamakua coasts of the Big Island and at Ewa on Oahu.[1] At the same
time, the application of United States labor laws to Hawaii spawned
an epidemic of petty strikes. Japanese workmen wanted a shorter
workday and an end to the inequitable docking-of-wages system;
they demanded the dismissal of sadistic lunas and the prompt removal of incompetent interpreters and physicians. The frequent
late payment of wages, the withholding of a part of their wages for
investment by the Japanese consul, and the shabby conditions of
many of the camps also gave rise to endless complaints.[2]

Distressed by the widespread strife and dissension on Hawaiian
plantations, Buddhist priests set out to encourage a state of more or
less permanent settlement, and Bishop Imamura personally resolved
to furnish his countrymen on all the major plantations with spiritual support through storm and stress. In a period of less than five
years, the Honpa Hongwanji built fifteen temples—'abodes of light
and love,' as Imamura dubbed them—in the midst of the largest
plantation districts of the Territory.[3] Between 1899 and 1902,
Imamura's Mission erected temples at Kealia and Lihue on Kauai; at
Ewa, Waipahu, Kahuku, Aiea, and Waianae on Oahu; at Honomu,

Papaaloa, Olaa, and Naalehu on the Big Island; and at Wailuku, Maui. During the next two years, seven more temples were raised on these islands: three more on Hawaii, at Honokaa, Holualoa, and Pahala; two others on Maui, at Hamakuapoko and Lahaina; and two more on Oahu, at Waialua and Waimanalo.

Temples were built by priests of the other sects, too. As early as 1899, Shizuka Sazanami, a priest of the Higashi Hongwanji, arrived in Hawaii and laid plans for the construction of a temple in Waimea on the 'Garden Island' of Kauai. In May 1902, Gyōun Takaki of the Nichiren-shū built a temple in Pahala on the southeast coast of the Big Island, and in 1903, Senyei Kawahara introduced Sōtō-Zen to the Hawaiian Islands. The first Sōtō temple, completed in 1905, was built on Waipahu plantation on the West Loch side of Pearl Harbor. A few years later, Ryūki Hirai, another Sōtō priest, supervised the construction of a temple at Waialua plantation on the north coast of Oahu. Meanwhile, Sōtō headquarters in Tsurumi had dispatched Ryōun Kan and Sogyō Ueoka to preach in the Islands. Kan eventually settled in Wahiawa on Kauai, and Ueoka went to Paia on Maui, and each priest built a temple in his respective locale. The Jōdo-shū, meanwhile, had built two more temples on the Big Island, in Olaa and Hakalau. By the end of 1906, there were more than thirty abodes of light and love in the Islands.[4]

Most of the plantation temples scattered throughout the Territory were simple frame cottages with graceful, overhanging roofs that 'reared above the huts of plantation laborers and broke the monotony of vast cane fields dotted here and there with clusters of camp houses.'[5] Within these walls, priests of Amida Buddha and the Wise Man of the Śākyas perpetuated ancient, familiar rituals. Temple gongs were sounded at regular intervals during chanted services to jolt professed followers of the Enlightened One out of their moral lethargy and to bid them forgo the grosser things of the world. Incense rose from temple altars recalling to the worshippers the impermanency of life and the fragrance of the Pure Land.

Most of the expenses connected with the building and furnishing of the temples were met by laborers earning a maximum of fifteen to twenty dollars a month. Between 1899 and 1902, the Buddhists of Honolulu, despite the severe monetary reverses suffered as a result of the plague and fire of 1900, donated thousands of dollars for the propagation of the Dharma throughout the Territory—an extraordinary testimony to the faith and devotion of the immigrants from Japan. The planters, too, soon began donating land and contributing money for the construction and maintenance of Buddhist temples.[6]

THE ROLE OF THE PLANTERS

Long before Oriental temples were built in Hawaii, plantation officials had demonstrated a commendable readiness to assist

Christian evangelists in converting 'many poor and needy souls.'
Jirō Okabe readily obtained pledges of support for his co-workers
in Hilo, and all expenses connected with the work of Shigehide
Kanda in Kohala were met by plantation managers. The Hawaiian
Board acknowledged the help of the planters in 'shedding Gospel
light,' and the *Friend* consistently urged Christian stockholders to
enlighten their 'ignorant human brethren' with the truths of the
Gospel in order to minimize 'the peril from the heathen Japanese.'[7]
In deepest sympathy with Christian workers was their kindest and
most generous friend, pioneer planter Henry P. Baldwin, son of the
late Reverend Dwight Baldwin who had long ago tried in vain to
convert the pious Heshero to Christianity. The work on Maui, in
fact, could never have been so successfully carried on had it not been
for the support of Henry P. Baldwin, 'Maui's most generous
giver.'[8]

While religious scruples deterred men like Henry Baldwin and
'Father' George Renton, manager of the Ewa plantation, from
extending similar assistance to Buddhist priests, most planters and
plantation officials had no such reservations. On the contrary,
planters freely donated land for the construction of Honpa Hongwanji temples (in Waipahu, Kahuku, Aiea, and Waianae on Oahu;
in Kealia and Lihue on Kauai; in Naalehu, Olaa, and Papaaloa on
Hawaii); they donated sites for Jōdo-shū temples (in Paauhau and
Hakalau on the Big Island, and in Koloa on Kauai); and they
allotted land for the Sōtō-shū temple in Waipahu on Oahu.
However, on the island of Maui, where Henry Baldwin was 'king,'
temples were usually erected (of necessity) on purchased property
—e.g., the Sōtō temple in Paia and the Honpa Hongwanji in
Wailuku.[9]

The generosity of the planters was prompted by enlightened
self-interest. Following annexation and subsequent abolition of the
contract labor system, Japanese migrated in droves to the U.S.
mainland where they could command higher wages. Within
five years, some forty thousand Japanese departed for the continen-
tal United States. In 1905, two thousand left in a period of just two
weeks. Not until 1907 was an immigration bill pushed through
Congress to restrict Japanese migration; in the meantime, the
planters had to find ways of enticing field hands to remain in the
Islands and were much too anxious to keep on good terms with
their laborers to coerce them in any way. Thus, there was no
opposition to Buddhism. On the contrary, as the U.S. Commissioner of Labor had noted, the planters 'rather encourage[d] the
building of temples.'[10]

The planters had observed, too, that Buddhism tended to
enhance the docility of their labor force. *Ando shugi*, the teaching of
peaceful cooperation, was a cardinal feature of the religion, and
patience in time of stress was exalted in the canons of the faith as
one of the Ten Perfections of the bodhisattvas. Buddhist priests,

furthermore, preached unceasingly against avarice and individual aggression, exhorting their countrymen to 'master regret, to endure pain, and to accept as eternal law the vanishing of things loved and the tyranny of things hated.'[11] The practical value of such a teaching soon became apparent to the planters—especially after Bishop Imamura's successful intervention in the strike of 1904.

THE SUGAR STRIKE OF 1904 AIDS THE GROWTH OF BUDDHISM

In July 1904, a protest strike broke out at Waipahu plantation on Oahu when the management refused to dismiss a vicious and much hated luna. The strike assumed alarming proportions and forty-six policemen were summoned to quell the riot. Consul General Miki Saitō and other influential leaders of the Japanese community rushed to the scene and pleaded earnestly with the strikers to return to work. Nothing happened. Men on the lowest rung of the social ladder have seldom complied with the demands of an insensitive intelligentsia. As a matter of fact, as the planters soon discovered, such persons seemed to have 'no influence whatever.'[12] At the most critical stage of the controversy (as a last resort, really), Yemyō Imamura was asked to see what he could do to restore order. Imamura's speech was neither eloquent nor persuasive, as his son Kanmo later recalled, but on such occasions his wide and deep understanding of the problems faced by the immigrants and his earnest wish for their happiness somehow came through. The Hongwanji bishop counseled his countrymen to cease their agitation and to put their trust in Amida Buddha 'who pours his boundless love upon us all.' The uproar on Waipahu plantation then quickly subsided, and the Japanese went back to work.[13]

Imamura's mediation in the settlement of the strike was duly noted and commended by the American press. The *Hawaiian Star* congratulated the Buddhist priest for his effective services, and even the *Friend* conceded that Imamura had come out frankly and helpfully on the right side. More important, the planters came to realize that 'For those who recognize only the supreme value of Amida's love, and never the claims of individual merit, such an arrangement no doubt involves the least danger of self-assertion.'[14] Before the close of the first decade of the century, more abodes of light and love were constructed in rural Hawaii, in most cases, with the hearty cooperation of the planters. The Jōdo sect built a new temple at Wailuku, Maui. The Honpa Hongwanji erected temples at Kohala and Papaiko on the Big Island; at Kilauea, Eleele, and Waimea on Kauai; and at Paia on Maui.[15]

The Christian community, of course, was appalled by the willingness of the planters to curry the favor of their labor force by supporting a religion which they at heart opposed. An aroused

KANMO IMAMURA

Puritan clergy, more determined than ever that pagan errors would not spread, angrily berated the planters for 'allowing sake free entrance to plantation camps . . . [for] winking at gambling fraternities' and, above all, for aiding and abetting Buddhism, 'an open enemy of our Master and His Kingdom of Righteousness.' At the suggestion of its Japanese evangelists, the Hawaiian Board passed a resolution to 'let each and all planters know what influence [and] effects should be brought to the plantations by the flourishing of' Buddhism.[16]

Christians had reason to be upset. Their efforts everywhere had been thwarted, as Superintendent John Wadman of the reactivated Methodist-Episcopal Mission reported, by Buddhist priests who were working harder than ever to hold the Japanese to the old 'superstitions.' Even those few 'converts' who were won to Christ before the introduction of Buddhism had reverted to the faith of their ancestors. In 1908 one of Wadman's evangelists optimistically reported that he had accomplished on Kahuku plantation the 'first Christian work . . . in a camp of several hundreds of Japanese in the very center of which [is] a big Buddhist temple.'[17] But only rarely did Christians make any headway in a rural area where one or more Buddhist temples 'stood as a challenge' to the Christian forces of the district. Even the most dedicated evangelists were finally compelled to acknowledge that Christianity and Buddhism were destined to be taught side by side, and before long, in many rural areas, a caustic rivalry sprang up between Christian zealots and Buddhist priests, who 'came, and saw, and conquered.'[18]

In the cities, the opposition from 'heathendom' was no less galling. Many Japanese had moved into urban districts at the turn of the century, and Buddhism moved in right along with them. In April 1904, the indefatigable Takie Okumura and a handful of devout Congregationalists in Honolulu organized the Makiki Japanese Christian Church in a little shed on Kinau Street. The Honpa Hongwanji then promptly constructed a temple nearby. In 1905, dejected evangelists in the Kakaako district complained that Buddhist priests were busily soliciting subscriptions for the construction of a Jōdo temple. At once the Christian work in Kakaako suffered a setback. Two years later, moreover, Jōdo-shū headquarters were transferred from the Big Island to Honolulu, and on Sunday, November 17, 1907, a jubilant throng of some one thousand persons gathered on South Street, in the heart of the city, to witness dedication rites for the Mission's new two-story temple, the first of this sect's to be built on the island of Oahu. Shinjun Shimizu, superintendent of the mission and 'seemingly a sort of bishop,' officiated at the dedication ceremony with much bowing before a bronze image of Amida Buddha. Assisting 'Bishop' Shimizu was the Reverend Enjo Itō, who had come from the Olaa temple on the Big Island to assume jurisdiction over Jōdo-shū affairs in Honolulu. The seven-thousand-dollar frame structure bore a striking resemblance, both inwardly and outwardly, to the other temple of Amida Buddha built earlier by the Hongwanji Mission.[19] Buddhism continued to flourish in Hilo also. A new Honpa Hongwanji temple built on Volcano Street in Hilo was formally dedicated in October 1907, and two years later, the Jōdo sect raised an equally imposing temple nearby on two acres of leased land.[20]

THE CHARTER ISSUE

In February 1906, Honpa Hongwanji headquarters had sent two men, Zuigi Ashikaga and Reishin Hayashi, to assess the effectiveness of Hongwanji missionary work in the Islands. Within a few weeks, these scouts sent a comprehensive and highly favorable report back to their superiors, and in May 1906, the home temple in Kyoto notified Bishop Imamura that the Hongwanji of Honolulu had been officially promoted to the status of *betsuin* (detached temple, branch headquarters).[21]

The Mission then applied for a charter of incorporation as a bona fide religious organization in the Territory. Governor George R. Carter flatly refused to grant it. Such a charter, Carter said, would not be compatible with 'the best future interests of this Territory.'[22] An irate Japanese press then launched forth a steady stream of invective upon the governor, denouncing him as a narrow-minded and bigoted officer who took it upon himself to think the Honpa Hongwanji Mission was more a patriotic organ than a religious one; and *this* in, of all places, a 'free country where the people are allowed free speech, free press, and free worship.'[23] The American press, on the other hand, considered Carter's suspicion that the Mission was inculcating Japanese patriotism to be a legitimate one.[24]

As a matter of fact, the governor's fears were not wholly without justification. The ardent national pride of the Japanese immigrants had been bolstered recently by another Japanese military triumph abroad which had produced disquieting outbursts of patriotic enthusiasm in Hawaii. As soon as Japan handed Russia a humiliating defeat in the Russo-Japanese War, newspaper editor Yasutarō Sōga boasted that 'Japan's rise as a power, her distinguished success in her great war [has] made her the cynosure of all eyes.'[25] Moreover, during the war, while the Kyoto Hongwanji hurried chaplains to the front lines, members of the Honolulu *betsuin* sent money to Japan to support the war effort and busily distributed, among local Buddhists, a pamphlet exhorting all young men departing for combat to be a credit to Nippon. Later, with the cessation of hostilities, Buddhist temples sponsored ostentatious victory celebrations and conducted elaborate memorial rites for those Japanese soldiers who had perished in battle.[26]

Governor Carter naturally looked askance at such effusions of patriotic fervor. He also viewed, with mounting apprehension, the increased frequency of petty strikes on Hawaiian plantations and the blustering arrogance of field hands who demanded their 'rights' as citizens of the 'most invincible power' in the Far East. Even before the charter issue came up, Carter had communicated his mistrust of Hawaii's Japanese to Secretary of State John Hay. Hay, in turn, had conveyed Carter's fears to President Theodore Roosevelt, and in February 1905, the president alerted Secretary of War William Howard Taft, as follows:

Dear Will: When you go to the Philippines next summer could you stop at Hawaii to look into the labor problem there and especially into the Japanese business. Carter has written a very interesting letter to Hay, which I would like you to send for. The Japanese have become very numerous in the Islands. They far outnumber the whites, and are now showing signs of an insolent temper, which may make them a most formidable problem. After reading Carter's letter . . . communicate with him and see if he needs a regiment or two of troops in the Islands.[27]

Taft courteously replied that he would do so, but there the matter rested.

On the charter matter, the Hongwanji bided its time, and as soon as Walter F. Frear succeeded Carter as governor, the Mission reapplied for a charter. Frear, unlike Carter, was not willing to risk incurring the wrath of the Japanese community. So in October 1907, the Honpa Hongwanji was incorporated as an ecclesiastical, eleemosynary, and educational organization and was authorized to hold property in the Territory up to the amount of two hundred thousand dollars.[28]

Ownership of all temples and properties was then consolidated and consigned to the *betsuin* in Honolulu, and the activities of branch temples throughout the Territory were coordinated with those of the Mission headquarters on Fort Street. A board of thirty-five laymen was elected to assist in the management of Mission affairs, and in February 1908, the first interisland Hongwanji conference was called in order to map out a centralized and systematic program of religious and educational propaganda.[29] Buddhism had become a permanent part of the religious life of the Islands.

BUDDHIST MORES IN HAWAII

In the early years of the century, Buddhism in Hawaii embodied the old country's ancient folkways and social mores which had been transplanted to the Islands along with the immigrants. Filial piety, a concept borrowed centuries ago from Confucianism, was exalted above all virtues and, from generation to generation, revivified the sense of the unity and continuity of the family. In the Japanese home, almost without exception, a *butsudan* (family altar) enshrined the *ihai* (ancestral tablets) on which were inscribed the posthumous Buddhist names of beloved family forebears. With the rising and setting of the sun, the Japanese father faithfully burned incense before the sacred *ihai*, and the Japanese wife and mother, as custodian of the household shrine, daily placed before the ancestral tablets offerings of flowers and freshly cooked rice. The ties of natural affection binding members of the family in both life and death were thus perpetually renewed. Ancestors, who dwelt in unseen worlds merited by the karma of their earthly thoughts and deeds, depended on living descendants to modify their bad karma and hasten their journey to the Pure Land. To neglect one's ancestors, therefore, was shameful, a sin against the dead. On the other hand, to do good for the sake of one's forefathers added immeasurably to one's storehouse of good karma.

The annual and popular *urabon* season, observed in Japan for centuries, is symbolic of the spiritual cohesion of the Japanese family and brings to mind the two pillars of Gautama's Dharma: *Wisdom*, the attainment of Enlightenment; and *Compassion*, the giving of all that one has and is, for the spiritual welfare of others.[30] The word *urabon* is derived from the Sanskrit *ullambana*, to hang upside down with suffering; and it is written in the *Ullambana Sūtra* that Moggalāna, Śākyamuni's beloved disciple, saw his mother hanging upside down with anguish in a purgatory caused by the karma of past selfish lives. To liberate her, Moggalāna practiced compassion and *dāna* (charity) to a heroic degree, forgetting himself altogether and offering up all the good karma accumulated thereby solely for her emancipation. In time, his selfless, bodhisattva-like love brought her to the shores of the Pure Land and Nirvana.

In Hawaii, as in Japan, the annual *urabon* festival, commencing on or about the fifteenth of July, was perennially observed in a spirit of joyful reverence. Every *butsudan* was scrupulously cleansed and adorned with fresh flowers from favorite florists, and pounded rice cakes or Japanese macaroni (*mōchi*) was offered on altars in place of the usual home-cooked rice. Colorful paper lanterns, *chōchin*, swayed from the verandahs of many homes and welcomed the spirits of departed ones who yearned to share the joys and griefs of the living. On the eve of *urabon*, priests visited the homes of the faithful to chant the *sūtras* while family patriarchs burned incense before memorial tablets of the beloved dead.[31]

It is also written in the *Ullambana Sūtra* that when Moggalāna saw his mother released at last from the hell-fires of greed and avarice, he danced with joy. Thus a traditional feature of the *urabon* season, popular with old and young alike, is the colorful Bon odori, or Bon dances, staged on temple grounds. At dusk, behind sugar mills throughout the Islands, exhausted and aging Japanese laborers, in preparation for holy *urabon*, taught their children and grandchildren the odori of joy.[32]

Buddhism thus made life on Hawaiian plantations more tolerable for the immigrants by strengthening and hallowing the sense of family kinship. It also elevated the morality of the Japanese by making them strictly accountable to the community for their conduct. Buddhist priests taught that every social relationship was a result of a long and complex karmic process persisting through countless lives and that the preservation of social harmony was a sacred obligation binding on each and every member of the community.[33] Every Japanese was therefore duty-bound to conform to a hierarchy of values rigidly defined by his socio-religious environment. In time these values also proved a boon to the wider community. In fact, it was said that had it not been for the influence of Buddhism, 'the [Hawaiian] government . . . might have found dealing with so many of these people [the Japanese immigrants] a very difficult problem.'[34]

In the meantime, the Christian clergy, stunned by God's reluctance to stay the march of heathendom, continued to do battle against the formidable foe. The Hawaiian Board employed more and more evangelists to work among the Japanese, and among the new recruits was one Frank Scudder, who, though reputedly an authority on the Shin sect, was horrified by the 'superstitious' custom of 'dancing at the festival of the dead:'[35] Scudder superseded Orramel H. Gulick as superintendent of the Japanese Department in 1907, and a few years later, John P. Erdman, another outstanding mission worker, superseded Scudder in the same capacity.[36]

With the addition of such 'experienced men' to its staff, the Hawaiian Board hoped that Buddhism could not survive the influence of the 'higher and purer' faith, and clerics took vigorous exception to suggestions from pagan circles that it was vain to carry the Gospel to the Japanese or that Buddhism was as good for them as Christianity. Orramel Gulick wrote on the eve of his resignation that no earnest Christian could be 'so benighted.'[37] But Buddhist missionaries came to the Islands as fast or faster than Christian evangelists, and most of the 'heathen priests' were every bit as solicitous of the spiritual and material welfare of the Japanese as were their Christian counterparts. In fact, they all too often gave a Christian exhorter 'the time of his life.'[38]

CHAPTER 7

The Buddhist Priesthood
in Hawaii

THE MAJORITY OF HAWAII'S JAPANESE
CAME FROM PREFECTURES OF SOUTHERN
Japan where the Jōdo-Shin-shū predominated. Most of the priests
who furnished the earliest moral and educational leadership of the
Japanese community in the Islands were also natives of the southern
provinces and, likewise, belonged to the True Pure Land sect.[1] The
following brief survey of the activities and accomplishments of the
early Buddhist missionaries, therefore, deals primarily (but not exclusively) with the priests of the Honpa Hongwanji of Hawaii.

THE PIONEER PERIOD

Long before the influx of Japanese women who, despite their
'heathen' training, helped to stabilize the domestic and social conditions in rural communities, itinerant Buddhist priests,* compelled
by circumstances to bear poverty with indifference and contempt
with equanimity, had discovered that the natural state of the immigrants, as Bishop Imamura put it, was 'a monstrous conglomeration
of "greed, passion, and folly." '[2] Many of the Japanese had 'banded
together . . . against law and order.'[3]

*Since there is no place for sacrificial rites or mediators between 'God' and man
in Gautama's teaching, strictly speaking, there is no priesthood in original Indian
Buddhism. However, those who have preached the Dharma and officiated at
symbolic religious ceremonies in Hawaii and elsewhere have customarily been
called 'priests.' The term has therefore been retained throughout this volume.

As the Japanese gradually lost touch with the homeland, as their spirits were weakened by a languorous climate, and as their characters were toughened by a hostile environment, traditional moral values and restraints were thrust aside. *Tabi no haji wa kaki sute*, Throw away shame when away from home, epitomized an attitude which soon became all too prevalent. The frequently reckless and lawless behavior of the Japanese sprang in large measure from resentment of a community that tolerated their presence merely as a necessary evil. Pressure was exerted on them by persons who cared nothing for their personal welfare, and their lives were controlled by a remote and indifferent society, totally inaccessible to them. As cane planters or harvesters, they were specialized functionaries with no personal identities. They lived in plantation-owned houses, bought their food and clothing from plantation-owned stores, and were treated by plantation-paid physicians.

Life on many Hawaiian plantations was truly wretched. More often than not, living quarters were unfit for habitation. Laborers working ten to twelve hours a day in cane fields or mills returned exhausted at twilight to dismal, termite-ridden bunkhouses. Conditions varied, of course, from plantation to plantation. But, as a rule, men were huddled together in barrack rooms which accommodated anywhere from six to forty men, and rough, one by twelve wooden planks served as beds. At one time, on some of the plantations along the Hamakua coast, as many as one hundred Japanese were cramped together in a single barrack. Married men were usually furnished with a small room for each family, but bachelors sometimes shared even these quarters. Privacy was a luxury enjoyed by few. Moreover, opportunities for amicable social intercourse were extremely rare. Before the construction of the Buddhist temples, the community bath house was the center of plantation life.[4]

Laborers were subjected to demoralizing and even abusive treatment by unfeeling lunas who, eager to impress employers with their 'efficiency,' were quick to use the whip. The language barrier frequently made it difficult for workmen to grasp what lunas expected of them, and the overseers in turn rarely tried to make any sense out of the broken Japanese and pidgin English of the field hands. Illness was often mistaken for laziness or an obstinate refusal to comply with orders. Sickness, moreover, was quite prevalent on Hawaiian plantations. The drinking water was bad, and there was seldom enough to go around. Dysentery and beriberi were common. Plantation doctors could not always be sure whether a man was genuinely ill or malingering. A few of them did not care, and some Japanese died of medical neglect.

The appalling conditions of their existence, inimical to their very survival and devastating to their self-respect, provoked the wrath of the Japanese and bred among them flagrant vice and a chaotic individualism. Some of them, a bit mad, became violent even over trifles, and crime and immorality spread with alarming rapidity. Between April 1894 and December 1895, alone, 14,492 Japanese were arrested; 10,109 were convicted. A few of the Japanese put an end to their misery by commiting *seppuku* (self-disembowelment). More of them just quietly despaired. '*Shikata ga nai,*' It is no use, they said. There was surely little evidence of the heroic Buddhist endurance of unalterable circumstances or of the faith that Nirvana comes with an extinction of the desire 'to want things to be other than they are.'[5] Buddhist admonitions against excessive drinking were totally ignored. Saloons situated on or near plantations all over the Territory, in fact, helped to provide whatever 'contentment' the Japanese enjoyed, which invariably came from 'much sake and gambling.'[6] Nor were murder and attempted murder uncommon. A Japanese policeman was murdered on Ewa plantation in September 1893, for trying to break up a nighttime gambling ring,[7] and murders were frequently incited by frenzied quarrels over the possession of paramours. A few of the most hated overseers and interpreters were either critically injured or done away with altogether. A gang of laborers at Makaweli, Kauai, made 'an almost fatal murderous assault upon their luna, J. Hasic, with their hoes,' and K. Wada, the detested Japanese interpreter at Spreckelsville Plantation No. 3, was murdered in a riot.[8]

Into the midst of this widespread wretchedness, rampant brutality, and pandemonium came the priests of the Enlightened One, preaching nonviolence, resignation, and *ando shugi* (peaceful cooperation). This was no mean task. Yet many of the priests who came to Hawaii remained in the Islands and, in good time, against seemingly countless odds, brought order out of the tumult and chaos of plantation life.[9] Some priests, like Hiseki Miyazaki, died in Hawaii. Others, like Shōi Yamada and Jōshō Yempuku, eventually carried the Dharma to the United States.[10]

EARLY BUDDHIST MISSIONARIES IN HAWAII

The burdens borne by the Buddhist priest both in body and in spirit were many. Married or single, he lived in cramped quarters in the rear of a plantation temple. He usually had charge of at least five or six camps, situated miles apart, which he visited on alternate evenings. On horseback it took him several hours, sometimes an entire day, to get from one camp to another. Reverend Hiseki Miyazaki regularly traversed eleven miles of rugged mountain terrain commuting between Koloa and Lihue on Kauai. Occasionally priests who visited until late hours of the evening with their countrymen were invited to sleep overnight in private quarters on plantation premises. But only rarely did priests enjoy a restful night. On one occasion, Reverend Hakuda Takeda was abruptly awakened late at night by a loud rapping on the door of a private home at a Makaweli camp. Takeda had fallen asleep in a room frequented by prostitutes, and (as he had neglected to turn off the light) a mob of raucous Japanese, gay on sake, had assumed that a harlot was making her rounds at an uncustomarily late hour. Upon discovering their error, but without a word about what had enticed them there, they remained to recite the nembutsu with their priest.[11]

Some of the Japanese still vividly remembered the 'Dark Ages,' so it sometimes took a *kaikyōshi* (missionary) much longer than he anticipated to win the confidence of his countrymen. In the meantime, suspect and unwelcome, the priest was frequently humiliated and ridiculed by his own people. The missionary was treated, according to Bishop Imamura's account, like a dog without a home. Imamura himself, shortly after his arrival in 1899, was greeted at one camp with such derision and vulgarity that he was tempted to pack his belongings and return to Japan.[12] Reverend Miyazaki, who appears to have had more than his share of problems, was once summoned to address a group of Buddhists at a spot some sixteen miles from the Lihue temple. Starting out on horseback in the early hours of a cold morning, he arrived at the appointed place at the appointed hour and found no one in sight.[13]

Priests were humiliated and even endangered by persons outside the Japanese community, too. On his way from Lihue to Koloa, Reverend Miyazaki was attacked one evening by a group of Puerto Ricans and was lucky to escape with his life. Reverend Jōshō Yempuku fled across cane fields between Waipahu and Ewa to elude a group of YMCA youths who had been goaded by a Christian zealot into hurling stones at 'the heathen priest.'[14]

Almost without exception, Buddhist priests were poor, and poverty in the midst of poverty did nothing to enhance a priest's popularity among the Japanese. Priests received no allotments from religious headquarters abroad and were thus heavily dependent on votary offerings.[15] Usually priests received a donation for officiating at funeral rites, and if the death rate was high in their particular locales, they fared fairly well; otherwise they were obliged to move on to other districts, surviving in the meantime on coconuts and bananas.[16] Occasionally a plantation manager who found it cheaper to keep a priest around than to employ policemen gave token support to a *kaikyōshi,* and priests who later taught in language schools received a monthly pittance of between ten and twenty-five dollars.[17]

To further complicate life for priests in the opening years of the century, impostors still appeared on the scene from time to time, excited the religious enthusiasm of the Japanese, pocketed large sums of money, and then hastily folded their *kesa* (surplices) and sailed away. A self-styled 'special emissary' from a Kyoto temple came to Honolulu on one occasion and collected fifty thousand dollars. Then he went on to California in the hope of emulating his success in Hawaii, but a San Francisco newspaper found out about him and he was forced to leave the West Coast under very awkward circumstances. Then, too, some bona fide priests were anything but exemplary. Once, a smooth-talking, well-dressed Nichiren priest arrived in Honolulu, delivered a fervid harangue of some sort before an enthralled crowd at the Asahi Theater, and absconded with forty thousand dollars. Later he was arrested in Japan for inveigling twenty thousand yen from a soap firm. His only other claim to fame was the Iji Gasho, a salvationist cult he founded in Hiroshima in his spare moments.[18]

But by the second decade of the century, swindlers and 'stray shepherds' rarely disrupted the work of the dedicated priests who had come to preach the Dharma and whose rewards were seldom commensurate with the services they performed. All bona fide priests officiated at temple rites and conferred posthumous names on the shin-botoke, newly dead; all of them celebrated weekly, monthly, and annual hōji, memorial services for the dead. In addition to their duties at the altar and at burial sites where (before cremation became fashionable) they consecrated graves and comforted the sorrowing, many priests chanted the sūtras at private services and presided over socio-religious gatherings on plantations. When the religious phase of such meetings was concluded, priests frequently laid aside their flowing koromo (priestly gown), sipped sake with their comrades, and joined in a lively discussion concerning the problems of the Japanese community.[19]

Priests were also called upon to perform a wide range of personal and social services. They wrote private and formal letters on behalf of their illiterate compatriots and acted as the go-between in arranging marriages. They also arbitrated in family disputes and settled violent quarrels between labor and management. As the producers and preservers of vital records, they registered births and deaths with the Japanese consulate.[20] In one capacity or another, they worked early and late (often to the detriment of their health), and in their 'spare time,' they organized fujinkai (women's associations), supervised Sunday schools, directed Young Men's Buddhist Associations, and taught Japanese youngsters the popular sport of jūjutsu (or jūdō, the art of self-defense) and the art of kendo (fencing) 'of the old school.'[21]

In time the Buddhist priest won the respect and admiration of his countrymen, who came to look upon him as their confidant and friend. Senyei Kawahara of the Sōtō-shū became exceedingly popular. So, too, did Yemyō Imamura, who had dotted the Islands with Hongwanji temples and extended the consolations of Buddhism wherever a considerable number of his countrymen were living. As early as 1912, a reporter for the *Honolulu Advertiser* wrote that the 'history of Buddhism here is essentially a one-man history, for behind the big work of building . . . temples for congregations of poor workingmen, organizing Sunday schools, Young Men's Buddhist Associations, the charitable societies which [are] a part of every church organism, night schools for working-men in every community and women's improvement societies, Rev. Y. Imamura has been the motive factor.'[22] Imamura's accomplishments in little more than a decade were a measure of, and a tribute to, the character and talents of the man. Of his many commendable qualities, the most conspicuous was his compassion. He possessed, too, a rare understanding of human nature which enabled him to evoke harmony from the greatest discord. He knew how to reach both the minds and hearts of his people, winning them over with a warmth of sentiment, a breadth of vision, and a direct-ness of purpose which inspired abiding confidence in those who relied on his judgment and integrity.

As Imamura and his fellow priests emphasized the dignity of manual labor and lauded the virtues of thrift and industry, com-plaints about conditions on the plantations quieted down. The emotional piety of the Pure Land sects and the preaching of patience and forbearance in the midst of adversity, by all priests, consoled and pacified even the most unruly. Bishop Imamura, visiting Hongwanji temples and plantation camps throughout the Territory, repeatedly reminded his countrymen that those who follow the Buddha were not defiant in attitude nor arrogant in spirit. A good Buddhist did not make, he counseled, 'one's little self one's own little god.' A good Buddhist, rather, endeavored to make his family, his community, and indeed the whole world an 'abode of thankful souls.' Shin-shū Buddhists, he believed, ought to have ever on their lips the nembutsu of thanksgiving and in their hearts the *Sho-shin-ge*, or Hymn of True Faith, recalling That Love which 'embraces all . . . though our eyes are so blinded by illusion that we do not discern that Light [which] shines upon all alike.'[23]

In the meantime, the Christian clergy, already much embittered by the willingness of plantation corporations and managements to assist Buddhist priests or their work, could find nothing good to say about the 'pagan priesthood' which everywhere exerted opposing influences. In 1903, Japanese evangelists of the Hawaiian Board petitioned the American clergy to 'set forth the character of the Buddhist priests and . . . the effects of their teachings to deter Christian people from contributing toward the upbuilding of Buddhism.'[24] Frank Scudder and Orramel Gulick obligingly pre-pared 'a memorial to the planters' on the dangers from Buddhism, and the *Friend*, with superb timing, asked how it was that plantation stockholders did not know the relation of Buddhist practice to the drink question. Buddhist priests, this Christian publication alleged, had not declared war on the evils which were daily sapping the moral health of thousands of Japanese in Hawaii. The attitude of the Buddhist priesthood toward vice and immorality, it was alleged, had never been one of uncompromising warfare and extermination. Christians had been working for the moral advancement of the Japanese, declared the *Friend*, but the Buddhist priesthood had not. Buddhism was said to have succumbed to the 'old Pagan foulness [while] Christianity batters it down and sweeps it away.'[25]

Such charges of moral apathy sprang from (among other things) an ignorance of Buddhist ethics. Aside from the fact that, to be heard at all, most priests had to approach their irascible flocks tactfully—with countenance benign, words gentle and kind, as one of them put it—no priest felt compelled to launch a moral crusade, nor did he recoil, as Christians thought he should, from the company of gamblers and pimps. He fraternized with anyone who could speak his language and yearned only to understand, not in order to forgive all (which is to stifle moral progress) but to feel a greater compassion for the folly and weaknesses of mankind. The Buddhist priest did not moralize, because his religion had taught him that morality could not be imposed from without and had little to do with outward conformity to any law. Moral perfection, if indeed there be such a thing, was a matter, according to the Buddha-Dharma, of inner purification effected through direct awareness of the folly of *trishnā* (selfish living) and a lasting gratitude for the compassion of the buddhas. Centuries ago the Wise Man of the Śākyas had admonished his disciples never to force maturity on that which was unripe. Be wise, rather, the Buddha had counseled, and wait for that maturity. Since every man was the result of his past karma, capable of only so much moral progress in a single lifetime, no man could guarantee that he, or anyone, would today or tomorrow be free from the envy, the greed, and the lust for life which binds men to the Wheel of Rebirth. Attainment of Enlightenment and release from saṁsāra could come only with the gradual modification of bad karma from one life to the next.[26] Thus loving-kindness, not stern morality, was the better part of goodness. The Buddhist priest, having learned forbearance and tolerance, rejoiced at the goodness in men and was saddened, but never discouraged, by their faults.

The views of the Christian clergy to the contrary notwithstanding, the United States Commissioner of Labor reported as early as 1902 that the moral and social influence of the priests was thought to be good, and a decade later, the American press conceded that the Japanese would have had no intellectual interests or moral restraint whatsoever had it not been for the efforts of the Buddhist missionaries from the Far East. In 1916 Consul General Rokurō Moroi declared that Buddhist priests had so elevated the moral standards of the Japanese immigrants that 'one can hardly believe they are the same [men] who came here a score of years ago.'[27]

Without doubt, the most lasting contribution of the Buddhist priesthood lay in the field of education. Bishop Imamura made certain that the Hongwanji priests who came to Hawaii were well educated. Most of them were graduates of Buddhist colleges, and many of them were authorities on the spirit of bushidō, the fine points of Japanese etiquette, and *shūshin* (ethics). Some had even cultivated intellectual hobbies. Reverend Hiseki Miyazaki was a collector of coins, stamps, and original Japanese woodblocks.[28] Before long, these men of liberal education and scholastic abilities, in fulfilling their role as guardians of tradition and the sacred learning, established schools in rural districts throughout the Islands to strengthen the ties of cultural affinity between the local-born Japanese and their parents. In so doing, many of them raised the intellectual level of their congregations to a degree 'which few Christian churches could parallel.'[29]

The earliest Buddhist 'schools' were started in 1898 by Reverend Kanayasu in Hilo and Reverend Sato in Kona. In a small room in the rear of plantation temples, these Hongwanji priests taught youngsters the rudiments of the Japanese language, *shūshin*, and the essentials of Japanese etiquette. In 1900 the Reverend Shōi Yamada in Kealia, Kauai, also began giving such *terakoya* (temple school) instruction, and two Jōdo-shū priests similarly tutored the children of Laupahoehoe and Paauhau on the Big Island.[30] The establishment of full-fledged primary and elementary schools lay several years in the future. In the meantime, Christian evangelists had opened up Japanese language schools in Honolulu and on the island of Hawaii.

THE CHRISTIAN LANGUAGE SCHOOLS

In 1890 a farmer named Fukuda opened a language school in Kula, Maui. It did not prosper and disappeared within a few years.[31] Six years later, in April 1896, the first Japanese language school of lasting importance was opened by Reverend Takie Okumura in a room in Queen Emma Hall in Honolulu. Soon after his arrival in the Islands, Okumura had noticed a Japanese child standing alone at the door of a church. When he asked where her mother was, she replied, '*Me mama hanahana yōkonai,*' meaning (as Okumura finally deduced), My mother works, cannot come. The child's 'mongrel' dialect horrified him. Considering it only proper that Japanese youths in Hawaii be given their national education, Okumura obtained the services of one Hideo Kuwabara (who had taught in Japan) and, with an initial enrollment of thirty, opened a school to educate Japanese 'in accordance with the prescribed rules of the Imperial Department of Education.'[32] Equipped only with a few crude benches and tables, Okumura's school provided instruction in oral and written Japanese for an hour a day after public school hours. As the enrollment increased, the Japanese evangelist raised funds and received donations from well-to-do members of the American community to purchase a piece of land at Nuuanu and Vineyard streets where a larger school building was constructed in 1899.[33]

The Okumura school had been established as much to convert the Japanese children to Christianity as to teach them the Japanese language, and before long other evangelists, representing the Congregational and Methodist-Episcopal churches, opened similar schools for the same purpose. During the first decade of the century, schools were established under the auspices of the Hawaiian Board at Hanapepe, Makaweli, and Lihue on Kauai; at Waialua and Ewa on Oahu; at Wailuku, Paia, and Kula on Maui; and at Waiakea, Hilo, and Kohala on Hawaii.[34] On the Big Island, in 1897, Shirō Sokabe founded the Honomu Gijiuku Gakuen, which offered a versatile curriculum featuring courses in religious education, geography, human psychology, science, American history, and 'The Story of Hawaii.'[35] By 1910 the Methodist-Episcopal Mission had opened throughout the Territory ten plantation day schools with a total enrollment of 275. Christian clerics were quite certain that these schools were needed and appreciated by Japanese parents. Without them, it was said that the Japanese children 'would receive no education in the use of their own language.'[36] As it turned out, this was wishful thinking.

THE BUDDHIST SCHOOLS AND BUDDHIST EDUCATION

Even before the turn of the century, fearing that Buddhists might start their own school and disturb the peace of the community, Takie Okumura had divorced his school from its religious affiliation and had transferred control of the institution to a board of thirty-three laymen under the supervision of Consul General Miki Saitō. Nevertheless, to the consternation of the entire Christian community, Buddhist sects soon established language schools of their own.

In his autobiography, *Seventy Years of Divine Blessings*, Okumura stated that he frankly discussed the school question with Bishop Imamura and obtained from the latter a promise that no competitive Hongwanji school would be built in Honolulu. But rumors reached Imamura that teachers in Okumura's school were openly mocking and debasing Buddhism. So in May 1902, a Hongwanji school was built on Fort Street with the financial assistance of the faithful Saiji Kimura and a few other affluent Japanese.[37] The primary purpose of the school, wrote Imamura, was to make certain that Japanese children, as 'the rightful heirs of the parental heritage,' would be 'taught to think and feel in sympathy with their parents.'[38]

In 1905 the Superintendent of Public Instruction reported that the number of Japanese children in public schools was increasing faster than that of any other nationality. To accommodate the accelerating number of Japanese youths, the Hongwanji Mission opened up schools, similar to the one on Fort Street, in many plantation communities on Oahu, Maui, Kauai, and Hawaii. The Jōdo-shū opened up additional schools at Hakalau, Olaa, and Kohala on the Big Island.[39]

The early school buildings, where priests of the Dharma and a few women trained in the normal schools of Japan taught *shūshin*, history, geography, penmanship, and the reading of Japanese ideographs, were poorly equipped, termite-ridden shacks.[40] All supplies for the schools came from Japan, and classes were held daily for an hour and a half in the morning before the public schools opened and for two hours in the afternoon after they closed. During the summer months, except for a two-week vacation, the schools were open daily from 9 A.M. to 3 P.M.[41]

Contributions from the Japanese community financed the schools, and occasionally donations trickled in from members of the imperial family. Once in a while, too, a small contribution was made by a home temple in Japan.[42] The planters, moreover, donated land and materials for the construction of the schools and turned over monthly allotments to the Japanese consulate for school maintenance in order to 'heighten the morale and loyalty of Japanese workmen.'[43]

The Japanese expected to return to their homeland upon expiration of their labor contracts; thus, a key objective of the Buddhist schools was 'to prepare the children as Japanese in the best possible way.' Discipline and instruction, wrote Bishop Imamura, were administered 'solely with that end in view.'[44] Loyalty to things Japanese was the focal point of instruction, and Buddhist priests, who revered the Imperial Rescript of 1890 enjoining fidelity to the distant kami, dutifully inculcated loyalty to *Hi-no-mikoto,* the Honorable Child of the Sun, the Emperor of Japan. Hongwanji priests even publicly announced that Buddhist organizations in Hawaii were committed to 'implanting the national spirit' and that all Buddhist institutions therefore must be 'in perfect accord' with any and all things which the 'imperial edict on education suggests.'[45] Religion and education were thus inseparably linked, and both, in the minds of many intensely nationalistic priests, revolved solely around loyalty to the imperial throne.[46]

Priests had resolved, too, that as long as Japanese children remained in Hawaii, they would be taught to be moral, diligent, and law-abiding. Most priests, strict disciplinarians that they were, demanded and received from their pupils obedience and respect; every priest expected his charges to defer to him in the age-old spirit of *shi-no-on*, gratitude for benefits conferred by educators. Youngsters who flouted priestly authority or behaved in an unseemly manner were not spared the rod. Another and most effective weapon against unruly young people was to make them feel *haji*, or shame.[47]

Priests admonished their students to practice kindness and magnanimity, respect for the aged, and reverence for life. They exalted *oya-on* (filial piety) as the 'most important virtue in the domestic and social life of the Buddhist'[48] and enjoined youngsters to protect, honor, and care for their parents. Since the family extends backward as well as forward in time, reverence for departed ancestors was an indispensable adjunct of *oya-on*. Another very important aspect of filial piety was *aikoku-shin*, or patriotism, a duty and sentiment based on *kō-on*, gratitude and devotion to the Japanese emperor as father of the national family.[49]

The seeds of kindness and compassion implanted by Buddhist priests evidently bore fruit. In September 1905, the *Paradise of the Pacific* magazine reported that quarreling was foreign to the nature of the children attending the Buddhist schools. Even more to these students' credit, it was said that they had refrained from 'imitating white youth in throwing stones at birds and animals and annoying Chinamen.'

Secular leaders of the Japanese community meanwhile continued to acknowledge the spiritual and educational leadership of the Buddhist priesthood. Consul General Miki Saitō wrote to the abbot of the Kyoto Honpa Hongwanji at least twice to praise the fine work of the priests in improving the morals of plantation workers and in educating the Japanese children.[50] The American community, however, was ill at ease. The Buddhist schools had caused many misgivings. The curriculum of the language schools had little in common with American educational ideas, and Buddhist priests daily obliged the second-generation Japanese to bow before the emblem of the Rising Sun and to sing the Japanese national anthem with deference and awe. The older Japanese, moreover, celebrated, on school grounds, all their national holidays and annual festivities in honor of the emperor's birthday.* The schools thus clearly represented, in the eyes of the American community, a potent influence in keeping the Japanese, old and young, loyal to Japanese institutions.[51]

As the Buddhist schools grew up like mushrooms, suspicion of them mounted. When the Hongwanji charter issue was reopened in 1907, attorneys for the Mission had advised Governor Frear that Carter's refusal to grant the charter sprang from a fear that Buddhist

*The Christian Japanese clergy (as well as the Buddhist priests) sponsored 'spirited' celebrations in commemoration of the emperor's birth and, in some cases, even converted their churches into centers of Japanese culture. But demonstrations of cultural pride or patriotic ardor became offensive only when advocated by Buddhist priests.

teachings were not encouraging the local-born Japanese to become good American citizens. But 'the high priest, Mr. Y. Imamura,' the attorneys recalled, had assured the community that such fears were altogether groundless. Moreover, with the aid of an interpreter, the lawyers had themselves gone through a half-dozen or more of the readers used in the schools and found 'absolutely nothing prejudicial' to the interests of American citizenship.[52] Nevertheless, Christian clerics, both American and Japanese, were certain that Japanese priests and parents were using every means to keep their children Japanese in spirit. Every day, wrote Bishop Henry Restarick of the Episcopal Mission, children were sent to a Buddhist priest and taught the Japanese language and patriotic principles. Thus the Buddhist schools, the clergy alleged, were a menace to the Americanization of the Territory.[53]

RELIGION AND THE STRIKE OF 1909

Throughout the decade 1900–1910, religious bitterness between the Japanese and the wider community was aggravated by developments on the domestic economic scene. On the eve of the 1904 strike at Waipahu plantation, the *Hawaiian Gazette* commented that Japan's rise as a Far Eastern power had made Japanese field hands more convinced than ever that 'even in the Hawaiian canefields they have their rights.'[54] Later the minimum wage of plantation workers was raised from sixteen dollars to eighteen dollars, but in 1907 a federal statute was passed regulating migration to the mainland, thereby giving planters the upper hand once more and enabling them to keep wages at a consistently low level. Finally, in May 1909, a well-organized strike broke out involving most of the large plantations on Oahu and cost the planters about two million dollars.[55]

The 1909 strike was precipitated by a critique of the labor situation written for the Japanese daily *Nippu Jiji* by Motoyuki Negoro, a graduate of the University of California at Berkeley. During the course of his studies, Negoro had managed (according to the *Honolulu Advertiser*) to get many violent ideas into his head, the most irksome of which was that Japanese workers in Hawaii ought to be making more than eighteen dollars a month. Shortly after the publication of Negoro's rousing exposition on economic justice, the Zōkyū Kisei Kai, Association for the Promotion of Higher Wages Question, was organized by Fred Higginbotham Makino, an influential and persuasive leader of the Japanese community,* referred to by the American press as the 'labor Pooh-Bah.'[56] In January 1909, this association submitted to the planters a demand

---

*Makino's mother was Japanese, and his father had been an English silk merchant. He had taken his mother's name, and his sympathies were unmistakably Japanese.

FRED HIGGINBOTHAM MAKINO, EDITOR OF THE
Hawaii Hōchi

for higher wages. It was ignored. On May 9, therefore, laborers on
the Aiea plantation quit work. A few days later, workers on Waipahu, Kahuku, and Waianae plantations followed suit.[57]

Incidents in connection with the strike did not alleviate anxiety
over the presence of alien institutions in Hawaii or win any plaudits
for Buddhist leadership. Bishop Imamura and most priests of the
old tradition took very seriously the Japanese-Buddhist concept of
nimmu, which obligated a man to perform his job honestly and to
the best of his ability with no questions asked. But a vocal part of
the labor force by this time was made up of a new breed of young
and militant Japanese, who did not share or sympathize with the
spirit of *nimmu* and *ando shugi*. Resignation to flagrant economic
discrimination, was an anathema to those young men who had been
taught in Hawaii's public schools to uphold the principle of

'equality and justice for all.' Nevertheless, Bishop Imamura again attempted to intervene. At the request of Japanese businessmen in Honolulu, he rode out in an auto to Ewa plantation with, of all people, Takie Okumura, and both men addressed the strikers at a mass meeting and tried to persuade the Japanese to return to work. A strike in Hawaii's main industry, they pleaded, would damage the whole social fabric of the Islands. Fourteen hundred men and women returned to work on June 7, but they soon struck again. Funds became scarce by July, and the strike was called off the following month.[58]

Fred Makino, in the meantime, had brought to the attention of the American community the increased burden imposed on the Japanese in connection with the education of their children and the expenses incurred in connection with their religion. In establishing, maintaining, and supporting educational and religious institutions, wrote the 'labor Pooh-Bah,' the Japanese had spent $101,750, a figure which represented investments in Hongwanji and Jōdo-shū institutions alone.[59] A pamphlet published by strike leaders confirmed Makino's statements and noted that the Japanese had 'expended some hundred thousand dollars, and [were] bearing current expenses of some $50 per month in average in each place.' It also reminded those directly concerned that religious institutions were just as important as bread and butter in the life of man and were veritably indispensable if planters desired 'intelligent, conscientious, and God-fearing laborers, instead of lazy, unscrupulous, selfish, and savage laborers.' Furthermore, the pamphlet pointed out that with 'the increase in the number of women and children, these churches and chapels [would] have to be enlarged in capacity and increased manyfold in number and improved in quality.'[60]

Making Hawaii Safe for Democracy—and Christianity

THE EXTRAORDINARY SUPPORT GIVEN BY BUDDHISTS TO ENSURE THAT THEIR temples and schools were indeed 'enlarged in capacity and increased manyfold' made it apparent to all concerned that the Japanese were determined to stoutly resist assimilation and to reinforce their own religious and cultural heritage. Furthermore, by the second decade of the century, many Japanese, like the Chinese before them, flocked into the towns and villages, became independent wage earners, acquired real property, and entered into 'distressful competition' with Caucasians and Hawaiians as merchants, storekeepers, mechanics, and artisans of every trade and occupation. Thousands more Japanese were added to the population as picture brides came to the Islands between 1911 and 1924 and kept home surroundings thoroughly Japanese. As the growth of the female Oriental population made it increasingly difficult to Americanize the Territory and as the economic competition between whites and Orientals became keener, Buddhist temples and schools became a convenient target for anti-Japanese propaganda. Bishop Imamura, meanwhile, did all he could to alleviate the growing fear of Buddhism. But when the Honpa Hongwanji extended its missionary work to the outside islands and built more and bigger schools and when Shinto and other Buddhist sects, including 'the most superstitious' Shingon-shū, infiltrated and became entrenched in the Islands, no one could quell the rancor in Christian circles. Then, too, Japan's aggressive foreign policy fed the flames of postwar American nationalism, and in 1919 anti-Japanese and anti-Buddhist ferment came to a head. Bills were introduced into the local legislature to 'regulate' the foreign language schools to safeguard for the nation a Christian-American citizenship in the Territory.

GROWING CHRISTIAN AND BUDDHIST RIVALRY AND THE STRUGGLE FOR DOMINANCE

In 1912 the *Advertiser* commented that despite the tremendous and devout following which 'Prince Gautama' had in the Islands, Buddhism had 'never aroused prejudice or antagonism.' Christian ministers, however, continued to deplore the vigorous propaganda of the Buddhist sects which had rendered the followers of Christ such a 'feeble folk' that an anxious clergy had begun to wonder, 'Which shall Hawaii be, Buddhist or Christian?' The Lord's work had suffered its most critical setback by the influence of Buddhism and the Asiatic standards of life, and it was becoming ever more difficult, the Hawaiian Board reported, 'to maintain the cause of Christ in the face of the highly organized religion which [has] for so many generations held sway' among the Japanese.[1] For a while, to be sure, it did seem that Buddhism was gaining the ascendancy.

At the opening of the second decade of the century, when the Honpa Hongwanji commenced missionary work on the outside islands, the home temple in Kyoto took a more direct interest in its Hawaiian Mission, and Bishop Imamura heralded the dawn of a Golden Age for Buddhism.[2] Additional abodes of light and love had already been constructed on the outside islands—at Kapaa and Koloa on Kauai; and at Hana, Kula, and Puunene on Maui—and early in 1912, Imamura's Mission announced its plans to enlarge the *betsuin*. Also, by this time, the Jōdo-shū (which had previously confined its propagandizing to the Big Island and Honolulu proper) likewise had extended its missionary activities to the other islands. Between 1910 and 1914, temples of this sect went up at Puunene and Lahaina on Maui, and at Kapaa and Koloa on Kauai. On Oahu, the Mission purchased and converted into a temple the Haleiwa Hotel, 'Honolulu's famous resort, on the line of Oahu Railway.'[3]

A hopeful Christian clergy endeavored to meet the challenge. Members of the Hawaiian Board and the Methodist-Episcopal Mission thought that, perhaps, services performed abroad by Red Cross workers during the Russo-Japanese War had created a more favorable feeling toward the Christian religion and that, thus, there had been a remission of bitterness in Hawaii toward Christian teachers and missionaries. Some evangelists even fancied that, with the growth of the new spirit of brotherliness, Buddhist temples would in time become Christian churches.[4] Such amity, if it existed at all, was short lived. Christians continued to build new churches all the same and to renovate old ones, while tireless evangelists sought out and won converts notwithstanding the activity of the Buddhist priesthood. Between 1912 and 1916, a whole new crop of Japanese Christian churches sprang up on Maui, Kauai, Oahu, and the Big Island, and in the next few years, the Japanese YMCA 'extended its work very much.'[5]

But it soon became apparent that only a few Japanese were 'progressive' enough to embrace the Gospel. The majority of them still considered Christianity an irrational and austere religion; thus, the Oriental membership in Christian churches remained negligible. As late as 1912, the Hilo Japanese Church had a discouragingly small membership, and on Maui, despite the efforts of the redoubtable Shirō Sokabe, the Honomu Church had gone deeply into debt with no prospective means of liquidation. Even by 1917, only 1,714 Japanese had formally accepted Christianity.[6]

Meanwhile the race between Buddhists and Christians to establish schools heightened hostilities between the rival religious camps. Christian evangelists, whose work was everywhere and always 'an uphill job,' grew increasingly resentful of the fact that Buddhists were making the Christian cause more and more tenuous by planting schools as widely as possible in the Islands—even in districts where Christian or nonsectarian schools already existed. The Buddhist sects stood ready to 'absorb' the so-called independent schools. Thus antagonism mounted steadily between spokesmen for the rival religions—especially in the old *pilikia* (trouble) spots (for example, in Wailuku and Paia on Maui; in Waimea, Kekaha, and Lihue on Kauai; in Honomu, Kohala, Olaa, and Hilo on the Big Island; and in Kahuku, Ewa, and Aiea on Oahu). In Honolulu there had been *pilikia* right along, ever since the Honpa Hongwanji opened its first language school in 1902 and the enrollment in Takie Okumura's school dropped overnight from two hundred down to seventy.

Buddhist priests, moreover, eagerly solicited enrollment for their schools. The U.S. Commissioner of Labor noted this and reported that, in conducting their 'quiet but persistent propaganda against Christianity,' priests of the Dharma had used their moral influence and a form of boycott to force Christian Japanese to send their children to Buddhist schools and to renounce their adopted form of worship. The Japanese Christian clergy pointed out, furthermore, that Buddhist priests, in order to discourage parents from sending children to the Christian schools, had spread the rumor that all rival institutions were run by flatterers of the Occidentals. It was also true that many priests artlessly spread the word that only in the Buddhist schools could prospective Japanese citizens receive the proper indoctrination in loyalty and patriotism to the emperor and the empire. The *Friend,* accordingly, issued a warning as early as 1911 that the Honpa Hongwanji schools, representing as they did the 'great aggressive sect of Japan,' had a 'very strong hold upon many of the people here' and was using patriotism as its 'trump card,' which it played to win.[7]

Competition was becoming keener between Buddhist and Christian Sunday schools also. As early as 1900, Mrs. Barber and another Caucasian woman organized the Children's Church, forerunner of the Honpa Hongwanji Sunday school, and a priest, Hōryū Matsumoto, began giving 'catechism' lessons at the *betsuin.* In 1912 the Mission made Sunday school attendance compulsory for boarders at the Hongwanji dormitory in Honolulu, and a few years later the Mission's Sunday school program was organized. Before long, grumbled Takie Okumura, the Christian Sunday schools were deserted.[8]

An alarmed and envious Christian clergy retaliated by seizing every opportunity to bring to the attention of the American community any reputedly un-American activities sponsored by Buddhist temples and schools. Reports of Buddhist activities abroad which in any way tended to confirm allegations made locally against Buddhist groups received exaggerated attention in the press. In 1913, the *Honolulu Advertiser,* quoting the *Christian Herald* (a weekly published in Japan), reported that Buddhism was a stumbling block to the maintenance of amiable Japanese-American relations on the West Coast. According to the *Herald,* the Honorable S. Ebara and a Mr. Yamamoto had gone to California to investigate conditions underlying the proposed anti-Japanese legislation. Yamamoto had concluded that the Japanese themselves were to blame for the agitation against them and that Buddhism was one factor working 'a lot of evils.' Buddhist priests, he said, had transplanted their religion to the United States without the least change and were unconscionably fostering Japanese jingoism in order to combat Christianity.[9]

Such anti-Buddhist propaganda did little to promote the Christian cause, and some Christian clerics became convinced, finally, that it was futile to try to compete with the more numerous and popular Buddhist schools. So, in an effort to at least neutralize the influence of these schools, they strongly advocated that Buddhist and Christian institutions be 'merged' and converted into plantation-owned, nonsectarian language schools. Buddhists, of course, considered the proposal inimical to their own interests, and nothing came of it.

Not only did Buddhists refuse to merge their elementary schools with Christian ones, but they began building high schools in several urban centers. With the assistance of Ryūsaku Tsunoda (who later became head of Columbia University's Oriental Library) and with a donation of three thousand dollars from Mrs. Mary E. Foster,

Bishop Imamura mapped out a comprehensive high school curriculum. In October 1907, his Mission opened a high school for boys in Honolulu; in April 1910, a similar school for girls was established. At the same time, the Jōdo-shū opened a secondary school for girls which, along with the usual academic subjects, provided instruction in the traditional Japanese arts of flower arrangement, brush painting, and tea ceremony. Later the Honpa Hongwanji built two more high schools in Hilo, one for girls in 1913 and another for boys in 1915. The Jōdo-shū built two more secondary schools, too, both of them for girls, one in Hilo and the other in Puunene, Maui. Christians meanwhile looked on helplessly as the Island-born Japanese were thus 'led [further] away from Christianity.'[10]

THE HONGWANJI EDUCATIONAL HOMES

In the first decade of the century, Takie Okumura had urged the creation of an association to embrace all language schools and language school teachers in the Territory. The time had come, he said, to formulate an educational policy which would guarantee the education of Japanese youths as American citizens and circumvent any further discord between Buddhists and Christians.[11] In response to the persistent entreaties of Okumura and others, the Japanese Educational Association, composed of school teachers throughout the Territory, was founded in 1914. At the initial gathering of Japanese pedagogues that year, Okumura strongly advocated a revision of the language school textbooks which were 'wholly unsuitable' for the training of American citizens.[12]

Bishop Imamura meanwhile had recognized the need for adjusting the language school program, and as early as 1910 the Honpa Hongwanji had notified the American public that its schools would be dedicated, henceforth, to 'the encouragement of American thought and system.'[13] Imamura consistently and vehemently admonished Hawaii's young Americans of Japanese ancestry to abide wholeheartedly by the principles of Americanism and instructed his priests to do likewise.[14] Early in 1915, spokesmen for the Mission announced that they had decided to revise the curriculum of their schools to better prepare local-born Japanese for American citizenship. Bishop Imamura declared that the old educational system must be given up at once and every Hongwanji school transformed into an 'Educational Home.' A circular, distributed by the Mission among plantation personnel and prominent educators, stated that while the original aim of the language schools had indeed been nothing more or less than to prepare the children as Japanese subjects in the best possible way, the immigrant Japanese had now forgotten their purpose of returning to their native land, thus, the aims and methods of Japanese-

Buddhist pedagogy would have to be set aside and a new educational philosophy put into practice. As a first step in this direction, the Mission was transforming its schools into so-called Educational Homes, which would serve as a link between public school instruction and the Japanese family.

The primary purpose of the Educational Homes, according to Mission spokesmen, was to keep the family together. Teacher-priests, it was said, would function solely 'as well-educated parents do towards their children.'[15] Japanese children, wrote Bishop Imamura, must not be merely the biological offspring of their parents yet alien in all other respects. Therefore, the task of the Educational Homes was to teach good morals and ethics (*shūshin*) and to fashion youths into 'the good second self' of the Japanese parent, who should not be deprived of communication of thoughts and feelings with his own flesh. It was all well and good for the public schools to educate the Japanese youth to be exemplary American citizens, but Buddhist children, Imamura wrote, were members of the family before they belonged to the community; hence, they must be taught to 'live, talk and work together in harmony with the seniors of the family.'[16] To the American community, Imamura's position at best seemed full of contradictions or, at worst, just so much double talk.

THE 'REVISION' OF LANGUAGE SCHOOL TEXTS

When, at the first meeting of the Japanese Educational Association in 1914, Takie Okumura demanded a complete, up-to-date revision of language school texts, Bishop Imamura agreed that the books would indeed have to be revised if the schools were to effectively carry out their stated purpose of adopting a philosophy and curriculum consonant with the aims of the American public school system.[17] In February 1915, just before the Honpa Hongwanji announced its Educational Home program, Imamura joined Takie Okumura and a group of distinguished pedagogues from Honolulu and the outside islands to discuss ways and means of revising the books. About seven months later, school teachers from the four major islands convened at the annual conference of the Japanese Educational Association and invited Professor Yaichi Haga of Tokyo Imperial University to undertake the revision of the language school textbooks. A special committee was spearheaded by Ryūsaku Tsunoda of the Honpa Hongwanji, and K. Kakehi, secretary of the YMCA's Citizenship Committee, was appointed to assist him.[18] Later, on May 22, 1916, at the suggestion of newly appointed Consul General Rokurō Moroi, a Central Educational Association was organized to standardize the curriculum of the Japanese schools in full cooperation with the Territorial Board of Education. Selected to serve on either the advisory or executive committee of the association were the consul general himself, Bishop Imamura, Bishop Enjō Itō of the Jōdo-shū, and the ubiquitous Takie Okumura. Rather than tend to the business at hand, Okumura immediately insisted that all Buddhist and Christian schools be converted into independent institutions and put under the joint supervision of American and Japanese educators. He was so obnoxiously persistent about the matter that, by his own admission, the Central Educational Association was 'forced to disband.'[19]

Nevertheless, in the late summer of 1916, Professor Haga came to Honolulu and edited a 'new' set of books. The American community, however, very quickly discovered that the 'revised' books were just Hawaiianized versions of the old ones. Haga had merely substituted a few lessons about American and Hawaiian subjects for those that were excessively Japanese in substance or spirit. The myths of Japan's divine origin remained intact and so did the lessons extolling loyalty to the distant kami. The alien Japanese were not pleased either. They resented all the deletions of patriotic material, and Takie Okumura wrote that they 'raised the usual big hullabaloo.'[20]

THE STORM GATHERS

Aside from the fact that the new texts had satisfied no one and despite Bishop Imamura's promises to 'Americanize' the Buddhist schools, the American community refused to believe that teacher-priests wholly unacquainted with English and out of sympathy with American ideals and institutions were either capable or desirous of educating the local-born Japanese for American citizenship. Americans continued to think that Buddhist teachers were focusing exclusive attention on subjects peculiarly Japanese, pursuing their original objective of fostering veneration of alien institutions, and strengthening Japanese religious and cultural values.[21] In the eyes of the American community, too, Buddhism was every bit as alien and antidemocratic as the slogan 'Loyalty to the Emperor and Country.' Buddhist educators, on the other hand, did not see how they could create the desired bond of sympathy and mutual understanding between the first- and second-generation Japanese without making the religion of the parents intelligible to the children. In the light of the crucial role played by Buddhism in the evolution of Japanese culture, they were no doubt correct in their insistence that an understanding of Japanese history and culture would be drastically impoverished, if not rendered altogether impossible, by divorcing Buddhism from the curriculum of the Japanese schools.

In subsequent years, religious antipathies generated innumerable petty quarrels between Buddhist and Christian educators and became increasingly a more significant factor in the ever widening breach between the American and the Japanese communities. Christian zealots did everything they could to persuade secular leaders that 'Christianization spells Americanization' and that Hawaii could not be American at all unless it remained solidly Christian. In 1915, Sidney L. Gulick, a former professor at Dōshisha University in Kyoto and son of Orramel H. Gulick, advocated that a Christian church be established as soon as possible in every village and pleaded with the planters to cooperate in every way to Christianize the Japanese. Hawaii with its large Oriental population could not be Americanized, he admonished, until Christianity displaced the superstitious Buddhist sects. No alien, he wrote, could be transformed into a 'whole hearted American citizen' unless he accepted 'the Christian ideals of personal responsibility, of duty to God and to fellow men.'[22] A year later, Episcopal Bishop Henry B. Restarick warned that the community was faced with a most serious question: Would Hawaii have a Christian population or one in which a majority of citizens were Shintoists or belonged to one of the Oriental cults? It was absolutely mandatory, declared Restarick, that Americans recognize the importance of teaching Japanese children the principles of Christianity lest the plurality of voters in Hawaii be adherents of a non-Christian faith. The *Friend* then pointedly asked, 'Why Buddhist Schools?' A College of Hawaii student warned that youngsters attending both the Buddhist schools and the public schools were receiving two distinct and diametrically opposed types of education. At the one, students were led toward the East, at the other, toward the West; at the one, to the gate of the Buddha, at the other, to the door of Christianity. The products of such a dual system of education, he concluded, were bound to be citizens who were 'neither Japanese nor American, neither Buddhists nor Christians.'[23]

Bishop Imamura argued to the contrary that Buddhism was in no way inimical to American political philosophy, and to prove his point, the Hongwanji enthusiastically joined the YMCA's citizenship drive in September 1915. Imamura pointed out that Buddhism had been gravely misunderstood by the American community. It was certainly not idolatrous, as those with a vested interest in Christian propaganda had alleged, and the Shin-shū Mission, the Hongwanji bishop emphasized, was no longer fostering Japanese nationalism. Pure Land Buddhists, furthermore, worshipped the Buddha of life, light, and love immeasurable, and the ideals of the sect were 'just as applicable to and for Americans as they [were] for Japanese.'[24]

While community opposition to Buddhism and the Buddhist schools continued to wax hot, other Buddhist sects became firmly entrenched in the Islands. In 1912 Gyōun Takaki of the Nichiren-shū had transferred the headquarters of his sect from Pahala on the Big Island to Honolulu, and five years later, in October 1917, a costly temple was erected on Liliha Street.[25] An independent Shin-shū Mission had already been introduced to Hawaii by two visiting priests who built a temple on Aloha Lane in Honolulu in 1914. In the same year, a Sōtō-Zen temple was erected in Honolulu under the direction of Bishop Hōsen Isobe, who had arrived the year before to assume jurisdiction over the Sōtō sect.[26] In 1916 the Sōtō Mission built another temple on an acre of leased land in Kealakekua in the Kona district of the Big Island, and a priest of the Higashi Hongwanji built a temple in Honolulu.[27]

By this time, the growing popularity of the 'superstitious' Shingon-shū was causing patriotic American students of the Hawaiian scene 'no little anxiety.'[28] Not only had this esoteric sect been associated for centuries with Shinto, but of all Buddhist sects, it was the most likely to be misunderstood. In Hawaii it had been misrepresented by ignorant and opportunistic 'lay priests' who had given the sect a bad name.[29]

Shingon Buddhism in Hawaii

The history of Shingon Buddhism in the Hawaiian Islands dates back at least to 1902 when an immigrant laborer, Hōgen Yujiri, opened a 'preaching hall' in Lahaina, Maui. A native of Yamaguchi Prefecture, Yujiri had worked in the cane fields of Aiea before moving on to Maui—and higher things. His popularity spread very quickly when word got around that he had been miraculously cured of an eye disease through the limitless compassion of Kōbō Daishi. In 1903, Kōdō Yamamoto, another native of Yamaguchi, came to Hawaii, went to the island of Kauai, and, with the help of a small group of devotees, built the 'Eighty-eight Holy Places of Hawaii's Garden Isle.' These small shrines, which dotted a secluded hillside a little off the main road at Lawai between Lihue and Hanapepe, were modeled after the famous Japanese shrines on the island of Shikoku. Over the entrance of each shrine was inscribed the Sanskrit name of a saint whose image, it was hoped, would soon adorn the shrine. Favorite saints (including Kwannon-sama and Amida Buddha) were believed to possess the power to restore bodily health, and it was said that persons afflicted with cholera, smallpox, eye trouble, lameness, and a host of other ailments had been completely cured through the intercession of these merciful bodhisattvas. Incidents of such marvelous cures led people in the neighborhood of Lawai to conclude that the Shingon-shū was the 'Christian Science' sect of Buddhism.

Shingon temples were built in Waimea on Kauai, and in Hilo on Hawaii, in 1908, and a layman named Kubo built a temple in the Pawaa district of Honolulu the following year. By 1911, two more *daishi-dō* (temples of Kōbō Daishi) had been built in Pahala and Honomu on the Big Island. Lay priests who specialized in healing the sick officiated at most of the temple rites. One of the most popular of these Shingon *kitōshi* ('healing priests') was a former railroad laborer who practiced his shamanism at the *daishi-dō* in Honomu. Before long, the enormous popularity of this man and a few others like him completely overshadowed that enjoyed by Hōgen Yujiri, and the latter, who did not welcome the competition, decided in 1913 to report the 'chaotic state' of Shingon affairs in Hawaii to officials of the sect in Japan.[30]

The teachings of the Shingon sect have traditionally been embodied in mystical symbolism, and its ritual consists of mantras (invocations) and intricate mūdras (movements and poses of the hands and fingers). A superficial grasp of the meaning behind the ritual could, and often did, lead to corruption and widespread misunderstanding of the religion. In Hawaii the authentic teachings of Shingon Buddhism were altogether lost in the vacuous repetitions of magical formulae and machinelike recitations of the sūtras by the *kitōshi*.

Priests of the other Buddhist sects soon took exception to the unorthodox practices of the *kitōshi* and their gullible followers. It was said that the Shingon lay priests were giving Buddhism a bad name. Spokesmen for the sects eventually conveyed their displeasure to the Japanese consulate, and Consul General Hisakichi Eitake was prevailed upon to write to Shingon officials in Japan and to the Japanese foreign minister demanding that a bona fide priest be sent to investigate conditions in the Hawaiian Islands.[31]

So in March 1914, on behalf of the Shingon temples of Daigo and majestic Kōyasan, Eikaku Seki came to the Islands and investigated Shingon activities on Oahu, Maui, and Hawaii. He discovered that less than a handful of the 'priests' who were busily erecting temples all over the Islands knew anything about Shingon Buddhism, and even among those who did know something about it, there was no unity of belief or practice. Every 'priest' was a law unto himself.[32]

Seki spread the word among his countrymen that he had come as a bona fide representative of the Shingon temples of Japan, and in June 1914, he opened a temporary mission hall in a residence near Thomas Square in Honolulu. The following year he collected about three thousand dollars and purchased a site for a temple on Sheridan Street. In July 1917, construction was completed of the seven-thousand-dollar detached temple of the Kongobuji, on Kōyasan,* and dedication ceremonies took place three months later.[33]

The Japanese consulate, in the meantime, continued to receive reports of unorthodox Shingon practices which evidently prompted Consul General Rokurō Moroi to decline an invitation to dedication ceremonies for the Sheridan Street temple. When asked

*The Kongobuji is the main temple of the Shingon sect. It was founded in A.D. 816 by Kōbō Daishi and is situated atop Mt. Kōya in Wakayama Prefecture.

by Seki for an explanation of his apparent animosity toward the sect, Moroi launched into a diatribe against the superstitious beliefs and practices of the Shingon Buddhists of Hawaii. Later on, during the regime of Consul General Chōnosuke·Yada, another unpleasant exchange took place. Kōō Kameyama, then bishop of the local sect, threatened to advise the Japanese foreign minister that the consul general was deliberately maligning Shingon Buddhism and its priesthood. Kameyama, seeing that Yada meant business, eventually and with little grace apologized to the Buddhist bishop, and the Shingon sect was taken off the consulate's 'black list.'[34]

Shinto in Hawaii

Between 1910 and 1918, Shinto, too, became a permanent part of the Hawaiian religious scene, giving the American community something more to fret about.* The construction of the earliest, small, wooden Shinto shrines in Hawaii actually preceded the establishment of institutional Buddhism. As early as 1898, Daijingu shrines with their quaint torii, or mystical gateways, were built in Lawai, Kauai, and in Hilo, Hawaii, in honor of the Sun Goddess, Amaterasu-Ō-Mikami. Later, in 1906, a group of devout Japanese, under the leadership of a priestess, Matsue Chiya, built a Daijingu shrine in the poor and rowdy Aala district of Honolulu. Six years later another shrine was constructed by a priest from Kochi Prefecture, Ritarō Kawasaki, who was personally responsible for the subsequent growth and popularity of the Daijingu in Hawaii. In 1907 Miyaō Katsuyoshi, a young priest from Hiroshima, took up residence on Beretania Street in Honolulu, collected money from his countrymen in and about the city, and eventually constructed an Izumo shrine† in the old Palama district (formerly a sacred and taboo enclosure for royal women of the mighty alii).[35]

Between 1907 and 1924, Shinto priests, performing an important social function, conducted numerous marriage rituals. Once the picture brides had begun to pour into the Islands, indignant moral uplifters, who maintained that these women were not married, raised a great commotion. Before leaving Japan, every picture bride had sworn to love, honor, and obey her husband, but that was hardly sufficient to pacify scrupulous Christian consciences. Shinto priests, therefore, were prevailed upon to improvise a nuptial

*Buddhism had been officially divorced from Shinto at the time of the Meiji Restoration in 1868, but the Japanese continued to profess and to practice both religions simultaneously. Members of the American community, ignorant of both Buddhism and Shinto, had no reason to assume the existence of any clear lines of distinction between the two.

†The Izumo Taisha, or Great Shrine of Japan, is the oldest shrine in Japan and is dedicated to Okuninushi-no-Mikoto, who is said to have introduced medicine, sericulture, and fishing in Japan. The shrine is situated at the foot of Mount Yakumo on the western coast. In October of every year, it is said, gods from all over the country assemble there to arrange marriages.

ceremony for the benefit of Christians, who objected to the moral turpitude of the 'Japanese-style hitch.' Some Izumo priests officiated at as many as thirty marriages a day.[36]

As time went on, more Shinto priests came to the Islands and more shrines were built in the environs of Honolulu and on the outside islands. In 1918, moreover, the flourishing Daijingu and Izumo shrines of Hawaii received official recognition as overseas branches, respectively, of the Grand Ise Shrine and the Izumo Taisha. The Daijingu organized a Sunday school, a night school, and even a 'Religious Institute' for the propagation of the faith. A few Shinto schools became popular, too, and one or two even tried to compete with the Buddhist schools.[37]

JAPAN'S FOREIGN POLICY AGGRAVATES OPPOSITION TO BUDDHISM

While Buddhist and Shinto groups were making inroads on the sacred precincts of Christianized Hawaii, Japan's aggressive foreign policy intensified the fear of persons and things Japanese. When Japan 'annexed' Korea in 1910, the Honolulu YMCA rejected an application for membership submitted by the then vice-consul, Rokurō Moroi. Moroi's nationality, officials of the association decided, was 'incompatible for membership.'[38] Between 1914 and 1918, moreover, militarists at the helm of the Japanese government thrust Nippon into a new series of foreign imperialistic adventures, and in 1915 relations between Japan and the United States were seriously strained when Japan issued the notorious Twenty-One Demands on China. The local American press reacted to the ultimatum with overwhelming disapprobation and ridiculed declarations by the Japanese press that Japan entertained 'no hidden ambition to establish a protectorate over China.'[39] The *Advertiser*, furthermore, painstakingly drew attention to the fact that Article 7 of Group 5 of the Demands forced China to agree that 'Japanese subjects shall have the right of missionary propaganda in China,' a provision which had created much uneasiness among the Chinese, who had reasoned that to come and preach Buddhism in China was 'like carrying coals to Newcastle.' In a story headlined 'Buddhists Plan China Campaign,' the *Advertiser* warned that the determination to propagate Buddhism throughout China was simply 'one of several demonstrations with which the Japanese [are] trying to emphasize their national spirit.'[40]

BUDDHISTS PUT ON THE DEFENSIVE

Such incidents on the international scene had immediate and lasting repercussions in Hawaii. In 1917, when the Honpa Hongwanji asked the Chamber of Commerce to endorse its plan to seek public support for its new one-hundred-thousand-dollar *betsuin*, the *Friend* immediately publicized its objections to the scheme and warned all gullible persons against contributing to the support of Buddhism, which was allegedly intensely nationalistic and hence strongly anti-American. Furthermore, Christian clerics emphatically pointed out that every dollar given to aid Buddhism fought every dollar given for the maintenance of Christian work.

Buddhists thus were put constantly on the defensive, and Bishop Imamura felt compelled many times over to point to the evidences of his Mission's good faith, both before and during the war years. Imamura recalled that the Hongwanji had participated in the YMCA citizenship drive and in 1918 had published the *Five Appeals to American Patriotism** to encourage Japanese youngsters to be 'faithful and obedient to the Land of the Stars and Stripes.'[41] The Mission had also participated in the Food Conservation Campaign and the Red Cross drives, and Buddhist priests had gone out of their way to urge plantation workers to support the War Savings Stamp Campaign.[42] During a series of missionary conferences held at the *betsuin*, the Mission issued a public statement that it could and would promote the Americanization of the Japanese.[43] This was promptly followed by a mass meeting of some eight hundred Mission members who, in an enthusiastic manifestation of the American spirit, promised to do their utmost to instill into the younger generation respect and loyalty to the United States.[44] The YMBA promptly began sponsoring lectures and debates on American citizenship in order to give the Japanese 'a better understanding of the conditions that surround them and a clear idea of how to conform to those conditions.'[45] Bishop Imamura wrote a twenty-nine page pamphlet entitled *Democracy According to the Buddhist Viewpoint*, which was immediately translated into English. In the pamphlet Imamura voiced his conviction (a puzzling one to the philosophically uninitiated) that, 'If autocracy has no absolute value, neither has democracy.' And if democracy were right, he continued, 'why should not autocracy be right also?' He wrote that Buddhists believed that 'in this world as well as in the ideal world there are no absolutely determined values or particular things that cannot be reduced to some other terms, and therefore that autocracy does not unconditionally exclude democracy.' Democracy and autocracy were, he concluded, 'two aspects of a thing which is in itself above such opposites.'[46] The pamphlet did more to confuse than to clarify the Hongwanji's position.

As a matter of fact, anything which Bishop Imamura might have said at this time, in an effort to repair the ever widening breach between Buddhists and Christians, would very likely have served

*The *Five Appeals* were the Declaration of Independence, Wilson's War Message, Washington's Farewell Address, President Monroe's Seventh Annual Message, and the Gettysburg Address.

to make Buddhism and its priesthood even more suspect. As it was, the American community thought it remarkably odd that priests whose entire upbringing was Japanese should suddenly begin professing wholehearted commitment to Americanism. The *Friend* wondered why several Buddhist temples and schools had overnight become 'centers of red hot Americanism,'[47] and Wallace R. Farrington, general manager of the *Star-Bulletin* who later became governor of Hawaii, was no less perplexed. In a congratulatory address at the dedication exercises for the new *betsuin*, Farrington had lauded the Hongwanji Mission for doing its part to bring about 'a natural assimilation of American ideals.'[48] But in a private memorandum he noted that Consul General Rokurō Moroi had tried altogether too hard to persuade him that the Hongwanji was trying in every way to Americanize Hawaii's Japanese. Moroi's enthusiasm, rather than inspiring confidence, had aroused further suspicion. The 'very powerful Buddhist Mission with its ten thousand school children in daily training' did indeed, Farrington mused, seem to be 'making a definite effort to convince the Americans of the city and outside islands that they are not only sincere but very enthusiastic in their effort to train the Japanese children born here [to] become good Americans.' But like other prominent citizens, Farrington puzzled over the sudden switch or swing to the other extreme. It was probably a new stratagem, he concluded, to strengthen the hold of Buddhism, a hold which was, in Farrington's eyes, 'as definitely Japanese as the evangelical or catholic [one] might be termed definitely American.'[49]

No doubt there was cause for bewilderment. On July 7, 1918, Bishop Imamura had stated that his mission advocated Americanizing the Japanese. Yet just the day before, the local *Advertiser* had printed an item from the Japan *Advertiser* lamenting that since Buddhists 'always represent the genuine nationalistic ideas, they encountered strong opposition on the part of Americans and [the] Christianized Japanese' in Hawaii.[50]

The Japanese Christian clergy was particularly unhappy about the continuous expansion of Buddhism in the Islands, and Bishop Imamura had very good reason to believe that his religion was being 'intentionally misunderstood by Japanese Christians and not understood by others.'[51] As pointed out earlier, no one was more resentful of Buddhist temples, priests, and schools than Takie Okumura, a man imbued with a sense of divine mission and motivated by a compulsive need to succeed. Before entering the ministry, Okumura had tried all sorts of callings—and failed. He participated in politics but gave that up after being chased out of Tokyo. Then he became an exporter, but 'not being versed in the fine art of [being] a merchant,' he had made a failure of that, too. Later he became a contractor but was duped and had to sell all his household goods to pay off creditors. Finding himself penniless, he left everything in his wife's hands and resorted to 'prayer and reading.'[52] Unsuccessful in the world and a failure in mundane affairs, Okumura fancied that he must have been chosen for a 'higher honor,' one reserved for a select group of initiates. As an ordained minister of the Most High, he would not, *could* not, fail. From the moment of his arrival in Hawaii, he 'worked aggressively to Christianize the Japanese'[53] and (along with his son Umetarō, who had acquired much of Takie's bigotry and self-righteousness) often led the American community astray in matters pertaining to Buddhism and Buddhist institutions. Be that as it was, Americans whom the Okumuras sought most to influence frequently seemed capable of deliberately misunderstanding the intentions of Buddhist priests without help from anyone. During dedication ceremonies for the new *betsuin* in 1918, Bishop Imamura had assured the American community that the Hongwanji harbored no injurious ideas against the public peace of the state. Buddhism, he stated further, could mold good American citizens because, like Christianity, it was for every nation and people. The *Star-Bulletin* interpreted his message to mean 'Buddhists Aim At World Influence.'[54]

GENESIS OF THE LANGUAGE SCHOOL BATTLE

About the time that the Hongwanji announced its Educational Home program, Sidney Gulick made an extensive investigation of conditions on Island plantations. He interviewed plantation managers, clerks, teachers, doctors, and priests and concluded, on the basis of what they had told him, that while the Japanese were slow to blend with other races and somewhat impeded in their assimilation of American ideas and ideals by their private schools, the evils of the schools were probably not as great as most critics had assumed. Moreover, Gulick thought it was very apparent that Japanese educators were seeking 'to make their schools contribute to, rather than to hinder the loyalty of their children to the United States.'[55] A few years later, Governor Charles J. McCarthy publicly endorsed the Japanese schools as a secondary system for the education of the Japanese.[56]

The Japanese naturally took enormous pride in their schools and believed, with Editor Yasutarō Sōga of the *Nippu Jiji,* that, in such a momentous period of transition, the Japanese children of the Territory should not lose what could be gained from the three thousand years of civilization that had prevailed in the Orient. No Japanese child, Sōga pleaded, should be compelled to remain ignorant of the old civilization. But public opinion against the schools was becoming more vocal. With America's entry into World War I, the *Friend* crusaded for a Hawaii 'Made Safe for Democracy.' American patriotism, it was said, must become the 'warp and woof' of Territorial life; aliens must be Americanized;

and the foreign language schools must go.[57] The *Advertiser* advocated that the Japanese schools in particular must be abolished in order to remove all suspicion of local-born Japanese.[58] Later, after the armistice in 1918, Hawaii was swept up in the contagious wave of nationalism which engulfed the mainland and 'at times amounted almost to hysteria.'[59] Hostility against the German press and language schools intensified abhorrence of all alien institutions, and the new nationalist consciousness, noted Lorrin A. Thurston, was an aftermath 'of just resentment against the propaganda and machinations of Germany and the Germans' and was evident in the renewed resolutions of Hawaii's Americans to suppress everything non-American in origin.[60] The foreign language schools were branded a menace to the peace and tranquillity of the Islands, and more persons came to agree with Sidney Gulick that, since 'American and Asiatic civilizations rest on postulates fundamentally different and antagonistic,' the two could not possibly be assimilated.[61]

With the exception of Takie Okumura, probably no one was more opposed to the foreign language schools (the Buddhist schools in particular) than Vaughan MacCaughey, an instructor at the College of Hawaii who later became superintendent of public instruction. MacCaughey, a South Dakotan born of Huguenot parentage, publicly grieved over the decline of Protestantism in Hawaii, which, he said, was due in large measure to the effective propaganda of the non-Christian faiths. He denounced the Buddhist schools as narrow, superstitious shrines for Mikado worship and predicted that, as long as 95 percent of the Japanese in Hawaii remained Buddhist, so long would Americanization be retarded. Since American democracy had been founded on the ideals and practices of the Christian home, it logically followed for MacCaughey that Buddhism was both undemocratic and un-American. The Japanese press took careful note of MacCaughey's tirades, and in February 1919, the *Hōchi* warned the Japanese community to expect real trouble in the near future.[62] Trouble came even sooner than expected. Before the year was out, the controversy over Hawaii's 163 Japanese language schools, with their enrollment of twenty thousand, became the hottest and most bitterly contested issue on the Hawaiian scene.[63]

THE LANGUAGE SCHOOL BILLS

In January 1919, attorney Albert F. Judd, grandson of an early medical missionary to the Islands, drafted an act to prescribe qualifications for school teachers. He hoped that this would 'safeguard for the nation a Christian-American citizenship in the Territory.' The proposed measure, referred to contemptuously in Japanese circles as the 'Judd Bill,' prohibited any instructor from teaching in the language schools without certification from the Department of Public Instruction that 'such teacher possesses [the] ideals of democracy and has a knowledge of the English language, American history and methods of government.'[64]

News of the Judd Bill quickly turned the Japanese community into a hotbed of lively discussions. The Japanese press, contending that any such bill would deal a fatal blow to all language schools, made a considerable to-do over the suspected conspiracy to abolish the schools. The *Advertiser* denied the existence of any 'plot' to liquidate the schools but warned that, because of the 'intemperate utterances' of the Oriental newspapers, the matter of abolishing the schools *had* been 'taken up for consideration' and that a bill 'aiming to do away with' the foreign language schools might yet be introduced in the legislature.[65]

A few weeks later, another measure against the schools was drafted by Lorrin Andrews, a 'Christian' attorney. The 'Andrews Bill' required all schools to be licensed by the Department of Public Instruction and to 'pursue a course of study calculated to inculcate in the pupils of such schools the ideals and principles of the form of Government of the United States.'[66] It also empowered the Department of Public Instruction to regulate school hours and to determine what texts could and could not be used.

Leaders of the Japanese community sprang into action. A flood of petitions protesting the passage of any bill that would place the language schools under the control of the DPI swamped the legislature. On March 10, 1919, two hundred Japanese crowded into the Asahi Theater in Honolulu to discuss the proposed school measures, and Lorrin Andrews received shortly thereafter a formal request from the Japanese Educational Association to withdraw his bill. Kusaka Haga, chairman of the mass meeting of March 10, wrote a letter to the president of the senate and protested the enactment of any legislation against the schools,[67] and on March 14, Ryūhei Mashimo of the Japanese Educational Association addressed a similar letter to the senate. Mashimo wrote that the teachers and principals of both the independent and the Buddhist schools were educating the Japanese youth in accordance with the true ideals and principles of the United States and were perfectly willing to 'co-perate to the best of their ability with the movement of the Americanization of the boys and girls now on foot.'[68] From a committee of the Hongwanji Educational Home in Honolulu came a resolution affirming that language school teachers were doing their utmost to Americanize Japanese youths and that the loss of the schools would impose a tremendous hardship on the entire Japanese community.[69] Letters poured in from the outside islands, too. A petition from Hilo pleaded that the schools were an absolute necessity because parents who worked in the cane fields until late hours had no time to look after their children. Educators in Kohala on the Big Island sent to the speaker of the house a letter with an attached petition signed by the manager of the Kohala Sugar Company that stated 'Any law passed that in any way attempts to dictate to a man what his language or religion shall be is . . . wrong.'[70]

Despite all the commotion created by the proposed legislation, Representative Henry J. Lyman introduced the Judd Bill in April 1919, as House Bill 277, and George P. Cooke introduced it in the senate as Senate Bill 137. Section B of the house bill, as amended by the Committee on Education, stipulated that beginning July 1, 1920, language school teachers would be given two years to cultivate the 'ideals of democracy, a knowledge of the English language, and [of] American history and government.' During that time, the teachers would be expected to pursue a course of instruction 'calculated to inculcate' the principles of American government and to discourage the teaching of anything 'to extol or exploit the ideals or principles of a government foreign to the government of the United States or anything not suitable for the training of youths for American citizenship.'[71]

The American press was, of course, solidly behind the move to regulate the schools. The *Advertiser* favored placing them under the control of the DPI as called for by the Andrews Bill and even accused government officials who did not favor such legislation of being 'against Americanism in the schools.'[72] The *Star-Bulletin* devoted much of its attention to an 'insidious lobby' led by the 'labor Pooh-Bah,' Fred Makino, against school legislation, and when the bills finally died in the senate, the press held the big plantation interests culpable.[73] The *Advertiser* reported that lobbyists had threatened that, if the schools were discriminated against, field hands would return to Japan; the *Star-Bulletin* quoted Senator Stephen Desha to the effect that the planters were indeed afraid that legislation would disturb labor conditions. Regardless of whoever or whatever was directly responsible for the death of the school bills, Editor Edward P. Irwin of the *Advertiser* warned that the Japanese were pursuing a dangerous course by insisting upon the perpetuation of institutions which were 'distinctly un-American.'[74]

At this point, a paranoiac fear of Japanese political domination of the Islands, bolstered by a phenomenal rise in the Japanese birth rate, intensified still further the opposition to all things Oriental. In January 1919, Judge Horace Vaughan of the Territorial district court had granted seventy-seven Japanese soldiers citizenship, in accordance with a United States naturalization act passed a few months before that authorized the naturalization of aliens who had served in the United States armed forces. William H. Ragsdale of the Board of Naturalization protested Vaughan's decision on the grounds that the term 'aliens,' as used in the act, did not apply to Orientals, and Irwin, with his unfailing genius for adding fuel to every fire, commented that Vaughan's ruling was 'fraught with possibilities of the gravest moment for Hawaii.' The Japanese consulate, meanwhile, had reported that the Japanese birth rate had catapulted to seven times the death rate, and a leading politician feared a movement might be under way to secure Japanese control of the house of representatives. In October 1919, an *Advertiser* headline shouted, 'Danger of Japanese Ascendancy in Hawaii Arouses Washington.' None of this could discomfit Judge Vaughan in the slightest,* and by December 1921, five hundred Orientals had been naturalized.[75]

RELIGION AND NATIONALISM

To add to the fears of Japanese political ascendancy, Christian clerics, solidly united in their animosity toward Buddhism and incessant in their reproofs, continued to stir up unrest with prophecies of an imminent Buddhist victory over Christianity. Their warnings became more ominous as it became apparent to more and more people that Buddhism, by preserving the language, habits, dress, and culture of Japan, was accentuating the differences between East and West. With the exception of Bishop Imamura, priests rarely expounded or exemplified the supranational ideals of Śākyamuni Buddha. The Buddhism preached in Hawaii was still, in too many places, inextricably tied up with Japanese nationalism. At the same time, the Christian ministers who accused Buddhist priests of fostering a rabid nationalism were themselves indulging in a great deal of flag-waving. As had happened so often in the past, religious and political fundamentalism joined hands in an unqualified condemnation of all things alien. As early as 1910, the *Friend* had observed that politics and religion mix a good deal in America and accurately predicted that the association was bound to become more intimate. When the United States entered the war in 1917, the bishop of the Hawaiian Episcopal Mission declared that patriotism was 'part of religion,'[76] and by the time the war was over, religion and patriotism had indeed become inseparable. In March 1919, Vaughan MacCaughey, soon to take office as superintendent of public instruction, asserted again that the political life of America depended ultimately and absolutely upon the Christian-American household and that the Americanization program of the public schools of Hawaii was being more or less completely neutralized by reactionary Buddhist priests who were teaching a medieval and intensely Japanese variety of Buddhism based on emperor worship and the veneration of ancient superstitions. The derogatory effects of such propaganda on genuine Americanization, he warned, were 'obvious even upon cursory examination.'[77] Hawaii's Japanese-

---

*Several years later, the Territorial attorney general reversed Vaughan's decision and the new ruling was upheld in 1926 by the U.S. Supreme Court.

Americans, moreover, had better stop shaping their lives by the beliefs of their forefathers, MacCaughey insisted, for as long as they continued to be guided by obsolete values, that is, by the 'Hand of the Dead,' Europeans and Americans would continue to look upon them with suspicion because Buddhist communities 'simply cannot be American.' Editor Irwin of the *Advertiser* enthusiastically applauded MacCaughey's 'logic' and contributed some of his own obtuse thinking to the subject. Certain tenets of Buddhism, he wrote, were 'incompatible with the Constitution of the United States.'[78]

BUDDHISTS BLAME THE CHRISTIAN CLERGY FOR THE SCHOOL CRISIS

In the face of such constant and militant opposition to the schools, it is hardly surprising that Buddhists traced the origin of the language-school feud to an outgrowth of religious strifes and jealousies. The Judd Bill, they contended, was primarily an effort by the Christians to suppress Buddhism. The editor of the *Hōchi* argued that the American community had become so wrought up against the Buddhists that perhaps if the schools were converted into Christian institutions opposition to them might cease. The *Jitsugyō-no-Hawaii* and the *Hawaii Chōhō* accused Takie Okumura of insti-gating the proposed language school legislation. Okumura was 'a wolf hidden under the mask of a sheep,' they charged, a traitorous rascal bent on 'selling his own country down the drain' and carrying on a seditious campaign against Buddhism.[79]

Certainly Okumura and his friends did nothing to discredit these allegations. As a matter of fact, soon after legislation against the schools had been tabled in the senate, Japanese Christians spread the rumor that a campaign was being widely conducted throughout the Islands to strangle Christianity and to inculcate Buddhism and Japanese radicalism.[80] A few months later, upon expiration of his term in office, Consul General Moroi confirmed suspicions that the Japanese Christian clergy was inciting agitation against the Buddhist schools. The Christianized Japanese, he said, had become jealous over the success of the Buddhist priests in maintaining the language schools and therefore had 'tried to mislead the American community [into] believing that these schools were obstructing the Americanization of the Hawaii-born Japanese children.' Thus, according to Moroi, the Japanese Christian clergy had paved the way for the language school crisis.[81]

Takie Okumura immediately asked Albert F. Judd to exonerate him of any responsibility for the Judd Bill.* In a brief and barely

---

*Before leaving office, MacCaughey's predecessor, Henry W. Kinney, had expressed his conviction that, although he had been assured to the contrary, the Judd Bill did indeed owe its origin to religious antagonisms. See *PCA* March 13, 1919.

EDWARD P. IRWIN, EDITOR OF THE *Honolulu Advertiser*

polite reply, Judd stated that he did not know what kind of statement Okumura wanted from him and that he had already informed the superintendent of public instruction that no Judd would be a 'stool pigeon' for the Okumuras. Furthermore, he (Judd) was not 'out gunning for the language schools' or involved in any conflict of religious beliefs.[82] Okumura, of course, continued to protest in the most solemn manner that he had not even the slightest idea of abolishing the language schools. He said nothing was further from his thoughts. Examination of his private papers, however, leaves little doubt that, while he was not directly responsible for initiating the language school bills, his peripheral activities and his later 'projects' for Americanizing the local-born Japanese were motivated by the desire to liquidate Buddhism and all Buddhist institutions.

The Japanese Buddhists were not alone in their suspicions that Christianized Orientals were conniving to abolish the Buddhist schools. Roderick O. Matheson, former editor of the *Advertiser* and a keen observer of men, events, and happenings, addressed an open letter to his former newspaper in December 1919 in which he advocated support of the language schools and immediate cessation of all criticism and efforts at suppression. The school controversy, Matheson wrote, showed that Hawaii was 'surfing on a crest of hysteria,' a deplorable situation brought about by the outgrowth of religious differences and aggravated by 'those who believe that Christianity embraces all that is good, moral and ethical and leaves nothing for other religions,' and by those who were 'anti-Japanese through unreasoning prejudices or blind ignorance.'[83] He wrote that the Japanese Christians were determined to suppress the Japanese schools because the majority of these were conducted under Buddhist missionary auspices. Moreover, propaganda alleging that these schools were hindering the Americanization process clearly overlooked the facts of the past ten years, which testified that the Japanese Buddhists had earnestly tried to revise their schools and textbooks. To attack the Buddhist schools was therefore un-American and smacked of bigotry. And, if teaching religion in private institutions was wrong, were those presently opposing the Buddhist schools going to agitate against Iolani (an Episcopalian high school) or St. Louis College (a Roman Catholic high school)? Were not these and other religious schools, Matheson asked, logically subject to the same opposition leveled against the Buddhist institutions? Or, was there, perhaps, a movement afoot 'to abolish religious freedom and make Christianity the state religion of Hawaii'?[84]

In reply to Matheson, Editor Irwin admitted that 'a wordy war' was going on between Buddhists and Japanese Christians, but he flatly denied that religious squabbles had affected the white population. The crux of the matter, he wrote, was not religion at all but, rather, the strong spirit of Americanism, which refused to truckle to expediency or bow to friendship and which insisted that children born on American soil and claiming American citizenship be educated as Americans in the language of America. Contrary to what Matheson prescribed, Irwin argued that what Hawaii needed was 'more nationalism and less internationalism.'[85]

In a desperate effort to resolve the mounting religious crisis, a number of Japanese teachers urged that the language schools be divorced from all religious affiliations. A few schools carried out the proposal. The Hongwanji Puuloa Educational Home was one, and the Jōdo-shū at Hawi, Kohala, was another. The Japanese Educational Association, moreover, formally voted to inaugurate radical changes in the curriculum and to discontinue all Saturday classes. Winter holidays, too, would coincide exactly with those of the American schools, the association promised, and new texts would be compiled to give 'special emphasis [to] the part that . . .

the Hawaii-born Japanese must play in creating a close bond of commerce and sentiment between Japan and the United States.'[86] Many schools also did away with elaborate observances of Japanese holidays, and the most important of these, the emperor's birthday, was celebrated in 1919 with little formal ceremony. But it was all too little and too late. Long before the heat generated by the proposed school measures could cool off and during the decade which followed, affairs took a turn for the worse. In 1920, cane workers on Oahu's sugar plantations called a general strike—the worst in Hawaii's history—and when Buddhist priests rushed to the defense of labor, they succeeded only in arousing additional malevolence toward their religion.

CHAPTER 9

The Troublesome
Twenties

THERE WAS NO RESPITE IN THE 1920S
IN THE CONFLICT OVER RELIGIOUS DIFFER-
ences. At the outset of the decade, Buddhist priests were blamed
for a critical sugar strike and the ever-inflammable language
school dispute that centered around the Honpa Hongwanji and
Jōdo-shū institutions. The stiffened opposition to Buddhism
eventually drove the embattled enemies of the 'alien seats of
learning' into the courts of the land in a desperate maneuver to
rigidly control or altogether eliminate the schools. Nevertheless,
for most Buddhist sects the decade was one of phenomenal growth
and successful adaptation. The 'formidable foe' grew ever more
formidable. Meanwhile, the Christian ministry, experiencing only
bitter frustration and envious disappointment, met every Buddhist
attempt to promote goodwill and mutual understanding with
derision and contempt. Takie Okumura, becoming more petty
and bigoted with age, continued to connive with the American
clergy in efforts to counteract the growing influence of Buddhist
institutions. He also patronized officials of the HSPA and even
convinced them that the Buddhist priesthood had long conspired
to stir up labor unrest. The deluded planters then donated
thousands of dollars to enable the Japanese evangelist to preach
against Buddhism in all the major districts of Hawaii. To repay
the planters for their generosity, Okumura and his friends concocted a number of ingenious schemes to help HSPA officials
keep the second-generation Japanese on the sugar plantations.

After the strike of 1909, the minimum monthly wage of Japanese laborers was raised from eighteen dollars to twenty dollars. Three years later, the HSPA inaugurated a bonus system. By 1916, nevertheless, a demand for still higher wages created a great disturbance in the community, and President A. W. T. Bottomley of the HSPA promised a new and even better wage scale. The earlier bonus system, based on 1 percent of the laborer's earnings for every $71.00 per ton of raw sugar and on 1 percent for every dollar per ton over $71.00, was increased by 50 percent. One-fifth of it was to be disbursed each month with the regular monthly wages; the remaining 80 percent was to be paid semi-annually in April and October. A laborer who had worked six months was to receive, based on the price of sugar at that time, $141.60 in wages and monthly bonuses and $86.40 in the semi-annual bonus—a total for the half year of $228.00, or an average monthly wage of $38.00. The bonus increase was calculated as follows: if the New York market averaged $71.00 per ton, the bonus would be $1\frac{1}{2}$ percent of wages; for every dollar paid over $71.00, the bonus would go up $1\frac{1}{2}$ percent. If sugar rose to $80.00 per ton, the bonus would be up 15 percent; if the market rose to $90.00, the bonus scale would be 30 percent, and so on. To discourage loafing and encourage efficiency, every laborer was required to work 75 percent of the time or a minimum of twenty days in order to share in the bonus.[1]

The American press reported that the Japanese were very much pleased with the announcement of the new bonus schedule, and Consul General Rokurō Moroi along with Masao Kawahara, president of the Japanese Merchants' Association, made their sincere appreciation known to the planters. Moroi was delighted with the planters' demonstration of concern for the welfare of the Japanese, and Kawahara was much relieved that the men, who were suffering from the high cost of living caused by World War I, could finally pay their debts. The *Advertiser* reported that, indeed, there had been a material improvement in the morale of cane workers after the new system had been explained to them and that the adjustment augured well for the prosperity, peace, and happiness of industrial Hawaii.

The Japanese press, too, was lavish in its praise of the new wage scale. Even Fred Makino's *Hawaii Hōchi* commended the 'broad-mindedness' of the HSPA.[2] The *Independent Review* alone sounded a discordant note. While half-heartedly acknowledging the 'liberality and wisdom' of the planters, the radical monthly expressed disappointment that wages per se had not been increased and that men unable to work a minimum of twenty days would not be permitted to share in the bonus. The *Review* alleged that the new scale had been, in fact, calculated 'arbitrarily and despotically' by men who wielded the power of feudal lords. There was thus a need for additional reform, since 'the Kingdom of God' could not be realized until 'there appears the perfect social and economic justice and fairness to all producers in this world.'[3]

A year later, a campaign for higher wages was under way and steadily gathered momentum. In July 1917, Fred Makino drew attention to the fact that, with the outbreak of the war, wages had been raised to meet inflation in every country except Hawaii. A couple of months later, the Association for Higher Wages Question, later called the Higher Wages Association, was formed. In November 1917, the association asked the HSPA for a wage increment. Retail prices had risen 62.3 percent, and the average cost of living for a single laborer was $24.81 per month. Yet most plantation workers were receiving only between $20.00 and $24.00. The bonus system was all well and good, but why should men who were making just a trifle over $24.00 or who were unable to work a minimum of twenty days a month be denied a share in the bonus? Such provisions, the association charged, were unfair.[4]

The American press did not go along with the logic behind the higher wages movement. Editor Roderick O. Matheson of the *Advertiser* (who was soon to take up the cudgels for the language schools) contended that since the bonus for 1917 would be a phenomenal 78 percent of regular wages, the plantation laborer was 'a fortunate individual in his employment.' The cost of living was higher, true enough, but the extra bonus money for the year would represent a 50 percent increase over the bonus of the previous year. As 1917 drew to a close, Matheson's paper reported that 'Never in the history of the industry has labor been so well paid or better satisfied than it has been during the past year.'[5]

The planters meanwhile did not budge. E. D. Tenney, president of the HSPA, stated flatly that an increase in wages was out of the question. The increased earnings of plantation laborers had already attracted a large portion of the floating population, and had resulted in the aggregate number of laborers becoming greater than before. Furthermore, while the bonus system had been established as a method under which the laborers would share in the prosperity of the plantations, the war had drastically changed conditions for management as well as for labor and brought largely increased production costs, excessive freight rates, and enormous taxes. To increase wages at that time would also have constituted 'an impossible burden for some of the smaller and less successful plantations.'[6] Rather than comply with the demands of the Higher Wages Association, the HSPA decided that labor should share the increased cost of production and raised the minimum base price upon which the bonus would be paid from seventy-one dollars to eighty-five dollars per ton. Nor did the planters heed the request that the bonus system be readjusted to allow those unable to work the minimum twenty days to share in the profits. The reason for initiating the profit-sharing plan in the first place, the planters pointed out, was 'to encourage regularity of service.'[7]

Officials of the Higher Wages Association promptly denounced the planters for their 'arrogance,' and the Japanese press protested that the new bonus system was 'illogical and unjust.' The *Hōchi* argued that it was grossly unfair to expect labor to share in the costs of production and that certainly no man who was not entitled to share in the bonus should be required to bear any part of such costs.[8]

The planters and Roderick Matheson disagreed. Matheson reasoned that since the bonus system was a profit-sharing plan, laborers should expect to have their profits cut by wartime inflation, just as stockholders must anticipate diminished incomes. The Japanese, nevertheless, continued to protest until Matheson appealed to their sense of duty and patriotic responsibility. Hawaii's Japanese should 'not be found wanting,' he said, at such a crucial moment.[9] The Japanese took Matheson's words to heart and waited out the war.

Once the war was over, the movement for higher wages was enthusiastically revived. The *Hawaii Chōhō* urged the Japanese to 'make their effort for the higher wages as effective as the effort against the school legislation,'[10] and the newly formed United Men's Association of the island of Hawaii issued a call for a well-organized drive to secure the rights of labor. Young Men's Buddhist Associations on Oahu dispatched notes to other youth groups throughout the Territory that urged united action for better wages. On October 23, 1919, the Japanese Society of Hawaii petitioned the HSPA for an eight-hour workday and a raise in the basic wage.[11] Nothing happened.

In November 1919, fifty-eight representatives from four labor unions met in Honolulu and formed the Japanese Federation of Labor,* which submitted three separate sets of demands to the HSPA asking (1) for an eight-hour day; (2) for an increase in the basic daily wage from $0.77 to $1.25; (3) that men who worked a minimum of fifteen (rather than twenty) days per month be entitled to share in the bonus; and (4) that plantation health and recreation facilities be improved. Moreover, since America was a Christian country where Sunday laws were vigorously enforced, it would also be 'most becoming,' proposed the federation, for Christian employers 'to offer a double pay for labor performed on Sundays which [the] Lord God [had] ordained specifically as a day of rest.'[12]

*The name was later changed to Hawaii Laborers' Association in an effort to dispel rumors that it was a 'nationalistic organization.'

In the meantime Filipino laborers* had submitted a similar set of demands to the HSPA. It too was flatly turned down. Therefore, on January 19, 1920, several thousand members of the Filipino Labor Union went on strike. Less than two weeks later, on February 1, 1920, after the planters defiantly refused to comply with the demands of the Japanese Federation of Labor, some twelve thousand Japanese quit work on Kahuku, Waialua, Waimanalo, Ewa, Waipahu, and Aiea plantations.[13]

The American community had been led to believe that the strike was precipitated and engineered by agitators. The *Advertiser* and the *Star-Bulletin* asserted that Japanese laborers had been perfectly content until they were 'stirred up' and pointed out that cane workers were receiving a bonus of 87 percent in addition to free rent, water, fuel, and medical care. The sums of money sent back to Japan through local banks and post offices showed no diminution whatsoever. In September 1919, just a month before the Higher Wages Association was formed, the American press recalled that the Japanese consul general had been most emphatic in a statement that plantation laborers were well treated and that relations between the planters and their field hands were 'most amicable.'[14]

This was not the first time that a strike was attributed to rabble-rousers. As early as 1900, inspector of immigrants C. A. Peterson informed the Board of Immigration that plantation workers had no minds of their own and blindly followed their leaders, who coerced them by threats of violence. The 1909 strike was also blamed on 'high-wages demagogues,' who had 'everything to gain and nothing to lose.'[15] The 1920 strike, likewise, was traced to the activities of a 'clever clique working along racial and nationalistic lines.'[16] As early as October 1919, the *Advertiser*, pointing to the fact that laborers had been absent from the governing body of the Higher Wages Association, took note of the fact that Buddhist teachers and newspapermen were piloting the executive committee of the newly formed Plantation Labor's Supporters Association. On the twenty-man executive committee of the association were three Buddhist teachers and three YMBA officials. The *Advertiser* concluded that, obviously, the higher wages movement was the undertaking of 'others than the plantation laborers.'[17]

Plantation officials, of course, did not need to be convinced that the trouble originated from the outside, and in a reply to a letter from the Japanese Merchants' Association, Royal D. Mead, secretary of the HSPA, made the position of the planters crystal clear. The HSPA could see no injustice in requiring able-bodied men to work an equivalent of four and a half days per week, and if the plantations were to pay, in addition to the bonus, the $1.25

*Filipino laborers were introduced to Hawaii as early as 1906 as an antidote to the influx of Japanese workmen.

minimum wage demanded by the Japanese Federation of Labor, they simply could not maintain their existence. As the day-wage increased, the turnout of laborers noticeably decreased. Last but not least, very few men had requested any financial aid from the Federation of Labor; the laborers admitted having sufficient funds on which to live for some months. The strike, Mead* concluded, had thus been brought about not by the conditions of employment but 'by the Japanese newspapers and agitators, aided and abetted by the Japanese school teachers and priests.'[18]

There was also a real fear in the community that the strike was part of a plan to compel land owners to yield control of the land to the Japanese. As early as January 1920, HSPA spokesmen saw in the pending labor crisis an anti-American movement designed to obtain control of the sugar business of the Hawaiian Islands. Soon after the strike was called, former governor George R. Carter wrote to evangelist Shigehide Kanda in Kohala that if the planters gave in and allowed the strikers to dictate wages, planters might as well give up running the sugar plantations. Japanese laborers, according to Carter, had told plantation managers that they did not want to strike but were obliged to do so lest they 'be reported to their government and their names . . . be published in Japan, so as to bring discredit upon their families.'[19]

Takie Okumura and other Japanese Christian clerics advised their congregations to oppose the strike because, as Shirō Sokabe put it, the planters had always been 'so good to the church.'[20] Buddhist and Shinto priests, on the other hand, openly sympathized with the campaign for higher wages, and on the eve of the strike, in a letter dated January 22, 1920, they pleaded with the HSPA to grant the demands of the Japanese Federation of Labor. Cane workers, burdened throughout the war by a fluctuating economy and unrelieved inflation, were in dire financial straits and were preparing for the worst, the petition warned. The Buddhist clergy thought it unjust to deny a share of the bonus to laborers who could not work a minimum of twenty days of every month. Some persons, they wrote, were legitimately unable to work twenty days out of every month; human beings, after all, were not machines. Furthermore, the bonus, as high as it was, did not compensate for the accelerated cost of living. As the spiritual leaders of the Japanese community, the priests felt compelled to take a stand for the right, as they saw the right. For years they had dutifully urged their countrymen to render faithful and honest service to the planters, but now the time had come to support the just claims of labor. The letter was signed by Bishop Yemyō

*Interestingly enough, just a decade before, Mead had said that the presence of Asiatics in Hawaii was 'no more felt than is that of the cattle on the ranges.' See Royal D. Mead, 'The Sugar Industry and Hawaii,' quoted by Hal Hanna, 'Big 5 Monopoly,' Hearings, 1946, p. 784.

Imamura of Honpa Hongwanji; Eikaku Seki of the Shingon-shū; Bishop Hōsen Isobe of the Sōtō-shū; Acting Bishop Ryōzen Yamada of the Jōdo-shū; Bishop Chōsei Nunome of the Nichiren-shū; and Kankai Izuhara of the Higashi Hongwanji. Chinjirō Sakaki, a Shinto priest, and Katsuyoshi Miyaō of the Izumo Taisha also attached their signatures to the letter.[21]

After receipt of the petition by the HSPA, the Buddhist priest-hood was caustically censured by the American press. Headlines in the *Star-Bulletin* of January 24, 1920, shouted: 'Buddhist Priests Interfere to Aid Strikers,' and excerpts from the priests' letter were taken out of context and translated by, of all people, Umetarō Okumura, and were publicized in a way which distorted both the meaning and the intent of the petition.*[22]

From then on, there was no convincing the non-Oriental community that the strike had not been started by Japanese newspapermen and Buddhist 'agitators.' The *Advertiser* editorial-ized at great length about an 'alien conspiracy' against Ameri-canizing the Islands and the 'brazen attempt' of Japanese editors and language school teachers to take over the sugar industry and to obtain 'soft jobs and fat salaries for themselves at the expense of their deluded followers.'[23] Pagan priests, it was said, had demonstrated beyond any doubt that they were hostile to American principles, and Editor Irwin of the *Advertiser* commented that, while the Constitution of the United States guaranteed religious freedom, it did not give alien priests the right 'to meddle with our affairs of government or stir up social and industrial distur-bances in this country.'[24] The strike on Oahu plantations was different from any preceding disturbance, warned the *Star-Bulletin*, because it demonstrated that 'Buddhism is pressing hard against the Christianity which has held sway here for a hundred years.' Buddhist spokesmen allegedly were taking a leading part as advisers and directors of the thrust against Hawaii's leading industry and thus were striking directly at the heart of American prestige. *Star-Bulletin* editor R. A. McNally wrote that the Japanese priests and teachers, without question, had furnished all the evidence a thinking man needed in order to conclude that the strike which they had provoked and spearheaded was perpetrated 'to compel the sugar planters to recognize them as the masters of Hawaii's Asiatic laborers.'[25]

Buddhist priests, all the while, remained adamant in their stand on behalf of labor. Most priests had come to the realization that the Japanese would no longer submit to economic injustices for the sake of *ando shugi* and had begun to focus more attention on Gautama's teaching (as set forth in the *Kūṭadanta Sūtra*) that, to prevent social and economic disturbances, men must be provided

*Umetarō Okumura was hired as the official translator for the HSPA on 19 January, 1920. See *Honolulu Star-Bulletin,* 23 January 1950.

opportunities 'for earning a sufficient income [so] they will be contented [and] have no fear or anxiety.'[26] Buddhist teachers on Kauai even solicited money to support the strike, and youth organizations associated with several of the rural temples came out actively in defense of the strike and sponsored talent shows to raise money for the striking laborers. Later, some three thousand strikers staged a protest march through Honolulu, and the Sōtō-Zen Mission gave them a portrait of Abraham Lincoln to carry through the streets.[27] An irate American press dubbed the march 'an insult' to the American public and alleged once more, with greater vehemence than before, that the labor crisis had been instigated by Buddhist rabble-rousers, who 'hate America, Americans and American institutions, and who set out to try to obtain economic dominance of the sugar industry.'[28]

Meanwhile, efforts to end the strike had come to naught. Dr. Albert Palmer, pastor of Central Union Church, pleaded with the planters that the Japanese did have some legitimate grievances. The field hands deserved at the very least, he said, a higher basic wage, a bonus adjustment of some sort, and better living conditions. At the very outset of the strike, Palmer and a few other concerned individuals had submitted to the HSPA and to the Japanese Federation of Labor the so-called Palmer Plan, which called for termination of the strike and the election by secret ballot on every plantation of an employees' committee to confer with management for the resolution of labor disputes. The Japanese Federation of Labor readily adopted the plan, but the HSPA rejected it 'flatly and unconditionally' on the grounds that the strike was *not* the outgrowth of genuine economic grievances.[29] A handful of Buddhist priests (who did not see eye-to-eye with their superiors on the labor crisis) had also tried, in their own way, to secure a settlement; and the *Advertiser* remarked that the 'educated' Japanese, indeed, seemed 'aggrieved' at the whole situation. But a few individuals, the paper concluded, could not hope to accomplish much now since they had made so little effort in the past to curb the intemperate utterances of the Japanese language press. The handful of Buddhist priests who dared to oppose the strike were thoroughly castigated by the Japanese press.[30]

Later, there were other complaints that most Japanese religious leaders did not have the courage to get out and face the Japanese community during the strike. A disappointed Lorrin Thurston said that not a single Japanese voice had been raised against any phase of the strike or against acts of terrorism committed by strike leaders and sympathizers. The 'more enlightened' Japanese were not in sympathy with the strike, he believed, but they 'either did not dare to oppose [it], or thought it would do no good.'[31] By the 'more enlightened,' Thurston probably meant the Christian Japanese; if so, he was quite right. The Okumuras and their friends walked a tightrope. They could not afford to offend the planters nor could they risk arousing the indignation of the older Japanese among whom they still hoped to make converts. Moreover, Thurston and those who shared his disappointment in the Japanese leadership had overlooked the fact that by this time some of the very worst agitators among the Japanese strikers were American-born Japanese, who flouted with indifference or outright insolence the authority of aging Buddhist and Christian clerics.[32]

The strike lasted five months. It was called off on June 30, 1920, at a special conference of representatives of the Japanese Federation of Labor. In the meantime, while Oriental laborers were threatening to cripple Hawaii's principal industry, confrontations between Buddhists and Christians over the language schools had become more acrimonious.

THE LANGUAGE SCHOOLS AND THE FEDERAL SURVEY COMMISSION

After the Judd and Andrews bills were defeated in the senate, the governor invited the United States Commissioner of Education to investigate the public and private schools of Hawaii and to make recommendations to the next legislature as to what would be necessary and proper to provide for the training and education of the pupils of all of the schools of the Territory, with the view of making the students loyal and intelligent citizens of the United States of America. Dr. Frank F. Bunker of the Federal Bureau of Education headed the commission. Assisting him were W. W. Kemp, chairman of the educational department of the University of California; Parke R. Kolbe, president of the Municipal University, Akron, Ohio; and George R. Twiss, state high school inspector and professor of secondary education, Ohio State University.[33]

When the commission arrived to conduct its investigation, opposition to the Japanese, heightened by postwar nationalism, the influx of anti-Japanese ideas from the Pacific Coast, and a profound distrust of Japanese foreign policy, was at fever pitch.[34] The Americanization movement was in full swing. The *Advertiser* sponsored essay contests on 'What Does It Mean To Be An American?' The YMCA advertised lectures on 'Christian American-ization.' The Honolulu post of the American Legion adopted the slogan 'America First and Always' and created an 'Americanism Commission' to launch a drive for the complete Americanization of the Territory.[35] The Christian clergy, incensed by Japan's crafty game in Asia, issued a warning to Hawaii's Japanese that they would be looked upon with suspicion (and often with hatred, added Arthur L. Dean, later president of the University of Hawaii) so long as Japan persisted in her drive for territorial expansion 'at any cost.'[36]

More than any other single factor, it was the strike of 1920 that once again stirred up fervid opposition to the Japanese language schools. Irwin of the *Advertiser* recalled that language school teachers had taken an active part in the assault on American industry in Hawaii,[37] and McNally of the *Star-Bulletin* pointed out that the agitators who had tried to exert absolute control over Hawaii's twenty-five thousand Japanese laborers were the very same Buddhist priests and teachers who had spearheaded the successful fight against language school legislation in 1919. The school bills had been defeated, McNally wrote, because of a fear that they would foment labor disturbances. Yet, ironically enough, a feeling of victory over the defeat of the bills had given the Japanese a new sense of power and an exaggerated confidence in their ability to change things to suit themselves. The newspaperman now feared that a 'dark conspiracy' was afoot to Japanize Hawaii. McNally's anxiety was caused, in part, by a statement made to the press at that moment by an anonymous local citizen who reportedly had 'very intimate' dealings with the Japanese, both in Hawaii and in Japan. The unnamed observer was 'astonished' that Buddhist priests had become so involved in labor disputes and alleged that Buddhism 'as developing in the territory of Hawaii' was 'an increasing menace' to American institutions.[38] After that, Irwin concluded that there was no point whatever in talking about Americanizing the Japanese until Buddhist upstarts were put in their place. Furthermore, he pontificated, the language schools should go, and the foreign language press must be curbed, or it, too, must go.[39]

RECOMMENDATIONS OF THE SURVEY COMMISSION

In the course of their investigation of Hawaii's schools, members of the Federal Survey Commission interviewed many American school teachers, members of the Chamber of Commerce, several members of the Daughters of the American Revolution, and key spokesmen for the Ad Club (an eight-year-old organization dedicated to the 'civic good' and boasting several unique features, like requiring all of its speakers to stand on their chairs). No language school teachers were consulted. The Chamber of Commerce recommended that all private schools be placed under the supervision of public authorities and that teachers in both the public and private institutions be obliged to confess democratic loyalties and to familiarize themselves with the fundamentals of American history and government. The Daughters of the American Revolution unqualifiedly opposed all the foreign language schools. The Ad Club advised that the schools be put under the supervision of the Board of Education, which, club members hoped, would adopt as its policy 'the gradual elimination' of these schools.[40]

Quite a few public school teachers, too, believed that the language schools were doing more harm than good. Some educators took the position that most youngsters were physically unable to do the extra work; boys and girls attending the language schools were often said to come to class tired and restless and were inattentive during the regular school hours. Others pointed out that it was very difficult to teach American patriotism to children who were being taught, both at home and in the Japanese schools, to be loyal to the Japanese government and to ignore American ideas and values. One teacher affirmed that the language schools were teaching loyalty to Japan 'under cover of religious instruction,' and another alleged that the religious beliefs of the language school teachers were clearly adverse to the making of 'real Americans.' Still another educator stated that the older Japanese teachers associated with the Buddhist missions were teaching a kind of divided allegiance theory, which fitted a child to be an American for the time being and a Japanese should the occasion arise.

The Christian clergy, meanwhile, had 'discovered' that, in addition to being agencies for the preservation of an alien culture, the language schools were 'retarding' the ability of the Japanese youth to speak and to write the English language.[41] The truth of the matter was that students who did well in one school usually did well in the other, while those who performed on a substandard level in the public schools blamed the language schools for their deficiencies. The following extract from a letter written to the *Advertiser*, by a student attending the Hongwanji High School in Honolulu, will illustrate the process of rationalization, which played conveniently into the hands of language school enemies.

I am one of the many young Japanese with a wide-awake modern ideas relating to at least something, and I want to tell you why the higher Japanese institutions of the Hawaiian Islands should be abolished if the Hawaiian Islands want pure patriotic and democratic American citizens out of the Japanese nationality. Since I am a student of the Japanese High School, I can only relate you my experiences of that school. What I am telling you is not at all an exaggeration but a real happened and is still existing fact as actually seen by me.

The Japanese High School teachers and Sept. [*sic*] Imamura are really very clever in trying to make the prominent local Americans believe that their work is not to make money like merchants, but to educate the Japanese; that the feelings of the future Japanese might be more Americanized. These facts are really true and are carried on. But are they the only things they do? No! These, they do, so that they can give an example to 'bluff' the Americans, but 90% of their work is devoted to make . . . not lively and socialistic Christians, but deadlike unsocialistic Buddhists. I can't express my thought very clearly, but I can interpret that in terms of people. For example, instead of producing practical people like engineers or bookkeepers who are useful directly to us, the Hongwanji Jap. High School produces people with perhaps . . . A.B. degrees, who, perhaps are important, but no so directly as others in the business world. . . .

This High School also teaches besides Lafcadio Hearn, a Buddhist and Japanese old spirits combined book, another book called Bushido, which is used as an English Japanese translating text book, but indirectly a text book used for stimulating the boys to become more Japanese-like. However, American civics text books are used in the lower grades, they are only used so as to 'bluff' the 'blindfolded' Americans. . . .

I am one of the many boys who is sent to the Japanese High School by force of the parents. I really hate to come to this school, but I have to, because if I object it, I have to suffer punishments by not being allowed to go even to the English School, which is my main thing, but more or less a nuisance to my parents. It is hard for me to do the English School work, since there is a great deal of home-work every day given by this School. I really pity those people who have to go to this school and to the high schools, especially to the Normal Schools, since they are not increasing their English vocabulary as they should do, and when the English school starts at 8:00, as is the case of the Normal School, we have to do a double time and quick time and all the known times to reach the school in time. You must know that all these are not done because we like, but the sake of the ignorant old ideaed [sic] parents. I have many more that I would like to tell you, but I cannot very well tell you in one letter, for I am not so very good in this line of work.[42]

While the balance of opinion was against the maintenance of the schools, a few of the public school teachers who were interviewed by the Federal Survey Commission expressed positive attitudes about the function and purpose of the Japanese schools. One teacher stated that the religious education given in these schools, along with the emphasis on strict discipline and good moral conduct, would prove a force for good in the community. Other teachers foresaw that should the schools be closed, the community would have on its hands (after public school hours) unsupervised boys and girls whose parents worked until late hours on the plantations. One teacher who favored retaining the schools pointed out, furthermore, that while the Japanese schools were indeed once a 'menace' to America, the curriculum of the institutions had been recently 'changed considerably along American lines.'[43]

Nevertheless, upon completion of its investigation of the schools of Hawaii, the Federal Survey Commission recommended that the next legislature abolish outright all foreign language schools. The commission proposed that whenever the demand became sufficient, foreign language instruction might be offered in the public schools for an hour each day after the regular school hours. Moreover, such classes were to be conducted solely by teachers regularly employed by the Department of Public Instruction.[44]

By the time the Territorial legislature of 1920 assembled, a number of bills had been drafted by various civic organizations to put the language schools under the absolute control of the

Department of Public Instruction. Among those who immediately protested all such measures was that curmudgeon for the defense, Lorrin Thurston. Thurston said that he could conceive of nothing more inexcusably tyrannical (referring specifically to the recommendations of the Federal Survey Commission) than to make it a penal offense for a man to teach his child his native language, without a knowledge of which the child could not communicate with his father or mother. Nothing, he said, was more un-American or devoid of the spirit of freedom and fair play. Thurston anticipated that in time the language schools would become obsolete and would die a natural death, so why, he asked, stir up a hornet's nest now by attempting to outlaw or rigidly control them? Furthermore, he warned, 'a persecuted religion [that is, Buddhism] thrives.'[45]

Japanese educators saw the handwriting on the wall. On November 15, 1920, asking that no law be enacted by the legislature to abolish the schools, these educators submitted to the Chamber of Commerce their own regulatory 'Act Relating to Foreign Language Schools and Teachers Thereof.' Like those preceding it, this measure was designed to fully safeguard the Americanization of all children attending schools in the Territory, and it specified that in order to teach or conduct foreign language classes, a teacher must have a reasonable knowledge of democratic ideals and American history and institutions, and must be able to read, write, and speak the English language. The provisions regarding a knowledge of English, however, were to be liberally construed during a two-year period up to July 1, 1922, at which time the act was to go into full effect. The proposed measure also stipulated that classes be held for one hour every weekday *prior* to the opening of public school classes, and it empowered the Department of Public Instruction to prescribe texts and courses of study for the schools 'from time to time.' The proposed act was signed by both lay and religious members of the Japanese Christian community and by Buddhist clerics, including Bishop Imamura and Bishop Tachikawa of the Jōdō Mission.[46]

The Chamber of Commerce immediately endorsed the measure and recommended its enactment to the legislature. Henry J. Lyman, Republican from Hilo, introduced the bill in the house; Harry A. Baldwin, Republican from Maui, introduced the measure in the senate as Senate Bill 18, 'An Act to prescribe qualifications for school teachers for the purpose of safeguarding American citizenship in the Territory of Hawaii.' Senate Bill 18 passed the senate unanimously on November 17, 1920, and with a few significant changes, the house concurred a few days later. As Act 30 of the Special Session Laws of 1920, the bill was signed by Governor McCarthy on November 24, 1920, and became effective on July 1, 1921.[47]

Act 30 provided: that no person might teach or conduct a foreign language school without a certificate from the Department of Public Instruction; that such a certificate would be issued only to a person conversant with American history, government, institutions, and ideals, and who could read, write, and speak the English language; that no foreign language school was to hold classes *before* or during the public school sessions; and that no pupil in a foreign language school was to attend classes for longer than one hour a day or six hours per week. With the passage of Act 30, the language school fracas subsided temporarily, but less than two years later, hostilities were resumed as fiercely as before.

THE GROWTH AND TRANSFORMATION OF BUDDHISM

Opposition to the language schools sprang primarily from their close association with Buddhist temples. The Federal Survey Commission had reported that ninety of one hundred ninety of the Japanese schools were directly operated under Buddhist auspices and that it was purely conjectural as to how many of the so-called nonsectarian schools were, in fact, independent. The Christian clergy continued to label Buddhist educational practices a Japanizing force responsible for Hawaii's social and religious problems. The schools run by the 'priests of paganism' thus continued to be condemned ipso facto as 'un-American in principle [and] subversive to patriotism.'[48]

By this time, too, there was a greater number of Buddhist temples and Buddhist-affiliated organizations in the Islands. The Hongwanji sect alone had constructed a total of sixty abodes of light and love in urban and rural districts, boasted a membership of at least seventy-five thousand, and sponsored thirty Young Men's Buddhist Associations and thirty-three Sunday schools with an enrollment of four thousand.[49] Other sects, too, were flourishing and were soon to give discomforting evidence of their growing popularity.

A disheartened Christian community, commemorating the one hundredth anniversary of the commencement of missionary work in the Islands, deplored the 'repaganization of Hawaii' as a process both 'subtle and sinister.' If Christianity failed in Hawaii, warned the Reverend Dr. Palmer of Central Union Church, it would set back the hope of humanity in a way terrible to contemplate. Reverend Henry P. Judd of the Hawaiian Board agreed with Palmer that Hawaii's most serious problem was neither racial nor political, but religious, in character. One-third of the population of the Islands, Judd calculated, were 'worshippers of Buddha or Shinto,' and the concern of the American community regarding the second generation Japanese thus naturally revolved around the fact that these young people who were coming of age were reared in Buddhism, surrounded by Buddhist influences, and instructed by Buddhist priests to worship idols and participate in heathen rites and ceremonies. Every time Islanders heard the booming of temple bells, Judd said, they were reminded of the process of repaganization. He charged that the Buddhist ideas taught in foreign language schools and in pagan homes clashed with American ways and principles. Scholar and scientist Arthur Dean, lamenting the fact that Hawaii was seething with bitter racial antipathies aggravated by the incessant quarreling between Christian churches and 'pagan temples,' conceded that Christian leaders had reason to be alarmed. The raucous and disreputable behavior of beachcombers and sailors in the early days of missionary activity were as nothing, he wrote, in comparison with the over-whelming challenge afforded now by the 'great ethnic faith.'[50] Summing matters up, Reverend John P. Erdman of the Episcopal Mission declared that the 'enterprise of winning the whole of Hawaii to Christ' had indeed become 'vital not simply for Hawaii, but for all the Pacific Islands.'[51]

During the next two years, in spite of all their efforts, the Christian clergy witnessed an even greater strengthening of Buddhist work, 'not only in Honolulu but all over the Territory.'[52] The Sōtō-shū replaced its six-year-old temple on Nuuanu Avenue with a new and costlier edifice, which was formally dedicated in August 1921, and the following year, Zenkyō Komagata, a young and capable priest, was appointed bishop of the Sōtō Mission of Hawaii. To keep pace with its steady growth, the Higashi Hongwanji also erected a new and costly temple in Honolulu in the summer of 1921.[53] The Nichiren-shū built two additional temples on Maui (one in Wailuku in 1920 and another in Puunene in 1922), and other Buddhist missions were established in the Pawaa and Moiliili districts of Honolulu.[54]

None of this activity escaped the notice of the American community, and the Okumuras made the most of every oppor-tunity to grieve publicly with Judd and other Christian clerics over the repaganization of Hawaii.[55] Word spread quickly that 'paganism is increasing and heretics is infesting the community.'[56] It seemed that Sidney Gulick had erred in his earlier prediction that the long persistence of Buddhism was improbable because Buddhism would 'undoubtedly die off with the present [first] generation of Japanese.'[57]

As the years went on, Buddhist priests gradually adapted their religion to Western ways to make it more acceptable to the younger Japanese, who were rapidly being transformed by values and life patterns very different from the traditions of their fore-fathers. This process of adaptation was greatly facilitated by the innate flexibility of Buddhism, which accounts for its success in countries with widely divergent cultural backgrounds, and by the disposition of the Japanese to reconcile religious teachings with the exigencies of time and space. (As early as 1902 the United States Commissioner of Labor had observed that the Japanese national trait of readily assimilating the exterior forms of Western civilization had reproduced itself 'peculiarly in religion.')

In some parts of the Orient, exponents of the Dharma had taken over 'wholesale' the methods of Christian propagandizing,[58] and this same phenomenon became apparent at a very early date in Hawaii. The *Friend* reported at the turn of the century that the Hongwanji had even appropriated the terminology of Christianity and altogether 'absorbed' the forms of the Christian religion. Temples were called 'churches' by Buddhist laymen, and priests were frequently addressed as 'Reverend.' The Honolulu Jōdo temple had installed 'benches like those in a Christian church,' and the new Honpa Hongwanji *betsuin* (built in 1918) was reported to be the only Buddhist temple in the world equipped with a pipe organ and an indirect lighting system. Buddhist Sunday or 'Sabbath' schools were conducted at several urban and rural temples, and the Hongwanji YMBA, which was modeled conspicuously after the YMCA, had over the years attracted many 'representative professional and business men.'[59] A Jōdo Mission *kanbutsue* (celebration of Buddha's birth) service in honor of Śākyamuni's birth was dubbed 'Buddhistmas,' and in 1923 the Honpa Hongwanji celebrated the 2,546th anniversary of Gautama's Enlightenment with 'pontifical vespers' and a Catholic-like 'pontifical ceremonial procession.'[60] By the 1920s, Buddhist gāthas, or religious songs (which were translated into English and patterned after old and favorite Christian hymns), were sung in unison to Western rhythms at the weekly English-language services. Among the most popular of these gāthas were 'Onward Buddhist Soldiers,' 'Buddha, Savior, Pilot Me,' and 'Joy to the World, the Buddha Has Come.'[61] In 1928 a Congregational minister who had attended a Hongwanji English service commented as follows:

I went into a Buddhist temple, which ministers to a Congregation of English-speaking young Oriental Americans. It is most tastefully appointed. Except for the altar equipment, which is, of course, pronouncedly Buddhistic in its symbolisms, you would almost have to be told you were in the courts of the 'heathen.' It looks much like a church. The Buddhists, physically, are made very much as we are, and, of course, have pews on which they sit—for all the world like Christians. They are very quiet—and come into their temple softly and silently, and while there, are deeply meditative, and never whisper—albeit, elsewhere the oriental is the world's most rapid and continuous talker. I purchased a little hymnal in the literature department of the temple. Much of the ritual is excellent, and with substitution of the name of Christ for that of Buddha could be heartily recommended to many of our churches in which worship has been neglected until it isn't even missed.[62]

By the 1920s the Honpa Hongwanji was also conducting full-fledged Western-style marriages,* complete with white gowns, bridesmaids, flower girls, and veil bearers.[63] In 1925 the first Caucasian couple married in a Buddhist temple in Hawaii were married at the Honolulu Honpa Hongwanji. Officiating at the ceremony with much pomp and little grace was a ruddy complexioned, crass convert from Anglicanism who referred to himself as the 'Archbishop Kirby, Ph.D.'[64]

THE HONPA HONGWANJI ENGLISH DEPARTMENT

When the new Hongwanji *betsuin* was dedicated in 1918, Bishop Imamura, in one of his finest moments, declared that 'true religion ought to rise above and be applicable to any country and nationality and so assimilate with every state and nation.'[65] Buddhism could not be preserved unmodified in a Western environment, and no one was more aware than Imamura that constructive changes would have to be made soon if Buddhism were not to lose out altogether to the dominant religio-cultural system of the Islands. Most important, the Hongwanji bishop realized that, if Buddhism were to become meaningful to Hawaii's Americans of Japanese ancestry, its priesthood would have to do more than imitate the forms and methods of Christianity. While continuing to afford the older generation a sense of cultural solidarity, priests would have to set aside their exclusively Japanese ways of thinking and focus more attention on the teachings of the historical Buddha, Gautama Śākyamuni. Above all, young Buddhists who understood only a little Japanese would have to be given a better understanding of the Dharma through a systematic exposition of the basic tenets of the faith. To accomplish these ends, the Mission would have to propagate Buddhism on a bilingual basis; only an English-speaking Buddhist could clarify the teachings of Buddhism for the second-generation Japanese and the community-at-large. Perhaps, too, Imamura hoped that Americans would take a more tolerant view of Buddhism if the Hongwanji established an 'English Department' and thereby assumed a major role in facilitating the assimilation of young Japanese.[66] Imamura's intentions were good and his reasoning was sound enough, but as soon as he announced his decision to propagate Buddhism among the English-speaking peoples of Hawaii, some of the older Japanese protested. Editor Yasutarō Sōga of the *Nippu Jiji* warned that the idea was ridiculous and impracticable. A Buddhist evangelical project at that time would merely, he prophesied, create more friction between Americans and Japanese, and the size of the new *betsuin* did not necessarily represent the

*As early as 1908 Bishop Imamura had obtained a license permitting him to officiate at weddings—an unheard of thing in Japan where no Buddhist priest had ever officiated at a nuptial ceremony.

spiritual importance of Buddhism in Hawaii.[67] Nevertheless, in November 1921, M. T. Kirby, a heavy-set, stern-looking convert from the Church of England, accepted Bishop Imamura's invitation to take charge of the Hongwanji's newly organized English Department. Kirby conducted his first 'American-Buddhist' service at the *betsuin* on Sunday, November 20, 1921. The topic of his sermon was 'True Religion and Its Spirit,' a subject about which he knew virtually nothing.[68]

Kirby's qualifications for the task he was summoned to perform (which demanded an extraordinary degree of forbearance and tact) were hardly impressive. In his youth, Kirby had been a cowpuncher, lumberjack, and farmer. He had also dabbled in theosophy. In 1913 he left his home in Vancouver, Canada, and went to Japan, where he taught briefly in a Hongwanji grammar school. Then he entered a Buddhist monastery in Kamakura. Later, for reasons clear to no one, he left the Orient and went to California, where he was recruited by Bishop Imamura to present 'the English exposition of Buddhism.'[69]

Kirby was in Honolulu less than three weeks when word reached the Christian clergy that he was 'ridiculing' Christianity. Reverend Albert Palmer, deciding to investigate the rumor, attended Kirby's 'Christmas' service at the Fort Street temple. According to Palmer, during the service Kirby strutted about in flowing yellow robes and, after uttering 'a sonorous ascription to the principle of all truth,' delivered a long and irksome 'tirade against Christianity,' admonishing his congregation of youthful Japanese to take the Bible and spirit of prophecy 'cum grano salis,' that is, with a grain of salt. Palmer quickly concluded that the Hongwanji Mission had brought in this 'insolent Father Kirby' to bolster the Hawaiian-born, English-speaking Japanese in their loyalty to Buddhism 'by discrediting Christianity.'[70]

In answer to Palmer's charge that Kirby had unjustly vilified the Christian faith, Kirby replied in the most stringent language at his command that, unless Christianity advanced along progressive lines by taking psychology and scientific scholarship into consideration, it would certainly 'reach its end.'[71] Kirby's reputation as an assailant of Christianity then spread with great rapidity. Henry Butler Schwartz of the Hawaiian Methodist-Episcopal Mission agreed with Palmer that Kirby's efforts did not really appear to be directed toward the conversion of Caucasians to Buddhism. Quite to the contrary, wrote Schwartz, the man seemed determined 'by a deliberate misrepresentation and disparagement of Christianity' to thwart the work of Christian missionaries among the English-speaking Japanese.[72] Kirby had hit the community like a bombshell. Editor Sōga's fears had been realized.

As an antidote to the 'poison' being disseminated by Kirby, the Methodist-Episcopal Mission summoned Dr. Y. Hiraiwa, a former bishop of the Methodist Church, to hasten to the Islands and set Hawaii's young Japanese straight on the merits of Christianity. Hiraiwa arrived from Japan in September 1922 and spent six weeks 'clearing the atmosphere,' said Schwartz, for 'the reception of our message.'[73] Takie and Umetarō Okumura, too, had resolved that Mr. Kirby's anti-Christian propaganda would not go unchallenged. In October 1922, Takie Okumura invited to the Islands the Reverend Mr. Kaku Imai, who would hopefully bolster Christian work among the Japanese. The *Friend* reported that Imai had long since passed 'out of darkness into light' and from 'winter into spring,' that is, he had renounced Shingon Buddhism for the Baptist faith. Speaking to Japanese throughout the Territory, Imai strongly counseled his youthful audiences not to listen to Buddhist priests, who had come up with the curious notion that Buddhists could be good Americans.[74] Encouraged and assisted everywhere by the Okumuras, Imai preached in the Islands against Buddhism for two months. By this time, the Okumuras had taken still other steps to counteract Buddhist propaganda and refute the idea, so popular in Buddhist circles, that the Dharma and Americanism could, and should, be reconciled.

THE OKUMURAS' 'EDUCATIONAL CAMPAIGN'

After the 1920 strike, many cane workers deserted the plantations and either returned to Japan or established businesses of their own as coffee or pineapple farmers, contractors or builders, truck gardeners, and small merchants. The planters therefore were again faced with the necessity of replenishing their labor supply. On April 20, 1921, the Territorial legislature created an Emergency Labor Commission, which was sent to Washington to seek Congressional help. The three members of the commission were Walter F. Dillingham, a prominent businessman, Charles F. Chillingworth, a Territorial senator, and Albert Horner, a sugar expert. Alleging that Hawaii's principal industry was in danger of passing into Japanese hands, Dillingham requested that Congress lift its ban on Chinese immigration. The payment of bonus money (in the sum of $25,878,996) had enabled many Japanese, Dillingham testified, to flee the less attractive field occupations. Of some one-hundred-nine thousand Japanese in the Territory, only twenty-five thousand were still at work in the cane fields.[75] In the meantime, George Wright, president of the Honolulu Central Labor Union, had despatched a wireless message to the legislative representative of the American Federation of Labor in Washington and charged that members of the so-called Emergency Commission had grossly misrepresented the labor situation in Hawaii. Wright himself then went to Washington and testified before the Committee on Immigration and Naturalization as the official delegate of the trade unions of Hawaii. Japanese laborers had been driven off the planta-

GEORGE WRIGHT, ENGLISH-LANGUAGE EDITOR OF THE
Hawaii Hōchi

tions, he affirmed, by intolerable conditions which had made it impossible for them to make a living. The 1920 strike, furthermore, had nothing whatsoever to do with a Japanese plot to seize control of the sugar industry, and the HSPA, he took care to point out, had categorically refused to consider any compromise or to cooperate in any way in order to terminate the strike. The 'Palmer Plan,' among others, had been summarily rejected in an autocratic and feudalistic manner. Thus, Wright contended that Hawaii's labor problem was due to overproduction, excessive capitalization, and gross mismanagement.[76] The upshot of all this was that the commission failed in its purpose. Congress refused to change its immigration statutes. So the planters once more had to resort to Filipino labor and to entice, if they could, the second-generation Japanese to remain on the plantations.

The Christian clergy, meanwhile, had capitalized on the labor crisis of 1920 to urge another full-scale 'Americanize and Christianize the Plantations' movement. Reverend Palmer, like Sidney Gulick before him, called for the establishment of a Sunday school on every plantation, and the Hawaiian Board, egged on by its Japanese members, passed a resolution to do everything possible to ensure that no plantation would give its support to any non-Christian faith. All members of the Hawaiian Board were counseled 'to use their influence to this end.'[77]

Takie Okumura was not to be outdone by the American clergy, and with the financial support of influential persons in Japan and well-to-do haoles in Hawaii, he conjured up an ingenious plan to preach Christianity and to combat Buddhism on Hawaiian plantations. In January 1921, he and his thirty-three-year-old son, Umetarō, inaugurated a Territory-wide 'Educational Campaign Among Japanese Labor on Various Plantations.' The purpose of the campaign, according to what the Okumuras told the American public, was to remove the causes of friction between the American and the Japanese communities. In reality, it was to disseminate the Okumuras' own variety of religious propaganda.

By his own admission, Takie Okumura frequently used a roundabout method to promulgate Christian doctrine. In the summer of 1920, to ensure the success of his projected 'Educational Campaign,' he made a trip to Japan, ostensibly to attend a Sunday school convention in Tokyo but in reality to solicit the endorsement of his proposed campaign by prominent politicians and government officials. Among Okumura's private papers was a memorandum marked 'Strictly Confidential,' which was 'not to be published' because it might cause undue sensation among the Japanese in Hawaii. The memorandum clearly stated that Okumura's trip was prompted not by any interest in a Sunday school convention but by the fear that he could not launch out on his proposed campaign without first obtaining something which would assist him and his co-workers against the dickerings and countercampaignings of Buddhist priests, newspaper editors, and school teachers. The Sunday school convention provided a convenient pretext for the trip.[78]

On August 3, 1920, addressing members of the Bankers' Club in Tokyo, Okumura declaimed the unfortunate presence of Buddhist institutions in Hawaii. Temples had been erected in every nook and corner of the Territory, he reported, and traditional Sunday services had given way to noisy festivals and wrestling tournaments at the temples and shrines. Americans, all the while, were obliged to sit quietly by and watch their country being repaganized. Still, he went on, it was not too late to smooth things over. Amiable relations between Americans and Japanese in Hawaii might yet be restored, Okumura affirmed, if Foreign Minister Uchida and other influential Japanese would graciously help the

Okumuras curb the power of the Buddhist priesthood in Hawaii. By the time the Japanese cleric returned to Honolulu, he had obtained written endorsements for his 'Americanization' program from several prominent Japanese businessmen and well-known government dignitaries like Viscount Shibusawa, Baron Morimura, and Foreign Minister Uchida.[79] In Hawaii the Okumuras won support for their project from sugar magnates William R. and George P. Castle, builder and banker Edwin I. Spalding, and two others who had occupied the highest position in the Territory, former governors George Carter and Walter F. Frear.[80]

Preaching that a radical difference in ideas was the chief cause of tension between the Japanese and Americans in Hawaii, the Okumuras annually toured practically every plantation in the Territory urging the Japanese to discard their mistaken ideas—especially Buddhism; to adapt themselves to American customs and manners; and to educate their children as good and loyal American citizens. The Japanese, old and young, were advised to always 'think and act American,' because they lived under the protection of the Stars and Stripes and enjoyed many privileges and blessings. The second generation was emphatically counseled to recognize their duties to the plantations and to discountenance 'the display of pagan rites at all times.'[81]

In the early months of the first Educational Campaign in 1921, a handful of well-meaning and unsuspecting Buddhist priests and teachers volunteered their services in many places to help put across the new 'Americanization' project. They distributed campaign literature and even invited crowds to hear the Okumuras hold forth on 'true Americanism.' Before long, however, rumors trickled back to the priests that the Okumuras were again disparaging Buddhism. Umetarō wanted the planters to outlaw the annual Bon dances because it was a crude native custom responsible for the low turnout of laborers in the cane fields. Both Okumuras continued to vociferously condemn HSPA officials for giving assistance to the Buddhist cause in order to 'hold the Japanese laborer.'[82] Before long, too, the Japanese Committee of the Hawaiian Board invited the Reverend U. G. Murphy of the American Bible Society to come to the Islands and parrot the propaganda of the Okumuras. Murphy, likewise, reprimanded the planters for aiding and abetting Buddhist temples and priests. It would seem impossible, he commented, that American plantation owners would support Buddhist temples and subsidize Buddhist priests. If ever a man did a foolish thing, Murphy said, that was it. Buddhism had allied itself, he went on, to the most backward part of the national life of Japan; an American Buddhist, therefore, was a practical impossibility. Furthermore, the excuse proffered by the planters, that it seemed only right to afford the Japanese the benefits of their own religious faith, had been a very poor one in view of the active part the priests had played in perpetuating the 1920 strike. Most plantation owners should realize by now, Murphy reasoned, 'that they have used very poor judgment in the selection of Buddhism as a means of keeping their employees in good humor.'[83]

With the circulation of such propaganda, the Buddhist priests who at first were in sympathy with the Educational Campaign turned on Christian workers with a vengeance and met them everywhere with fierce opposition, even employing, Takie Okumura alleged, 'all sorts of tricks' to discourage plantation workers from going near the Christian evangelists. Worst of all, Buddhist priests had the gall, Okumura wrote, to 'mistake' his Americanization campaign for 'a clever scheme of proselyting.'[84]

About a year after the inauguration of the Educational Campaign, Takie Okumura (along with other Christian leaders) was to even further alienate the Buddhist clergy by attempting once more to deal a fatal blow to the language schools.

THE JOINT COMMITTEE FOR THE REVISION OF TEXTBOOKS

Pursuant to the provisions of Act 30 requiring language school teachers to obtain a license from the Department of Public Instruction certifying that they were conversant with the English language and acquainted with American history and political theory, a five-months course of study was opened in January 1921, under the auspices of the DPI, in order to instruct Japanese language teachers in subjects upon which they were subsequently to be examined. Six months later, some three hundred Japanese teachers passed the required examination and were issued licenses to teach in the foreign language schools, and 128 Japanese schools, by November 1921, had been authorized to conduct classes in the Japanese language. Japanese school teachers and principals thus had clearly demonstrated a willingness to cooperate with the Territorial Board of Education.[85] But shortly afterward, when a joint committee of Japanese and Americans was appointed to revise the language school texts (also pursuant to the provisions of Act 30), the cooperative spirit manifested by Japanese teachers and principals vanished.

In July 1922, Consul General Chōnosuke Yada selected the following thirteen well-known members of the Japanese community to revise the textbooks in use in the Japanese schools: Iga Mori, Tasuku Harada, Takayuki Asano, Ryūhei Mashimo, Seishi Masuda, Ichirō Nakao, Kazuhiko Ogata, Tetsujirō Oki, Yasutarō Sōga, Tetsuzō Takamura, Takashi Uzawa, and the Reverends Taiji Fukao and Takie Okumura. Upon the request of these men (most of whom were associated with the non-Buddhist schools), six Americans were invited to assist in revising the texts. The Americans appointed by former governor W. F. Frear were: Dr. K. C. Leebrick, C. F. Loomis, A. E. Robinson, Mrs. Maud Tucker—and two men who were unequivocally in favor of abolishing the schools—Dr. Arthur L. Dean and Dr. Henry Butler Schwartz, superintendent of the Japanese Mission of the Methodist-Episcopal Church.[86]

Rather than tend to the business of revising the textbooks, the American members of the Joint Committee proposed that the course of instruction in the language schools be shortened from eight to six years and that the kindergartens and first two grades be eliminated altogether. The Japanese members said they were totally unprepared for such a suggestion. But when the Americans 'hinted' that, if the kindergartens were not abolished voluntarily, the next legislature would do away with them anyway, the Japanese consented in deference, they said, to the spirit of cooperation and harmony.

The official 'Recommendations of the Joint Committee' as submitted to the Department of Public Instruction stipulated that: beginning in September 1923, foreign language school texts would contain English equivalents for foreign words and idioms and would be based on the principle that the pupil's normal medium of expression was English; the course of instruction in the Japanese schools would cover a period of six, not eight years; and the kindergartens and first two grades would be discontinued according to the following plan. No children would be admitted to kindergarten or to the first grade during or after the school year beginning September 1922; no children would be admitted to kindergarten or to the first or second grade during or after the school year beginning in September 1923; and, as of September 1924, only children who had completed the second grade in a public school would be admitted to a foreign language school.[87]

Upon publication of the Joint Committee's recommendations, the Japanese press and influential Buddhists made it clear that they would not accept any abridgement of the language school curriculum. The Japanese Educational Association pointed out that, if the early grades were eliminated, children would show little interest later in learning Japanese and that youngsters would be placed at the mercy of 'the evil influences of hoodlums' after public school hours.[88] Fred Makino of the *Hawaii Hōchi* argued long and hard, both then and thereafter, that the schools had been fulfilling a mission in cementing relations between East and West and that Americanization, after all, was 'not a superficial process like applying a coat of paint.'[89]

The *Advertiser*, meanwhile, had gone to press with the 'news' that 'a careful reading' of the reports of the Joint Committee indicated that the recommendations were inspired by the Japanese committeemen, who would have gone 'even further' had not the

American minority advised that reforms were liable to be more effective 'if gradually made.' A fired-up Japanese community then immediately went to work on the 'traitorous' Orientals who were apparently making another attempt to eliminate the competitive Buddhist schools. The *Nippu Jiji* of August 8 noted that the most popular language schools were still operated under Buddhist auspices and again expressed the suspicion that the religious issue was underlying the whole affair. If the language schools had long ago severed their affiliation with Buddhist temples, this troublesome problem, the paper commented, might not have come up. Unfortunately, the independent schools now had to share the fate of the Buddhist institutions. Thus Buddhism, the *Nippu Jiji* concluded, was 'responsible for the decline of the Japanese language education in Hawaii.'[90] The *Hōchi*, too, repeated its conviction that the school controversy had stemmed from Christian opposition to the aggressive activities of Buddhist groups and even dared the American community to be honest about its 'high-handed' measures against the schools. Why did not Americans speak out frankly, the paper asked, and admit that the real motive behind the recommendations was to abolish the Buddhist schools?[91] Riley H. Allen of the *Star-Bulletin*, like Irwin of the *Advertiser*, argued that the language school controversy had nothing whatever to do with religion. He was certain that the community objected to the schools simply because they were 'alien culture centers.'[92] Even so, the Japanese were substantially correct in viewing the school issue as a religious conflict. Christianity and Buddhism had for centuries formed the intellectual and spiritual bases of two unique, very different, and often mutually antagonistic cultures; and two radically dissimilar sociopolitical traditions had in turn allied themselves with, and become virtually inseparable from, differences in religious outlook. This helps to explain why the Hawaiian Board felt dutybound to pass a resolution that Japanese youths be encouraged first to 'participate in Hawaii's best Christian education, and *then invited* [italics mine] to take up the burdens and privileges of American citizenship.'[93]

Some of the Japanese members of the Joint Committee were unquestionably opposed to Buddhism. Takie Okumura was one. Another was Dr. Tasuku Harada, professor of Japanese history at the University of Hawaii and one of Okumura's intimate friends. According to Harada, Americanization without Christianization was but 'sounding brass or a clanging cymbal.' The Christianization of the Japanese, he wrote, was urgent, not only for the sake of their individual salvation but for the safety and welfare of the community. Buddhism representing, as it undoubtedly did, the 'difference of religion between Americans and Japanese,' was, he insisted, the 'first retarding factor' in the process of assimilation.[94]

Despite their unabashed hostility toward Buddhism, the

Japanese members of the committee, against whom much criticism had already been directed, keenly resented all insinuations that they had proposed the regulations restricting the course of study in the schools. Protesting their innocence in an article which occupied a full page of the *Nippu Jiji*, they declared that they had been forced to choose between the lesser of two evils. The Japanese committeemen claimed that the American members of the committee had admonished that, if the lower grades were not voluntarily done away with, the legislature would abolish the schools altogether. Thus the Japanese were allegedly forced to choose between seeing the schools vanish immediately or seeing them prolonged as long as possible.[95] Consul General Keiichi Yamasaki was then informed that the Japanese members regarded as a personal rebuke the slurs made upon their integrity, and in a huff, infuriated by the ingratitude with which their services had been requited, the offended parties submitted their resignations. Two of them also wrote a letter to the superintendent of the Department of Public Instruction, Vaughan MacCaughey, insisting that the Japanese members of the committee had no intention of abridging the course of instruction in the schools. On the contrary, it was the American members who had insisted upon a six-year course. The Japanese members had reluctantly accepted the proposal in an effort to show the public their 'willingness to cooperate.'[96] In reply, MacCaughey stated that the American community had every reason to assume that the Japanese committeemen represented the language schools of Hawaii and that he, personally, had no reason to believe that anyone had been 'forced' into anything.[97] Riley Allen of the *Star-Bulletin* came to MacCaughey's support. While every effort had been made by the Japanese members to fix responsibility for the committee's recommendations on the American members alone, the conclusions of the committee, Riley wrote, were joint conclusions reached after many weeks of discussion, during which time there had been no talk of coercion.

The evidence suggests that there was, in fact, a meeting of minds. A letter to the Department of Public Instruction (submitted with the committee's recommendations and signed by both the American and the Japanese members) stated that committee meetings had been marked by 'greatness' in the discussions and presentation of opinions and that the committee's recommendations were the result of the friendly cooperation of all the committeemen. Even before that, Arthur Dean had written a letter to MacCaughey expressing the appreciation of the American committeemen for the friendly and fair-minded spirit with which the Japanese members had carried on their part of the work.[98]

As soon as the Department of Public Instruction officially approved the Joint Committee's recommendations, the Japanese press called for a Territorial conference of Japanese parents in order to devise effective countermeasures.[99] On August 16, 1922, Bishop Imamura and the other directors of the Japanese Society of Hawaii presented a petition to MacCaughey protesting the proposed curtailment of the school curriculum. The regulatory measures would, it was anticipated, 'seriously affect the financial arrangement of the Japanese schools and [the] supervision of children attending the schools.'[100] That same evening a mass meeting of Japanese young men's associations, presided over by T. Terada, secretary of the YMBA, was held at the Asahi Theater to arouse Japanese parents to the gravity of the situation.[101] The following day another mass meeting was staged. Sixty delegates representing both the independent and the Buddhist schools gathered at the Japanese Central Institute and voted unanimously to petition MacCaughey for modification or abrogation of the committee's recommendations. The next day, twelve of the school representatives adopted a resolution to formally petition the DPI to reject the proposals of the Joint Committee.[102] Other petitions were sent to Superintendent MacCaughey. One of them contended that the so-called progressive Japanese members of the committee did not represent the bulk of the Japanese community and that most Japanese in the community were 'thunderstruck' by news of the regulations. But MacCaughey, who had lost none of his compulsion to rid the community of the 'heathen' schools, replied superciliously that the recommendations nevertheless *should* have expressed the united will of the Japanese community and that, therefore, he expected Japanese throughout the Territory to put them into effect.[103] On August 26, the commissioners of public instruction declared that the measures of the Joint Committee would become effective September 1, 1922, and MacCaughey notified language school principals that 'no pupils will enter kindergarten or first grade foreign language school classes in September, 1922.'[104]

Ironically enough, as soon as the regulations went into effect, public school officials discovered that they were unable to accommodate the overflow enrollment. To meet the emergency, the Honpa Hongwanji Mission placed a number of its empty classrooms at the disposal of the DPI—a most humiliating development 'on the heels of the language school controversy and the regulations just adopted.'[105] A far more serious problem created by the 'regulatory' measures was how to keep the Japanese children out of mischief while their parents were at work in the cane fields. As a possible solution to this dilemma, and on behalf of the now rather chagrined American members of the Joint Committee, Arthur Dean wrote a letter to Richard Cooke, chairman of welfare work of the HSPA, requesting that welfare workers be engaged to supervise activities in connection with school playgrounds after school hours. Cooke in turn referred the proposal to the Industrial Committee of the HSPA, and, at a subsequent meeting of the trustees, a letter was despatched to the plantations directing that prompt attention be given to the matter. In January 1923, the Hawaiian Evangelical Association, likewise, asked its members and friends to help care for Japanese children during those hours when they would otherwise have been attending the 'pagan schools.'[106]

In the meantime, Lorrin Thurston had again come to the defense of the language schools. The Joint Committee had gone beyond the original purview of its appointment, and there was no necessity, he said, for the precipitancy of the action taken. The committee had been assembled only *to revise textbooks*, yet he noted that the present books were to continue in use for another year while on snap judgment, practically without notice and without opportunity for public hearing or full consideration, nineteen persons had taken it upon themselves to abolish parts of the schools. Thurston thought this was serious business, for if the Board of Education could 'regulate' parts of the schools right out of existence, it could just as easily do away with the rest of the language school system. He wanted to know why the pertinent and 'serious textbook question' had been set aside while 'the comparatively unimportant question' of what was to be done with four- and five-year-old children had 'been dealt with drastically and immediately.'[107]

Two weeks after Thurston expounded his views on the matter, a Japanese-American by the name of Shean Okazaki set forth his opinions on the action taken by the Joint Committee. Okazaki wrote that the selection of the Japanese members of the committee by former Consul General Yada had been a contravention of proper procedure. Appointment of the Japanese committeemen should have been left up to the *Fukei-kai*, Japanese Parent-Teachers' Association. The Joint Committee's action, furthermore, was grossly unfair to the young children who attended the schools and whose loyalty to the Stars and Stripes could hardly be jeopardized by the fairy tales and nursery songs taught to them by Buddhist teachers. Okazaki surmised that Japanese Christians, in their concentrated efforts to thwart Buddhism, had precipitated every bit of the unpleasantness connected with the school crisis. The move to abolish part of the school curriculum, he charged, was a religious scheme, pure and simple, dressed up in the 'guise of a patriotic project.'[108]

TESTING THE CONSTITUTIONALITY OF HAWAII'S
LANGUAGE SCHOOL STATUTES

The new regulations, lacking the signature of the governor, did not go into effect on September 1, 1922, but it was only a matter of weeks before Governor Farrington approved them. Farrington was in complete agreement with the recommendations.[109] He thought the language schools represented 'a daily effort to keep the children as fully alien as the teaching of an alien language in an alien atmosphere and under alien ideals can make them'; the language schools were thus the 'greatest stumbling block in [the] pathway toward statehood.'[110] In November, Farrington signed the regulations and declared that the new measures, effective January 1, 1923, represented the conclusions of the best educational leaders of Hawaii. He said there was 'no more friendly spot for alien races under the flag than here in Hawaii.'[111]

But the Japanese saw nothing friendly about the outlawing of a vital part of their educational program, and they would not permit the schools so necessary to the preservation of their culture to be needlessly jeopardized. On September 20, 1922 (before Farrington had approved the regulations), Lightfoot and Lightfoot, attorneys for the Japanese Society of Hawaii, had filed with the Governor a brief challenging the constitutionality of the new regulations. The brief stated that the Japanese members of the Joint Committee did not represent those whose interests were involved and that Act 30 had given the DPI the authority only to *regulate* the schools, not to abolish them. As Thurston had pointed out, if the government could eliminate three grades, it could just as readily abolish the entire system. To 'regulate' any part of the curriculum out of existence was an unwarranted interference with the liberties of the Japanese. The brief also pointed out—suggesting that religion was indeed at the heart of the issue—that a number of Christian teachings had been copied from Buddhism and that many people in the world believed that Buddhism was 'a better and more rational religion than Christianity.'[112]

Most of Hawaii's Buddhists clearly favored contesting the legality of the new regulations. Bishop Imamura, in fact, had pointed out that, since the supervisory measures were designed to expel children who had enrolled in the kindergarten and first grade before January 1, they were at the very least ex post facto laws.[113] So on December 26, 1922, the principals and teachers of seven Japanese language schools in Honolulu sent a petition to Governor Farrington pleading for leniency in the execution of the regulations. Since the schools had admitted children to their kindergartens and lower grades prior to the governor's decision to endorse the Joint Committee's recommendations, the educators asked that the regulations not be made retroactive, that is, that children already enrolled in the schools be permitted to continue in attendance. Farrington ignored the petition. The Palama Japanese language school, therefore, promptly instituted a case in the Territorial Circuit Court to test the legality of Act 30 and the new regulations. A few weeks later, six more schools, independent and Buddhist, petitioned to be included as plaintiffs in the suit, and a temporary injunction was obtained to restrain the attorney general and the superintendent of public instruction from putting the regulations into effect.[114] In January 1923, the *Fukei-kai* unanimously passed a resolution to challenge the legality of Hawaii's language school statutes, and the following month, four more schools became parties to the test suit.[115]

In February 1923, Circuit Court Judge James J. Banks tried the case and handed down the decision that Act 30 was constitutional. Valid, too, was Regulation No. 3 of the Department of Public Instruction, which stipulated that new texts must contain English equivalents for foreign words and idioms and must be based on the principle that a pupil's medium of expression was English. But those provisions in the new regulations which reduced the course of instruction from eight to six years were declared illegal, as they clearly exceeded the limits of authority delegated to the DPI by the legislature. Attorneys for the Territory and the schools then appealed the case to the Territorial Supreme Court.[116]

Things quickly went from bad to worse. When the legislature convened in 1923, W. A. Clark of Paia, Maui, introduced a bill to amend Act 30. It passed the senate unanimously and was signed by Governor Farrington on May 2, 1923, as Act 171.[117] This 'Clark Bill' empowered the DPI to stipulate attendance requirements and approve or disapprove the textbooks and curriculum of the schools. It also revoked all permits, licenses, certificates, or consents of every kind or nature previously issued to persons or schools connected with conducting foreign language classes irrespective of the law or laws under which the same were issued. It stipulated that after September 1, 1923, all language schools would be obliged to pay a fee of one dollar per pupil (calculated on the average attendance of the previous year).[118] On May 5, 1923, pursuant to Act 171, all language school permits expired. Attorneys for sixteen Japanese schools then filed for an injunction and obtained a temporary restraining order from Circuit Court Judge Frank Andrade. Act 171, they charged, violated the Fifth and Fourteenth Amendments.[119]

As the weeks went by, more schools joined the ranks of the litigant institutions, especially after the U.S. Supreme Court in *Meyer* v. *Nebraska* handed down the decision that foreign language school statutes were unconstitutional.[120] On July 28, 1923, six of the litigant schools issued a public statement explaining their position. Most of the private language schools, the statement read, had willingly abided by the initial supervisory measures. They had agreed to shorten their classes to one hour per day, and their teachers had passed the examinations administered by the DPI. But now, the new 'regulatory' measures had clearly overstepped the boundaries of reason and fair play. By imposing a fee of one dollar per pupil, the legislature was inflicting an intolerable financial burden on the schools. Act 171, in fact, gave the DPI the power of 'life and death' over the Japanese language schools. The statement was signed by representatives of the Fort Street and Palama Educational Homes, the Jōdo-shū High School in Honolulu, and the Moiliili, Manoa, and Waikiki language schools.[121]

Such 'discourteous' rebuffs infuriated Governor Farrington, who declared that they merely served to prove that the Japanese 'aim to dictate.' The inciters of the school controversy were acting in bad faith, he warned, and had raised serious doubts about the desire of the Japanese to be assimilated.[122] Even so, more schools abandoned the ranks of the so-called cooperating schools, and by 1925, of some 140 language schools 84 had become litigants to test the constitutionality of Act 30 as 'amended' by Act 171. The Japanese community, meanwhile, had raised $25,481 to cover the legal expenses in connection with litigation.[123]

In May 1925, over the protests of the attorney general, Governor Farrington, and the superintendent of public instruction, the plaintiff schools brought suit in the federal court and obtained a temporary restraining order from Judge John T. De Bolt. On July 2, however, De Bolt dissolved the restraining order—'a distinct victory for the territory,' reported the *Advertiser*.[124] The plaintiff schools then filed an injunction against the Territory, whereupon De Bolt quickly changed his mind and granted the injunction to restrain Territorial officials from enforcing the school regulations. Attorneys for the Territory immediately protested, and De Bolt, in disgust, referred the case to the Ninth Circuit Court of Appeals in San Francisco. On August 8, 1925, the case went before that tribunal. By this time, legislative and legal proceedings had been going on for three years.

Meanwhile, in Honolulu, Fred Makino of the *Hawaii Hōchi* had complicated matters by publicly accusing DPI officials of squandering public funds to solicit opposition to the litigant schools. Will C. Crawford, newly appointed superintendent of public instruction, emphatically denied the charge. Crawford affirmed that funds appropriated by the 1923 legislature for the revision of texts and for supervising the teaching of the said schools had been legitimately distributed among those who had helped to revise the texts or performed other related services. Makino retaliated by threatening to obtain and publish a detailed account from the auditor of the Territory which would show that Henry Butler Schwartz, staunch Methodist-Episcopal cleric and supervisor of the foreign language schools, had scattered money about 'like the proverbial drunken sailor.' When these expenditures were made, furthermore, 84 of 140 schools were involved in litigation; thus the duties of Schwartz, Makino said, pertained to only 56 Japanese schools and a dozen or so institutions operated under Chinese or Korean auspices. And if supervision of 56 schools between June 2, 1923, and April 30, 1925, had cost $20,486.55, the taxpayers had better know about it. The truth was, according to Makino, that public funds had been distributed exclusively to persons who had spent a great deal of time disseminating propaganda in favor of the foreign language school laws of the Territory. At least two of the teachers employed to compile the new texts (which were to contain English equivalents for foreign words and idioms) did not know English, and one of the teachers who was paid for revising the texts—a task which Crawford had sworn was performed in Honolulu—had never left the island of Kauai. These men were obviously paid not for preparing texts, Makino concluded, but for other reasons. As for the texts, they were too full of errors to be usable. Makino noted that in one volume alone there were over six hundred mistakes. Even the nonlitigating schools had rejected them. Crawford then reminded Makino that the principals of the litigating schools were largely to blame for the textbook errors since they had obstinately refused to lend a hand in revising the books. Makino retorted that this lack of cooperation was due to the fact that the government had insisted that the *Star-Bulletin* would print the texts. That newspaper, Makino said, was, and always had been, the arch enemy of the schools. Furthermore, he charged that Superintendent Schwartz had traveled 'madly all over the country,' not for the purpose of supervising schools but, rather, to dissuade other schools from becoming litigants or paying 'even one cent' for attorneys' fees and other expenses in connection with the test case. Crawford countered to the contrary. Not one penny, he argued, had been spent for anything in connection with litigation. Makino asserted that he could prove otherwise.[125]

While Makino and Crawford were busily exchanging words, the test case had gone before the Appellate Court in San Francisco, and in March 1926, that tribunal ruled that the injunction granted by De Bolt was valid and that Hawaii's language school laws were unconstitutional. At the end of the year, Attorney General William B. Lymer filed for a review of that decision by the Supreme Court of the United States. On January 18, 1927, attorneys for the plaintiff schools filed their brief charging that the prohibitory foreign language school statutes of Hawaii were an encroachment upon the fundamental rights of Japanese in the Territory.[126] Finally, on February 21, 1927, the U.S. Supreme Court delivered the unanimous verdict that Hawaii's language school laws were unconstitutional and represented a deliberate plan to bring such schools under strict government control for which the record discloses no adequate reason.

The Japanese had won their seven-year-old legal fight, but the taste of victory was bittersweet. The long years of dispute had further alienated the American community and had seriously strained relations between the first-generation Japanese and their offspring. Many of the Nisei, or second-generation Japanese, who were already drifting steadily away from the cultural heritage of the.old country, had intensely resented the religious conflict which had underlain the school dispute and had strongly opposed contesting the legality of the language school statutes. On July 26, 1923, spokesmen for the Society of American Citizens of Japanese Ancestry had called on Bishop Imamura, who, they said, had more power than anyone else over the denominational schools. Recognizing the strong influence Imamura wielded, they asked the Buddhist leader to discourage other schools from joining hands with the litigating schools. Imamura said he was powerless to interfere, and the young Japanese went away disappointed. They had felt certain that the Hongwanji bishop could have resolved the school crisis 'if he desired to do so.'[127]

Before long, life was further complicated for the Nisei by incidents abroad. In 1924, Congress passed the Exclusion Act prohibiting Japanese immigration to the United States. The law naturally aroused the indignation of the alien Japanese and gravely aggravated for Hawaii's Japanese-Americans the already touchy problem of dual citizenship. In May 1924, the Society of American Citizens of Japanese Ancestry passed a resolution condemning dual citizenship. An expatriation drive got under way the following year, after the Japanese government passed a nationality law stipulating that children born in the United States prior to December 1, 1924, could expatriate themselves merely by foreswearing any allegiance to Japan. One thousand eight hundred twenty-eight Japanese renounced their alien citizenship between November 30, 1925, and January 1926. But the enthusiasm was short-lived. As late as 1933, only fifty-five hundred of sixty-six thousand Nisei had expatriated themselves. Moreover, the Japanese nationality law had also stipulated that Hawaiian-born children would *not* lose their alien citizenship if their parents deposited a written request at the Japanese consulate to have those citizenship rights retained. Between December 1, 1924 (the date of the nationality law), and November 30, 1925, of 5,024 Japanese births, 3,645 had been registered at the Japanese consulate. As time went on, a staggering number of additional dual citizens was created by Japanese parents who were reluctant to have their offspring become citizens of a country which had excluded Orientals from its shores while preaching justice, humanity, and brotherhood.[128] To make matters even more unpleasant for the Nisei, ardent American patriots persisted in confusing dual citizenship with dual allegiance.

By this time, the sugar planters (though they did not worry much about problems of dual citizenship) had also begun to take a very special interest in the Nisei. When Japanese laborers deserted the plantations after the 1920 strike, the planters had again resorted to Filipino cane workers, who once more proved 'difficult.' Now, in addition to the dilemma of unsatisfactory labor, there was the fear that Congress might restrict alien immigration altogether. In the hope of finding a solution to these problems, the HSPA turned its attention to devising ways and means of recruiting native-born labor.

Takie and Umetarō Okumura offered to help. The Okumuras had collaborated with the planters frequently in the past, and in their annual Educational Campaigns they continued to remind cane workers in every locality of the many 'blessings' conferred upon them by the planters. In 1927, Umetarō Okumura wrote a letter to plantation manager B. D. Baldwin in which he frankly stated that the yearly Educational Campaigns (conducted ostensibly to remove the causes of friction between Americans and Japanese) had been purposely designed 'to make the Japanese laborers see the value of labor on the sugar plantation and [to] encourage the young element to follow the footsteps of their parents.'[129] Okumura also asked Baldwin to remain silent about the real intent of the campaigns and, above all, not to divulge the fact that trustees of the HSPA were financing these annual crusades. The Japanese, he wrote, were still under the illusion, which he and his father did not wish dispelled, that monetary support for the work of the Okumuras had come from 'intimate associates' and Japanese dignitaries like Viscount Shibusawa 'and his friends in Japan.'[130]

THE OKUMURAS' NEW AMERICANS CAMPAIGN

In the early months of 1927, the Okumuras concocted still another scheme to eliminate 'prejudices against sugar plantations [and to] encourage return to farm, or plantation work.'[131] In the summer of 1927, they inaugurated the annual New Americans Conferences. These were gatherings of citizens of Japanese ancestry, who were invited to Honolulu from urban and rural districts of Oahu and from the outside islands to discuss in open forum 'problems vitally affecting their status in Hawaii.'[132] The Okumuras had on several occasions informed the public that the purpose of these conferences was to make good citizens of the Hawaiian-born Japanese by enabling Nisei youngsters to become better acquainted with prominent industrial and political leaders of the community. A typed manuscript among Okumura's private papers, however, states matter-of-factly that the Okumuras were 'quietly working . . . under cover of "New American Conference" to break down the deep-seated prejudices against sugar plantations which were sown by [the] older Japanese [and] to win back the confidence of youths.'

In exchange for assisting the planters, the Okumuras expected the 'moral support' of the HSPA in 'protecting' Hawaii's citizens of Japanese ancestry from 'the adverse alien influence of Buddhism.'[133]

As a matter of fact, the Okumuras failed to convince the second-generation Japanese that plantation work was a desirable occupation. The Nisei, encouraged by Buddhist priests and teachers to aspire to higher things, had come to disdain plantation work as beneath the dignity of educated men. Most of the second-generation Japanese were high school graduates capable of making good wages, so why, the New Americans asked, should they be expected to work the rest of their lives as field hands.[134] Japanese parents naturally resented the Okumuras' 'Back-to-the-Plantations' campaign, and supported by their priests and language school teachers, they emphatically encouraged the Nisei to aspire to 'a greater career than that of a plantation laborer.'[135] The Japanese press, meanwhile, had detected that the Okumuras' 'Return-to-the-Farm' project was a scheme of the clerics and sugar planters to keep the Nisei on the plantations. The New Americans Conferences had been designed, the paper warned, solely 'to place youngsters in such a position that they [could] easily be pulled by[their] noses'—especially in the direction of Christianity.[136]

It soon became evident, however, that neither the Educational Campaigns nor the New Americans project was making the desired number of converts, old or young. Less than 3 percent of the Japanese population had become Christian, and by the end of the decade, Buddhism was in many ways more formidable than ever. The shrewd and effective propaganda techniques employed by its alert priesthood had successfully countered every Christian effort to proselytize, and the Christian clergy was asking, with greater urgency than before, 'Will Hawaii at last be American or Japanese? Will it be Christian or Buddhist?'[137]

Eager to see the question resolved in their favor, Buddhists continued to build more temples and schools, especially in Honolulu and on the Big Island. The Honpa Hongwanji boasted a membership now of one hundred thousand, approximately two-thirds of the entire Buddhist population, and had erected eleven new temples since the opening of the decade, bringing the tally of its mission stations and temples in Hawaii to seventy-one. In February 1926, the Honorable Sonyū Ōtani, abbot of the home temple in Kyoto, went to the United States to confer with American religious leaders. His purpose was to get their views as to the difficulties encountered by Christian workers in their work so as to plan more carefully for 'the future of Buddhist work in America and Hawaii.'[138] Other sects, too, continued to prosper. The Jōdo-shū obtained a charter of incorporation and in 1928 purchased the Makiki Hotel property in Honolulu for a reported price of fifty-nine thousand dollars. In June 1927, the Sōtō-shū

Guzeji of Kaunakakai, Molokai, which had been founded to propagate the teachings and doctrines of the Sōtō sect, filed articles of incorporation with the Territorial treasurer and obtained a charter permitting it to own property valued up to one hundred thousand dollars. The Higashi Hongwanji showed no signs of decline either, and when 1926 drew to a close, the Shingon-shū had twenty-five temples in the Territory.[139]

By this time, Buddhism was coming more frequently to the attention of the public because of the growing popularity of its youth movement. Membership in the Hongwanji YMBA had nearly tripled since 1918, and in June 1924, the youth organization built a larger, two-story headquarters on Fort Street directly across from the *betsuin*. The new terra-cotta edifice, replacing the Beretania Street center, cost sixty thousand dollars and contained a large recreation hall, auditorium, and library.[140] Three years later, in June 1927, the first annual Inter-Island YMBA Convention was held in Honolulu to arouse religious interest among the younger Japanese. Some 1,950 delegates from Oahu, Hawaii, Kauai, Maui, and Lanai attended the four-day conference to discuss means of unifying the activities of the numerous young men's clubs scattered throughout the Territory. To facilitate dissemination of Buddhism, the delegates decided to consolidate the propaganda departments of all Buddhist youth associations into a 'Society for the Promotion of Buddhist Knowledge.' The Inter-Island YMBA Federation was also formed at this time to coordinate Buddhist activities throughout the Islands.[141]

Two months later, the priests and lay officials of the Honpa Hongwanji gathered for their annual conference and drew up plans for the extension of Buddhist propagation among the English-speaking peoples of Hawaii.[142] By this time, moreover, there had come to the fore a new English spokesman for Buddhism who, unlike the 'Archbishop Kirby, Ph.D.,' nobly exemplified the spirit of Gautama's Dharma and did more than anyone else in subsequent years to make Buddhism intelligible to the second generation Japanese.

THE REVEREND ERNEST HUNT

Christian resentment of Kirby's 'cum grano salis' approach to the Bible did not in the slightest deter the English Buddhist from pontificating at great length on topics like 'The Making of the Pentateuch,' 'The Prophets,' 'God,' and 'Did Jesus Really Live?'[143] Especially exasperating and indeed infuriating to the Christian clergy were Kirby's relentless assaults on the orthodox doctrine of the immortality of the soul, which, he insisted, showed 'lack of intelligence and [lack of] a sane view of life.'[144] Actually, there was reason to question Kirby's sanity. Hatred was the ruling passion of his life, and his animosity toward the Christian religion was surpassed only by the contempt he felt for his own father. After more than five years of irreparable disservice to Buddhism in Hawaii, Kirby left the Islands, to the great relief of his Buddhist colleagues who were disgusted with his pompous arrogance and who recognized that his hatred of Christianity bordered on the psychotic. Kirby spent two years in Japan after his departure from Hawaii, and then he went to Europe. He eventually settled in Southeast Asia, where he frittered away the remainder of his life. In time he abandoned Buddhism, which he had never really practiced, and he died ignominiously in a Salvation Army camp, cursing the Dharma as fit only for the 'dirty Niggers' of Ceylon.[145]

Ernest Hunt, the gentleman who replaced Kirby as head of the Hongwanji English Department, was an Englishman by birth and 'an internationalist in spirit.'[146] Born on August 16, 1876, in Hoddesdon in the county of Hertford, he attended St. Paul's school in London and graduated from Eastbourne College in Sussex. Even in his kindergarten days, Hunt was drawn to religion. Later he studied for admission to Anglican Orders, but, on the eve of ordination, he set aside Christianity and embraced Buddhism. His parents were shocked and heartbroken, yet the decision was not as precipitant as it appeared. As a young midshipman in the British Merchant Marine, Hunt had become acquainted with an Indian Buddhist, who introduced him to the teachings of Gautama. With its emphasis on Wisdom and Compassion rather than faith and authoritarian loyalties, Buddhism seemed preferable to Christianity which demanded of Hunt an acquiescence he could no longer in good conscience abide.

Hunt came to Hawaii in 1915, worked for a few years as a book-keeper at Waipahu plantation on Oahu, and then moved to Kohala on the island of Hawaii. In the early 1920s, while Kirby was disparaging Christianity at the Honpa Hongwanji in Honolulu, Ernest Hunt and his wife Dorothy opened up Buddhist Sunday schools in plantation camps and villages along the east coast of the Big Island and taught Japanese youths to respect what was noble and good in all religions.[147]

On August 11, 1924, at the Honolulu *betsuin* during ceremonies for the first Buddhist ordination in the Territory of Hawaii, Bishop Imamura invested Ernest and Dorothy Hunt with the robes of the Mahāyāna Order. On that solemn and happy occasion, Ernest Hunt took the befitting Buddhist name Shinkaku, which means 'true-light bearer.'[148] To the young Buddhists of Hawaii he became, and remained, exactly that.

Immediately following their ordination, the Hunts resumed their work on the Big Island, speaking at annual YMBA and Sunday school rallies and encouraging young Buddhists to dedicate their hearts and lives to 'the great Buddha-Heart of Infinite Com-

ERNEST SHINKAKU HUNT

passion.' They also gave public lectures at Hongwanji temples in and around Hilo, urging their youthful audiences to carefully ponder such questions as, 'What is Buddhism?' and 'What Does Buddhism Mean to the World?'[149]

On the eve of Kirby's departure for Japan, the Hunts moved to Honolulu, and when Kirby left Hawaii in January 1927, Ernest Hunt succeeded him as head of the Hongwanji English Department.[150] Thinking first of the children, who were always closest to his heart, Hunt started a special Children's Sunday Service. Then he took over the weekly English services for young adults and compiled the *Vade Mecum,* a book of Buddhist ceremonies in English, which subsequently went through several editions and was used in temples throughout the Territory. Talented Dorothy Hunt composed numerous gāthas, or Buddhist hymns, for the English services.[151]

Hunt's mind was clear and logical, if not brilliant, and he possessed a dignity of bearing and magnanimity of spirit which gave an irresistable force to his words. Before long, he attracted much attention by conducting open forums on philosophical and religious issues of the day. In July 1928, of some sixty Caucasians who had begun diligently studying Buddhism under the 'haole priest,' the following persons were formally initiated into the Buddhist religion at an impressive ceremony at the *betsuin*: Adolph Constable, Carl Scheid, Mrs. Flora Maddock, Miss Gloria Wall, Julius Goldwater, Merlin McGrew, and Mr. and Mrs. George W. Wright (Mr. Wright was editor of the English section of the *Hawaii Hōchi* and president of the Central Labor Union).[152] At Hunt's suggestion, the newly confirmed Buddhists immediately organized a nonsectarian branch of the Mission for the purpose of spreading Buddhism among Occidentals. At the same time, they issued a public statement explaining why they had become Buddhists. Affirming the Dharma to be wholly compatible with the highest ideals of Western civilization, they argued defensively that Buddhism was really the only great religion distinctively Aryan, having originated in India, the starting point of the Indo-European branch of the Caucasian race which spread westward into Europe. Buddhism, they continued (as if this point were really important), was 'more directly and intimately the religion of our own race than any of the offshoots of Semitic origin that have been grafted with the paganism of the early Mediterranean tribes!'[153] They concluded their apologia (published in the *Star-Bulletin,* July 16, 1928) by inviting to the Hongwanji English service all who felt the need of a religion or philosophy of life that was based upon simple common sense and was in full accord with all that modern science had to teach.

But few persons have ever been drawn to a religion only on the basis of its simple, common sense and its full accordance with modern science. As a matter of fact, the progressive strengthening of Buddhism in the Islands and the Hongwanji's determination to 'make our Buddhism for Hawaii' struck the American community as nothing short of catastrophic. Christian clerics lamented that after 108 years of missionary efforts in Hawaii, the Protestant churches had a membership of only slightly more than 3 percent of the total population. Immigrant Orientals had stubbornly resisted the light of the Gospel, the *Advertiser* reported, and Buddhists now comprised some one hundred twenty-five thousand persons of a population of three hundred thirty-three thousand.[154]

Buddhists continued withal to try to win the friendship of

Christian spokesmen. As soon as Ernest Hunt took charge of the Hongwanji English Department, he pleaded with Buddhist and Christian leaders for mutual cooperation, and Buddhist priests traveling to and from Japan continued to urge Americans and Japanese to work together to make the most of the rich potential in both religious traditions. One Buddhist priest, en route to his homeland from the Congress of World Religions held in San Francisco in 1915, pointed out that Buddhists and Christians who were at war with one another, in truth, showed no real understanding of the religions they professed. In June 1921, the Right Reverend Sekizen Arai, who had come from Japan to dedicate the new Sōtō temple, pleaded for mutual cooperation and goodwill, emphasizing that Buddhism was a peaceful religion whose principal aim, like that of Christianity, was 'to make mankind better and happier.'[155] In 1924, Richard Kaneko, a young Honolulu Buddhist who had won second prize in an essay contest sponsored by the *Friend* on the subject of 'What is My Religion and What Are My Reasons for Choosing It,' wrote that he preferred Buddhism because of its traditional attitude of respect for other religions. In keeping with the spirit of tolerance and goodwill which he understood to be essential to the teachings of his chosen faith, Kaneko extended an invitation to the Buddhists and Christians of Hawaii to throw overboard their narrow prejudices and bigotries and to blend both faiths into a unique religion that could be 'the guiding, enlightening torch of all peoples and the strengthening of the ties of brotherhood.'[156]

But these and other such pleas for mutual appreciation fell on deaf ears. Christians, taking to heart the admonition of St. Paul, refused to be 'unequally yoked together with unbelievers.' Buddhism, furthermore, was pessimistic and passive, they said; hence, it was inferior to Christianity, which was optimistic and active. According to Dr. M. H. Alexander of the Methodist Church, Buddhism was selfish and without social responsibility, a religion which inculcated submission, resignation, indifference to the allurements of sense and passions, and deadness to the world and the things of the world. Forgetting that Gautama the Buddha, having set aside his own inclinations entirely, had voluntarily abandoned a life of contemplation and solitude to go and actively preach the Dharma, Alexander charged that Buddhism had always reserved its highest blessing for the contemplative, who 'could pass through the world as a stick floats down the river unattracted to either bank.'[157] Christians also found offensive the pragmatic Buddhist notion that the *source* of an idea was of no particular importance and that what mattered was what the idea did to, or for, human beings. On the contrary, the Protestant clergy insisted that divine revelation was all-important as was the acceptance of Christ as Savior of the world. As far back as 1916, Bishop Henry

Restarick of the Episcopal Mission had made the Christian position unmistakably clear when he declared that the important issue for the community to decide was not whether Oriental religions had been of some benefit to the Japanese, but whether or not 'Christ is the Light of the World.'[158] Several years later Reverend H. V. White of the local Christian Church stated, in all seriousness, that any cooperation with Buddhists would be conditional on their acceptance of the Christian doctrine concerning Jesus Christ. After all, he said (as equally small-minded clerics had asserted before him), 'Buddha has been the light of Asia, but Christ is the Light of the World.' As the Reverend Dr. Alexander had concluded, there was little ground for positive cooperation between Buddhists and Christians since the latter announced they would not be 'seduced' into hauling down their 'standard of truth' in deference to any 'fancied liberality of thought.'[159]

Buddhism and orthodox Christianity, furthermore, were predicated on radically dissimilar views concerning the nature and destiny of man. A few Christian clerics conceded that original Buddhism did have something in common with the ethical teachings of Jesus, but Christianity also involved a belief in personal immortality and a certain definite belief and attitude toward God as the controller of human destiny. Buddhism had nothing whatever to say about 'God,' and to persons like the Reverend Henry P. Judd, who understood nothing about the Dharma, Buddhism taught only the complete effacement of the individual, a belief which Judd saw as perilous to American ideals.

Under these circumstances it was extremely difficult, virtually impossible, for Reverend Hunt or any other Buddhist to make his own beliefs intelligible. In October 1928, a few weeks after a young Japanese, Miles Fukunaga, had kidnapped and murdered a Caucasian boy in a senseless and unprovoked crime that shocked the community, a reporter for the Star-Bulletin interviewed Hunt to get the Buddhist 'verdict' on what would become of Fukunaga once 'justice' was meted out by the law. Hunt tried to explain the Buddhist belief that no one is lost and that, between one cradle and one grave, no man could merit eternal punishment or everlasting bliss. Fukunaga may still stumble and stagger in subsequent rebirths, but eventually love would triumph over hate, wisdom would overcome ignorance, and the karmic stream would be cleared. One day, along with all mankind, even this tragic young slayer would know the mercy of the Enlightened Ones and attain Nirvana.[160] No one, Hunt affirmed, could judge the heart of another person, and no one could predict the spiritual fate of others. One thing only was certain: someday, somehow, everyone would reap what he had sown. All of this, of course, sounded like sheer nonsense—or madness—to Christian clerics, who took very seriously visiting Biblical scholars who had announced that 'This Generation Will Attain Eternal Life Hoped for through the Ages' and who sponsored public debates on topics like 'Did Voltaire Go to Hell When He Died?'[161] Christians, in fact, remained confident that cooperation with Buddhists was not possible, and that 'the question of its desirability [should] not be raised.'[162]

An incident which forcefully demonstrated the intensity of Christian animosity toward Buddhism and the Buddhist priesthood took place in the lobby of the Alexander Young Hotel in Honolulu on July 9, 1929. At the invitation of the Reverend Henry P. Judd, secretary of the Hawaiian Board, a group of priests and ministers had gathered at the hotel to discuss how to make religion more appealing and meaningful to the younger generation. Among the invited guests, strangely enough, was Ernest Hunt. During the exchange of introductions, Bishop Stephen Alencastre of the Roman Catholic diocese, glaring at the Buddhist priest with obvious contempt, refused to shake hands with him. 'I love Protestants,' the bishop shouted, 'but I hate Buddhists!' An Anglican dean then stepped up to Alencastre's side and proclaimed that he, too, hated all Buddhists and 'apostates.' The two outraged Christians stomped off in the direction of the door, but Hunt was a step ahead of them. 'Do not go,' he said. 'You are of greater importance at this meeting than I. I am the one who will leave.'[163] Once the 'heathen' priest had departed, the Catholic bishop, the Anglican dean, and their fellow clerics, united more by an ecumenism of hatred than by the spirit of Christian fellowship, settled down to the business at hand and discussed community problems involving the education of youth along moral, ethical, and cultural lines from a nonsectarian standpoint.[164]

CHAPTER 10

The Critical Thirties

LESS THAN A DECADE AFTER BISHOP
IMAMURA ESTABLISHED THE HONGWANJI
English Department in order to facilitate the dissemination of
Buddhism among the second-generation Japanese, his Mission
reported that its Hawaiian-born adherents far outnumbered its
alien members. Even so, many of the Nisei were rejecting Buddhism. With their strangely hybrid minds, they belonged neither
to the old world nor to the new; they lived in a 'no man's land,'
'twixt east and west.' In their struggle to be accepted and to get
ahead in the American community, quite a number of them found
it expedient to embrace Christianity. Many more, 'thoroughly
confused by the backgrounds of Oriental customs and loyalties in
which they were raised,'[1] lost interest in religion altogether. So in
the third decade of the century, Buddhist leaders, as before, were
faced with the task of making their religion attractive and meaningful to the second generation. Also, they were constantly obliged to
confute allegations that Buddhism was un-American. In the 1920s,
under the enlightened leadership of Bishop Imamura and Ernest
Hunt, Buddhism was providently transformed to coincide more
closely with what Hunt called the American trend of thought.
But the progress made by the Hongwanji in this direction and
Hunt's concentrated efforts to foster a spirit of intersectarian
cooperation came to a standstill soon after the untimely death of
Bishop Imamura in 1932. In the late 1930s, a resurgence of Japanese
nationalism again reignited local opposition to Buddhism, and as

the Okumuras once more helped to rekindle the flames of religious dissension, Buddhist temples and schools were branded as hotbeds of sedition.

BUDDHISM V. AMERICANISM?

Throughout the 1930s, as in earlier decades, secular and religious leaders of Hawaii insisted that Oriental youths must be Christianized lest they fail to understand the basic principles of American life. Takie Okumura continued to preach that Americanization was a matter of spirit and that no Japanese could be considered a true American until he could say to all Americans, 'Your country is my country; your God is my God.'[2] So positive were the Okumuras that Buddhism was incompatible with American ideals that even Buddhist Boy Scouts were taunted for not being 100 percent American. Since Buddhist boys did not believe in 'God,' they could not be Boy Scouts, the Okumuras contended, because every Scout was expected to take a pledge honoring God and Country.*[3]

Buddhists continued to refute as best they could the virulent propaganda, which depicted their religion as an insurmountable obstacle to Americanization and assimilation. In articles written for the *Dōbō* (organ of the YMBA), Ernest Hunt affirmed that Buddhism and genuine Americanism had much in common. He wrote that a true American, like a good Buddhist, was one who believes in absolute religious freedom and equal opportunity for all irrespective of race, color, or creed. A true American, like a good Buddhist, was one who 'tries by his words and actions to hasten the day of universal brotherhood and peace.'[4] Later, the renowned English Buddhist, Bernard L. Broughton (who had been informed 'on good authority' that there was a tendency among the English-speaking Japanese of Hawaii to be ashamed of their faith) exhorted the Nisei to 'Rally to the Diamond Banner' and to pay no heed to the self-righteous snobs who had told them that no Buddhist could be a good American. Buddhism, he wrote, was not an outworn faith, as they had been told, or one which no decent Westerner would profess. Such talk was as absurd as it was vicious. There were numerous and distinguished Buddhists in both Europe and America.[5] Later, an American Buddhist, Denzel Carr, wrote from Kyoto that he, too, had heard that influential persons in Hawaii had been persuaded by specious arguments that no Americanization was possible without Christianization. He argued that Buddhism was not a tribal or exclusively racial cult like Shinto or Judaism; like Christianity, it was a universal religion adaptable to any race, country, or culture. In no way was it alien to the spirit of the founders of America. To be sure, a Japanese might from time to

*In the late 1930s, to counteract discrimination against Buddhist boys, the Hongwanji organized its own Boy Scout troops.

time express anti-American sentiments, but it was crucial to discern whether he was talking as a Japanese, as a Buddhist, as both, or as neither.[6]

The Nisei, nevertheless, through constant exposure to Christian ideas and principles in the public schools, were coming to understand the nature of God, as Takie Okumura put it, and did not 'know Buddha.' The first-generation Japanese took their religion as a matter of course and spoke little or no English and thus were unable to conceptualize the teachings of Buddhism for their children. Only on rare occasions did they require their youngsters to attend temple services, and some were even willing to let their offspring adopt what they had been told was the 'American religion.' A great number of young Japanese, thus, grew up with little or no understanding of Buddhism, and many of them, under the persuasive influence of their Christian associates, had come to the conclusion that the faith of their ancestors was 'merely a form [with] no moral precepts or living values.'[7]

Most bewildering to the young Nisei was the glib manner in which the Buddhist sects had assimilated the functions and trappings of the Christian churches. One Nisei wrote that it was becoming, in some ways, increasingly more difficult to discern which church was Christian and which one was Buddhist. If Buddhism could not 'stand by itself against Christianity,' he reasoned, why not profess the genuine article rather than an ersatz, 'strangely concocted religion.'[8] Some youths defected to Christian denominations simply to enjoy a more diversified round of social and recreational events. Others soon discovered that, as 'converts' to Christianity, it was much easier to get white-collar jobs, higher wages, and loans from local banks. It was undoubtedly true that the Nisei who publicly professed Christianity gained enormously in social prestige with influential members of the American community. Even the youngest among them found it a great relief not to be harassed any longer by their Christian peers as 'dirty little heathens and idol-worshippers.'[9] So, in effect, the 'Christianizing-of-Orientals' movement (as YMBA spokesmen noted) had made snobs and hypocrites of many of the Nisei by giving the impression that in order to be accepted as part of the American community they must profess Christianity. And as prominent Christians made social privileges and economic advantages conditional on the acceptance of Christianity, Orientals who had but little genuine interest in the Gospel 'flocked to their gates.'[10]

Buddhist leaders were sorely disappointed in the Nisei who renounced the Dharma for material and social advantages and who took to publicly censuring their Oriental heritage. What a pity it was, wrote Ernest Hunt, that 'we find many of those born in Hawaii of Japanese parents slowly but surely losing touch with the East [and] hear some of them speaking scornfully of old customs and despising, through ignorance, the glorious literature of their past.'[11] In fact, most of the Japanese who openly disavowed Buddhism and embraced Christianity, in brazen opposition to their immediate environment, became exceedingly unpopular among their own people, and in some places were even 'boycotted and ostracized.'[12]

No matter which way they went, the Nisei were bound to step on sensitive toes; hence, it was hardly surprising that the majority of Japanese youths decided not to commit themselves to either Buddhism or Christianity. Some straddled the fence and hoped to satisfy both their parents and the American community by attending both Buddhist temples and Christian churches. Many others simply banished religion from their minds. As far back as 1916, Episcopal Bishop Henry Restarick had observed that the youngsters being educated in the public schools knew little about Buddhism 'and cared less.' Another Christian minister wrote later that the Hawaiian-born Japanese were afflicted with a 'deep-rooted indifference to any religion,'[13] and in 1923, C. N. Kurokawa, secretary of the YMCA, reported that a survey of the religious affiliations of the second-generation Japanese showed that of a group of sixty-five hundred boys, twelve years of age and older, more than four thousand were 'not touched' by any religious organization. Confusing Buddhism with the men who espoused it, Kurokawa commented on the survey findings as follows: 'Buddhism with its sweeping assumption of . . . dominance over the Japanese because of race . . . has gone to extremes.' So-called Americanization Workers, he noted, had caused much religious strife, and the consequences of the irrational religious propaganda disseminated by exponents of *both* religions had been very serious. Far too many youngsters had become 'passive in their religious life.'[14]

Meanwhile, Christian clerics who said that Buddhism alone was responsible for the absence of religious enthusiasm among the Nisei resolved to show 'kindness' to the 'disillusioned' young people of Buddhist ancestry who had rejected their parents' religion and had as yet found no substitute. Moreover, since it was Buddhism that had allegedly hindered the young folk from having any religion, all Christians had an obligation, the clergy announced, to 'double their efforts' to evangelize the Japanese 'no matter how much [they] might appear to compete' with the rival faith.[15]

As more and more Nisei lost interest in Buddhism, it did indeed look as if the religion would decline despite the expressed determination of its priesthood that 'Buddhism shall not die in these Islands.'[16] But the young Japanese who retained their Buddhist faith were also determined that the light of the Dharma would not go out. A few of them even outlined and proposed specific reforms in the hope of injecting new life into Buddhism and leading the 'lost sheep' back to the fold. One of these was Katsumi C. Yamasaki of Lihue, Kauai, who voiced a number of complaints and made the following observations about the status of Buddhism in Hawaii:

In most of the Buddhist temples of Hawaii, Buddhism in its ritual and formula is an exact replica of the system in vogue in Japan. Few of our Japanese priests have made any real effort to keep up with the times or to adapt themselves to this country or try to understand the young people of their own blood, born here. They conduct their ceremonies for the youth in a manner highly uninteresting and utterly unsuitable to local conditions.

Owing to this sad state of affairs, religion has become in the minds of many a dead, meaningless custom instead of a living spiritual force. I know people who only turn to religion in times of misfortune such as sickness and death. To others, religion is a matter of chanting of sutras, the saying of nembutsus through whose magical virtue or agency they fondly imagine they will be transferred at death to a Paradise.

It is hard to believe that such ignorance could prevail among any who call themselves Buddhists. The interpretations and superfluous dogmas . . . which were perhaps suitable for the time, age and conditions in which they were propagated have served their purpose and should be respectfully laid to rest.

So far, my criticism has been of a destructive nature; one must pull down before one can build up. I am now, however, going to offer something in the line of constructive thought, not in my own name alone but in the name of thousands of young Hawaiian-born Buddhists who are tired of the fairy tales they hear in the Sunday Schools, yet who want to remain Buddhist if it is possible, because they know in their hearts that Buddhism in its essence and purity is the finest system ever developed to enable man to help himself, and desire earnestly to Rightly Understand the Teaching of the historical Buddha Sakya-Muni.

The following are some of the constructive features I would suggest:

1. That the priests in charge of temples study the needs of the younger generation and attempt to fill those needs. This they must do at once if they look for our support when our parents pass away.

2. That all fairy tales (this does not mean stories with a real Buddhist moral) be abolished from the children's Temple Schools.

3. That a system of religious instruction be adopted whereby the children and young people learn some of the real Teaching of the Buddha and how to apply that Teaching in their daily lives. I would suggest a catechism and a textbook in both the Japanese and English languages; the English being the more important should be given wherever possible . . . .

4. That the simple ceremony in the Vade Mecum be used uniformly in all services for the English-speaking youth. That some one with qualifications should be engaged, for a short period at any rate, in every large centre to train the youth in the singing of gathas.

5. The establishing in Honolulu of a school for Temple School teachers in the English language under a competent English-speaking Buddhist. (How about Mrs. Hunt?) Pupils to be sent from all islands on some plan to be arranged either for the summer months or all the year

round. Perhaps some of these pupils would eventually become candidates for ordination as bhikshus [priests] or bhikshunis [priestesses] later on.

6. The abolition of all sect teaching. The bringing together of young people of all sects as often as possible.

7. To begin now to prepare to bring about a financial foundation which will enable us to have one good English-speaking teacher resident on each island.

These suggestions are only meant to be tentative; doubtless they can be improved upon. If they serve to bring our needs before the public and cause those in authority to think, they will have served their purpose.

Through the visits of Oriental men of culture and Caucasian Buddhist Bhikshus and the reading of Buddhist books written by men like Silacara, Dahlke, Suzuki, Goddard, Holmes, Rhys Davids, and last but not least Sir Edwin Arnold, we young people have caught a glimpse of real Buddhism and we do not feel like being cheated with an inferior brand or put off with fairy tales any longer. . . .[17]

A few steps had already been taken in an effort to meet the needs of the Nisei. Long before Yamasaki brought up the matter, Bishop Imamura had recognized that priests born and educated in Japan were not equipped to preach Buddhism to the second generation; as early as 1918 he declared that the creation of a local, English-speaking clergy had become an absolute necessity. Later, at Imamura's suggestion, Abbot Sonyū Ōtani of the Kyoto Hongwanji inaugurated a policy of awarding five-year scholarships to local high school graduates who agreed to study for the priesthood and after ordination return to Hawaii to preach. In the summer of 1926, for the first time, two English-speaking, Hawaiian-born youths went to Ryūkoku University, in Kyoto, on scholarships. The next year, three more went to Japan. Among them was a young Caucasian, W. E. McGuffin, who believed that, since orthodox Christianity could 'no longer satisfy thinking people,' Buddhism would succeed where Christianity had failed. In 1928 Bishop Imamura announced that additional scholarships* would soon be available, and by November 1931, more than fifteen boys and girls were preparing for the priesthood in Buddhist colleges in Japan.[18]

In the meantine, Ernest Hunt had discovered that a good many young Buddhists, such as Katsumi Yamasaki, wanted to set aside petty sectarianism and study their religion as it had been when first given to the world by the Wise Man of the Śākyas. Hunt also was eager to eliminate sectarian jealousies, which were a form of selfishness, the cardinal Buddhist 'sin.' Urgently needed, he wrote, were not sectarian thinkers but men who were willing to devote their energy to 'furthering the Buddha Ideal of Unity, Compassion and

*The practice of sending local people to Japan did not work out very well. Those who attended Buddhist colleges on scholarships often did not return to Hawaii at all, or they came back with no intention of fulfilling their agreement to preach Buddhism in the Islands.

Brotherhood.'[19] In time, primarily due to the English priest's efforts, the leaders and spokesmen of Hawaii's six Buddhist sects began to move in the direction of mutual cooperation, and in April 1929, they jointly inaugurated the annual Hanamatsuri, or Flower Festival, in honor of the birth of Gautama. On a Sunday morning at Kapiolani Park, at the first of these colorful intersectarian celebrations, priests of every sect dressed in their formal ceremonial attire, chanted the sūtras together, and addressed their congregations from a common platform.[20]

THE HAWAII BRANCH OF THE INTERNATIONAL BUDDHIST INSTITUTE

By this time, a renewal of interest in Buddhism was taking place on a world-wide scale, and Buddhist centers had been established in key cities throughout Europe. A large new monastery had been built in Hamburg, and two Buddhist societies had been founded in England—the Buddhist Lodge in London and the British branch of the Maha Bodhi Society in Liverpool. The Dharma was beginning to 'catch on' in the United States also, especially in New York and on the West Coast. In 1930, the Honolulu *Advertiser* noted that Buddhism was indeed enjoying an unprecedented popularity in Europe, Canada, and the United States. In California alone, thousands of Buddhists were worshipping at shrines in nearly every city and town. Hawaii, too, the paper observed, was rapidly becoming a beehive of Buddhist activity.[21]

On April 12, 1929, a few days after the first Hanamatsuri celebration, Abbot Tai Hsü of the Lin Yin Temple in Hangchow stopped briefly in Honolulu en route back to the Orient from the Pacific coast. An outstanding promoter of the Buddhist revival in China, Tai Hsü had traveled extensively in Europe and inspired the founding of the Les Amis du Bouddhisme, the Buddhist Society of Paris. Arriving in Hawaii with letters of introduction from prominent European Buddhists, he talked at great length with Bishop Imamura and Ernest Hunt about establishing a Hawaii branch of the newly formed International Buddhist Institute, which was dedicated to breaking down sectarian barriers and working for a united Buddhism everywhere. Other branches had already been established in London, New York, and Chicago.[22]

Soon after Tai Hsü returned to China, Imamura and Hunt acted on the monk's proposal and organized the Hawaiian branch of the International Buddhist Institute, a rigidly nonsectarian association dedicated to the preservation of Buddhist unity. The Hawaii IBI was a youth movement, too, committed, first and foremost, to helping Hawaiian-born Japanese to understand the outstanding features of Buddhism. Bishop Imamura was elected lifetime president of the institute, and Hunt became its first vice-president.

'Buddhism Shall Not Die in These Islands' became the motto of the organization, and its members pledged to seek Wisdom and to practice Compassion in the spirit of the Blessed One who long ago had said, 'Hatred is not overcome by hatred, hatred is overcome by loving kindness. This is the Everlasting Law.'[23]

The IBI sponsored a comprehensive program of activities designed to promote a better understanding of Buddhism among the English-speaking peoples of Hawaii. Hunt officiated at a number of special services for children and young adults at the Hongwanji *betsuin*, and with the assistance of a handful of Caucasian Buddhists and the *bhikshuni* Shinkoh (Mrs. Ernest Hunt), he conducted public and private study classes and presided at monthly forums for high school and college students.[24]

Ernest Hunt firmly believed that Enlightenment came with the discovery of the innate value of all human beings and that the surest way to Nirvana was through the practice of *mettā* (active goodwill). Therefore, he organized a social service branch of the IBI whose members were encouraged to add to their storehouse of good karma by paying regular visits to hospital patients and the inmates of penal institutions. As head of the Social Service Department, Hunt personally officiated at weekly services for bedridden tubercular patients at Leahi Home, and those most in need of religious solace, he visited daily.

On behalf of the IBI Hunt also visited Buddhist youths in plantation districts throughout the Islands and presided at annual YMBA and Sunday school rallies. More importantly, he revitalized the Hongwanji Sunday school program. Twelve thousand eight hundred six Buddhist children in one hundred twenty-five Sunday schools were, by 1931, studying their religion from new 'catechisms' written by the English priest.[25] The IBI also collaborated with the Hongwanji press in publishing scholarly dissertations on Buddhism—most of them written by Hunt. In 1929 the Mission published *An Outline of Buddhism: The Religion of Wisdom and Compassion*, a thesis for which Hunt received the Burmese Theravāda ordination and the degree of Doctor of the Dharma.[26] The following year, the institute made available to the public the first of four issues of the *Hawaiian Buddhist Annual,* a first-rate and lushly illustrated publication featuring philosophical essays on the Dharma written by renowned Buddhist scholars the world over. Ernest Hunt edited all four issues of the *Annual* in addition to the cyclostyled magazine, *Navayana*, official organ of the IBI.[27]

THE GROWTH OF THE BUDDHIST YOUTH MOVEMENT AND THE CHRISTIAN COUNTERBLAST

The young Buddhists of Honolulu, meanwhile, had dedicated their own publication, the *Dōbō*, to the propagation of Buddhism.

In the summer of 1930, to publicize their religion on a world-wide scale, they sponsored the first Pan-Pacific YMBA Conference, one of the most significant events in the annals of Buddhism. Religious and lay leaders of the Hongwanji Mission had set aside a thousand dollars the previous year to meet expenses in connection with the proposed conference, and Ernest Hunt was sent on a tour of Europe and the United States to solicit the cooperation of Buddhists abroad.[28] The first of its kind to be held anywhere in the world, this international forum, inspired and planned for by Hawaii's young Buddhists, who wanted to strengthen Buddhism as a unified system of teachings, was held in Honolulu in July 1930 and was attended by about 170 delegates from the United States, Hawaii, Canada, China, Japan, Korea, Thailand, India, and Burma. Roundtable discussions during the six-day convention focused on two key issues: how to propagate Buddhism among the young people of the world and how to do away with sectarian cleavages. As an initial step toward solving the first problem, the young Buddhists nominated Hawaii as the logical 'nucleus from which nonsectarian Buddhism, adapted to Western countries, may be spread to Pacific countries.'[29]

By this time, the Hongwanji YMBA had expanded its schedule of social and athletic events, and its junior youth program was gaining momentum. At the fifth Inter-Island YMBA Convention in 1931, the Hawaii Federation of Young Buddhists was organized to coordinate activities of all Buddhist youth groups in the Territory.[30]

Ernest Hunt continued to plead with the American community for a meeting of minds, both East and West. 'I feel very strongly,' he wrote to Reverend Henry P. Judd, 'that appreciation of other faiths is becoming more and more necessary if the forces working for the uplift of humanity are to cope with the forces working for evil.'[31] At the Pan-Pacific Conference, Hunt expressed his confidence that progressive American people could, and would, appreciate Buddhism if they could only come to understand it. On a placard in front of the Honolulu YMCA were inscribed the words 'Mutual tolerance is a necessity for all times and all races.' But tolerance, as Hunt wrote to the editor of the *Advertiser*, implied 'a measure of concession,' and concession suggested 'offensive superiority.' Mutual appreciation, not tolerance, was really what was needed.[32]

Mutual appreciation, however, lay in the distant future. There were, to be sure, a handful of Christians who had retracted their earlier wholesale indictments of Buddhism. Sydney Gulick, who years before had alleged that 'superstitious' Buddhism was unquestionably an obstacle to the Americanization and assimilation of Hawaii's Japanese, came to recognize that Buddhism had actually rendered a valuable service to members of the rising generation, who would 'otherwise not [have] come under any religious influence.'[33] Most Christians, however, aware that Buddhist churches (with a following of one-third of the entire local population) represented the largest religious group in the Territory, continued to grieve over the 'repaganization' of Hawaii. The growing popularity of the International Buddhist Institute, with its slogan 'The World for Dharma and Nirvana for All,' did nothing to relieve their anxiety, and to add even further to their uneasiness came the news that Hawaii had been nominated by young Buddhists as the potential center for the 'spread of Buddhism throughout the world.'[34]

Most disconcerting to the Christian clergy was the fact that Buddhist priests continued to copy Christian methods of proselytizing. Ernest Hunt insisted that they were merely following 'the American way' in devising schemes which, while unaltered in their Buddhistic essence, could make the Dharma more intelligible to the English-speaking peoples of the Territory. But Christian clerics countered that Buddhists were camouflaging their religion day by day under the cloak of Christianity and were making frantic efforts to show that God and the Buddha were one and the same. A Japanese-Christian pastor wrote: ' "Buddish" Priests are always saying that Christianity and Buddhism are same "so stick to old Buddah." '[35] The Right Reverend Samuel Harrington Littell, the new bishop of the Episcopal diocese, even charged that, by organizing YMBAs, Sunday schools, women's associations, and social work projects, Island Buddhists were not doing what was 'essentially Buddhistic' and had thus been 'repudiated in the Orient.'[36] His remarks did not set well with Ernest Hunt, who was personally responsible for most of the more recent innovations. One ought not to make assertions, Hunt retorted, which, when examined, are proved historically inaccurate. Hunt challenged the Episcopal prelate to prove that the Buddhists of Hawaii had been repudiated in the Orient. As a matter of fact, said Hunt, Littell's remarks were absurd; were it otherwise, the Young Men's Buddhist Associations of Japan would surely not have cast a unanimous vote to hold the first Pan-Pacific YMBA Conference in Honolulu, under the auspices of the Hongwanji Mission. Nor would His Eminence Tai Hsü have suggested Hawaii as a site for a branch of the International Buddhist Institute. Nor would Indian, Sinhalese, and Burmese Buddhists have placed their imprimatur on literature published by the local Hongwanji Mission.[37]

Littell's remarks had provided Takie and Umetarō Okumura with another pretext for impressing upon the Nisei the fact that Christianity and Buddhism were indeed not the same. Kaku Imai, the Buddhist who became a Baptist, was invited back to again tell the uninformed wherein lay the difference between truth and error and why it was not folly for the Japanese to become Christians.

A little later, to gain an even stronger hold on Japanese youths, Takie Okumura selected for his proposed new Maikiki Church a forty-thousand-dollar site directly across the street from McKinley High School, which had the largest enrollment of students of Japanese ancestry of any school in the Territory. The Buddhist priesthood was fighting desperately to hold its own, the Okumuras declared, so all Christians must now 'work harder than ever before to gain an access.'[38]

THE OKUMURAS' CHAIN-SCHOOL STRATEGY

No one had worked harder over the years to gain an access to Christianizing the young Oriental Buddhists than did the Okumuras, and by this time they had devised still another scheme to counteract the influence of Buddhism and the Buddhist schools. As soon as the Federal Survey Commission recommended that foreign language instruction be given in public schools whenever the demand arose, the Okumuras began campaigning for support of the commission's proposal. Later they persuaded influential Americans that language school teachers had retrogressed after their victory in the Supreme Court, were again displaying the real color of Japanism, and were requiring young Japanese-Americans to shout banzai to the emperor and Japan.

So in 1929, with the financial and moral support of prominent citizens like Theodore Richards, the patriarchal John P. Erdman, and Frank Atherton (an almost perfect personification of the Gospel of Wealth of late nineteenth-century America), the Okumuras formed the Japanese Language Education Association, which was publicized as a nonsectarian and nonpolitical organization founded to give children free instruction in the Japanese language and to foster good character, in cooperation with the public schools. Members of the Christian clergy were made honorary members of the association, and its first officers were Dr. Iga Mori, Reverend John P. Erdman, Umetarō Okumura, and Reverend K. C. Kondo, an American-trained, English-speaking Japanese evangelist.[39] The executive committee of the association was spearheaded by Dr. Tasuku Harada and Takie Okumura.

The first thing the Japanese Language Association did was to publicly announce that it was unnecessary and unwise to waste the money of the community to operate separate Japanese schools. Then, in the hope of replacing the private institutions and influencing some fifteen hundred children (as Reverend Kondo .admitted), the association initiated its own 'Chain-School' program in the public schools of Honolulu. In September 1930, with the blessing of the Superintendent of Public Instruction, Will C. Crawford, the association opened classes in six schools in the city. Every weekday afternoon, for one hour, instruction in oral and written Japanese was provided—along with moral education as part of the machinery of Americanization. Spokesmen for the chain schools promised DPI officials to disbar all subjects which tended to teach Japanism and to make every effort, in accordance with the policy of the public schools, to Americanize the local-born Japanese. By 1933, instruction in the Japanese language, chain-school style, had been introduced in nine of Honolulu's schools: McKinley High School; and Central and Washington Intermediate schools; and at the Lanakila, Royal, Kaahumanu, Waikiki, Kuhio, and Waialae Elementary schools.[40]

The alien Buddhist community immediately saw through the new stratagem, and Honolulu's young Buddhists deplored the almost indecent haste with which certain misguided people intended to 'place the bible and Christianity in . . . the public institutions of Hawaii.'[41] Buddhists suspected who was behind the chain-school program, and Takie Okumura made no effort to deny that the idea was his. He did affirm once again, however, that he was not out to destroy Buddhism. He wrote that there were some persons who, by confusing the work of the Okumuras with religion, had 'misrepresented' the school question as 'the issue of Christianity versus Buddhism.' Buddhists were always ready to attack any effort to better the schools as a conspiracy against their religion.[42]

The Buddhist institutions were already in cutthroat competition with each other and did not welcome the competition afforded by the chain schools. Over the years, much of the friction between the Japanese on Island plantations had centered around Buddhist schools, and priests and teachers who belonged to the various sects had fought incessantly with each other for control of the independent schools.[43] So Buddhist educators (those 'die-hard conservatives' who, as Takie Okumura put it, were 'sweating mightily' to ensure Buddhist supremacy over 'a doomed institution') met the chain-school program with fierce opposition, even boycott and intimidation. In some sections of the city, private school principals turned out en masse on the opening day of public schools to dissuade Japanese mothers from registering their children in the chain-school classes.[44] In August 1933, influential Buddhists who most resented the 'fly-by-night' schools submitted a petition to the superintendent of public instruction complaining that: the use of public school buildings to teach foreign language classes was neither equitable nor just to taxpayers; such classes interfered too much with the work of those teachers whose rooms were being used; the nominal rent being charged for the use of the classrooms by sponsors of the chain schools was hardly enough to cover depreciation and damage done to the buildings constructed and maintained from the taxpayers' money;

and there was plenty of available space in private schools maintained 'for the particular purpose of giving instruction in foreign
languages.'[45]

But the chain schools prevailed. Neither the opposition of
ignorant parents nor the vicious progaganda of a strong clique
of Buddhist priests could eliminate them, boasted Takie
Okumura. Time alone would take care of that.[46]

Meanwhile, at the peak of the chain-school storm, the Buddhist
community suffered the loss of Yemyō Imamura, and following the
untimely death of the Hongwanji bishop, control of the most
influential Buddhist sect in Hawaii fell into the hands of men who
were not as tolerant or as committed to the spirit of internationalism as were Imamura and his friend Ernest Hunt.

THE DEATH OF YEMYŌ IMAMURA

Early on the morning of December 22, 1932, Ernest Hunt and
Yemyō Imamura sat in the bishop's office discussing Hunt's recent
visit among the young Buddhists of Lihue, Kauai, and making
plans for a trip together to Japan. Suddenly Imamura excused
himself and walked briskly over to his residence adjoining the
temple on Fort Street. Presently, a male member of the temple,
hysterical with grief, ran into the study where Hunt was awaiting
Imamura's return. 'Bishop Imamura *make**! Bishop Imamura
make!' he shouted. Hunt dashed over to the bishop's residence and
found the sixty-five-year-old Hongwanji leader stretched out on
his bed, dead of a heart attack.

For weeks, bereaved Buddhists mourned Imamura's death in
private and public services throughout the Islands, and religious
spokesmen, Christian as well as Buddhist, paid tribute to the
memory of one of the most extraordinary religious leaders in
Hawaiian history. The Japanese and American press both testified
to the key role that he had played in the religious and cultural life
of the Islands. The *Nippu Jiji* recalled that the humble and dedicated
priest, who had risen to 'the most exalted position among the
Japanese of the territory,' had always exercised his authority
judiciously. The *Star-Bulletin* characterized him as a modest and
unassuming man who, in ministering to the faith of a multitude,
had always taken 'positive positions without arousing serious
antagonism.' A grief-stricken Ernest Hunt recollected that the late
bishop had many times brought harmony and peace out of what
threatened to be grave disorder. The American press conceded that
men with narrower vision 'would have made more noise and
accomplished less.' Imamura's goodwill and sense of fair play had
always been evident, even to those who did not agree with his
*The Hawaiian word for dead.

policies, and he possessed the gift of tact and had a quiet charm sadly lacking in most of his successors. The Hongwanji home temple in Kyoto posthumously bestowed upon Imamura the Jishin Tokujyu Grade 1, the highest honor to ever be awarded a Hongwanji priest, and Japanese Foreign Minister Uchida cabled the *betsuin* that the Imperial Government had posthumously bestowed on the late bishop the Sixth Order of Merit, the first such honor ever to be conferred on a priest engaged in overseas missionary work.

On the morning of December 28, a three-hour funeral service, one of the most impressive ever conducted in Honolulu, was celebrated for Imamura at the Fort Street Mission. Following the temple rites, more than a thousand persons, in a torrent of rain, marched behind black-gowned priests and the floral-laden casket to Nuuanu Cemetery, where Imamura was cremated at 1 P.M. Two months later, Imamura's widow returned to Japan aboard the *Taiyo Maru* to bury the ashes of her husband in the family ancestral plot in Fukui Prefecture.[47]

In October 1933, Zuigi Ashikaga was appointed by the home temple to succeed Imamura. Ernest Hunt later described the interim bishop as a fine gentleman, and the work begun by Imamura and the English priest continued to prosper for a while. Upon Imamura's death, Hunt was elected president of the International Buddhist Institute, and membership in the organization grew steadily during the next few years. The popularity of the IBI was due primarily to the enormous popularity of Hunt, whose broadness of vision in transcending national and sectarian boundaries had won worldwide recognition among Buddhists of both the Mahāyāna and the Theravāda. The IBI became a Territory-wide association and even adopted a constitution and set of by-laws to clarify its objectives and to centralize its 'energetic promulgation' of Buddhism.[48]

BISHOP GIKYŌ KUCHIBA ALIENATES MORE OF THE NISEI

On March 12, 1935, Bishop Ashikaga returned to Japan. Gikyō Kuchiba succeeded him as bishop of the Honpa Hongwanji. Kuchiba was a fanatic Japanese nationalist and a zealous Shin-shū Buddhist, who was diametrically different from his predecessors and wholly opposed to Americanizing Buddhism.[49] Kuchiba had no sympathy with Ernest Hunt's nonsectarian, internationalist views which (as Kuchiba said later) had influenced Hawaii's young Japanese to profess a form of Buddhism that 'follows the stream of Japanese Buddhism [but] is not Japanese Buddhism.'[50]

The Nisei quickly became disenchanted with Kuchiba when for no good reason he abruptly fired Ernest Hunt and discontinued the Hongwanji English Department. With Hunt gone, many more second-generation Japanese abandoned Buddhism. The Nisei who remained Buddhists simply ignored Kuchiba and went their own way and supported and participated exclusively in their own YMBA programs. In 1934, two hundred of Hawaii's young Buddhists attended the second Pan-Pacific YMBA Conference held in Tokyo. The following year the Inter-Island YMBA became the Hawaii Federation of Young Buddhist Associations, and in 1937 the Hawaii branch of the Pan-Pacific YMBA was organized. But interest in the Buddhist religion, as Christian workers noted, had declined noticeably. The Nisei 'tie-up' with the Buddhist youth movement, as one evangelist put it, was superficial when it came to religious values and most young Japanese were still wholly ignorant of the teachings of the Buddha.[51]

Even the sacred Bon festival had lost much of its religious significance. The annual Bon odori (Bon dances) were performed in the summer months on temple grounds or at the Honolulu Stadium where pink, paper cherry blossoms and dozens of glittering, breeze-blown lanterns dipped and swayed in the moonlight. But by this time, rhythmic *ondo* (modern Japanese folk dances) with fast and furious tempos were incorporated into the Bon program and were performed solely for pleasure to the accompaniment of saxophone, guitar, and violin.[52] The Bon dances were staged on a commercial basis, too, and before long they became a popular tourist attraction. The Nisei, thus, had casually transformed what was once a holy festival into a gala social event and money-making project. To the older generation this was indeed appalling, despite the fact that all profits realized from odori concessions were turned over to charitable institutions.[53]

But the most serious rift between the first and second generation, in comparison with which the heated disputes over the Bon odori were as nothing, had been brought about by the furor over the Buddhist schools. Few of the Nisei who had attended the language schools could read or write Japanese correctly, and many of them had no desire to learn the language. As the Nisei became Americanized and were strongly admonished by Christianized Japanese to disown their Oriental heritage, they saw no necessity for learning Japanese and increasingly resented being compelled to attend institutions operated by priests, who for years had been suspected of strengthening cultural and national ties with an alien empire. The Nisei, it will be recalled, had strongly opposed the test suit to challenge Territorial language school statutes and had publicly expressed their disapproval of the noncooperative attitude taken by the litigant schools. A group of Japanese-Americans had even openly encouraged students enrolled in the large Hongwanji school in Honomu, Maui, to withdraw from the Buddhist institution and to establish an independent, cooperating language school that would abide by the Territorial regulations.[54] As far as the Nisei were concerned, the real issue had been, not the constitutionality of Hawaii's language school statutes, but rather, their own status and prestige as citizens of an American community. They feared that as long as Buddhism was suspect, schools sponsored by the Buddhist sects and flourishing in such impressive numbers would continue to be, as Governor Farrington had warned, a base from which attacks would be made upon the sincerity of those Americans who were 'required by [their] alien parents to attend these schools.'[55]

Interestingly enough, although there was lingering animosity of the Nisei toward alien institutions, community disapproval of the foreign language schools had abated somewhat in the early 1930s. After the 1927 Supreme Court decision, an irate American press had warned that, while the Territory could no longer exercise any control over the schools, there would be no change in popular sentiment against them.[56] But three years later, the Governor's Advisory Committee on Education found that the schools had not only become slightly less alien in their control and influence, but were performing an important and useful function as a bridge between the two cultures. In the future, too, the committee pointed out, the schools would become 'increasingly important as commercial and other contacts increase between the Orient and America.'[57] On the eve of Bishop Imamura's death, prominent educators in the community submitted statements to the Department of Public Instruction reflecting, for the first time, genuine approval and, in some instances, heartfelt appreciation of the schools. Even Arthur L. Dean, who had once strongly urged the abolition of the kindergartens and early grades, had concluded that the purpose of the schools was, in fact, not to inculcate loyalty to Japan, but, rather, to teach children the language of their parents and to give them a knowledge of Japanese ethics and manners. Dean, to be sure, still did not particularly like the idea of the schools, but he saw clearly that without them problems of social adjustment would be aggravated. W. Harold Loper, supervising principal of Honolulu schools, stated that the language schools were no longer being operated for nationalistic motives. Dr. William H. George, dean of the University of Hawaii's College of Arts and Sciences, wrote that the schools were actually a benefit to the community and that the attempt in the 1920s to abolish them had indeed been, as Roderick Matheson had said, the result of hysteria. O. W. Robinson, supervising principal of rural schools, noted a marked trend in the Japanese schools toward the employment of local-born and American-trained teachers. Miles E. Cary, principal of McKinley High School, reported that he had had close associations with young Americans of Japanese ancestry and could not recall a single instance in which a pro-Japanese or anti-American sentiment had been voiced among them—despite the fact that most of them had attended (or were still attending) the language schools. E. V. Sayers, director of the school of elementary education at the University of Hawaii, reported that at one time, like other

American educators, he believed that the Japanese schools were a disintegrating influence in the community and should therefore be strictly regulated or abolished. But over the years he had changed his mind and had come to look upon the schools as constructive social institutions and stabilizing agencies. They had rendered a valuable service to youths who were in danger of losing the social benefits of home and family 'before they had sufficiently accepted [the] customs and institutions of the American community.'[58]

In the early years of the decade the focus of community attention had been deflected toward the depression, the sensational Massie rape and murder case, and the Jones-Costigan Sugar Act that was believed to discriminate against Hawaiian sugar. The language school controversy had thus temporarily faded into the background. But with the resurgence of Japanese nationalism and Japan's aggression in the Far East, the schools again fell into disrepute as more alien teachers were brought in to accommodate a steady increase in enrollment, which had risen from 19,648 in 1925 to 42,665 in 1935.[59]

THE RESURGENCE OF JAPANESE NATIONALISM

Japan's abortive steps toward representative democracy and cooperation with other nations in the late 1920s were halted in the following decade by a rapid about-face in domestic and foreign policies. The industrial growth and commercial expansion of the country had enormously increased the national wealth and whetted the appetite of militarists, who had infiltrated the government and had begun to think more and more of war and conquest.

Consummate strategy was employed to mobilize Japan for her Far Eastern campaign. The Departments of Education and War collaborated to contaminate the nation with jingoistic propaganda. Films and pamphlets glorifying the emperor and the country were widely distributed to indoctrinate the people and to work up fanatic demonstrations of *yamato-damashii*, the Japanese nationalistic spirit.[60]

The militant nationalism, which finally reduced Hankow and Canton to ashes and sacrificed tens of thousands in the holocausts of Nagasaki and Hiroshima, was essentially religious. Japan's drive for imperialistic domination had for its rationale the Shinto-inspired myth of divine favor.* History books were distorted

*The myth of divine favor is an ancient one with many variants. The Israelites, who wrested the Promised Land from the Canaanites, believed they had fulfilled the Divine Purpose, and Rome, ex post facto, 'discovered' she was destined by her gods to conquer the world.

to make room for the myth of divine origin, and teachers were compelled to teach the imperial cult. Militarists decreed that the distant kami, as the divine son of Amaterasu-Ō-Mikami, must be the center of all loyalties and that Japan had a sacred mission to extend her 'protective suzerainty' over lesser nations and to create a 'New Order' in East Asia.

Japanese Buddhists, who for centuries had subordinated the ethics of Gautama to Japanese ethnocentrism, served the militarists well. The Wise Man of the Śākyas had denounced all pretensions to racial superiority, and his earliest disciples had strongly admonished against alliances with emperors and kings. But of paramount importance to Japanese Buddhists through the centuries was the preservation and prosperity of 'Dai Nippon Koku,' the Country of Great Japan. Buddhism became the body by which the germ plasm of Shinto was transmitted. The great heroes, founders, saints, and eminent priests of Japan fervently preached, as a vital element of their faith, that dedication to the imperial throne was indispensable to national unity, security, and prosperity.[61] Eisai, Zen leader of the twelfth century and founder of the Rinzai-shū, propagated the doctrine of 'Kōzen Gokoku,' Zen for the protection of the country; and Dōgen, founder of the Sōtō-Zen, used his influence in Kamakura to accelerate restoration of imperial rule. Rennyo, an early Pure Land evangelist, taught that loyalty to the distant kami was the basis of all Buddhist conduct. Nichiren, founder of the most avidly nationalistic Buddhist sect, rhapsodized, 'How true it is that our land of Japan is above all nations.'[62]

After the Manchurian affair in 1931, a flood of patriotic literature gushed forth from the Buddhist press in Japan, exalting 'Patriotism and Buddhism' and dealing at length with topics like 'Buddhism and the Japanese Spirit' and 'Buddhism and the New Mission of the Japanese Race.' A book published by the Buddhist Federation of Japan emphasized that Japanese Buddhism was unique and different from the Buddhism of India or China, primarily because of its intense nationalist spirit and historic connection with the imperial throne.[63]

Gautama had preached pacifism and reverence for life, and there were no allusions in the Buddhist sūtras to holy wars. But to the Japanese any war involving their homeland was a holy war. Three years after Japan issued the notorious Twenty-One Demands on China, Shin-shū Buddhists published a pamphlet which decried the world's poor opinion of Japan and yet asserted that, since Shinran had never forbidden 'a just war,' Buddhists would always rise to arms whenever their ancestral home was threatened or if ever their imperial house were put in danger.[64] In the late 1930s when militarists sought to boost the power and majesty of the imperial house and augment national defense,

Japanese priests rose to the occasion and, with rifles slung over their shoulders, demonstrated their preparedness by marching in military drills on temple grounds.

The Buddhist clergy in Hawaii did not march up and down on temple grounds. But as militarists usurped control of the Japanese government, Hawaii's priests, especially those of the Honpa Hongwanji, were suspected of being 'the political right arm of the Japanese government.'[65] The Hongwanji sect had for centuries been intimately associated with the imperial throne and represented, in the minds of Americans, a close tie-up with the imperial cult. This association of ideas was reinforced when Emperor Hirohito, characterized by the American press as 'the high Shinto priest of his nation,' issued a special proclamation in 1928 awarding Bishop Yemyō Imamura the Sixth Order of the Sacred Treasure thus making the Hongwanji leader 'the holder of the highest imperial decoration granted by the Japanese government to a Japanese in the Territory.'[66]

Other things escalated suspicion of Buddhism. Too many Buddhist priests continued to remain aloof from the wider community; only a few showed any interest in promoting good relations between Japanese and Americans.* Moreover, priests and Buddhist educators from Japan who visited Hawaii in the 1930s made enthusiastic public statements about Oriental culture, which were grossly distorted by the American press. At the first annual Inter-Island YMBA Convention in 1927, Consul General Kazuye Kuwashima had made the innocuous statement that without a knowledge of Buddhism it would be difficult to understand Japanese culture and that young Buddhists had 'a peculiar mission' to clarify the teachings of Gautama for non-Buddhists.[67] In 1934, Shinryū Umehara, a Buddhist educator returning to Kyoto from the mainland, addressed the young Buddhists of Hawaii in a similar vein. By this time, however, Japan's international relations had taken on such an ominous aspect that Umehara's words seemed to have a distinctly sinister ring. Like Kuwashima, Umehara urged young Buddhists to study and appreciate the contributions of Buddhism to Japanese culture. He also expressed regret that suspicion of Japanese institutions had become so widespread that many of Hawaii's Japanese felt ashamed of their Oriental heritage. America had made room for great diversity of race and religion, Umehara

---

*Bishop Imamura was the exception who proved the rule. A year before his death, Imamura had returned from a sojourn in Japan with no less than three thousand volumes on various phases of Japanese life. These were to be the first collection of a proposed Hawaii Japanese Cultural Center, a project which he envisioned as a means of promoting good relations between Hawaii and Japan and Americans and Japanese in Hawaii. See the *Honolulu Advertiser*, 30 October and 15 November 1931.

noted, and young Buddhists should identify and refine those elements of Japanese culture which could enrich the American tradition.[68] Later, in local papers and at Statehood Hearings, Umehara's words were repeatedly taken out of context, blown up, and translated to mean that Hawaii's Buddhist temples and language schools were a 'hot-bed of racial consciousness.'[69]

Such misrenderings in translation or interpretation (usually the work of Takie and Umetarō Okumura) were soon taken at face value by a community made increasingly uneasy by a handful of itinerant aliens who, in fact, did try to work up *yamato-damashii* among Hawaii's resident Japanese. In August 1933, six months before Umehara's arrival, a Buddhist priest arrived in Honolulu and delivered a series of lectures at Island temples. In the course of his talks, he made some contemptuous remarks about the 'sanctimonious hypocrisy' of the American government whose '*Hokkekyō*' was its bank account and whose 'flagrant vices' had disgraced humanity. He also heartily approved of Japan's 'mandate' to wage a 'holy war' against the United States.[70] This tactless, outspoken critic of American materialism was none other than Bernard L. Broughton, a distinguished Oriental scholar and one of the pioneers of Buddhist activities in Britain. Broughton, a militant man 'with too many degrees,' as Ernest Hunt later recalled, had traveled extensively in Asia, where he met and married a devout Nichiren Buddhist.[71] It was evidently impossible to reason with this man; in fact, he rarely stopped talking long enough to hear what anyone else had to say. On one occasion he totally ignored three polite requests to close a long address and had to be silenced by the loud clang of a temple gong.[72] Buddhist leaders breathed a sigh of relief when Broughton left the Islands, but he had succeeded in stirring up additional ferment.

At about this time, too, the Counter Intelligence Police was informed that a recent arrival from Japan, a certain Mr. Tsunemitsu, had distributed among YMBA youngsters an ultra-secret pamphlet entitled '*Zai' Nippon* and was scheming to reorganize the YMBA along lines 'more effective and helpful to Japan.'[73] Alien parents, meanwhile, encouraged their youngsters to make trips to the homeland, and the United Young Buddhist Association, backed financially by religious dignitaries and prominent Japanese businessmen, sponsored trips to Japan during the summer months.[74]

The nationalist fervor of the older generation was bolstered at this time, too, by itinerant Japanese newspapermen who extolled the righteousness of Japan's Far Eastern policy. In October 1937, Shingorō Takaishi, the editor-in-chief of the *Tokyo Nichi Nichi*, one afternoon sat on the terrace of the Royal Hawaiian Hotel on Waikiki Beach and publicly expounded at great length on the justice of Japan's holy war. Nippon's Far Eastern campaign, he said, was intended to make China grasp the 'true' state of affairs in Asia, to stabilize conditions in the East, and to bring 'peace' to the Orient.[75]

In the closing years of the decade, as the tide of nationalism abroad swelled, the patriotic fervor of alien residents became increasingly evident. Japanese women scurried along Fort and King streets in congested Honolulu, soliciting from passers-by stitches for their *sennin-bari* bands.* Language school teachers raised money for the 'holy war' against China, and members of the Hongwanji *fujinkai* (women's associations) collected money to send comfort bags to Japanese soldiers. Films were imported which glorified Japan's military conquests and the superiority of the Yamato race.[76]

Along with this surge of nationalist spirit, more Shinto shrines were constructed, and some of the new, Shinto-oriented religions of Japan that had made their way to Hawaii somewhat earlier became exceedingly popular. By the late 1930s, more than fifty thousand Japanese were participating faithfully in elaborate celebrations at Shinto shrines in honor of the emperor's birthday, and after the capture of Hankow and Canton, elaborate thanksgiving and memorial services were held at all the shrines of Hawaii.[77]

The enthusiasm of practicing Buddhists was no less apparent. More and bigger temples had gone up—even in the midst of the depression. In Honolulu, devout Jōdo-shū Buddhists went heavily into debt to build a large, imposing concrete temple on Makiki Street. Dedicated in July 1932, the edifice represented a total investment of close to one hundred thirty thousand dollars.[78] A little later, the Ken-Hokkekyō, a subsect of the fanatically nationalistic Nichiren-shū, erected a temple in Nuuanu Valley, where picturesque cherry blossom parades were staged in commemoration of the death of the fisherman's son who centuries ago had promised to be 'the eyes and pillar of Japan.'[79] In 1937, the Honpa Hongwanji† built on the main highway,[80] in Kapaa, Kauai, one of the largest Buddhist temples, and by the end of the decade, Christian pastors on Hawaii estimated that on the Big Island alone, Buddhist temples outnumbered Christian churches by two or three to one.[81]

Even more ominous than the construction of larger and costlier temples were the reported 'changes and reversals' effected at this time by the Kuchiba administration. Takie and Umetarō Okumura had spread the word among government and military officials that the Hongwanji bishop was acting as a 'watchdog' of the Kyoto

*These were good luck charms sent to relatives serving in the Japanese army or navy. See *Honolulu Advertiser,* 4 September 1937.

†The Hongwanji appears to have constructed more new temples during the decade than all other sects put together. Compare the figures given by the *Honolulu Advertiser,* 15 November 1931, and the *Nippu Jiji,* 22 December 1932, with statistics in the *Dōbō,* May 1941.

temple, which exercised 'absolute power' over the temples in Hawaii. Hongwanji buildings and properties were estimated by the Okumuras to be worth about four million dollars and were said to have been deeded by Kuchiba to Hongwanji headquarters in Kyoto, and the bishop was reported to be in 'regular communication' with officials of the Japanese government. It was even said that Kuchiba had the power to cause the 'removal or recall' of consul generals.[82]

The Okumuras capitalized again on every opportunity to cast suspicion on Buddhist priests and institutions. After the Manchurian crisis, they proclaimed that the language schools had once more become infected with the virus of imperial propaganda. Ever since 'the Manchurian fiasco,' wrote Umetarō, teachers who were 'swept up in the rising tide of Japanese nationalism' had openly declared that they were 'teaching Japanese spirit through [the] medium of [the] Japanese language.'[83] Brazen Buddhist priests, added his father, were again preaching loyalty to the distant kami, who was deified by the priests and exalted as being coeval with heaven and earth.

By the time the Congressional Investigation Committee on Statehood arrived in Hawaii in October 1935,* an aroused and vocal part of the American community was geared once more to disparaging the Japanese schools as an anachronism and serious obstacle to the full assimilation of the Japanese. Local and mainland opposition to statehood, revolving around the 'professed inability to judge the loyalty of the Japanese,' was traced invariably to 'the existence of [the] Japanese language schools and . . . non-Christian religions.'[84] In defining its policy on statehood, the *Advertiser* accused the Japanese schools of teaching principles and traditions distinctly at variance with American ideals. These schools and the temples closely allied with them, the paper stated, were faced with a steady decline in attendance, but the community nevertheless felt that Japanization played a dominant part in the purpose of the schools. Instruction in the schools went beyond the surface curriculum, the *Advertiser* charged, and however innocuous the textbooks might appear, another strain of thought, which was not in accord with American ideals, was being conveyed to Hawaii's Japanese-Americans.[85] Takie Okumura's advice that every obstacle in the way of statehood be swiftly removed—

*The notorious Massie rape and murder case of 1932 had brought with it the threat of commission government and (along with the Jones-Costigan Sugar Act) converted many people in the Islands to the cause of statehood. Hawaii had always been subjected to all the taxes imposed on the states, and the Territory annually paid millions of dollars to the federal government. Yet the Islands had been excluded from many benefits conferred on the states. Congress, moreover, could take away, with one stroke, what it had granted in the Organic Act. But by 1935, under increasing pressure from influential Island residents, Congress had begun to take more seriously Hawaii's pleas for statehood.

especially the Buddhist schools—was enthusiastically applauded and reechoed by the American press. Other 'reliable sources,' too, were quoted by the local papers regarding the allegedly subversive activities and propaganda of alien institutions. Dr. Fry of the Methodist-Episcopal Mission testified that the biggest stumbling block to the language schools could be removed if they had no connection whatsoever with the Buddhist religion; and Dr. Palmer of Central Union Church asserted that Buddhist influence in the maintenance and control of the schools of Hawaii had all along been subtle, hidden, and imponderable, though never expressed openly. In an Open Letter to the Japanese Education Association, the *Advertiser* asked pointedly why it was that Takie Okumura's proposal to abolish the private language schools and to teach the Japanese language in the public schools had been rejected by Oriental educators. The Japanese Education Association replied that the character of the language schools had been deliberately maligned, and their purpose deliberately misunderstood. Despite all propaganda to the contrary, the schools were doing their very best, the association affirmed, to rear those of Japanese ancestry as loyal and useful citizens. Furthermore, it would only be a matter of time before all teachers in the schools would be American citizens. Okumura's chain-school project as a 'substitute' for the private institutions was thus 'neither practicable nor desirable.'[86] Yasutarō Sōga of the *Nippu Jiji* replied, as he had in the past, that the schools were playing a vital role in preserving and transmitting to the second generation what was best in Japanese thought and culture.[87] The *Advertiser*, he contended, had made the 'ridiculous charge' that the language schools were teaching loyalty to the emperor when, in fact, the opposite was true, and they were advancing a program designed to develop good American citizens.[88]

Whatever the case (and few Americans believed that the schools were working hard at molding exemplary American citizens), other factors were at work to intensify opposition to Oriental institutions. In 1937, there were 151,141 Japanese in the Islands of a total population of 396,715. The Japanese electorate had increased phenomenally, and quite a few Japanese-Americans had made successful bids for public office. As the Nisei became more numerous, fear mounted once more that they would secure political control of the Islands by voting as a racial bloc.[89]

In the late, turbulent years of the decade, the Christian clergy, led by the Okumuras, continued to preach with monotonous, irritating regularity that two things remained at the root of all doubts concerning the loyalty of citizens of Japanese ancestry— dual citizenship and the inculcation of Japanism. Both, the clergy charged, were being fostered by Buddhist priests and educators, who were associated with the language schools. Takie Okumura incessantly exhorted the Nisei to expatriate themselves and become 'simon-pure' Americans.[90] They could do this best, he said, by getting rid of language school teachers, who had allegedly opposed expatriation, and by abolishing as rapidly as possible the schools which were allegedly inculcating Japanism.[91] Also, the Nisei must provide for instruction in the Japanese language in some other way—namely, in the chain schools.[92] Above all, they must abandon Buddhism, which was diametrically different from the religion of America.[93] A religion with 'no-God and no-soul' was declaimed by Okumura as wholly incompatible with American thought, and Buddhist priests, by 'deliberately stuffing Buddhism' into the minds of Hawaii's Japanese-Americans, had strengthened 'the sense of difference by adding to the different racial color, the totally different religious or moral force.'[94]

The Okumuras (in whose minds fact often seemed inextricably mingled with fiction) also disseminated erroneous data alleging that the number of schools affiliated with the Buddhist temples had increased with alarming rapidity. Quite a few new temples had been erected, but less than a handful of Buddhist schools had been built during the decade. The Nichiren-shū and the Sōtō-shū each established one school in Honolulu at the opening of the decade, and in some of the more populous rural areas, new and larger buildings had been constructed to accommodate the increased enrollment. By 1937, however, only 45 of 186 Japanese schools were affiliated with Buddhist temples, and in May 1941, the statistics on the Buddhist schools and their enrollments were as follows:

SECT	NO. OF SCHOOLS	NO. OF TEACHERS	STUDENT ENROLLMENT
Higashi Hongwanji	None	—	—
Honpa Hongwanji	23	151	9,829
Jōdo-shū	12	40	2,084
Nichiren-shū	1	4	78
Shingon-shū	None	—	—
Sōtō-shū	10	35	1,648[95]

As the mouthpiece of the Buddhist community, the Japanese press again took offense at the erroneous propaganda promulgated by the Okumuras. The *Hawaii Hōchi*, deploring all efforts to prevent the sprouting of so-called dangerous thoughts, objected strenuously to standardized concepts of Americanism as defined by narrow-minded and bigoted Americanists.[96] Buddhist newspapermen were incensed by the fact that hysteria had again infected the community as the result of the malicious propaganda spawned by Japanese-Christian evangelists. Leading members of the American community, as the *Hōchi* recalled, had previously testified at Statehood Hearings that the schools were by no means the menace that some persons had thought them to be, and following the 1937 Hearings, the chairman of the Joint Committee on Hawaii had concluded that, despite the 'fuss' which had been made over them, the Japanese schools had served 'a real purpose in the adjustment of an immigrant group to new conditions.'[97] But Christian zealots had again gone out of their way to stir up opposition to the schools. In an editorial entitled 'Abolishing the Language Schools,' the *Hōchi* of July 22, 1938, set forth once more its views on a controversy which had now raged for more than three and a half decades. There had been persistent influences at work to discredit the language schools, the paper noted, and the bitterest opposition to them had always come from persons within the Japanese community who sought their own advancement by attacking the Buddhist institutions. Arguments against the schools conjured up by such persons were invariably based upon false premises, bolstered with gross exaggerations, and used to play upon religious and racial prejudice and a general ignorance of the real nature and purpose of the language schools. Commenting on the DPI proposal recommending the dissolution of the private schools and the teaching of Japanese in the public schools, the *Hōchi* stated that such a proposal failed 'to take into consideration the larger field being occupied by the private schools in addition to the simple function of teaching Japanese.' Some of the schools, the paper frankly admitted,

also specialize in the teaching of Buddhist principles and the religious ideology of the Orient. This is a perfectly natural requirement for children from non-christian house-holds and one that certainly could not be undertaken by the public school system. In exactly the same way the Catholics maintain private educational institutions and colleges where children from Catholic families are taught the rudiments of their religion in addition to subjects of general knowledge. The same is true of other Christian sects. In a country of religious freedom without a state religion the oriental beliefs stand on an equal footing with all others and there is no justification for any infringement of this right of parents to send their children to schools where the emphasis is placed upon their own natural religion.

There should be no objection, the *Hōchi* concluded, on the part of tolerant and fair-minded Americans to the 'continuance of such education under private control.'

Nevertheless, when the New Americans convened in July 1940, Takie Okumura clamored once more for the removal of the schools. Americans, he persisted, were convinced that the language schools were part of a concerted program to win Americans of Japanese ancestry to a basic and underlying loyalty to Japan. At the Okumuras' invitation, Judge Alva E. Steadman instructed the New Americans to turn their backs on the language schools, because the alien institutions were an 'item of friction . . . suspicion and distrust.'⁹⁸ At the Okumuras' invitation, Major General Charles D. Herron of the United States Army warned the New Americans that the schools were suspect because they employed a preponderance of alien teachers—'an intolerable affront' to the American community.⁹⁹

A 'Memo,' marked 'Strictly Confidential,' among Takie Okumura's private papers records the reaction of the Buddhist community to the Okumuras' 1940 crusade against the language schools (conducted ostensibly on behalf of statehood). Suspecting that General Herron and Takie Okumura were conspiring to abolish the language schools, a group of Buddhist priests and school teachers called on Consul General Gunji to ask his help in 'crushing' the New Americans Conferences. According to the 'Memo,' Gunji's visitors emphasized that whatever was aired at these conferences eventually appeared as a measure in the Territorial legislature and that Okumura was particularly adept at firing a signal for impending legislation. If the conferences were wiped out, the priests pointed out, there would be no danger of bringing up questions like those of the language schools or of expatriation, and the Japanese in Hawaii would forever be at peace. Gunji, refusing to be 'stampeded,' replied that the New Americans Conferences were doing splendid work in breaking down prejudices against the local industries, citizenship, and the American people. The 'Memo' also stated that Buddhist priests 'kept on coming to the consulate day after day,' and on July 25, 1940, officers of the Japanese Education Association demanded that Gunji take 'drastic measures' to offset any attempt to abolish the schools. General Herron's proposal that only American citizens be permitted to teach in the schools would appear, the association feared, as a bill in the forthcoming legislative session unless something were done immediately. Buddhist priests, meanwhile, continually harped on the activities of the Okumuras, who, they were certain, were hatching another conspiracy to wipe out the schools. The consul general, however, still would not listen, the 'Memo' stated, and Buddhists were finally told to go home and cool off.

But the Buddhists did not cool off. On August 12, Fred Makino of the *Hōchi* summoned a meeting of language school officials and swore that he, personally, would fight to the last breath for the preservation of the schools. Governor Poindexter was not an enemy of the schools, Makino said, and with the governor's assistance, he could 'quash' any legislative measure that would do away with the schools. Language school officials then promptly made preparations, grumbled Takie Okumura, 'to raise big campaign fund for the "Protection Of Language Schools",' whereupon Gunji became firmly convinced, with the help of the Okumuras, that 'Makino is a real cancer of the community.'¹⁰⁰

The following year, things were no better. At the New Americans Conference in 1941, the Okumuras again summoned influential Americans to denounce and to cast more aspersions on the language schools. By now, too, a larger number of alienated and disgusted Nisei were actively opposing the schools. In January 1941, the Hawaii Japanese Civic Association sponsored a forum at the Nuuanu YMCA to discuss the question 'Should We Continue the Japanese Language Schools?' J. Garner Anthony, a well-known attorney, answered in the negative. Unrest over the schools, he affirmed, had been occasioned as much by political as by educational considerations. In 'the light of Japan's current foreign policy,' alien institutions, he warned, would continue to breed doubts about the loyalty of the American-born Japanese. Another lawyer, Philip Cass, was convinced that the schools were instruments of the Japanese government intended 'to undermine the loyalty' of Japanese-Americans.[101]

As the relentless language school controversy went on and on, even more of the Nisei eschewed all things reputedly un-American and summarily renounced and denounced the Dharma. Attendance at religious services became 'more and more perfunctory,' enrollment in Buddhist Sunday schools decreased alarmingly, and membership in the Hongwanji YMBA dropped to half of what it had been under the leadership of Ernest Hunt and the late Bishop Imamura.[102]

Japanese delinquency statistics went up, too. In previous years, due in large measure to the religious and moral training provided by Buddhist priests and teachers, the crime and delinquency rate for the Japanese had been remarkably low. Seth Richardson, a Washington lawyer who made a thorough investigation of crime and law enforcement in Hawaii in 1932, had found that the Japanese, old and young, were a decent, law-abiding people. Even Consul General Gunji, despite his opposition to the schools, observed that the boys and girls who had received moral instruction from Buddhist educators were 'by and large more law-abiding than the other Japanese children.'[103] But by the end of the decade, much of the control formerly exercised over Japanese youths by their parents and priests had disintegrated. Many Nisei had dropped out of the language schools and, imitating the rugged individualism of their public school friends, had insolently refused to be shackled any longer to the outworn and unpopular value system of their elders. Probation officers were thus no doubt correct in attributing the rising rate of delinquency to ethical confusion and moral chaos among the second generation. Too many alien parents and teachers, as police officials noted, had failed altogether to make clear to their children the meaning of Japanese religious concepts and values.[104]

On the other hand, interestingly enough, most of the Nisei who remained Buddhists also were law-abiding and exemplary citizens. In 1937, a Honolulu probation officer reported that the results of a case study by the juvenile court concerning the relations between religion and delinquency showed that the delinquency ratio of Buddhists to Christians was very low in favor of the former.[105]

While the American community, kept in perpetual anxiety by certain Christian clerics, continued to harbor doubts about the Nisei and to wonder if Buddhism were not in truth a force tending to weaken rather than to strengthen democratic values, Hawaii's young Buddhists continued to reaffirm their loyalty to America. They conducted their own expatriation drives, welcomed every opportunity to point out that the ideas of Buddhism were not at all incompatible with genuine Americanism,[106] and publicly swore to defend the Constitution against all enemies and to bear true faith of allegiance to same. In August 1941, when President Roosevelt declared a state of national emergency, officials of the Hawaii Federation of Young Buddhists (who for years had been led by both Buddhist and Christian clerics to identify religion with nationalism) veritably 'mobilized' the Noble Eightfold Path. Right Aspiration was defined as the determination to preserve the democratic system of government, and Right Effort meant proving oneself worthy of 'the greatest form of government' in the world.[107]

At this time, Bishop Kuchiba, a fanatic patriot in his own right, exhorted a large audience of Japanese-Americans at the annual YMBA Convention to prove through the Buddhist faith their readiness and loyalty to the Stars and Stripes. Kuchiba, expressing a conviction popular for centuries among men who were Japanese first and Buddhists second, said Buddhism had always taught that a man's greatest obligation was his duty to his country, even if that duty meant forsaking parental love. Young Buddhists listened to Kuchiba (many of them for the first and last time) and formally pledged their lives to America. They were prepared, they said, 'for any emergency.'[108] A few weeks later, on December 7, 1941, the imperial forces of Japan attacked Pearl Harbor.

CHAPTER 11

War and Restoration

WORLD WAR II TOTALLY DISRUPTED
BUDDHIST ACTIVITIES IN HAWAII. SCHOOLS
and temples were closed and most priests were interned. More of
the Nisei abandoned the old restraints and the old faith, and the
alien Japanese, scorned as the 'enemy' by their own children,
wandered about pathetically in a desperate search for moral
support and religious solace. Many of the first-generation Japanese
flocked to faith-healing cults which promised them health,
salvation, and the safe return of their heroic sons, who were to
become among the most decorated soldiers in the United States
Army. Later, with the cessation of hostilities and the return of
Island priests, who renewed their resolution that Buddhism shall
not die in the Territory, Buddhism enjoyed a rapid and healthy
revival. This chapter concerns the hardships endured by Hawaii's
Japanese during the war years and the successful revival of Buddhism in the postwar decades. In the 1950s and the early 1960s,
the future of Buddhism looked promising indeed. With the
growth of the new ecumenical spirit, opposition to the Dharma
all but disappeared, and Christian and Buddhist clergymen moved
steadily forward in the direction of the mutual understanding and
appreciation which Bishop Imamura and Ernest Hunt had worked
for and pleaded for over the years. Buddhist spokesmen came to
the realization, too, that the success of their religion in Hawaii
would depend primarily on how effectively they cooperated with

one another in propagating the teachings of the Indian sage who, centuries before the Christian era, had preached an inexorable law of moral responsibility and had taught that kindness and compassion were the highest rule of conduct.

At 10:45 A.M., December 7, 1941, three hours after Japanese torpedo planes and bombers had immobilized the American fleet at Pearl Harbor in an inferno of fire and smoke, Governor Joseph B. Poindexter declared a state of emergency. At 2:45 that afternoon, the governor issued a formal proclamation of martial law and General Walter C. Short, commanding general of the Hawaiian Department, became military governor of Hawaii. The next day, martial law went into effect, and provost courts were established. All Japanese language schools were closed, and temples were evacuated. The Jōdo-shū temple on Makiki Street was converted into the headquarters of an infantry battalion, and the Hongwanji Educational Home on Fort Street became an army billet. The largest abode of light and love in Hilo was plundered and desecrated, apparently by military personnel. The large brass lamps disappeared, and costly ceremonial vestments were stolen. Authorities were notified immediately, but no redress was made. Aged and heartsick Japanese, their eyes moist with tears, peered sadly into their deserted temples and pondered 'the transiency of the world.'[1] The most suspect among the Japanese were quickly rounded up and interned at Sand Island or at relocation camps on the mainland. A year later their sons went to war.

THE NISEI GO TO WAR

On January 28, 1943, the War Department called for fifteen hundred volunteers from Hawaii. More than ten thousand Japanese-Americans responded, and of some thirty-three thousand citizens from Hawaii who joined the armed forces, 52 percent were of Japanese ancestry.[2] Commanding generals in the Hawaiian Department, recalling how the second generation had been 'indoctrinated' in the language schools, wondered (as so many civilian Americans did) if the Nisei would be loyal to the United States. Ironically enough, the alien community harbored no such doubts—not ever. More than three decades before Pearl Harbor, the *Nippu Jiji* had confidently stated that American citizens of Japanese ancestry would 'never choose to neglect their obligation to America, even at the cost of their lives,' and in 1916 a priest from the Kyoto Hongwanji (while visiting briefly in the Islands) prophetically remarked that, since Hawaii's young Japanese were being well schooled in patriotism and loyalty and were acquiring the true spirit of bushidō, 'when their patriotism is transferred from a former allegiance to another . . . patriotism for America and American ideals will come naturally to them.'[3] And so it did. Hawaii's celebrated war heroes demonstrated unexcelled courage and heroism on the battlefields. All Hawaii was proud of them—and both the Christian and Buddhist clergy claimed them.[4]

When the war broke out, Takie Okumura acknowledged that most of the one hundred twenty thousand Hawaiian-born Japanese were nominal or practicing Buddhists; even at that late date, he lamented, comparatively few were Christians. During the war, Ernest Hunt had received a great deal of mail from Nisei soldiers who composed the 100th Infantry or 'Purple Heart' Battalion and was thus quite certain that most of the boys were Buddhists.[5] But Christians refused to believe that Hawaii's 'fightingest' men were Buddhists. Chaplain Corwin H. Olds of the Pacific Base Command estimated that only 25 percent of the inducted troops were Buddhists, and after the war, Reverend Hiro Higuchi, a Honolulu Congregational minister and a member of the famed 442nd Combat Team, challenged the editor of the *Pacific Citizen* in Salt Lake City to prove his assertion that more than half of the soldiers of the 442nd were Buddhists. The Chaplain's Office of the 442nd, Higuchi recalled, had taken a census of the religious preferences of some five thousand men in the regiment. The results of the survey had proved only that to the average Nisei religion was not very important. Of the group that participated in the census, 35 percent preferred Protestantism; 13 percent Buddhism; 5 percent Catholicism; and 1 percent Mormonism. Forty-six percent had no religious preference at all.[6]

But no matter what percentage of Hawaii's soldiers openly professed Buddhism (and in order to avoid the epithet 'buddha-heads,' some were careful not to 'prefer' Buddhism), the extra-ordinary heroism of the Nisei must be explained, at least, in part, by the values that they acquired from their parents and educators. No one can wholly divorce himself from the culture that nourished him in his youth, and no matter how much the Nisei may have hated the language schools, most of them attended the institutions and listened to Buddhist priests fervently extol the virtues of patriotism (aikoku-shin) and selfless, single-minded dedication to duty (giri). As far back as 1905 a handful of farsighted Japanese had predicted that Hawaiian-born Japanese would be made better Americans by the 'moral maxims [and] instruction in patriotism found in their schoolbooks.'[7] Some forty years later, the patriotism exemplified by Hawaii's heroic Nisei and immortalized by their far-famed battle cry Go for Broke! earned the enduring gratitude of all their fellow Americans and hundreds of Purple Hearts, Bronze and Silver Stars, and Distinguished Service Crosses.[8]

The day after the attack on Pearl Harbor, Hawaii's Buddhist priests were interned. Three hundred seventy aliens, many of them religious leaders and educators, had been sent off to concentration camps by the evening of December 8, 1941.[9] Bishop Kuchiba of the Honpa Hongwanji and Bishop Zenkyō Komagata of the Sōtō-shū were among the first to be interned at Sand Island, on the west side of the entrance to Honolulu Harbor. Among the other detained priests were Honpa Hongwanji's first postwar bishop, Ryūten Kashiwa, who received the most mail, and the Reverend Nishu Kobayashi, who received the most mail from women. Seventy-two-year-old Bishop Kyokujo Kubokawa of the Jōdo-shū was also confined at Sand Island. Not understanding why he had been taken from his temple and put behind barbed wires, Kubokawa refused even to take off his priestly robes and indignantly shuffled about the camp reciting the *nembutsu* with bowed head and folded hands. Cooperation with camp authorities was evidently the farthest thing from his mind. But when the horror of Pearl Harbor hit him, he was so appalled and overcome with shame that he volunteered for the heaviest work in the camp.[10]

None of Hawaii's priests complained of ill treatment during internment. Reverend Hiseki Miyazaki, an old-timer who had preached on Kauai and worked for years with Bishop Imamura and Ernest Hunt, wrote: 'When we were first confined . . . we felt as though we were thrown into a hell. But contrary to our expectations, we [were] treated well.'[11] Confinement was actually a blessing in disguise to some of the older priests who were never able, given even the best of abilities, to satisfy both the alien parents and the American community wherein they had functioned 'as cultural outposts and, as many thought, also as spies.'[12] But most of the younger priests, worried about their families, lonely, and lacking the spiritual and emotional maturity of the older men, found internment intolerable. The behavior of the most embittered was not becoming. Yasutarō Sōga of the *Nippu Jiji* was interned with quite a few of the priests, and some of them, he wrote, with 'faces like buddhas,' performed acts 'less than human.' As the weeks and months dragged on, some priests, disgusted and frustrated, forgot that they were married. Others suffered the embarrassment of having their most intimate secrets exposed. One priest had worked for years to build up a reputation for sanctity, and, on the eve of the war, some of his parishioners had begun to call him *hotoke*, saintly one. But when FBI agents arrested him, they found more than a thousand dollars in cash in the pockets of his frayed garments along with a passionate love note from a married woman. There were supercilious priests, too, who kept their hands in their pockets and refused to do any menial work. By all accounts, Zen priests, long accustomed to rigorous discipline, behaved the best.[13]

Quite a number of the priests who had been stationed at mainland temples were openly anti-American. One of these, a priest from the Fresno Hongwanji who completely went to pieces when news of Hiroshima and Nagasaki reached him, circulated a rumor among the internees of the Roseberg camp in New Mexico that Japan had won her 'holy war' against inhumane and unscrupulous adversaries. Most priests from Hawaii, however, tended to shy away from publicly venting their innermost feelings or convictions, though the older men, wherever they came from, lived in an ivory tower, as Sōga put it, and refused to believe that Japan could or did lose the war. Bishop Kuchiba, among many others, refused to accept the reality of his country's defeat.[14]

Unrealistic as the priests often were, and however uninspired their leadership on occasions, their absence from certain detention camps was painfully evident. Most of the 'incorrigibles' among the alien Japanese had been sent to the notorious Tule Lake relocation center in northern California. Only a few priests were interned there; hence, religious leadership in the camp was 'exceedingly weak.'[15] Strikes and riots were commonplace, and in November 1943, a mob of violent Japanese, in an attempt to take over control of the camp, seized federal employees and held them prisoners. Order was not restored until a Buddhist priest interceded and pacified the rioters.[16]

Throughout the war years, with the assistance of devout internees, many priests conducted Buddhist rites and presided at traditional Buddhist festivals. Japanese at the Santa Fe camp in New Mexico sponsored very elaborate Bon odori celebrations, and at Camp McCoy in Wisconsin, Śākyamuni's birth was commemorated annually with much solemnity and with no little nostalgia. On one such occasion, Hawaii's Reverend Hakuai Oda, an expert in the art of flower arranging, converted a leafless oak branch into a blooming tree and fashioned cherry blossoms out of toilet tissue dyed with beet juice. Then the venerable and bearded Reverend Nago of Honolulu delivered a moving address and reminisced about the colorful prewar Hanamatsuri festivals at Kapiolani Park at Waikiki.[17]

THE HOME FRONT

Regular Buddhist services and activities in Hawaii were terminated immediately after the sneak attack for the duration of the war. Only a handful of Japanese priests and priestesses were not interned. Sixty-five-year-old Ernest Hunt, a free British subject, conducted services in private homes and in the classrooms of his own Island

Paradise School, doing all that he could to bring comfort and hope to the Japanese of Honolulu. He also obtained permission from General Delos C. Emmons to hold public services in temples on rural Oahu and on the island of Hawaii. Everything went along smoothly for Hunt until he reached the Olaa temple on the Big Island where, in the middle of a service, a military official grabbed him by a sleeve of his priestly garment and shouted, 'Are you Japanese?' More than a little startled, Hunt replied that he had always thought of himself as a Caucasian. 'Well, then, what are 'ya doin' here?' came the contemptuous reply. Hunt explained that he was a Buddhist priest and had every right according to the United States Constitution to conduct a bona fide religious service in a temple of his own faith. He got no reply at first, but his interrogators finally departed when he showed them a letter of authorization bearing General Emmons' signature.[18]

Meanwhile, persons who had always hated or feared the language schools set out to make certain that they would never be reopened. As it turned out, Nisei boys who understood the Japanese language were able to make vital contributions to their country as interpreters, censors, and intelligence workers. But the fact that a knowledge of the language had enabled these young men to save the lives of thousands of their fellow-Americans made no impression at all on Takie Okumura and his co-workers, who were bound and determined that the language schools must go. In January 1943, the Okumuras dispatched to prominent citizens and politicians a form letter which read as follows:

Dear Sir,

We are sending you herewith a memorandum on the language school problem. This memo presents briefly a plan of establishing language classes in public schools [or 'chain schools'] as an alternative in the event that abolition or supervision measure is found to be inadvisable.

Even today quite a number of local Japanese are thinking of reviving the language schools after the termination of the war, and we believe we must do something right away in order to prevent the reappearance of foreign language schools as separate institutions in American community.

From now on every possible effort must be directed toward a thorough Americanization, and make Hawaii truly impregnable as an outpost of America in the Pacific. We do not want to see Hawaii become a victim of another treacherous attack.

We believe if we start early, we can work up the community sentiment in favor of rigid supervision of the schools, or placing language instruction in the public schools, and thus have a good measure introduced in the coming session of the Territorial legislature.

Your earnest consideration and frank expression are therefore urgently sought.[19]

In 1943, the legislature passed Act 104, designed to prevent the schools from reopening in the future. No child, the measure stipulated, could undertake the study of a foreign language until he had completed the fourth grade in a public school or attained his fifteenth birthday. The act alleged that foreign language instruction at too early an age had, in many cases, caused serious emotional disturbances, conflicts, and maladjustments. It was therefore only 'fitting and proper' that such foreign language studies be put aside in order to 'promote the health and welfare, of children of tender age.'[20] On February 20, 1943, three days after the legislature had convened, Umetarō Okumura wrote a letter to David Y. K. Akana, who had introduced the school bill in the senate. The letter read as follows:

Dear Sir:
    Father and I want to express our thanks for your courage in leading the move to wipe out from this community the foreign language schools. Your proposed measure will place the language schools in such a condition that they can not possibly revive after the war.
    Enclosed is a memo and circular letter which we passed sometime in January among our friends. We did not think of health angle, limiting the school hours of each child. We were anxious to bring about the abolition through licensing and restricting of teachers to only qualified American citizens with supervisory director under the Territorial Superintendent of Education. Your proposed measure will simplify the whole problem.[21]

Takie Okumura also asked his old friends among the sugar planters to help abolish all language schools and Buddhist temples on plantation premises.[22] In March 1943, Kenneth B. Carney of the Public Relations Committee of the HSPA obligingly proposed that the planters subsidize a 'broad educational campaign' to Americanize Hawaii's Japanese-American population. Carney had been persuaded that the sugar magnates were being held responsible by the whole nation for having created a Japanese problem by importing Oriental labor in the first place. The planters had better boost their efforts, he wrote, to see that in the future Japanese-Americans obtain their 'culture appreciation' in American schools and along 'approved lines' rather than in separate institutions 'where opportunity and incentive permit their teachers to instill un-American ideas.'[23]

The war years, of course, afforded the Okumuras an excellent opportunity to reach the Japanese youth. In their annual Educational Campaigns, they continued to admonish youngsters ad nauseam to throw Buddhism overboard, thus proving loyalty to the United States.[24] Disappointingly, a number of young people buckled under the pressure. This is not to say that some of the new converts were not sincere. As a matter of fact, quite a number of them identified with the fundamentalist sects, suggesting that there were indeed some 'truth-seekers' among them, as one Seventh-Day Adventist elder put it, as well as the 'half-baked' ones who just followed the crowd. But in most instances the Nisei just did not dare to be Buddhists during the war. Christian ministers had threatened them with internment should they persist in professing an alien creed, and Ernest Hunt recalled that some of his own young parishioners felt so intimidated that they refused to walk on the side of a street where a Buddhist temple was situated.[25]

As more Japanese youngsters abandoned Buddhism and felt compelled to denounce all things 'un-American,' including their parents, the alien Japanese, stunned and horrified by the attack on Pearl Harbor, floundered in a desperate and pathetic search for moral and psychological reassurance. The first-generation Japanese had always thought of themselves and their country as decent and honorable, and some of them never recovered from the shock of December 7, 1941. Others were irrational for months, even years. In the weeks that followed the Day of Infamy, a group of the most distraught aliens circulated a rumor that the sneak attack was not, indeed could not have been, the work of Japanese bombers. It was provoked, they said, 'by an evil human-faced cow possessed of supernatural powers and . . . beyond human control.'[26] The alien Japanese, in fact, exhibited many strange forms of psychic disorders. Some of them set fire to emblems of the Rising Sun and portraits of the imperial family, others discarded the kimono and obi for American clothes, and some even changed their names (the Oharas became the O'Haras). The Japanese Charity Hospital suddenly became Kuakini Hospital, and the word 'Japanese' was dropped from Christian churches formerly so designated.[27]

The closing of the temples put the mental health of the older Japanese in further jeopardy, and the internment of their priests had an absolutely 'paralyzing effect' on them.[28] Without the temples, where they had congregated for years to worship and socialize, and without the priests, whom they had relied on for moral and spiritual guidance, they were deprived of everything that gave meaning to their existence. Without their priests and temples, they could not bury their dead in the time-honored tradition, and the discontinuance of the all-important memorial rites for their beloved deceased caused them untold mental and emotional anguish.[29] Even private worship was threatened. Early in the war years, an elderly Buddhist came to Ernest Hunt in tears. FBI agents, he said, had raided his home and ordered him to get rid of his *butsudan*. 'Can they do such a thing in this country?' he asked. Hunt replied in the negative and promised to report the incident to the proper authorities. Then Hunt promptly paid a call on General Emmons, who, incensed by such a flagrant infraction of one of the Four Freedoms, took immediate steps to make restitution to the old man.[30]

In the absence of their priests, the Japanese went about pathetically from place to place 'looking for someone or something to give them again a sense of direction.'[31] A few, very few, turned to Christianity. Many more flocked to religious cults which were being popularized by fellow members of their alien community and which promised them *yokigurashi*, a happy life free of disease and pain. Ethnic pride and family solidarity had once kept the Japanese faithful to the religious beliefs and values of their ancestors. After the attack on Pearl Harbor had shattered their pride in their country and even turned their children against them, they became willing, even anxious, to try anything which might restore some small measure of their self-respect and help them to identify with some new and noble cause. Several of the *shin shūkyō*, or syncretist 'new religions,' of Japan met those needs. These curious cults, introduced to the Islands before or during the war, were popularized forms of Shinto or Buddhism spiced with Christian odds and ends.

Tenrikyō, the Religion of Divine Wisdom, was the oldest and most popular of the Shinto-oriented cults which found their way to Hawaii. It was founded in 1838 by a Mrs. Miki Nakayama, a visionary daughter of a farmer. As a young girl, she had planned to become a Buddhist nun. Instead she married and suffered a series of domestic crises centered around a perpetually ailing husband. Soon after her marriage, she became a medium and received the gift of 'mystical healing.' She was also 'descended upon' by Tennō Shōgun, the Heavenly General, who, she said, had created mankind from an expanse of muddy waters.[32] Followers of the Tenrikyō in both Japan and Hawaii firmly believe that the mind of Mrs. Nakayama was 'replaced' by the mind of God 'at the very moment He took up habitation within her body.'[33] Mrs. Nakayama, of course, had never doubted her own divinity and, in fact, had insisted upon being treated like a unique phenomenon even to the point of requiring her rice to be cooked on a separate fire and in a separate kettle to be used by no one else. She wore spectacular red garments, too, to impress upon her followers that she was no ordinary person.[34]

Tenrikyō was introduced to Hawaii in 1929. The following year the Tenrikyō Pacific Church was erected on McCully Street in Honolulu, and within a few years, fifteen Tenrikyō meeting places were established in the city. In 1965, a two-story temple of the cult was built on the Pali Highway, not far from the Honpa Hongwanji *betsuin*.[35]

Of all the *shin shūkyō* which came to Hawaii, the *Seichō no Ie*, or House of Growth, was the most eclectic, borrowing its doctrines from Shinto, Buddhism, and Christian Science. During the war years, it was also, by far, the most popular. The founder of the Seichō no Ie was Masaharu Taniguchi, born in Kobe, Japan, in 1893. As a young man, Taniguchi suffered two very disappointing love affairs. One of these involved a ten-year-old girl who became his 'true lover' until his aunt discovered the affair and discontinued her nephew's allowance. When word got around of his predilection for girls aged ten to seventeen, schools closed their doors to him, and he had to find a job. He found work, finally, in a spinning factory in Osaka where he soon became involved in a new series of illicit affairs and contracted a venereal disease. Then his thoughts turned to religion and to problems relating to sickness and its spread and cure. Before long he began to hear voices which assured him that sickness was all in the mind.[36]

Seichō no Ie was introduced to Hawaii in the early 1930s but remained inconspicuous until the outbreak of the war. The cult became popular because of its emphasis on faith-healing and the cleverness with which its 'priesthood' preyed upon the loneliness and spiritual confusion of the disillusioned Japanese. Seichō 'priests' conducted services in private homes, prayed fervently over photographs of Nisei boys at war, and promised their safe return.* In November 1944, leaders of the cult obtained permission to hold public services, and its members then met regularly at the two Higashi Hongwanji temples in Honolulu.[37]

Not among the *shin shukyō*, but nevertheless very popular with aliens who chose to isolate themselves altogether from a hostile community and to cling tenaciously to old customs and beliefs, was the *Tōdaiji*, a cult established in Honolulu by 'Bishop' Tetsusho Hirai, another woman who had seen visions. She claimed to be an exponent of the ancient Kegon school of Buddhism,† but the Buddhist clergy in Hawaii challenged her competency to expound the Kegon teachings. This, of course, merely enabled her to pose as a martyr. 'I have been subjected,' she complained, 'to under-served [*sic*] and unexpected criticism from priests belongin[g] to other Buddhist sects.'[38] She was not long-suffering about it either. She threatened to put a curse on Ernest Hunt.[39]

In 1941 permission was obtained to organize the first overseas Tōdaiji Mission, and in 1956 Honolulu devotees built for Bishop Hirai a gorgeous temple on Jack Lane in Nuuanu Valley. Hirai remained close to the common people, sharing their superstitions

---

*In 1944, Dr. J. Leslie Dunstan of Central Union Church wrote to his Japanese clergymen about 'a matter of deep concern to us all.' It had been reported to Dunstan that the Seichō practice of exhibiting and praying over photographs of soldiers had crept into Christian memorial services. The Christian clergy, Dunstan warned, must not 'depart from the essential truths' of Christianity in such a manner—not even to help people with sons at war. The use of names or pictures might have 'a place in Buddhism', he fancied, but certainly not in Christianity. See Dr. J. Leslie Dunstan to Rev. Paul Tamura, 20 June 1944; Dr. J. Leslie Dunstan to his fellow pastors, 12 June 1944, Japanese Department, HMCS.

†Kegon Buddhism, founded in China in the seventh century, was introduced to Japan in A.D. 736. The mother temple, the Tōdaiji at Nara, is reputed to be the largest wooden structure in the world.

and fortifying many of their illusions. She believed, as they did, in many spirits and in thirteen gods. Fūdo-sama, the god of fire, occupied a prominent place in her pantheon, and before his fierce, scowling image, she celebrated 'fire masses' twice a month. Knowing, too, that virtue and wealth are causally related in the Japanese mind, she lived in luxury as evidence of divine approbation. The Japanese were in awe of her 'healing powers,' and many of them referred to her as their *Ikigami*, or living goddess.[40]

Some aliens who 'lost face' during the war eventually drifted into cults whose practitioners promised to make them physically and spiritually 'fit' to play a key role in the construction of a future 'paradise on earth.'[41] Among the cults which capitalized on this approach was the Meshiya-kyō, or Church of World Messianity. Known in Japan as the Sekai Kyūseikyō, it was easily the most specialized of the so-called healing religions. Its founder, Mokichi Okada, had suffered numerous illnesses (rheumatism, catarrh of the stomach, heart disease, nervous prostration), and, like Miki Nakayama, he had been 'possessed' by deities. After giving the matter thought, Okada came to the realization that although Christ, Buddha, and Mohammed had been great saints, only he was 'truly united' with the divine.[42] In 1963, members of the Honolulu Meshiya-kyō purchased a two-hundred-thousand-dollar estate in upper Nuuanu Valley for the construction of a new temple, which was completed and dedicated in 1968.[43]

After the war, the most popular of the *shin shūkyō* was the Tenshō-Kōtai-Jingū-kyō. Like the Church of World Messianity, this 'new religion' guaranteed the Japanese a role in the spiritual regeneration of the world. Tenshō was founded in Japan by Mrs. Sayo Kitamura, better known as the 'Dancing Goddess,' 'The Prophet of Tabuse,' or simply as 'Ōgamisama,' the Great God. According to Mrs. Kitamura, God descended into her body, more specifically into her 'belly,' on May 4, 1944. She then became 'His perfect mediator,' and all her words became synonymous, she said, with the 'Voice from Heaven.'[44]

Ōgamisama came to Hawaii for the first time in May 1952. In her first sermon in Honolulu, she declared that, while the Japanese had in the past taken up weapons and attacked other countries, the time had come for them to stand up and make strenuous efforts to establish the Absolute Peace of the world. They must now repent of their sins and make themselves loved by all the peoples of the world.[45] The Dancing Goddess had borrowed freely from both Shinto and Buddhism in framing her own set of beliefs, yet she ordered all of her followers to burn their Shinto shrines and Buddhist ancestral tablets—it being only common sense to cast 'the remains of the dead into the sea.'[46]

The appeal of Tenshō was simple and direct. Ōgamisama welcomed into her fold anyone who was willing to 'polish' his soul by practicing charity and brotherhood. Her ability to 'heal' won many converts, and social outcasts and discontents from every walk of life came to her seeking a miraculous cure for physical or psychosomatic illnesses. The ritual of Tenshō consisted of public testimonials, confessions, and an 'ecstasy dance' led by the Dancing Goddess and dedicated to 'chasing out maggots' and to ridding the world of evil. There was also the *Oinori no kotoba*, or special prayer beseeching God to give mankind a heavenly kingdom pleasant to live in. Salvation depended on 'cutting bad karma' by prayer, faith in Ōgamisama, and the elimination of illicit desires. Those who did not polish their souls and who preferred to satisfy wicked passions would be washed away, she warned, 'by God's exorcism into abysmal darkness with the evil spirits.' The Dancing Goddess died on December 28, 1967,* and was succeeded by her teenage granddaughter who dances but apparently does not preach.[47]

By the mid-1960s, the fastest growing of the *shin shūkyō* was the Nichiren Shōshū Hawaii Kaiken, a local branch of the militant Sōka Gakkai, or Value-Creation Society. A subsect of the Nichiren-shū, the Sōka Gakkai has been described as the most 'vigorous, exclusivistic, belligerent, and self-confident' of the 'new religions' of Japan. Isolated members of the cult in Hawaii met for the first time in October 1960 to welcome Daisaku Ikeda, president of the Sōka Gakkai, who had stopped briefly in Honolulu on a trip around the world. About two years later, in January 1963, the Hawaii General Branch of the cult was officially organized. Sōka Gakkai membership in Hawaii was and still is made up of persons who seem to be easily won over by the cult's exaltation of the pursuit of personal profit. The Nichiren Shōshū has also attracted a great many dissatisfied refugees from Buddhist and Christian sects. In contrast to the gentle, peace-loving Gautama, who maintained a Noble Silence about issues which inevitably led to anger and fruitless bickering, Sōka Gakkai members, who believe that theirs is 'the one true faith,' have had a tendency to sneer at the great religions of the world. In Japan, some of them practice *shakubuku*, an aggressive method of making converts, which involves browbeating into submission 'by determined argumentation . . . or fearsome warnings.'[48]

THE REVIVAL OF BUDDHISM

The first Buddhist priests to return to Hawaii after the war arrived aboard an army transport which cruised into Honolulu Harbor in November 1945. Others soon followed. Only the most embittered

---

*Following Ōgamisama's death, recordings of her old sermons were played during Tensho services.

and disconsolate men, like Gikyō Kuchiba, returned to Japan— and the shock of reality.[49]

Temples which had been neglected for years stood in need of major repairs, and once-exotic temple gardens were parched and weed-ridden. But priests went to work quickly, and in a short time even the shabbiest temples were respectable looking again. Soon, too, new and bigger ones were under construction. Priests immediately began to celebrate memorial rites for American Buddhists killed in action and to console bereaved parents with the faith that 'while lives pass, Life never dies' and that 'all who love each other will someday find each other.' In a short time, most of the priests resumed all of their prewar functions and responsibilities.

Meanwhile, the return of the Shinto priests had created a flurry in the community. In an editorial entitled 'The End of a Phoney Religion,' the *Advertiser* warned the alien Japanese that Japan's defeat had better be a lesson to them and advised 'fake former Shinto priests' returning from internment camps to recognize that 'the door is slammed on their racket.' The paper's remarks were obviously intended for Buddhists as well. The days 'of beating gongs and burning punk' were over, too, it stated. The paper felt confident that the language schools had been relegated to 'a limbo from which there can be no return.'[50]

Hawaii's Nisei heroes led the agitation to throw off the control of the Shintoists. With the enthusiastic support of the American Legion, they strongly urged the deportation of Shinto priests— and the newspapers applauded their stand. There was no longer 'even the shadow of an excuse,' the *Advertiser* asserted, for Shinto priests to remain in Hawaii.[51]

Some Christian clerics also advocated the closing of the Shinto temples. Takie Okumura was one. Another was Dr. E. Tanner Brown of the Episcopal Mission, who reported that a University of Hawaii professor had informed him that priests at the 'Yodo Shinto Shrine' (actually, the Jōdo-shū temple) in Honolulu had been 'stuffing' young Japanese full of *yamato-damashii*. Another Episcopalian minister, Reverend H. H. Corey, countered that it was not really necessary to deport any priests. Corey had once been a missionary in Japan, and he had found that the best way to handle Shinto was 'by laughing at it.'[52]

At this point, the Executive Board of the Hawaii Interracial Committee took a determined stand against deporting the priests. In a statement issued by Bernhard L. Hormann, then an assistant professor of sociology at the University of Hawaii, the board stated that the agitation to get rid of Shinto priests sprang from ignorance. Concerned persons, Hormann said, had failed to distinguish between State Shinto (the imperial cult) and privately supported Shinto sects. Prior to the outbreak of the war, the statement read, Shinto shrines were no more tied up officially with State Shinto than was Buddhism.[53] In the end, the move to deport the Shinto clergy failed.

There was little community opposition to the return of the Buddhist priests, but ironically enough, Buddhist rather than Shinto clerics became the foci of reactionary religious movements. Not all of them were aliens, either. On March 1, 1946, young Jisho Yamazaki of the Sōtō-shū was arraigned in Circuit Court and indicted by the grand jury on charges of disloyalty to the United States. In letters and postcards written to men interned at the Honouliuli camp on Oahu, Yamazaki had declared that Japan had won the war, that the Japanese fleet was keeping a close eye on Hawaii, and that American soldiers who had dared to set foot in Japan were being used by the Japanese as 'laborers.'[54] Once out on bail, he continued to propagate his bizarre delusions, and on April 9, 1946, decked out in formal priestly attire, he exhorted a crowd of more than seven hundred alien Japanese to demonstrate the Yamato spirit. The purpose of all such grotesque goings-on, the *Advertiser* commented, was 'to bring the United States of America into disrepute and contempt.'[55] A priest of the Shin sect, too, spread the lie that Japan had won the war. 'If Japan was completely defeated,' he assured his fellow countrymen, 'I would have committed "seppuku" [self-disembowelment].'[56]

Such a large number of aliens swallowed the propaganda circulated by these and other disaffected men that other priests, worried about the mental state of their parishioners, hesitated to break the news that Japan had lost the war. Some well-meaning priests knew better but supported the rumors that Japan had been victorious. Those who told the truth were called traitors and were ostracized by the men and women who had lost all touch with reality.[57]

Students at the University of Hawaii Research Laboratory, meanwhile, had made an extensive study of the postwar delusions of the Japanese and had come to the conclusion that some way must be found for reviving the 'recognized forms' of the Oriental religions.[58] So despite all the commotion over Shinto and despite the fact that many Americans still saw no clear lines of distinction between Shinto and Buddhism, few people openly opposed the revival of Buddhism. Reverend E. Tanner Brown continued to fret about 'queer happenings' at the 'Yodo' temple—but he was finally quieted down by a government official who reminded him that in America 'there was religious freedom.'[59] In May 1946, the Honolulu Council of Churches, representing thirty-six Protestant churches in the Islands, issued a statement that, while the Christian clergy did not encourage the revival of Buddhist activities, Oriental priests, 'acting solely as religious leaders,' had the legal and moral right to give solace and guidance to their followers and to conduct religious services.[60]

In the meantime, Buddhist boys back from the war front had become incensed by the false propaganda spawned by reactionary Buddhist priests. Walter S. Kadota, a veteran of the 'Purple Heart' Battalion, wrote: ' . . . if our Buddhist brother [Jisho Yamazaki] has been so ill-advised as to preach and indoctrinate the out-dated rule of "might makes right" . . . we suggest he peddle his idea of a new social order somewhere else. . . . It is regrettable that the good name of the lord Buddha should have been so grossly exploited to influence a cause that bears all the earmarks of another world war in the making. . . . Such remarks only tend to arouse suspicion and alienate the cause of Buddhism in the eyes of the public.'[61] Kadota's public denunciation of Yamazaki appeared first in *The Forum,* postwar organ of the reactivated Honpa Hongwanji YMBA.

REORGANIZATION AND EXPANSION OF
BUDDHIST YOUTH PROGRAMS

Soon after it was reorganized in 1946, the YMBA greatly expanded its program of social, educational, and recreational activities. In April 1947, the association was incorporated as an eleemosynary organization and officially designated as the Young Buddhist Association (YBA) of Honolulu. Under the capable and enterprising leadership of a popular hero of the 442nd Combat Team, Mineo Yamagata, who became executive secretary of the YBA in 1951, the association's program was extended to include a busy schedule of oratorical and essay contests; song and dance festivals; judo, ballet, and physical fitness classes; picnics and bazaars; and bowling, tennis, swimming, golf, and volleyball tournaments. The annual Inter-Island Convention was revived, too, and again became one of the most effective means of strengthening the ties of friendship and unity among the young Shin-shū Buddhists of Hawaii. Convention themes have focused on the role of Buddhism as an instrument for the promotion of world peace and as a bridge between East and West.

A number of YBA projects soon attracted community and national attention as it became evident that the postwar Buddhist youth movement in Hawaii was the finest of its kind anywhere in the world. In 1948, the YBA erected and dedicated, on the Honpa Hongwanji grounds, a memorial plaque bearing the names of 374 American Buddhists who had perished in the war. At the same time, members of the association dispatched a petition to Secretary of Defense James Forrestal asking that a Buddhist priest be awarded a chaplaincy in the United States Army. Then, too, since it had come to the attention of YBA officials that hundreds of Buddhists had perished in the war with misleading identification tags,* the Hawaii Federation of Young Buddhists sent a request to the War Department that the letter 'B' for Buddhist be included among religious identification tags. No action was taken on the petition for a chaplaincy, but the letter 'B' was eventually added to the government's identification system.

There were other landmarks in the postwar history of the Honpa Hongwanji youth movement. In 1948 a 'Rainbow' Chapter of the YBA was organized at the University of Hawaii, and in 1949 the YBA became a participating member, a Red Feather agency, of the Honolulu Community Chest. In 1951 the Quartermaster General in Washington, D.C., notified the Hawaii Federation of Young Buddhists that the Dharma Cakra (Buddhist wheel symbolizing the Noble Eightfold Path) had been accepted by the War Department as an appropriate grave marker for the Buddhist war dead. After February 21, 1951,† the symbol was inscribed on headstones in national cemeteries at the expense of the government.[62] In 1954 the National Boy Scout Council officially recognized the Buddhist Boy Scout Sangha Award (a ribbon to which was attached the Dharma Cakra). Four years later, the YBA initiated the Sangha (Brotherhood) Club program designed to supplement the extracurricular activities of the public schools. Sangha Club members were dedicated to the promotion of fellowship and responsible citizenship. In recent years, too, the YBA has sponsored lectures and debates on topics like 'The Morality of American Involvement in the Vietnam War,' 'The Morality of the Now Generation,' and other contemporary issues directly affecting the youth of America.

After the war, youth groups associated with the other sects were also reactivated. The Sōto-shū Young Buddhist Associations began holding annual conventions shortly after the conclusion of hostilities, and the Young Shingon Buddhists' Associations (YSBA) have met annually since 1962.

Religious festivals were also revived—not without some curious results. On one occasion, as a regular part of every summer's Bon season, the Jōdo Mission cast adrift an eight-foot skiff full of vegetables, fruits, and burning incense. The Coast Guard did not get word of what the Mission was doing, and in response to many phone calls and reports of 'fire,' 'smoke,' and 'flashing lights,' a cutter was dispatched to the waters off Waikiki to find out what was happening. The ever popular Bon dances were revived and once again became a colorful attraction of the summer

*The only identification marks authorized by the Armed Forces were 'P' for Protestant, 'H' for Hebrew, and 'C' for Catholic. Buddhists had been lumped together and classified under 'P.'
†The government also agreed that markers prior to 1951 would be similarly inscribed if the next of kin requested it.

months for residents and tourists alike. Among other popular tourist attractions was the annual Hanamatsuri, featuring pageants dramatizing the birth and death of Śākyamuni and celebrated, as in prewar years, in April at Kapiolani Park.[63] At the present time, the biggest tourist attraction appears to be the projected Lahaina Buddhist Cultural Park featuring a twelve-foot replica of the famed Buddha of Kamakura. The park has already drawn thousands of curious visitors, and the Jōdo Mission of Lahaina, sponsor of the park project, hopes to have a new temple building on the property by 1974—in time to honor the eight hundredth anniversary of the founding of the Jōdo sect.

Even Buddhist Sunday schools enjoyed a healthy revival. By 1951 the Honpa Hongwanji was operating three hundred such schools. The language schools were also reopened, although they never regained their prewar popularity. It will be recalled that after the war the American press emphatically warned priests returning from the detention camps that Hawaii would not tolerate the revival of the language schools or 'the habits and customs they taught.'[64] In 1946, however, a small group of the Chinese language schools decided to challenge the constitutionality of Act 104. The case was eventually taken to the Ninth Circuit Court in San Francisco, and Act 104 was declared unconstitutional. Once lawyers for the Chinese schools had begun litigation, an aggressive campaign to reopen the Japanese schools was undertaken by Buddhist priests, who were eager to regain their prestige as the educational leaders of their communities. By 1948, fifteen Japanese schools were in operation with a teaching staff of 246 and an enrollment of 13,470. In 1967, the Hongwanji Mission established the first Buddhist English school in America in order to 'provide a sound, liberal primary and elementary education' for Hawaii's English-speaking Buddhists. The old Japanese High School, built in the second decade of the century, was torn down to make room for the new $289,000 school building.[65]

By the 1950s, community opposition to Buddhism and Buddhist institutions had virtually disappeared. No sane person could question any longer the loyalty of Hawaii's Japanese-Americans, and many of the most intransigent Japanese Christians, those champions of a lost cause who had worked like men possessed to curb or eliminate the influence of Buddhism, were no longer among the living. Reverend Shirō Sōkabe, the 'cross between a New England Puritan and a devotee of Bushido,' succumbed on July 2, 1949. Reverend Takie Okumura, who had done all that one man could do to fan the flames of religious bigotry and who persisted to the end in thinking that anyone who criticized him or his policies was ignorant or malicious, died in Queen's Hospital in Honolulu on February 10, 1951, at the age of eighty-seven.[66]

REPLICA OF KAMAKURA BUDDHA AT
LAHAINA BUDDHIST CULTURAL PARK, LAHAINA, MAUI

Okumura's last ambition, characteristic of his boundless and irrational zeal, was to convert the whole Japanese nation beginning with Hirohito. He had even written to General Douglas MacArthur 'advising' that the reconstruction of Japan begin with the immediate Christianization of the country. He volunteered to undertake the project himself, but MacArthur flatly refused him entrance to Japan.[67] Okumura, after all, was not a peacemaker. Painfully conscious of his own rectitude and believing he was justified of all his deeds, he saw no merit in ideas other than his own, and he set out to abolish anything that threatened to foil his plans. Criticism merely enabled him to pose as a martyr. No one, he wrote, had been 'more frightfully misunderstood, attacked, misrepresented and ridiculed than myself,' yet abuses, in the end, he boasted, were his big nourishment.'[68]

In the 1960s, Hawaii's Buddhists, confident that their religion could exert a beneficent and lasting influence on the social and religious life of the Islands, tried in various ways to win public recognition for Buddhism. In January 1963, the Hawaii Buddhist Council circulated a petition (bearing forty-three thousand signatures) to make 'Buddha Day,' April 8, a state holiday so that 'American tolerance and acceptance of "Freedom of Religion" [might] be visibly demonstrated and exemplified to the entire world.'[69] Buddhist priests hoped the bill would provide an impetus for Christians to learn what Buddhism was all about and lead to a better understanding between Christians and Buddhists.[70] The

Star-Bulletin commented, moreover, that the Buddha Day issue aroused some interesting speculation as to the proper role of the government with respect to religious holidays. If only Christian holidays were recognized, did this not constitute an 'establishment of religion' in violation of the First Amendment? Perhaps, too, the paper speculated, to designate only Christian holidays as state holidays was to neglect the rights of the minority.[71] In any case, when Senator Kazuhisa Abe proposed a 'Buddha Day Bill' to establish April 8 as a legal holiday, the press came out solidly in favor of it. In view of the 'large number of Americans of Oriental descent in Hawaii who are followers of the Buddha,' the *Advertiser* commented, Senator Abe's measure 'deserved thorough and respectful consideration.'

Christian clerics were divided on the merits of the bill. Bishop Harry S. Kennedy of the Episcopal Mission saw no reason why Christians should contest it, and a priest of the Honolulu diocese of the Roman Catholic Church was totally in favor of it. But Monsignor Charles A. Kekumano, also of the Honolulu diocese of the Roman Catholic Church, along with Reverend Seido Ogawa, executive director of the Honolulu Council of Churches, had no comment. To spokesmen for the fundamentalist churches, the bill was bad news. Stanton H. Nash, executive secretary of the Hawaii Southern Baptist Convention, strongly opposed it with the fatuous remark that, 'If everybody wanted a holiday for his own faith, I don't know where it would end.'[72]

Things at first looked hopeful. In the state House of Representatives, Democrat Jack Suwa introduced a bill similar to Senator Abe's which passed both the House Government Efficiency and the Public Employment committees. But Senator Abe, meanwhile, had introduced with his Buddha Day measure a companion bill which called for the abolition of Christmas and Good Friday as legal holidays. With this faux pas, the press quickly changed its attitude. Abe's dramatization of Buddhism, the *Advertiser* commented, amounted to an attack on another religion. Nevertheless, a bill fixing April 8 as Buddha Day finally did pass the senate, but not without the provision that April 8 'shall not be construed to be a State holiday.'[73]

In attempting to put their religion before the public in the best possible light, a few Buddhists, understandably enough, became extremely sensitive. In 1965, the Reverend Ryōshō Kondo complained that he and other Buddhists in the community had been 'deeply offended' by the retailing of Zen bath soap, perfume, and cologne in Honolulu stores. The year before, Kondo recalled, a Buddhist group had discussed the matter in detail with the manufacturing company and obtained what appeared to be a sincere apology and a promise that the products would be taken off the market.* Alas, they had not been. Zen cosmetics and toiletries, Kondo thought, were 'in very poor taste and a disgrace to [the] 50,000 Buddhists in the State of Hawaii.'[74]

In the 1960s, in keeping with the new ecumenical spirit in Christian circles, Buddhist priests were occasionally invited to participate in interfaith rites. In January 1966, in an ecumenical first for Hawaii, a multifaith ceremony marked the dedication of the new chancel of Central Union Church. Protestant and Catholic clergymen took part in the service along with a Jewish rabbi with his prayer shawl and Torah and a Buddhist priest attired in traditional *koromo* and *kesa*. The ceremony was concluded with an Old Testament benediction and a message from the Wise Man of the Śākyas delivered by a priest of the Honpa Hongwanji. Dr. Thomas L. Crosby of Central Union correctly observed, 'We made history.'[75] The Christian clergy had, indeed, come a long way since Archbishop Alencastre declined to sit at the same table with Ernest Hunt because Alencastre 'hated' Buddhists.

While Buddhism thus seemed at last to be winning the long battle for community endorsement, Buddhists had not yet solved many of the problems which for decades had crippled the effectiveness of their propaganda. There was still an urgent need for dynamic, English-speaking leaders with the wisdom, tact, and dedication of the late Ernest Hunt.† As late as the mid-1960s, only a dozen or so Buddhist priests could speak English, and without exception, these few were born and educated in Hawaii and were the sons of early missionaries. Most of the priests serving in the Islands were still, as one young priest put it, 'Made in Japan.' There were some Caucasians in Hawaii and on the mainland who

---

*One wonders how Kondo would have reacted to an advertisement that appeared in the *Hilo Tribune* of 22 October 1898. 'Nirvana Tea,' it read, 'is something new in Hilo. Try it.'

†The Venerable Ernest Shinkaku Hunt died at his home in Honolulu on February 7, 1967, at the age of ninety. Following his dismissal from the Honpa Hongwanji and up to the time of his death, he was associated with the Sōtō temple in Honolulu, where he taught the essentials of Buddhism to young members of the Mission, officiated at weddings and funerals, and delivered Sunday morning talks on the Dharma to hundreds of curious tourists. In 1953 he received the Sōtō-Zen ordination at the hands of the Venerable Archbishop Rōsen Takashina, who came from Japan to dedicate the magnificent new Zen temple on Nuuanu Avenue. In 1963 Hunt became the only Caucasian priest in the Western world to receive the high rank of Oshō, and in May of the following year, he was honored at a testimonial dinner at the Reef Hotel in Waikiki. In attendance were prominent secular leaders of the community as well as members of the University of Hawaii's history and philosophy departments. The late Professor Charles A. Moore, founder of the East-West Philosophers' Conferences, was guest speaker. The foregoing was based on personal interviews and the author's presence at the testimonial dinner. See also *Honolulu Star-Bulletin*, 21 September 1963 and 25 May 1964; *Honolulu Advertiser*, 14 September 1963.

sympathized with the teachings of Buddhism and who had even, it was said, expressed an interest in the priesthood. But these haoles, it was observed, did not feel at home in most Buddhist 'churches.' Architecture and religious artifacts which remained distinctly Oriental were thought to alienate Occidentals.[76] Priests were not well paid, and this, more than any other factor, was enough to discourage young men of any race from entering the priesthood. As late as 1963, the highest paid Honpa Hongwanji priest received a salary of about six hundred dollars a month.[77] Immediately after the war, in the hope of inducing boys to enter the priesthood, there was talk of establishing a Buddhist seminary in Hawaii which would at least eliminate the necessity of sending boys to Japan to study for ordination. Later, in 1948, the YBA of Honolulu passed a resolution urging the Hongwanji Mission to promptly establish a seminary and to 'proceed in the training of students desirous of receiving training for the priesthood.' But funds were insufficient and facilities remained inadequate to undertake and subsidize such a project.

In the absence of exemplary, English-speaking leadership, Japanese youths in the postwar decades continued to shift away from Buddhism to Christianity, and many of those who professed Buddhism remained as ignorant as before of the fundamental teachings of the religion. Senator Abe, sponsor of the Buddha Day Bill, admitted, 'I don't know why I'm a Buddhist . . . I don't fully understand the Buddhist religion.'[78] Some Nisei, as they had done in the past, superciliously wrote Buddhism off as, at best, an innocuous opiate for old folks. If the temples and priests could somehow 'rehabilitate' the first-generation Japanese and 'make them feel comfortable in this new atomic age,' wrote a member of the younger generation, Buddhism would have accomplished 'its greatest good.'[79]

Dedicated young Buddhists, however, saw a great future for their faith as an active force for good in the world. The only problem in their minds was how best to clarify the Dharma for non-Buddhists and whether or not to proselytize. At the thirty-second annual Inter-Island YMBA Convention, Larry Ronson, vice-president of the then First National Bank of Hawaii (now the First Hawaiian Bank), advised Buddhists to 'merchandise' their religion —to 'utilize the techniques of persuasion.'[80] Older Buddhists recalled that aggressive missionary endeavor had never been a part of the Buddhist tradition. But Buddhist youths remembered that Gautama had sent out some sixty disciples in all directions from Benares to preach the Dharma and that Shinran had preached his *tariki-kyō* in the provinces and villages of Japan in a manner which could hardly have been described as passive.[81] At mid-century, when groups like the Sōka Gakkai were giving Buddhism a bad name abroad, and later on, when Gautama's teachings were exploited in Southeast Asia by fanatics and warmongers, Hawaii's conscientious young Buddhists reasoned that to set forth and clarify the teachings of Śākyamuni had become a moral imperative.

The Honpa Hongwanji also resolved to boost its efforts to put Buddhism before the public. The Mission began to broadcast its English services, and in August 1965, the legislative assembly of the Mission resolved to create a research and planning committee for matters involving 'overseas propagation.'[82]

By this time, Buddhists, old and young, with an eye on the future, were doing some serious thinking about certain vital questions. Did Buddhism, as it was being preached in Hawaii and on the mainland, accurately represent the teachings of the Enlightened One? What teachings and values within the rich tradition of Buddhism were most applicable to the contemporary needs of Western man? What ought to be emphasized by Buddhist spokesmen in their efforts to adapt the Dharma to Western cultures and civilization?

Unfortunately, errors of the past were not exposed and corrected. In the name of tolerance, but at the expense of philosophical integrity, Buddhist priests and teachers had for centuries permitted their followers the luxury of professing and practicing every kind of superstitious nonsense in the name of Buddhism. As Western writers had been quick to point out, such persons, for all their scholarly pretensions, had prostituted the teachings of Gautama by abiding a nauseating amount of 'accumulated rubbish.'[83] As late as the 1960s, in family worship among the Japanese, the Buddha shared honors with the Christ and the Shinto fox deity—so far had the principle of accommodation (*hōben*) exceeded the dictates of reason and common sense. To acknowledge and respect the merits of religious beliefs and practices which lay outside the pale of Gautama's teaching was one thing; to expediently incorporate such beliefs or practices into the Body of the Law, however irreconcilable they may have been with the essential Dharma, was quite another.

Then there was the serious and still unresolved problem of how Buddhists ought to respond to the commands of Caesar. A universal religion which wholly adapts or too readily submits to national or ethnic considerations sooner or later defeats itself. Men like Jisho Yamazaki were certainly a disgrace to Buddhism. Yet to boast, as some Buddhists did, that postwar Buddhism was 'strongly imbued with the American spirit'[84] was not necessarily a step in the right direction.

Shin-shū Buddhists did take a step in the right direction, however, when they resolved after the war to run their own affairs. Before the war, bishops of the Honpa Hongwanji had been appointed by the chief abbot of the home temple in Kyoto, but in August 1946, priests and lay officials of the Honpa Hongwanji elected their own bishop for the first time.[85] Later on, in August 1967, another event of exceptional significance took place. At a two-day 'diocesan meeting,' the Mission elected its first English-speaking bishop. The new *rinban* was Kanmo Imamura, Hawaiian-born son of the late Bishop Yemyō Imamura. In the spirit of his distinguished father, the new Bishop Imamura declared that the message of Gautama was one that 'all the world can understand and [one] that all the world needs.' The American press, listening to his message *and* the spirit in which it was uttered, expressed confidence that the new bishop (whose tolerance seemed to be based not on indifference but on a genuine interest in ideas other than his own and in the people who upheld them) would not only widen the Mission's influence, but also contribute to 'a broadened understanding of Buddhism.'[86]

OUTLOOK FOR THE FUTURE

Today these expectations seem likely to be fulfilled if Buddhists of all sects fully cooperate with each other in devising effective and appropriate methods of expounding and propagating the Dharma. Soon after the war, one priest affirmed that a very important thing for the future of Buddhism in Hawaii was 'the unification of all Buddhist sects.'[87] That may be so, but even more important is the selection by all Buddhist sects of persons with great tolerance and tact to preach the Dharma. Another 'Archbishop Kirby' would be disastrous. In a country where belief in a transcendent deity and immortality of the soul continue to have a hold on so many people, there are some things about which all spokesmen of the Dharma might do well to maintain a Noble Silence. On the other hand, some things ought to be emphasized. One of these is the close kinship Buddhism has with America's noblest ideals. Buddhism's teaching that life is One is certainly democratic in the best sense of the word, and no other religion has with greater insistency stressed the American faith in equality of opportunity. Siddhārtha Gautama believed in an aristocracy, not of birth, privilege, or rank, but of spiritual and moral accomplishment alone. He was thus, as Ernest Hunt said long ago, the first great democrat.

Another prominent local Buddhist, George Wright, once affirmed that the greatest lesson Buddhism had to teach the West was that of direct, individual responsibility. This is another valid and timeless point deserving of emphasis. In Buddhism, man's position is supreme; he alone, individually and collectively, is responsible for his past, present, and future. At its best, Buddhism implicitly warns against attributing to legendary or mythical beings those powers, good and evil, which lie within the human mind and heart; at its best, it explicitly condemns idolatrous submission to the state and the blind submission of individuals to mass movements. No religion, moreover, has had greater respect for the sanctity of the individual than Buddhism. Decades ago, the *Friend* remarked that the Christian idea of the inherent worth of the individual was not shared by Eastern philosophies of life. Nothing is further from the truth. As a young Shin-shū priest stated in 1963, Buddhism teaches that the whole business of life is the fulfillment of the individual personality. According to the *Buddha-Dharma*, however, such fulfillment means cultivating one's unique and only half-developed talents for the moral enlightenment and spiritual enrichment of mankind. It does not connote, as it so often has in the West, a kind of carefree 'rugged individualism.' There is no room in the Buddha's thought for an individualism which exploits others or ignores discipline in the name of 'freedom' or for one which wallows in sensuality or self-pity, doing little or nothing to alleviate the suffering of other men. Moreover, where Christian theologians have traditionally taught that man is unique because he has an 'immortal soul' destined for union with God, the Buddha taught that preoccupation with one's own 'soul' frequently made a man vain or selfish and too often obscured his vision of That One Reality which underlies and permeates all life. The Wise Man of the Śākyas believed that men were precious, not because they had separate souls, but because they were the supreme architects of the moral universe and because their gradual spiritual maturity from life to life revealed the 'infinite possibilities of the innate Buddha-nature.'[88]

Whatever the future holds for Buddhism in the United States, its spokesmen in the Hawaiian Islands confidently met and overcame a series of initial setbacks and persistent obstacles in order to provide the necessary moral and spiritual leadership of the Japanese community in Hawaii for more than a half century. Descendants of the early missionaries thus can take just pride in all those 'fine and elevating deeds that the pioneers accomplished'[89] as they transmitted to a new land and a new breed some of the finest elements of Eastern thought and culture. Two decades ago Governor Ingram M. Stainback paid a well-earned and fitting tribute to Buddhist leadership and influence in the Islands. Buddhism, he said, had undoubtedly contributed to the welfare and good of the community. 'Its teachings made its followers good citizens, good neighbors, kindly men and women.'[90] No religion could be expected to do more.

Bishops of the Honpa Hongwanji Mission of Hawaii

Bishop Yemyō Imamura (1899–1932)
Bishop Zuigi Ashikaga (1933–1935)
Bishop Gikyō Kuchiba (1935–1946)
Bishop Ryūten Kashiwa (1946–1948)
Bishop Kōdō Fujitani (1948–1952)
Bishop Zenu Aoki (1952–1958)
Bishop Chitoku Morikawa (1958–1963)
Bishop Shojitsu Ohara (1963–1967)
Bishop Kanmo Imamura (1968–)

Notes

DOCUMENTARY MATERIALS FOR
THIS STUDY ARE IN THE EXTENSIVE FILES
of the State Archives which contain the correspondence and
reports of Hawaiian officials and important political personages.
The Hawaiian Sugar Planters' Association Library contains
valuable 'Project Files,' Department of Commerce Bulletins,
surveys on labor conditions, and the annual reports of various
sugar companies. The author also had access to the HSPA Public
Relations File (1933–1946) from a private collection.

Portions of the private papers of such individuals as Frank C.
Atherton, former president of Castle & Cooke, Ltd., and former
governor Wallace R. Farrington were invaluable in evaluating
the reaction of prominent Americans to Buddhist penetration of
the Islands. The private collection of the late Venerable Ernest
Shinkaku Hunt, including personal letters written by and to the
English *bhikshu*; newspaper clippings; and articles from the
British Buddhist and the *Buddhist Child* were most helpful in
assessing the work of the Honpa Hongwanji English Department,
1927–1936.

On file at the Hawaiian Mission Children's Society Library
are the correspondence and official reports of Christian clergymen
which reflect the Christian reaction to the extension of Buddhist
propaganda in the Islands. Also at the HMCS Library are the
annual reports of the Hawaiian Evangelical Association; issues of
the highly informative Christian periodical, the *Friend*; Minutes of

the Japanese Committee of the HEA; and the *Official Minutes* and *Journals* of the annual sessions of the Pacific Mission of the Methodist-Episcopal Church. *Year Books* of Central Union Church are on file at the church library on Beretania Street in Honolulu. Most helpful in appreciating the impact of Buddhist propagandizing on the Christian community were the private papers of the Reverend Takie Okumura, 'leader of the opposition.'

Data relating to the origins of Buddhism in Hawaii were obtained primarily from Japanese sources in the Oriental Collection, University of Hawaii Library. Among the most useful of these were Sakae Morita's *Hawaii Nihonjin Hattenshi* [History of the Japanese Development in Hawaii], Hidegorō Fujii's *Shin Hawaii* [New Hawaii], and Yemyō Imamura's *Hawaii Kaikyōshi* [History of the Hawaiian Missionary Work]. Supplementary information concerning the expansion of Buddhism in Hawaii was pieced together from local newspapers, annual reports of youth groups affiliated with the Buddhist sects, books, pamphlets, and reports of missionary activities published by Buddhist organizations. Some of these printed materials are currently available at the HMCS Library. The writer also had access to rare copies of the *Dōbō*, a YMBA publication, which are part of the private collection of the late Ernest Hunt. Annual reports of the Hawaii Federation of Young Buddhists were made available to me by Mineo Yamagata of the YBA of Honolulu.

With the exception of an interview with Ernest Hunt conducted by Mrs. K. Culver and a report by Dr. Adeline Babbitt for UNESCO (both reflecting the religious confusion of the Japanese in Hawaii during the war years), very little material on Buddhism is contained in the Hawaii War Records Depository at the University of Hawaii.

Occasional papers of the Hawaiian Historical Society and several issues of *Social Process in Hawaii*, copublished by the Sociology Club and the Romanzo Adams Social Research Laboratory of the University of Hawaii, provided corroborative data on significant prewar developments on the Hawaiian political scene and facets of postwar Buddhist history.

A wealth of information, unattainable elsewhere, was obtained through personal interviews with Buddhist and Christian clergymen and prominent members of the secular Buddhist community. Letters to the author from the Reverend Kanmo Imamura, son of the late Bishop Yemyō Imamura and now bishop of the Honpa Hongwanji, also contained much helpful information.

ABBREVIATIONS

AH	Public Archives of Hawaii
AJA	Americans of Japanese Ancestry
CIP	Counter Intelligence Police
FBI	Federal Bureau of Investigation
HA	*Honolulu Advertiser*
HEA	Hawaiian Evangelical Association (the Hawaiian Board)
HHS	Hawaiian Historical Society
HMCS	Hawaiian Mission Children's Association
HSB	*Honolulu Star-Bulletin*
HSPA	Hawaiian Sugar Planters' Association
HWRD	Hawaii War Records Depository
IBI	International Buddhist Institute
PCA	*Pacific Commercial Advertiser* (later the *Honolulu Advertiser*)
UHOC	Oriental Collection, University of Hawaii Library
YBA	Young Buddhist Association of Honolulu
YMBA	Young Men's Buddhist Association
YSBA	Young Shingon Buddhist Association
YWBA	Young Women's Buddhist Association

CHAPTER I

1. Hermann Oldenberg, *Buddha: His Life, His Doctrine, His Order* (London, 1882), p. 276.
2. August Karl Reischauer, *Studies in Japanese Buddhism* (New York, 1917), p. 210; Maurice Percheron, *The Marvellous Life of the Buddha* trans. Adrienne Foulk (New York, 1960), p. 5; Oldenberg, *op. cit.,* p. 182; W. E. Soothill, *The Lotus of the Wonderful Law or The Lotus Gospel* (Oxford, 1930), p. 30.
3. Edmund Holmes, *The Creed of Buddha* (London, 1957), p. 199.
4. Christmas Humphreys, *A Popular Dictionary of Buddhism* (New York, 1963), p. 32 (hereafter cited as *A Popular Dictionary*).
5. Ernest S. Hunt, *Essentials and Symbols of the Buddhist Faith* (Honolulu, 1955), p. 11 (hereafter cited as *Essentials and Symbols*).
6. *Ibid.,* p. 8.
7. Christmas Humphreys, *Buddhism* (Great Britain, 1954), p. 109.
8. Humphreys, *A Popular Dictionary*, p. 34; A. J. Bahm, *Philosophy of the Buddha* (London, 1958), p. 93.
9. Max Weber, *The Religion of India*, trans. and ed. by Hans H. Geith and Don Martindale (Glencoe, Illinois, [1958]), pp. 243, 254; Humphreys, *Buddhism*, p. 49.
10. Hunt, *Essentials and Symbols*, p. 10.
11. Soothill, *op. cit.,* p. 44; Weber, *op. cit.,* p. 254.
12. Soothill, *op. cit.,* p. 2.

13. Junjirō Takakusu and Charles A. Moore, eds., *The Essentials of Buddhist Philosophy*, 3rd ed. (Honolulu, 1956), pp. 127–128.
14. Ernest R. Hughes, *Religion in China* (New York, 1950), p. 69; Humphreys, *A Popular Dictionary*, p. 110.
15. Ryūsaku Tsunoda, William de Bary, and Donald Keene, comps., *Sources of Japanese Tradition* (New York, 1959), p. 93.
16. *Ibid.,* p. 99; Kenneth Scott Latourette, *A Short History of the Far East*, 3rd ed. (New York, 1957), p. 200.
17. Hajime Nakamura, *The Ways of Thinking of Eastern Peoples* (Tokyo, 1960), pp. 288, 292–293; Shao Chang Lee, *Popular Buddhism in China* (Honolulu, 1939), p. 8.
18. Hughes, *op. cit.,* pp. 67, 68; Herrlee G. Creel, *Chinese Thought from Confucius to Mao Tse-Tung* (New York, 1960), p. 158; Arthur F. Wright, *Buddhism in Chinese History* (Stanford, 1959), pp. 98–100; Sir Charles Eliot, *Japanese Buddhism* (New York, 1959), pp. 94, 96–97.
19. W. G. Aston, *Shinto: the Way of the Gods* (New York, 1905), pp. 7–9.
20. Tsunoda, de Bary, and Keene, *op. cit.,* p. 24.
21. *Ibid.,* pp. 268–269.
22. A. K. Reischauer, *op. cit.,* p. 211.
23. Basil Hall Chamberlain, *Things Japanese* (London, 1905), p. 78; Daisetz T. Suzuki, *Buddhist Philosophy and Its Effects on The Life and Thought of The Japanese People* (Japan, 1936), pp. 17, 18 (hereafter cited as *Buddhist Philosophy and Its Effects*).
24. D. T. Suzuki, *Buddhist Philosophy and Its Effects*, p. 18; Edwin O. Reischauer, *Japan Past and Present* (New York, 1956), p. 71.
25. Tsunoda, de Bary, and Keene, *op. cit.,* pp. 284, 285.
26. *Ibid.,* pp. 176, 287, 288.
27. *Ibid.,* 116, 120.
28. *Ibid.,* p. 116.
29. E. O. Reischauer, *op. cit.,* pp. 45–49; Latourette, *op. cit.,* p. 215.
30. Tsunoda, de Bary, and Keene, *op. cit.,* p. 191.
31. R. F. Johnston, *Buddhist China* (London, 1913), pp. 96, 97; A. K. Reischauer, *op. cit.,* pp. 111, 222; Kenju Masuyama, trans., *The Tanni Shō* (Kyoto, 1962), p. 92.
32. Beatrice Lane Suzuki, 'The Conception of the Bodhisattva According to the Shin Sect,' *Hawaiian Buddhist Annual* (Honolulu, 1931), p. 5.
33. A. K. Reischauer, *op. cit.,* p. 110.
34. Yejitsu Okusa, *Principal Teachings of the True Sect of Pure Land* (Tokyo, 1910), pp. 4–6; Beatrice Lane Suzuki, 'Jiriki and Tariki: Two Aspects of Mahayana Buddhism,' *Hawaiian Buddhist Annual* (Honolulu, 1934), p. 63.
35. Masuyama, *The Tanni Shō*, p. 54.
36. Suzuki, 'Jiriki and Tariki,' p. 65.
37. Nishu Utsuki, *The Shin Sect: A School of Mahayana Buddhism* (Kyoto, 1937), p. 27.
38. Tsunoda, de Bary, and Keene, *op. cit.,* p. 219.
39. *Ibid.,* p. 220.

40. Takakusu and Moore, *op. cit.*, p. 179; Tsunoda, de Bary, and Keene, *op. cit.*, p. 224; Latourette, *op. cit.*, pp. 221, 222; Humphreys, *A Popular Dictionary*, p. 135; Humphreys, *Buddhism*, pp. 174–175.
41. A. K. Reischauer, *op. cit.*, p. 124.
42. *Ibid.*, p. 117. For a detailed study of the impact of Zen discipline on the *samurai* class, see Kaiten Nukariya's *The Religion of Samurai* (London, 1913).
43. Ernest S. Hunt, *Gleanings from Soto-Zen* (Honolulu, 1960); A. K. Reischauer, *op. cit.*, p. 117; Takakusu and Moore, *op. cit.*, p. 161.
44. Lafcadio Hearn, *Kokoro* (London, 1905), p. 252; Daisetz T. Suzuki, *Outlines of Mahayana Buddhism* (New York, 1963), p. 47.
45. Arthur L. Sadler, *A Short History of Japan* (Sydney, 1946), p. 88.
46. Hideo Kishimoto, comp., and John F. Howes, trans., *Japanese Religion in the Meiji Era* (Tokyo, 1956), p. 101.
47. E. O. Reischauer, *op. cit.*, p. 78.
48. Tsunoda, de Bary, and Keene, *op. cit.*, p. 314.
49. Utsuki, *op. cit.*, p. 32; E. O. Reischauer, *op. cit.*, p. 78.
50. Tsunoda, de Bary, and Keene, *op. cit.*, pp. 307, 311; E. O. Reischauer, *op. cit.*, pp. 85, 86.
51. Utsuki, *op. cit.*, pp. 35, 36.
52. Tsunoda, de Bary, and Keene, *op. cit.*, pp. 443, 445; Toshimitsu Hasumi, *Zen in Japanese Art: A Way of Spiritual Experience* (New York, 1962), p. 61.
53. Hasumi, *op. cit.*, pp. 45, 46.
54. E. O. Reischauer, *op. cit.*, pp. 103–104, 106.
55. Tsunoda, de Bary, and Keene, *op. cit.*, p. 642.
56. Robert N. Bellah, *Tokugawa Religion* (Illinois, 1957), pp. 98, 99, 101–103; Tsunoda, de Bary, and Keene, *op. cit.*, pp. 593, 594.
57. Arthur Hyde Lay, 'Japanese Funeral Rites,' *Transactions of the Asiatic Society of Japan* 14 (1891): 532, 534.
58. E. O. Reischauer, *op. cit.*, p. 97.
59. Tsunoda, de Bary, and Keene, *op. cit.*, pp. 314, 617.
60. E. O. Reischauer, *op. cit.*, pp. 110, 112, 114.
61. Ralph S. Kuykendall, 'The Earliest Japanese Labor Immigration to Hawaii,' University of Hawaii *Occasional Papers* 25 (1935): 10, 11–12 (hereafter cited as 'Earliest Japanese Labor').

CHAPTER 2

1. Ralph S. Kuykendall, *The Hawaiian Kingdom, 1854–1874: Twenty Critical Years* (Honolulu, 1953), p. 136; Hilary Conroy, *The Japanese Frontier in Hawaii 1868–1898* (Berkeley, 1953), p. 9; Theodore Morgan, *Hawaii: A Century of Economic Change 1778–1876* (Cambridge, Mass., 1948), pp. 140–145.
2. Ralph S. Kuykendall, *The Hawaiian Kingdom, 1778–1854: Foundation and Transformation* (Honolulu, 1947), pp. 325–326.
3. Kuykendall, *The Hawaiian Kingdom, 1854–1874*, p. 143.
4. *Hawaiian Almanac and Annual for 1894*, p. 72.
5. Kuykendall, *The Hawaiian Kingdom, 1854–1874*, p. 76.
6. *Ibid.*, p. 77.

7. Ernest K. Wakukawa, *A History of the Japanese People in Hawaii* (Honolulu, 1938), p. 16; Ralph S. Kuykendall and A. Grove Day, *Hawaii: A History* (Honolulu, 1961), p. 126.

8. Kuykendall and Day, *op. cit.*, p. 126; Kuykendall, *The Hawaiian Kingdom, 1854–1874,* pp. 153, 180.

9. Kuykendall, 'Earliest Japanese Labor,' p. 4; Kuykendall, *The Hawaiian Kingdom, 1854–1874*, p. 183.

10. Conroy, *op. cit.*, p. 16.

11. Kuykendall, 'Earliest Japanese Labor,' p. 10; Conroy, *op. cit.*, pp. 9, 27; Y. B. Goto, 'Samurai Who Came in 1868 Likes Islands,' *HSB*, 19 February 1935.

12. Conroy, *op. cit.*, p. 23.

13. *Ibid.*, p. 24.

14. *Ibid.*, p. 15.

15. Ryūkichi Kihara, *Hawaii Nihonjin Shi* [A History of the Japanese in Hawaii]. (Tokyo, 1935), p. 398; Conroy, *op. cit.*, pp. 21, 27; *HSB*, 19 February 1935.

16. Yasutarō Sōga, *Gojūnenkan no Hawaii Kaiko* [Reflections on Fifty Years in Hawaii]. (Osaka, 1953), p. 137 (hereafter cited as *Gojūnenkan*).

17. *HSB*, 19 February 1935, 22 September 1960.

18. Conroy, *op. cit.*, p. 27; Wakukawa, *op. cit.*, p. 28; Sōga, *op. cit.*, p. 137; Kihara, *op. cit.*, p. 211; Aston, *Shinto: The Way of the Gods*, p. 66; *Sunday Star-Bulletin and Advertiser,* 5 May 1968.

19. David J. Lee to Board of Immigration, 19 June 1968, Department of the Interior, AH; Kihara, *op. cit.*, p. 401; *Hawaiian Almanac and Annual for 1910*, p. 158; Conroy, *op. cit.*, p. 27.

20. 'Local Happenings Fifty Years Ago,' *HA*, 16 June 1918; Conroy, *op. cit.*, p. 28; Kihara, *op. cit.*, p. 404; *HSB* 19 February 1935.

21. *PCA*, 1 July 1871, 13 January 1872.

22. Kihara, *op. cit.*, p. 405; Conroy, *op. cit.*, p. 28.

23. *Hawaiian Almanac and Annual for 1917*, p. 153; *PCA*, 23 May 1909.

24. *PCA*, 21 October 1871, 27 April 1872.

25. *HSB*, 7 March 1914; Sanford B. Dole, 'The Old Bethel,' *Friend,* December 1913; *Friend,* November 1937.

26. George L. Chaney, *Aloha!* (Boston, 1880), p. 264; Ethel Damon, *The Stone Church at Kawaiahao* (Honolulu, 1945), pp. 94–95.

27. *PCA,* 7 May 1870, 18 February 1871.

28. Kuykendall and Day, *op. cit.*, pp. 77, 133; John P. Erdman, 'The Hawaiian Board of Missions,' *Friend,* April 1937.

29. Kuykendall, *The Hawaiian Kingdom, 1778–1854*, pp. 101, 126; Kuykendall and Day, *op. cit.*, p. 76.

30. *PCA*, 27 April 1872.

31. Kuykendall, *The Hawaiian Kingdom, 1778–1854*, p. 174.

32. 'Memo of Japanese for "Scioto,"' Department of Interior, AH; Conroy, *op. cit.*, p. 29.

33. Memorandum for Bishop & Co., 17 March 1870; M. McInerny to J. W. Hutchison, 3 August 1868; J. H. Wood to F. W. Huchison [*sic*], 26 January 1870; Theo. H. Davies to C. T. Gulick, Secretary

of Board of Immigration, 21 January 1870, Department of Interior, AH; *PCA*, 11 July 1868, 27 February 1869.

34. Sakae Morita, *Hawaii Gojūnenshi* [A Fifty Year History of Hawaii] (Honolulu, 1919), pp. 132, 331; *PCA*, 1 January 1870; Conroy, *op. cit.*, pp. 35, 41.

35. Morita, *Hawaii Gojūnenshi*, p. 331; Conroy, *op. cit.*, pp. 40, 41; Zengi Yagisawa, 'Hawaii ni okeru Nihon iminshi no issetsu' [A Chapter in the History of Japanese Emigration to Hawaii], *Shakai Keizai Shigaku* [Studies in Social and Economic History], 4, no. 5 (August 1934): 46, 47.

36. Conroy, *op. cit.*, pp. 42, 43.

37. 'Local Happenings Fifty Years Ago,' *HA*, 30 June 1918; Takie Okumura, *Seventy Years of Divine Blessings* (Honolulu, 1939), p. 83, (hereafter cited as *Seventy Years*); *Hawaii Buddhist Annual* (Honolulu, 1932), p. 205; *HSB*, 19 February 1935, 22 September 1960; Bradford Smith, *Americans from Japan* (New York, 1948), p. 34.

38. Conroy, *op. cit.*, pp. 16–17, 44; Kuykendall, 'Earliest Japanese Labor,' pp. 25–26.

39. A. F. Judd to Rev. J. R. Boydd, 18 January 1873; 'Lunalilo, The Sixth King of Hawaii,' HHS *Annual Report*, 1935, p. 27.

40. A. F. Judd to Rev. J. R. Boydd, 20 January 1873, 26 February 1874; HHS *Annual Report*, 1935, pp. 30, 34.

41. 'Sketch of Lunalilo's Life,' HHS *Annual Report*, 1935, p. 43; Kuykendall and Day, *op. cit.*, p. 143.

42. Wakukawa, *op. cit.*, p. 43; Kuykendall and Day, *op. cit.*, pp. 156, 165; William N. Armstrong, *Around the World with a King* (New York, c. 1904), p. 84.

43. Conroy, *op. cit.*, p. 59.

44. *PCA*, 9 February 1885; *Planter's Monthly*, March 1885, p. 663.

45. Conroy, *op. cit.*, p. 67; Smith, *op. cit.*, p. 38.

46. *PCA*, 12 February 1885; Tsuncichi Yamamoto, 'Japanese Yesterdays in Hawaii,' *HSB*, 14 October 1967.

47. *PCA*, 17 February, 3 March 1885.

48. Conroy, *op. cit.*, p. 68.

49. *Ibid.*, p. 81.

50. Lafcadio Hearn, *Glimpses of Unfamiliar Japan, II* (Boston, 1894), p. 482.

51. *Hawaii Hōchi*, 16 February 1935.

CHAPTER 3

1. See Sir Henry Howorth, 'Buddhism in the Pacific,' *Journal of the Royal Anthropological Institute of Great Britain and Ireland* 51 (1921): 284–286.

2. 'Delano's Account of the Shipwrecked Japanese,' extract from *A Narrative of Voyages and Travels . . . in the Pacific Ocean and Oriental Islands. Papers of the HHS*, no. 18, 27 October 1931, p. 22.

3. *Polynesian*, 1 August 1840; Morita, *Hawaii Gojūnenshi*, p. 91.

4. James J. Jarves, *Scenes and Scenery in the Sandwich Islands* (London, 1844), pp. 77–78.

5. *Ibid.*, p. 78; *Polynesian*, 1 August 1840.

6. Rufus Anderson, *History of the Mission of the American Board of Commissioners for Foreign Missions to the Sandwich Islands* (Boston, 1874), p. 234; Morita, *Hawaii Gojūnenshi,* p. 110; Wakukawa, *A History of the Japanese People in Hawaii*, p. 6.

7. Yamato Ichihashi, *Japanese in the United States: A Critical Study of the Problems of the Japanese Immigrants and.Their Children* (Stanford, 1922), p. 222.

8. Hidegorō Fujii, *Shin Hawaii* [New Hawaii], (Tokyo, 1902), p. 172; Morita, *Hawaii Gojūnenshi*, p. 397.

9. *PCA*, 28 February, 4 March 1889.

10. *Daily Bulletin*, 2 March 1889.

11. Alfred S. Hartwell, 'Forty Years of Hawaii Nei,' HHS *Annual Report*, 1947, p. 10; *PCA*, 20 November 1888; *Friend*, May 1890.

12. Elmer Hill, *Six Months in Honolulu* (Santa Barbara, 1885), p. 7.

13. *Friend*, February 1889; *Daily Bulletin*, 4, 28 March 1889; *PCA*, 27 February, 4 March 1889; 'A Steamer Arrival in 1889,' *HSB* (Annual Progress Edition, IV), 29 January 1963.

14. 'Royal Hawaiian Band Organized in 1871,' *Paradise of the Pacific*, January 1888; Albert P. Taylor, *Under Hawaiian Skies* (Honolulu, 1922), p. 234.

15. *PCA*, 22 January 1900; Sereno E. Bishop, 'Religion in Hawaii,' *Paradise of the Pacific*, February 1894; *Friend*, February 1888; Mary Dillingham Frear, 'A Brief Record of Kaumakapili Church,' *Friend*, April 1938.

16. Yemyō Imamura, *Honpa Hongwanji Hawaii Kaikyōshi* [A History of the Missionary Work of the Honpa Hongwanji in Hawaii] (Honolulu, 1918), p. 75 (hereafter cited as *Hawaii Kaikyōshi*); Sakae Morita, *Hawaii Nipponjin Hattenshi* [History of the Japanese in Hawaii] (Honolulu, 1915), p. 326; Morita, *Hawaii Gojūnenshi*, p. 398; *Gomonshu Gojunkyō Kinen Hawaii Honpa Hongwanji Kyōdan Enkakushi* [A History of the Hawaii Honpa Hongwanji Mission] (Honolulu, 1954), pp. 4, 11 (hereafter cited as *Hawaii Honpa Hongwanji Kyōdan Enkakushi*); Fujii, *op. cit.*, p. 172; Kihara, *Hawaii Nihonjin Shi*, p. 219; *Friend*, April 1889.

17. *Daily Bulletin*, 2, 4 March 1889; *Friend*, May 1889; *Annual Report*, HEA, 1889.

18. Lorrin A. Thurston, *Memoirs of the Hawaiian Revolution* (Honolulu, 1936), p. 44 (hereafter cited as *Memoirs*).

19. Hartwell, *op. cit.*, p. 16.

20. Thurston, *Memoirs*, p. 26.

21. Kuykendall and Day, *Hawaii: A History*, p. 166.

22. Hill, *op. cit.*, p. 16.

23. Thurston, *Memoirs*, pp. 129, 130; Sanford B. Dole, *Memoirs of the Hawaiian Revolution* (Honolulu, 1936), p. 47.

24. Kuykendall and Day, *op. cit.*, pp. 170, 171; Dole, *op. cit.*, p. 50.

25. Ethel M. Damon, *Sanford B. Dole and His Hawaii* (Palo Alto, 1957), p. 215.

26. Robert N. L. Lee, 'Vertical Mobility Among the Chinese in Hawaii' (master's thesis, University of Hawaii, 1951), pp. 17, 19; *Friend*, October 1888.
27. *Friend*, January 1887, May 1889.
28. *Hawaiian Almanac and Annual for 1890*, p. 89; *Hawaiian Almanac and Annual for 1894*, pp. 73, 75.
29. *Friend*, October 1887; Herbert H. Gowen, *The Paradise of the Pacific: Sketches of Hawaiian Scenery and Life* (London, 1892), p. 138.
30. S. W. Thwing, 'Chinese New Years,' *Friend*, March 1904; *PCA*, 7 February 1902, 5 October 1903.
31. E. Z. Simmons, 'Why Chinamen Worship,' *Friend*, January 1889.
32. Kum P. Lai, 'The Natural History of the Chinese Language School in Hawaii' (master's thesis, University of Hawaii, 1935), p. 30; Harry T. Morgan, *Chinese Symbols and Superstitions* (California, 1942), p. 54.
33. *PCA*, 24 September 1870.
34. 'Meeting of Stockholders of Kohala Sugar Co., 26 October 1864,' Frank C. Atherton Papers, Honolulu, Hawaii.
35. John P. Erdman, 'A Brief Historical Sketch of the Hawaiian Board of Missions,' *The Centennial Book: One Hundred Years of Christian Civilization 1820–1920* (Honolulu, 1920), p. 77 (hereafter cited as *The Centennial Book*); Mrs. Charles M. Hyde, 'The Work Among the Chinese, Japanese and Portuguese Races,' *Friend*, December 1902; William Kwai Fong Yap, 'Early Chinese Christians in Hawaii,' *Friend*, June 1928.
36. *PCA*, 11 July 1868, 24 September 1870; *Friend*, 1 May 1868, 2 August 1869, 1 January 1870, June 1870, January 1872.
37. *Friend*, January 1882, September 1885, August 1877; Chaney, *Aloha!*, p. 17.
38. Chaney, *op. cit.*, p. 17.
39. Yap, *op. cit.*; *Friend*, January 1881, January 1882, June 1928.
40. *Friend*, October 1881, December 1883, June 1889.
41. 'Address at the Chinese Church, 2 January 1881, by Rev. S. C. Damon,' *Friend*, 4 January 1881.
42. *Friend*, June 1881, March 1904.
43. *Friend*, October 1887.
44. Morgan, *Hawaii*, p. 150.
45. *Friend*, July 1882.
46. Edwin G. Burrows, *Hawaiian Americans* (Connecticut, 1947), p. 53; *Friend*, April 1882, October 1887.
47. *Friend*, July 1882, January 1887.
48. *Friend*, April 1882; *Daily Bulletin*, 18 December 1883.
49. C. K. Yang, *Religion in Chinese Society* (Berkeley, 1961), pp. 58–63.
50. See Morgan, *op. cit.*, p. 103; Johnston, *Buddhist China*, p. 101.
51. Hughes, *Religion in China*, pp. 73, 80; Soothill, *The Lotus of the Wonderful Law*, p. 31.
52. Hearn, *Glimpses of Unfamiliar Japan*, II, p. 486.
53. A. K. Reischauer, *op. cit.*, p. 109.
54. *Friend*, October 1887.

55. Gowen, *op. cit.*, p. 138.

56. *Friend,* April 1889.

57. *Daily Bulletin,* 22 March 1889.

58. *Hawaiian Almanac and Annual for 1890*, pp. 11, 27; Yagisawa, 'Hawaii ni okeru Nihon no issetsu,' p. 60.

59. Imamura, *Hawaii Kaikyōshi*, p. 97.

60. G. O. Nakyama [*sic*] to Minister Foreign Affairs, 26 October 1886, Department of Interior, AH; Imamura, *Hawaii Kaikyōshi*, p. 97.

61. *Kona Echo,* 27 March 1898; Morita, *Hawaii Nipponjin Hattenshi*, p. 327; Conroy, *The Japanese Frontier in Hawaii*, p. 87.

62. Imamura, *Hawaii Kaikyōshi*, p. 97; Kihara, *op. cit.*, p. 219.

63. Morita, *Hawaii Nipponjin Hattenshi*, p. 327; Morita, *Hawaii Gojūnenshi*, p. 398.

64. Yemyō Imamura, *Hawaii Kaikyō Shiyō* [Summary History of Missionary Work in Hawaii] (Honolulu, 1918), p. 253; D. Howard Hitchcock, 'Town of Hilo,' *Paradise of the Pacific,* August 1895; *Hawaii Honpa Hongwanji Kyōdan Enkakushi*, p. 139; 'Local Happenings Fifty Years Ago,' *HA,* 9 June 1918; *PCA,* 9 March 1919; Morita, *Hawaii Nipponjin Hattenshi*, p. 343.

65. *PCA,* 12 November 1888.

66. *Daily Bulletin,* 29 May 1889; Imamura, *Hawaii Kaikyōshi*, p. 75.

67. Jirō Okabe to Rev. Dr. Hyde, 15 July 1889, HMCS.

68. *Friend,* July 1888.

69. Conroy, *op. cit.*, pp. 86, 87.

70. Imamura, *Hawaii Kaikyōshi*, pp. 75–77.

71. See passenger list for *Kinau* in the *Daily Bulletin,* 8 June 1889.

72. Jirō Okabe to Dr. Hyde, 15 July 1889, HMCS.

73. Imamura, *Hawaii Kaikyōshi*, p. 75; *Hawaii Honpa Hongwanji Kyōdan Enkakushi,* p. 11.

74. Kihara, *op. cit.*, p. 219; Fujii, *op. cit.*, p. 173; Morita, *Hawaii Nipponjin Hattenshi*, p. 326; Imamura, *Hawaii Kaikyōshi*, p. 75.

75. Morita, *Hawaii Nipponjin Hattenshi*, p. 326; Morita, *Hawaii Gojūnenshi*, p. 397; Fujii, *op. cit.*, p. 173.

76. Fujii, *op. cit.*, p. 173; Morita, *Hawaii Nipponjin Hattenshi*, pp. 326, 327.

77. Albert M. Craig, John K. Fairbank, and Edwin O. Reischauer, *East Asia: The Modern Transformation* (Boston, 1965), p. 268; Kishimoto and Howes, *Japanese Religion in the Meiji Era*, p. 113.

78. Kishimoto and Howes, *op. cit.*, pp. 115, 121; G. B. Sansom, *The Western World and Japan: A Study in the Interaction of European and Asiatic Cultures* (New York, 1950), pp. 389, 469; Daniel Holtom, *Modern Japan and Shinto Nationalism: A Study of Present-Day Trends in Japanese Religions,* rev. ed. (Chicago, 1947), p. 127; Eliot, *Japanese Buddhism*, pp. 315, 316.

79. Utsuki, *The Shin Sect,* pp. 34, 35; Sansom, *The Western World and Japan*, p. 469; Kishimoto and Howes, *op. cit.*, pp. 131, 132, 141, 143.

80. Kishimoto and Howes, *op. cit.*, pp. 146–151; Craig, Fairbank, and Reischauer, *op. cit.*, p. 270.

81. Morita, *Hawaii Nipponjin Hattenshi*, p. 327; Morita, *Hawaii Gojūnenshi*, pp. 398, 402; Fujii, *op. cit.*, p. 173; Imamura, *Hawaii Kaikyōshi*, p. 76.

82. *Friend,* June 1889.

CHAPTER 4

1. Imamura, *Hawaii Kaikyōshi*, pp. 78, 79–81; Lillian S. Mesick, 'Buddhist Propaganda in Hawaii,' *Paradise of the Pacific*, March 1903; Morita, *Hawaii Gojūnenshi*, p. 423.

2. Imamura, *Hawaii Kaikyōshi*, p. 78; Morita, *Hawaii Gojūnenshi*, p. 400; Fujii, *Shin Hawaii*, pp. 173–174; Morita, *Hawaii Nipponjin Hattenshi*, pp. 328–329; passenger manifest, *Yamashiro Maru*, 1 October 1889, 3 April 1890, AH.

3. Jirō Okabe to O. P. Emerson, 28 May 1890, HMCS.

4. *Ibid.*

5. Kihara, *Hawaii Nihonjin Shi*, p. 219; Fujii, *op. cit.*, p. 173; Morita, *Hawaii Gojūnenshi*, p. 400; Morita, *Hawaii Nipponjin Hattenshi*, p. 328; passenger manifest, *Yamashiro Maru*, 28 April 1891, AH.

6. *Friend*, December 1890, June 1891; Jenichiro Oyabe to Rev. Emerson, 13 July 1895, HMCS.

7. *Friend,* June 1891.

8. *Friend,* May 1888.

9. *Friend,* March 1885.

10. *Friend,* May 1887, May 1888; *Annual Report,* HEA, June 1888.

11. *Friend,* June 1890; John P. Erdman, 'The Hawaiian Board of Missions,' *Friend*, April 1937.

12. *Friend,* November 1887, May 1888.

13. Kihara, *op. cit.*, p. 212; *Friend*, November, December 1887, August 1888; Bishop J. P. Newman, *Story of the Japanese Methodist Episcopal Church in Hawaii*, HMCS; *Official Journal* of the Fourth Annual Session of the Pacific Japanese Mission of the Methodist-Episcopal Church, 1903, pp. 7, 27.

14. *Friend,* December 1887, January 1888.

15. *Friend,* August 1888; *PCA*, 19 July 1888.

16. *Friend,* March, July 1888, April 1889; *PCA*, 27 July 1888.

17. Okumura Papers, Honolulu, Hawaii.

18. *Friend,* February 1889; *PCA*, 19 July, 13 November 1888.

19. *Friend,* December 1888, February 1889; Sōga, *Gojūnenkan*, p. 137; *PCA*, 13 November 1888.

20. *Friend,* August 1888; Rev. William D. Westervelt, *The Japanese Consul,* (pamphlet, n.d.) HMCS.

21. *Friend,* August 1888.

22. Westervelt, *op. cit.*; *Friend,* August 1888.

23. *Friend,* July 1888.

24. *Friend,* August, December 1888, February 1889.

25. *Friend,* May, December 1888; Tarō Andō, 'The Origin of Temperance Work in Hawaii,' in T. Okumura, *Seventy Years*, pp. 76, 78;

Mrs. C. M. Hyde, 'The Work Among the Chinese, Japanese and Portuguese Races,' *Friend,* December 1902, February, October 1889.

26. *Friend,* February 1889.
27. *Friend,* July 1888; *Daily Bulletin,* 4 March 1889.
28. *Friend,* February 1889.
29. *Daily Bulletin,* 5 October 1889; *Friend,* November 1889, May, September 1890; *Official Journal,* Pacific Japanese Mission of the Methodist-Episcopal Church, 1903, p. 27.
30. John P. Erdman, 'The Hawaiian Board of Missions,' *Friend,* April 1937; T. Okumura, *Seventy Years,* p. 16; Rev. F. S. Scudder, 'Our Japanese Mission,' *Annual Report,* HEA, 1910, p. 35; *Friend,* August 1895.
31. T. Okumura, *Seventy Years,* p. 16; *HA,* 30 November 1939; 'History from Our Files,' *HA,* 9 January 1941; *Friend,* February, June 1891, September 1892.
32. *Friend,* August 1913.
33. Jenichiro Oyabe, *A Japanese Robinson Crusoe* (Chicago, 1898), pp. 201, 205.
34. *Ibid.,* p. 205; Jenichiro Oyabe to Rev. Emerson, 13 July 1895, HMCS.
35. *Kona Echo,* 2 October 1897; *Friend,* November 1895, HMCS.
36. Rev. F. S. Scudder, *op. cit.,* p. 34; Kihara, *op. cit.,* p. 212; Morita, *Hawaii Gojūnenshi,* p. 375; *Friend,* August 1889.
37. Jirō Okabe to Rev. O. P. Emerson, 24 February 1890; *Friend,* March 1890; *Annual Report,* HEA, June 1890.
38. *Annual Report,* HEA, June 1893; *Friend,* September 1892, January 1905; Morita, *Hawaii Gojūnenshi,* p. 378.
39. Jirō Okabe to O. P. Emerson, 28 May, 13 November 1890, HMCS.
40. Jirō Okabe to O. P. Emerson, 20 January 1891, HMCS.
41. K. Hoshina to O. P. Emerson, 17 February 1892, HMCS.
42. Thurston, *Memoirs,* p. 228.
43. *Ibid.,* p. 229.
44. Alfred S. Hartwell, 'Forty Years of Hawaii Nei,' HHS *Annual Report,* 1947, p. 20; Thurston, *Memoirs,* pp. 64, 65.
45. See Ralph S. Kuykendall, *The Hawaiian Kingdom, 1874–1893: The Kalakaua Dynasty* (Honolulu, 1967), p. 603.
46. *PCA,* February to 22 March 1894, inclusive.
47. Wakukawa, *Japanese People in Hawaii,* pp. 84–86.
48. See Wray Taylor to T. Masaki, Esq., Consul for Japan, 9 November 1891, Department of the Interior, AH.
49. *Hilo Tribune,* 8 August 1898.
50. *Friend,* July 1889, July 1895.
51. Ken'ichirō Hoshina to O. P. Emerson, 28 March 1892; Jirō Okabe to O. P. Emerson, 18 March 1892; *Friend,* April 1892.
52. *Friend,* March 1951; T. Okumura, *Seventy Years,* pp. 93, 99, 101, 106, 181, 182, 187; Umetarō Okumura, *My Father* (pamphlet, n.d.), p. 3.
53. U. Okumura, *loc. cit.*; T. Okumura, *Seventy Years,* pp. 105, 112.

54. T. Okumura, *Seventy Years*, p. 112.

55. *Ibid.*, p. 12; *Friend*, February 1912.

56. T. Okumura, *Seventy Years*, pp. 21, 22.

57. U. Okumura, *My Father*, pp. 19, 20; *Friend,* March 1902; Jisoo Sanjume, 'An Analysis of the New Americans Conference from 1927–1938' (master's thesis, University of Hawaii, 1939), p. 7; Okumura Papers.

58. John P. Erdman, 'A Brief Historical Sketch of the Hawaiian Board of Missions,' in *The Centennial Book*, p. 77; Rev. F. S. Scudder, *op. cit.*, p. 35; *Annual Report*, HEA, 1924, p. 23; *PCA*, 7 October 1913; T. Okumura, *Thirty Years of Christian Mission Work Among the Japanese in Hawaii* (Honolulu, 1917) (hereafter cited as *Thirty Years of Christian Mission Work*); *Friend*, April 1892, November 1895, August 1898; T. Okumura, *Seventy Years*, p. 17.

59. T. Okumura, *Seventy Years*, p. 17; Imamura, *Hawaii Kaikyōshi*, p. 78; Morita, *Hawaii Nipponjin Hattenshi*, pp. 328–329; Kihara, *op. cit.*, p. 219; *Friend*, March 1896.

60. *Friend*, December 1890; T. Okumura, *Thirty Years of Christian Mission Work*.

CHAPTER 5

1. T. Okumura, *Seventy Years,* p. 19; U. Okumura, *My Father*, p. 10.

2. Morita, *Hawaii Gojūnenshi*, pp. 420–421; *Yōjō no Hikari, Dendo Kinen* [Mid-Ocean Illumination, Commemorating Missionary Work] (Hawaii: Jōdo Mission of Hawaii, 1934), p. 4 (hereafter cited as *Yōjō no Hikari*); Kihara, *Hawaii Nihonjin Shi*, p. 219; Morita, *Hawaii Nipponjin Hattenshi*, pp. 345, 346.

3. Morita, *Hawaii Nipponjin Hattenshi*, p. 329; Fujii, *Shin Hawaii*, p. 174; Imamura, *Hawaii Kaikyōshi*, p. 78; Kōdō Matsunami, *A Glimpse of Hawaii Buddhism* (pamphlet, n.d.), p. 2.

4. *Hawaiian Almanac and Annual for 1898*, pp. 47, 133.

5. Morita, *Hawaii Nipponjin Hattenshi*, pp. 328, 329; Fujii, *op. cit.*, p. 174; Imamura, *Hawaii Kaikyōshi*, p. 78; 'The Center of Buddhism in Hawaii,' *PCA*, 28 April 1912; Lillian S. Mesick, 'Buddhists Build New Temple in Hawaii,' *Paradise of the Pacific*, December 1918; Morita, *Hawaii Gojūnenshi*, p. 401; Matsunami, *op. cit.*, p. 2.

6. *Yamato Shimbun*, 26 January, 6 February 1897, in Katsuhiro Jinzaki, *Selected Translations from The Yamato (renamed as the Yamato Shimbun in 1896 and currently published under the name of the Hawaii Times), the Oldest Existing Japanese Newspaper in Hawaii, 1895–1898*, from *Bulletin* of Faculty of Liberal Arts 4 (Nagasaki University, 1964).

7. Imamura, *Hawaii Kaikyōshi*, pp. 79–83.

8. *Hawaii Honpa Hongwanji Kyōdan Enkakushi*, p. 140; Morita, *Hawaii Nipponjin Hattenshi*, p. 330.

9. Morita, *Hawaii Nipponjin Hattenshi*, p. 330; Imamura, *Hawaii Kaikyōshi*, pp. 84, 85; Kihara, *op. cit.*, p. 219; 'The Center of Buddhism in Hawaii,' *PCA*, 28 April 1912.

10. Yemyō Imamura, *Chōshōin Kaikoroku* [The Recollections of

Chōshōin] (Hawaii, 1937), p. 153; Mesick, 'Buddhist Propaganda in Hawaii'; idem, 'Buddhists Build New Temple in Hawaii'; Morita, *Hawaii Nipponjin Hattenshi*, p. 331; Yemyō Imamura, *History of the Hongwanji Mission in Hawaii* (Honolulu, 1918), pp. 2, 15.

11. Imamura, *Hawaii Kaikyōshi*, pp. 85, 86, 90, 420; Morita, *Hawaii Nipponjin Hattenshi*, pp. 329–331; Sōga, *Gojūnenkan*, p. 132; Imamura, *History of the Hongwanji Mission in Hawaii*, p. 2; Lillian S. Mesick, 'Buddhism in Hawaii,' *Paradise of the Pacific*, October 1906; idem, 'Buddhist Propaganda in Hawaii' and 'Buddhists Build New Temple in Hawaii.'

12. 'The Center of Buddhism in Hawaii,' *PCA*, 28 April 1912; Morita, *Hawaii Nipponjin Hattenshi*, p. 330; Imamura, *Hawaii Kaikyōshi*, p. 86.

13. *Hilo Tribune*, 1 October 1898.

14. *Nippu Jiji*, 30 December 1932.

15. Passenger statement, *Gaelic*, 21 February 1899, AH; Mesick, 'Buddhists Build New Temple in Hawaii'; 'The Center of Buddhism in Hawaii,' *PCA*, 28 April 1912; Morita, *Hawaii Nipponjin Hattenshi*, pp. 331, 337; Imamura, *Hawaii Kaikyōshi*, p. 87.

16. Imamura, *Hawaii Kaikyōshi*, p. 86; Fujii, *op. cit.*, p. 175; Bureau of Conveyances, Book 189, pp. 109–111, AH.

17. Morita, *Hawaii Nipponjin Hattenshi*, p. 331; Fujii, *op. cit.*, pp. 177–178; Imamura, *Hawaii Kaikyōshi*, pp. 94, 97; *Friend*, February 1898.

18. Joseph Barber, Jr., *Hawaii: Restless Rampart* (New York, 1941), pp. 131–132; Kuykendall and Day, *Hawaii: A History*, p. 190; Imamura, *Hawaii Kaikyoshi*, pp. 90, 93; Morita, *Hawaii Nipponjin Hattenshi*, p. 332.

19. Morita, *Hawaii Nipponjin Hattenshi*, p. 332; Imamura, *Hawaii Kaikyōshi*, pp. 89, 90, 92; T. Okumura, *Thirty Years of Christian Mission Work*; T. Okumura, *Seventy Years*, pp. 24–25; Sōga, *op. cit.*, p. 132.

20. Imamura, *Hawaii Kaikyōshi*, pp. 89, 93; Kihara, *op. cit.*, p. 219; Morita, *Hawaii Nipponjin Hattenshi*, p. 331; *Hawaii Honpa Hongwanji Kyōdan Enkakushi*, p. 14.

21. *PCA*, 26 November 1900.

22. Imamura, *Hawaii Kaikyōshi*, pp. 91, 95.

23. *Friend*, August 1900; *Yamato Shimbun*, 24 July 1900, 21 May, 20, 23 July 1901; *PCA*, 20, 22 July 1901; *Golden Anniversary Edition, YBA 1900–1951*; Imamura, *Hawaii Kaikyōshi*, pp. 92, 95, 103; *Hawaii Honpa Hongwanji Kyōdan Enkakushi*, p. 15.

24. Morita, *Hawaii Nipponjin Hattenshi*, pp. 345–346; Morita, *Hawaii Gojūnenshi*, p. 421; Fujii, *op. cit.*, p. 183; Kihara, *op. cit.*, p. 219; *Yōjō no Hikari*, p. 4.

25. *PCA*, 10 February 1899; *Annual Report*, HEA, June 1898; *Friend*, June, July 1898, August 1900.

26. Kuykendall and Day, *op. cit.*, pp. 187, 189, 194; William A.

Simonds, *Kamaaina: A Century in Hawaii* (Hawaii, 1949), pp. 59, 61.

27. *Hawaiian Almanac and Annual for 1900*, p. 160.
28. *Hawaiian Almanac and Annual for 1900*, pp. 160, 161; *PCA*, 2 February 1899; *Friend*, February 1899.
29. *PCA*, 22 November 1899.
30. Kuykendall and Day, *op. cit.*, p. 190; *PCA*, 22 November 1899; Barber, *op. cit.*, p. 132; *Hawaiian Almanac and Annual for 1900*, pp. 163, 164; *Yamato Shimbun*, 2 August 1900; Wakukawa, *Japanese People in Hawaii*, p. 125.

CHAPTER 6

1. *Yamato Shimbun*, 13, 20, 27 August 1898.
2. *Hawaiian Almanac and Annual for 1901*, pp. 173–174; Barber, *Hawaii: Restless Rampart*, pp. 132–133; *Hawaii Hōchi*, 16 February 1935; Miki Saito to Agents of the Japanese Emigration Companies, 18 September 1899, AH; C. A. Peterson to Hon. Alexander Young, President, Board of Immigration, 4 May 1900, AH; Fujii, *Shin Hawaii*, pp. 419–424; *PCA*, 26 September 1903.
3. Yemyō Imamura, *A Short History of the Hongwanji Buddhist Mission in Hawaii* (Honolulu, 1931), p. 3 (hereafter cited as *A Short History*).
4. Imamura, *Hawaii Kaikyōshi*, pp. 93, 100, 104–105, 107–109; Imamura, *History of the Hongwanji Mission in Hawaii*, pp. 16, 17; Morita, *Hawaii Nipponjin Hattenshi*, pp. 330, 334, 335–336, 337, 339, 341, 342–343, 346–347, 350–351, 355–356, 359; *Yōjō no Hikari*, p. 4; Fujii, *Shin Hawaii*, p. 183; Kihara, *Hawaii Nihonjin Shi*, pp. 213, 221; *Yamato Shimbun*, 25 March 1905; *Nichiren-shū Rikkyō Kaisō Nanahyakunen Hawaii Kaikyō Gojūshūnen Kinen Dai Keisan-e; Kinen Shashin Narabini Hosshu Godairi Junkyō Kiroku* [Great Commemorative Celebration of the 700th Anniversary of the Establishment and the 50th Anniversary of the Beginning of Mission Work in Hawaii of the Nichiren Sect; Commemorative Photographs and Records of the Propagation of the Teachings by Representatives of the Lord Abbot], (Nichiren Mission of Hawaii) pp. 4, 5 (hereafter cited as *50th Anniversary of the Beginning of Mission Work in Hawaii*).
5. Yemyō Imamura, 'The Propaganda of the Island Buddhists,' *PCA*, Fiftieth Anniversary Edition, 2 July 1906, p. 89; Kiyoshi K. Kawakami, *Asia at the Door* (New York, 1914), p. 229; *Friend*, August 1904; Souno Inouye, 'How the Japanese Came to the Islands,' *HA*, 30 April 1935.
6. Matsunami, *A Glimpse of Hawaii Buddhism*; Miki Saitō to Agents of the Japanese Emigration Companies, 18 September 1899, Department of the Interior, AH; *Yamato Shimbun*, 31 August 1899; Mesick, 'Buddhist Propaganda in Hawaii'; Imamura, *Hawaii Kaikyōshi*, p. 143; *Friend*, August 1903.
7. *Friend*, February 1894, March 1898, May 1899; *Annual Report*,

HEA, 1894; *Kona Echo*, 11 Dec 1897; *Official Minutes*, Hawaiian Mission of the Methodist-Episcopal Church, 1906, HMCS.

8. *Friend*, April 1892; *PCA*, 6 February 1908; *Annual Report*, HEA, 1909; *Official Minutes*, Hawaiian Mission of the Methodist-Episcopal Church, 1906 and 1907, HMCS; 'Educational Campaign Among Plantation Japanese For the Year 1934,' Okumura Papers.

9. 'Educational Campaign Among Plantation Japanese For the Year 1934,' Okumura Papers; Morita, *Hawaii Nipponjin Hattenshi*, pp. 334–335, 337, 339, 341, 343, 346–348, 351–353; Imamura, *Hawaii Kaikyōshi*, p. 269; Morita, *Hawaii Gojūnenshi*, pp. 423–424.

10. U.S. Commissioner of Labor *Reports* for 1901 and 1902, *Senate Documents*, No. 169, 57th Cong., 1st sess., 1902, and No. 181, 57th Cong., 2nd sess., 1903; *PCA*, 17 April 1905; Morita, *Hawaii Gojūnenshi*, p. 343; Wakukawa, *Japanese People in Hawaii*, pp. 135, 143.

11. Imamura, *A Short History*, pp. 4, 9, 10; idem, *Hawaii Kaikyōshi*, p. 143; Tachibana, *The Ethics of Buddhism* (London, 1926), p. 134; Hearn, *Kokoro*, p. 37.

12. Imamura, *Chōshōin Kaikoroku*, pp. 159–160; Wakukawa, *op. cit.*, p. 131; C. A. Peterson to Hon. Alexander Young, 4 May 1900, AH; *PCA*, 21 July 1904; Fujii, *op. cit.*, p. 417.

13. Sōga, *Gojūnenkan*, p. 134; *Hawaiian Star*, 1 August 1904; Kanmo Imamura to Louise Hunter, 28 August 1963.

14. *Dōbō*, May 1941; *Hawaiian Star*, 1 August 1904; *Friend*, August 1904; Tsunoda, de Bary, and Keene, *Sources of Japanese Tradition*, p. 212.

15. Imamura, *Hawaii Kaikyōshi*, p. 120; Morita, *Hawaii Nipponjin Hattenshi*, pp. 338, 342, 349–350; *Hawaii Honpa Hongwanji Kyōdan Enkakushi*, pp. 20, 22.

16. *Friend*, August 1903, July 1904, April 1905, May 1906.

17. T. Okumura, *Thirty Years of Christian Mission Work*; *Friend*, August 1904; *PCA*, 6 February 1908; *Official Minutes*, Hawaiian Mission of the Methodist-Episcopal Church, 1907, p. 24; *Official Minutes*, Hawaiian Mission of the Methodist-Episcopal Church, 1908, p. 18.

18. *Friend*, October 1903, January, April, August 1904; Morita, *Hawaii Nipponjin Hattenshi*, pp. 292, 334–335, 337, 339, 340, 346–348, 350–351, 353, 387, 390; *Annual Report*, HEA, 1906, p. 54; *PCA*, 2 October 1907; Morita, *Hawaii Gojūnenshi*, pp. 373, 380, 381–382, 385–386, 387; *Official Minutes,* Hawaiian Mission of the Methodist-Episcopal Church, 1907; Imamura, *Hawaii Kaikyōshi*, pp. 100, 104, 119–120, 259, 270, 348, 508.

19. Morita, *Hawaii Gojūnenshi*, pp. 379, 388; idem, *Hawaii Nipponjin Hattenshi*, pp. 344–346, 349, 350; Imamura, *Hawaii Kaikyōshi*, pp. 108–109; T. Okumura, *Seventy Years*, p. 180; *Annual Report*, HEA, 1906, p. 83; *PCA*, 17, 18 November 1907; *Yōjō no Hikari*, pp. 4, 5; Kihara, *op. cit.*, p. 221.

20. Morita, *Hawaii Nipponjin Hattenshi*, pp. 344, 347–348; *Hawaii Honpa Hongwanji Kyōdan Enkakushi*, p. 142.

21. *PCA*, 17 February 1906; Imamura, *Hawaii Kaikyōshi*, pp. 111–112; Morita, *Hawaii Nipponjin Hattenshi*, p. 333.
22. Carter to A. J. Campbell, Esq., 9 July 1906; *Executive Document* 4526, AH.
23. Quoted in *PCA*, 10 August 1906.
24. *PCA*, 12 July 1906.
25. *Yamato Shimbun*, 17 July 1905.
26. Kishimoto and Howes, *Japanese Religion in the Meiji Era*, p. 168; Imamura, *Hawaii Kaikyōshi*, pp. 108–109, 115–116; *Yamato Shimbun*, 5 January, 2 March 1905.
27. Theodore Roosevelt to William H. Taft, *Theodore Roosevelt Letters*, *IV* (Cambridge, Massachusetts: Harvard University Press, 1951–1954), p. 1118. Selected and edited by Elting E. Morison.
28. Thompson and Clemons to Hon. Walter F. Frear, 24 September 1907, AH; *PCA*, 5 October 1907; Morita, *Hawaii Nipponjin Hattenshi*, p. 333; *Hawaii Honpa Hongwanji Kyōdan Enkakushi*, p. 19.
29. Imamura, *Hawaii Kaikyōshi*, pp. 117–119, 120; *Hawaii Honpa Hongwanji Kyōdan Enkakushi*, pp. 20, 142.
30. Interview with Rev. Yoshiaki Fujitani, 9 July 1963; Rev. Ernest Hunt, 'The Buddhist Bon Festival,' *HA*, 20 August 1958.
31. *PCA*, 18 August 1918.
32. *HSB*, 14 August 1924.
33. Masaharu Anesaki, *Religious Life of the Japanese People* (Tokyo, 1938), p. 78.
34. Mesick, 'Buddhism in Hawaii,' p. 18.
35. *Friend*, November 1909.
36. George F. Nellist, ed., *The Story of Hawaii and Its Builders* (Honolulu, 1925), p. 759; *Annual Report*, HEA, 1924, p. 18; *PCA*, 2 October 1907; 'A Brief Historical Sketch of the Hawaiian Board of Missions,' *Friend*, April 1937.
37. *Friend*, May 1902; *Year Book*, Central Union Church, 1907, p. 49.
38. *PCA*, 2 October 1907; *Friend*, February 1909.

CHAPTER 7

1. Imamura, *Hawaii Kaikyōshi*, pp. 562–566.
2. *Official Minutes*, Hawaiian Mission of the Methodist-Episcopal Church, 1906, p. 28; Imamura, *History of the Hongwanji Mission in Hawaii*, pp. 11–12.
3. *PCA*, 7 February 1899.
4. *Friend*, May 1899, August 1902; *Yamato Shimbun*, 21 August 1905; *Kona Echo*, 2 October 1897; Sōga, *Gojūnenkan*, pp. 11–17; Fujii, *Shin Hawaii*, pp. 412–416; Miki Saitō to Agents of the Japanese Emigration Companies, 18 September 1899, AH; C. A. Peterson to Alexander Young, 30 October 1899, AH; *Labor in Hawaii*, 5 January 1900, Bureau of Foreign Commerce, Department of State, HSPA Library; U.S. Commissioner of Labor Report for 1901, *Senate Documents*, No. 169, 57th Cong., 1st sess., 1902.

5. W. O. Smith to Henry E. Cooper, 17 November 1897, AH; Tachibana, *The Ethics of Buddhism*, pp. 127, 270; A. J. Bahm, *Philosophy of the Buddha* (London, 1958), p. 79; *Friend*, March 1898.

6. *Friend*, October 1893, January 1897, March 1903, September 1905.

7. *Hilo Tribune*, 4 January 1893, 26 March 1898; *Friend*, October 1893.

8. Conroy, *The Japanese Frontier in Hawaii*, p. 86; *Hilo Tribune*, 30 April 1898; *Kona Echo*, 27 March 1897; *Hawaii Herald*, 11 November 1897.

9. Fujii, *op. cit.*, p. 176; Imamura, *Hawaii Kaikyōshi*, p. 76.

10. *HA*, 7 July 1928, 23 September 1960; *HSB*, 22 August 1946; *Hawaii Honpa Hongwanji Kyōdan Enkakushi*, pp. 31, 47.

11. Imamura, 'The Propaganda of the Island Buddhists'; idem, *Hawaii Kaikyōshi*, pp. 87, 350, 551–554, 555–556; idem, *Chōshōin Kaikoroku*, pp. 156–157; John F. Embree, *Acculturation Among the Japanese of Kona, Hawaii* (Wisconsin, 1941), pp. 105–106 (hereafter cited as *Acculturation*); *PCA*, 18 November 1907; Mesick, 'Buddhists Build New Temple in Hawaii'; Kawakami, *Asia at the Door*, p. 231; *Hawaii Hōchi*, 16 February 1935.

12. Imamura, *Chōshōin Kaikoroku*, p. 155; idem, *Hawaii Kaikyōshi*, p. 77.

13. Imamura, *Chōshōin Kaikoroku*, p. 155; idem, *Hawaii Kaikyōshi*, pp. 556–557; *Hawaii Hōchi*, 16 February 1935.

14. Imamura, *Hawaii Kaikyōshi*, p. 558; *Hawaii Hōchi*, 16 February 1935.

15. During the early missionary period in Hawaii, the Honpa Hongwanji in Kyoto delegated all available funds to the propagation of the faith in Korea and China. See Imamura, *A Short History*, p. 28.

16. Embree, *Acculturation*, pp. 106, 107; *Yōjō no Hikari*, p. 4.

17. *Friend*, August 1903; U.S. Commission of Labor *Report*, *Senate Documents*, No. 432, 4th Cong., 1st sess., 1915, p. 60; Fujii, *op. cit.*, p. 153.

18. Sōga, *op. cit.*, pp. 275, 276; *Nippu Jiji*, 24 April 1934; *HSB*, 28 June 1924; *HA*, 24 July 1924; Kawakami, *op. cit.*, p. 232.

19. Embree, *Acculturation*, pp. 46–47, 107, 114; personal interviews with Rev. Yoshio Hino, 25 January 1965 and Dr. Kazuo Miyamoto, 16 January 1965.

20. Fujii, *op. cit.*, p. 184; personal interview with Rev. Kōdō Matsunami, 26 March 1964; *Hawaii Hōchi*, 16 February 1935.

21. *Hawaiian Star*, 13 July 1904.

22. Mesick, 'Buddhists Build New Temple in Hawaii'; 'The Center of Buddhism in Hawaii,' *PCA*, 28 April 1912.

23. Imamura, *History of the Hongwanji Mission in Hawaii*, p. 13; idem, *Hawaii Kaikyōshi*, p. 68; Sōga, *op. cit.*, p. 280; Imamura, *A Short History*, p. 22.

24. Minutes of the Japanese Committee, HEA, 29 July 1903, HMCS.

25. *Friend*, August 1903.

26. Oldenberg, *Buddha* p. 91; Okusa, *Principal Teachings of the True Sect of Pure Land*, p. 15; Hideo Kishimoto, 'Some Japanese Cultural

Traits and Religions,' *Philosophy and Culture East and West* (Honolulu, 1962), p. 251; interview with Rev. Yoshio Hino, 25 January 1965.

27. U.S. Commission of Labor *Report* for 1902, *Senate Documents*, No. 181, 57th Cong., 2nd sess., 1902, p. 37; 'The Center of Buddhism in Hawaii,' *PCA*, 28 April 1912; *HA*, 31 July 1916.

28. *HSB*, 16 February 1935.

29. 'The Center of Buddhism in Hawaii,' *PCA*, 28 April 1912.

30. Imamura, *Chōshōin Kaikoroku*, p. 160; idem, *Hawaii Kaikyōshi*, pp. 46, 383, 460; Kihara, *Hawaii Nihonjin Shi*, p. 225; Morita, *Hawaii Gojūnenshi*, pp. 424, 478; Fujii, *op. cit.*, p. 183; *Hawaii Honpa Hongwanji Kyōdan Enkakushi*, pp. 46, 140; Morita, *Hawaii Nipponjin Hattenshi*, pp. 389, 390, 392.

31. Umetarō Okumura to Dr. Gulick, 25 November 1935, Okumura Papers.

32. *Hawaiian Gazette*, 27 August 1889; *A Survey of Education in Hawaii* (Washington 1920), Bureau of Education, Department of the Interior, *Bulletin* No. 16, pp. 108–109 (hereafter cited as *A Survey of Education*); Takie Okumura, 'My Attitude of Japanese Language School Problem,' Okumura Papers.

33. *PCA*, 13 February 1899.

34. Orramel H. Gulick, 'Hawaii and the Far East,' *Annual Report*, HEA, 1907, p. 82.

35. Katsumi Onishi, 'A Study of the Attitudes of the Japanese in Hawaii Toward the Japanese Language Schools' (master's thesis, University of Hawaii, 1943), p. 9; Frank S. Scudder, 'Work of Rev. Sokabe, 1893–1920,' Minutes of the Japanese Committee, HEA, January 1917–1 January 1925, HMCS; A. G. Hamilton Colket, 'Japanese Schools in Hawaii,' *Friend,* October 1923.

36. *Official Journal,* Pacific Japanese Mission of the Methodist-Episcopal Church, 1903; *Official Minutes*, Hawaiian Mission of the Methodist-Episcopal Church, 1910, HMCS.

37. T. Okumura, *Seventy Years*, p. 41; idem, *Taiheyō no Rakuen* [A Paradise in the Pacific] (Tokyo, 1917), p. 222.

38. T. Okumura, *Seventy Years*, p. 41; Imamura, *Hawaii Kaikyōshi*, pp. 47, 70, 184, 229; *Yamato Shimbun*, 5 May 1902; Imamura, *Chōshōin Kaikoroku,* p. 160.

39. *PCA*, 31 July 1905; Morita, *Hawaii Nipponjin Hattenshi*, pp. 335–336, 337, 387, 389, 390, 391–392; idem, *Hawaii Gojūnenshi*, pp. 424, 480, 482; Imamura, *Hawaii Kaikyōshi*, pp. 259, 267, 274, 281, 288, 298, 303, 317–318, 333, 402–403, 424, 452, 468, 508.

40. *A Survey of Education*, p. 113; statement of the Hon. Samuel W. King, *Hearings* Before the Committee on the Territories, 74th Cong., 1st sess., 1935, p. 13.

41. *Yamato Shimbun*, 10 January, 31 July 1905; letter from Secretary of Labor, *Senate Documents* No. 432, 4th Cong., 1st sess., 1915, pp. 60–61; *A Survey of Education*, p. 114.

42. U.S. Commissioner of Labor *Report, House Documents*, No. 580, 59th Cong., 1st sess., 1906, p. 126; *Senate Documents*, No. 432, 4th

Cong., 1st sess., 1915, p. 60; Imamura, *Hawaii Kaikyōshi*, pp. 231, 232.

43. *Friend,* August 1903; *HA*, 8 January 1923, 30 April 1925; Kawakami, *op. cit.*, p. 228; Albert W. Palmer, *The Human Side of Hawaii* (Honolulu, 1924), p. 107; Morita, *Hawaii Nipponjin Hattenshi*, pp. 334–336, 344, 355–356, 377–379; *Senate Documents*, No. 432, 4th Cong., 1st sess., 1915, p. 60; *A Survey of Education*, p. 113.

44. Imamura, *Chōshōin Kaikoroku*, p. 160; idem, *Hawaii Kaikyōshi*, p. 55; idem, *History of the Hongwanji Mission in Hawaii*, p. 21; U.S. Commissioner of Labor *Report*, *House Documents*, No. 580, 59th Cong., 1st sess., 1906, p. 126.

45. *PCA*, 20, 22 July 1901.

46. *Ibid.*; *PCA*, 6 July 1918; see also Wakukawa, *Japanese People in Hawaii*, pp. 266–268.

47. *Yamato Shimbun*, 15 May 1905; personal interview with Rev. Kōdō Matsunami, 26 March 1964.

48. Tachibana, *op. cit.*, p. 219.

49. Walpola Rahula, *What the Buddha Taught* (New York, 1962), pp. 78–79; Okusa, *op. cit.*, pp. 62–63.

50. Imamura, *Hawaii Kaikyōshi*, pp. 97, 98, 106–107, 112–113.

51. U.S. Commissioner of Labor *Report, Senate Documents* No. 181, 57th Cong., 2nd sess., 1903, p. 37; U.S. Commissioner of Labor *Report, House Documents*, No. 580, 59th Cong., 1st sess., 1906, p. 126; Imamura, *Hawaii Kaikyōshi*, pp. 140, 238; personal interview with Rev. Kōdō Matsunami, 26 March 1964.

52. Thompson and Clemons to Hon. Walter F. Frear, September 1907, AH.

53. *PCA*, 18 May 1907.

54. *Hawaiian Gazette*, 6 May 1904.

55. Barber, *Hawaii: Restless Rampart*, pp. 134, 135.

56. *PCA*, 21 May 1909; 19 June 1909; *Hawaiian Star,* 19 June 1909.

57. Wakukawa, *op. cit.*, p. 179.

58. *PCA*, 8 June 1909; *Hawaiian Star*, 7 June 1909; Wakukawa, *op. cit.*, pp. 179, 182.

59. Fred K. Makino to Hon. W. O. Smith, Secretary, HSPA, January 1909, Department of the Interior, National Archives, *Bureau of Immigration and Naturalization, 1900–1924*, NJE–29, Roll 5 (microfilm).

60. Quoted in *Bulletin* of the Bureau of Labor: Report on Hawaii, Department of Commerce and Labor, May 1911, pp. 740, 741, HSPA Library.

CHAPTER 8

1. *Annual Report*, HEA, 1905, p. 15; 'The Center of Buddhism in Hawaii,' *PCA*, 28 April 1912; Doremus Scudder to W. W. Hall, 18 January 1904; Minutes of the Japanese Committee, HEA, HMCS; *Year Book,* Central Union Church, 1912, p. 61; Rev. William Brewster Oleson, 'The Scribe's Corner,' *Friend*, October 1912; *HA*, 29 December 1919.

2. Imamura, *Hawaii Kaikyōshi*, pp. 129, 132, 530.

3. Imamura, *History of the Hongwanji Mission in Hawaii*, p. 17; Morita, *Hawaii Nipponjin Hattenshi*, pp. 338, 339, 340, 343, 348–349; Imamura, *Hawaii Kaikyōshi*, pp. 61, 64, 66, 124, 126, 128, 131, 135; *PCA*, 24 July 1905; *HA*, 26 May 1926; *HSB*, 16 February 1935; *A Survey of Education*, pp. 110–111.

4. *Annual Report*, HEA, 1906, p. 31; *Official Minutes*, Hawaiian Mission of the Methodist-Episcopal Church, 1907, pp. 19–20.

5. Frank S. Scudder, *Thirty Years of Mission Work for the Japanese of Hawaii and The Call of the Next Decade* (Honolulu, 1917), p. 3; *PCA*, 2 October 1907; *HA*, 20 March 1915; *Annual Report*, HEA, 1916, pp. 41, 65; *Friend*, October, November 1912; T. Okumura, *Seventy Years*, pp. 48, 49; Morita, *Hawaii Gojūnenshi*, pp. 374, 379, 380–381, 382–383, 386–387, 388–389.

6. Scudder, *op. cit.*, pp. 3, 4; *Friend*, April, October 1912, November 1913; Morita, *Hawaii Gojūnenshi*, p. 378; Minutes of the Japanese Committee, HEA, January 1917–1 January 1925, HMCS.

7. Frank S. Scudder, 'The King's Highway,' *Annual Report*, HEA, 1914, pp. 20, 21; *Annual Report*, HEA, 1920, p. 29; U. Okumura, *My Father*, Okumura Papers, p. 18; T. Okumura, *Taiheiyō no Rakuen*, pp. 222, 223; Imamura, *Hawaii Kaikyōshi*, p. 179; *Yamato Shimbun*, 9 March 1905; Morita, *Hawaii Gojūnenshi*, p. 386; *Friend*, April, August 1903, July, October 1911; T. Okumura, *Seventy Years*, p. 41; U.S. Commissioner of Labor *Report, Senate Documents*, No. 181, 57th Cong., 2nd sess., 1903, pp. 36, 37; William Pullar, manager, Honomu Sugar Co., to Mr. George P. Cooke, 15 January 1920; Minutes of the Japanese Committee, HEA, January 1917–1 January 1925, HMCS; Kawakami, *Asia at the Door*, p. 230.

8. Imamura, *Hawaii Kaikyōshi*, pp. 183–190; Kenju Ohtomo, 'Buddhism in Hawaii,' *Pan-Pacific* 4 (January to March 1940): 21; Umetarō Okumura, *Japanese Sunday Schools in Hawaii as Americanization Agencies* (Honolulu, n. d.), Okumura Papers.

9. *PCA*, 21 October 1913; Sidney L. Gulick, *The American-Japanese Problem: A Study of the Racial Relations of the East and the West* (New York, 1914), pp. 109–110.

10. Morita, *Hawaii Nipponjin Hattenshi*, pp. 390, 393; Imamura, *Hawaii Kaikyōshi*, p. 386.

11. Takie Okumura, 'My Attitude of Japanese Language School Problem,' *Paradise Times*, March 1927, Okumura Papers; idem, *Taiheiyō no Rakuen*, p. 231.

12. *Paradise Times*, March 1927, copy in Okumura Papers; *Education of Japanese in Hawaii in Their Own Language*, (Honolulu: Japanese Educational Association, 1919), Misc. File Coms. 1–45, AH.

13. *Hawaiian Almanac and Annual for 1910*, p. 35.

14. Testimony of Wilfred C. Tsukiyama, *Hearings*, Statehood for Hawaii, 75th Cong., 2nd sess., 1938, pp. 470, 471.

15. Imamura, *History of the Hongwanji Mission in Hawaii*, pp. 7, 8, 22, 23; Imamura, *Hawaii Kaikyōshi*, pp. 54–57; Arthur F. Griffiths, *More Race Questions* (Honolulu, 1915), p. 3.

61. Gulick, *Hawaii's American-Japanese Problem*, p. 16.
62. *HA*, 15 August 1918, 11 March 1919; Vaughan MacCaughey, 'Americanization and the Schools of Hawaii,' reprinted from *School and Society* 8, no. 184 (1906–1924): 24–26, Department of the Interior, National Archives, Bureau of Immigration and Naturalization, 1906–1924 (microfilm); *Hawaii Hōchi*, 3, 7 February 1919.
63. Wist, *op. cit.*, p. 171.
64. 'Letters from the People,' *HA*, 4 January 1919.
65. *HA*, 30 January, 7 February 1919; *Hawaii Hōchi*, 15 February 1919.
66. *HA*, 7 March 1919.
67. Misc. File Coms. 1–45, AH; *HA*, 31 March 1919.
68. Misc. File Coms. 1–45, AH.
69. *HA*, 31 March 1919.
70. Misc. File Coms. 1–45, AH; *Senate Journal*, 10th Leg., Reg. Sess. (Honolulu, 1919), pp. 1107, 1189; *HA*, 31 March 1919.
71. *House Journal*, 10th Leg., Reg. Sess. (Honolulu, 1919), pp. 1082–1083; *Senate Journal*, 10th Leg., Reg. Sess. (Honolulu, 1919), p. 762, AH.
72. *HA*, 17 March, 19, 22 April 1919.
73. *HSB*, 17, 28 April 1919.
74. *HA*, 23 April, 2 December 1919; *HSB*, 29 April 1919.
75. *HA*, 8, 20, 28 January, 2, 4 September, 21 October 1919; *HSB*, 17 April 1919; 14 December 1921.
76. *Friend*, October 1910; *HA*, 4 October 1917.
77. *HSB*, 29 March 1919.
78. *HA*, 17 March, 18 October 1919.
79. *Friend*, February 1919; *HA*, 7 February 1919.
80. *HA*, 5 May 1919.
81. *HA*, 5 September 1919.
82. A. F. Judd to Takie Okumura, 19 March 1919, Okumura Papers.
83. *HA*, 29 December 1919.
84. *Ibid.*
85. *HA*, 29 December 1919.
86. See *HA*, 25, 26, 27 July, 6 August, 11 September 1919; *A Survey of Education*, p. 115.

CHAPTER 9

1. *HA*, 2, 4 May 1916.
2. *HA*, 5, 10 May 1916, 14 June 1916.
3. *HA*, 15 May 1916.
4. *HA*, 29 July, 21 September, 23 November 1917; Edward Johannessen, *The Hawaiian Labor Movement: A Brief History* (Boston, 1956), p. 67.
5. *HA*, 2 November, 3 December 1917.
6. *HA*, 23 November, 4 December 1917.
7. *HA*, 3, 8 December 1917.
8. *HA*, 9 December 1917.
9. *HA*, 9, 10 December 1917.

10. Quoted in *HA*, 12 October 1919.

11. *HA*, 24 October 1919; Takashi Tsutsumi, *Senkyūhyaku-nijū Nendo Hawaii Satō Kōchi Rōdō Undō Shi, I* [An Account of the Labor Movement on Sugar Plantations in Hawaii in 1920] (Honolulu, 1921), pp. 68, 75–78.

12. *Controversy Between Japanese Labor and the Sugar Planters of Hawaii* (Honolulu: Federation of Japanese Labor, 1920), pp. 1–2, 7; *Facts About the Strike on Sugar Plantations in Hawaii* (Honolulu: Hawaii Laborers' Association, 1920), AH.

13. Wakukawa, *Japanese People in Hawaii*, pp. 238, 247–248; *Proceedings of the Fourth Annual Meeting of the HSPA*, 29–30 November 1920, p. 5; Johannessen, *op. cit.*, p. 68.

14. *HA*, 5 September, 5 December 1919; *HSB*, 18 February 1920.

15. C. A. Peterson to Hon. Alexander Young, 4 May 1900, Department of the Interior, AH; *Annual Report*, Hawaiian Commercial and Sugar Co., April 1910, p. 9; *PCA*, 14 May 1909.

16. *Proceedings of the Fourth Annual Meeting of the HSPA*, pp. 6–7; *Labor Problems in Hawaii,* 67th Cong., 4th sess., *House Documents,* No. 1717, p. 1.

17. *HA*, 31 October 1919.

18. *HA*, 19 February 1920.

19. 'The Oriental Question,' *The American Legion*, 1923, p. 19; *HA*, 6 January 1920; George R. Carter to Mr. S. Kanda, 24 February 1920, Okumura Papers.

20. T. Okumura, *Seventy Years*, pp. 57–58; extracts from letter of Royden Susumago to Theodore Richards, 13 February 1930, Honolulu Christian Church File, HMCS.

21. Tsutsumi, *op. cit.*, pp. 244–247.

22. *HSB*, 24 January 1920.

23. *HA*, 4 February, 26 March 1920.

24. *HA*, 5 February, 1 March 1920.

25. *HSB*, 7, 25 February 1920.

26. Rahula, *What the Buddha Taught,* p. 82.

27. *HA*, 4, 9, 22 February 1920; *HSB*, 19 February 1920; Tsutsumi, *op. cit.*, pp. 69, 402, 419, 421; *HA*, 4, 5, 27 April 1920.

28. *HA*, 5 April 1920.

29. Wakukawa, *op. cit.*, p. 256; *HA*, 28 February 1920.

30. *HA*, 18, 20 April 1920; *Labor Problems in Hawaii*, serial 7, part I, 67th Cong., 1st sess. (Washington, 1921), p. 235; Tsutsumi, *op. cit.*, p. 372.

31. *Labor Problems in Hawaii*, serial 7, part I, 67th Cong., 1st sess. (Washington, 1921), p. 229; Lorrin A. Thurston, 'The Language School Problem. Why It Has Become a Controversial Issue,' *HA*, 12 September 1922.

32. *HA*, 2 March 1920; *Labor Problems in Hawaii*, serial 7, part I, 67th Cong., 1st sess. (Washington, 1921), p. 232; personal interview with Rev. Yoshio Hino, 25 January 1965.

33. *Senate Journal*, 10th Leg., Reg. Sess. (Honolulu, 1919), p. 1709; *A Survey of Education*, p. 7.

34. Arthur L. Dean, 'Japanese Language Schools,' *Friend*, August 1920.

35. *HA*, 24 October 1919, 1, 3 April 1920.
36. *HA*, 6, 9, 11, 27 October 1919; Arthur L. Dean, 'What of the Future?' *The Centennial Book*, p. 87.
37. *HA*, 8 February 1920.
38. *HSB*, 7, 11 February 1920.
39. *HA*, 10 February, 1 March, 6 April 1920.
40. *Hawaiian Almanac and Annual for 1922*, pp. 152, 153; *A Survey of Education*, pp. 134–139; *HA*, 21 October 1919, 23 May 1920.
41. *A Survey of Education*, pp. 129–130, 131, 133; *HA*, 23 October 1919.
42. *HA*, 4 March 1919.
43. *A Survey of Education*, pp. 126–127.
44. *Ibid.*, p. 145.
45. Lorrin A. Thurston, *The Japanese Problem in Hawaii*, an address before the Japanese Language School Teachers' Convention, 29 July 1919; *The Foreign Language School Question*, address before the Honolulu Social Science Association, 8 November 1920, pp. 16–17, 19.
46. *HA*, 16 November 1920; Thurston, *The Foreign Language School Question*, pp. 27–29.
47. *Senate Journal*, 11th Leg., Special Sess., 10–24 November (Honolulu, 1920), pp. 51, 87, 164; *House Journal*, 11th Leg., Special Sess. (Honolulu, 1920), p. 54.
48. *HA*, 25 January, 23 February 1920; *HSB*, 9 February 1920; Albert W. Palmer, 'The Task of the Hawaiian Board Today,' *The Centennial Book*, p. 82; Doremus Scudder, 'The Language Schools,' *Friend*, January 1920.
49. *A Survey of Education*, p. 111.
50. Dean, 'What of the Future?' pp. 80, 86; Scudder, 'The Task of the Hawaiian Board Today,' *The Centennial Book*, p. 80; *Friend*, July 1920; *HA*, 18 May 1920.
51. John P. Erdman, 'A Brief Historical Sketch of the Hawaiian Board of Missions,' *The Centennial Book*, p. 79.
52. *HA*, 5 July 1921; Kihara, *Hawaii Nihonjin Shi*, p. 221; Henry Butler Schwartz, 'Report of the Japanese Field Secretary,' *Official Minutes*, Hawaiian Mission of the Methodist-Episcopal Church, 1922, p. 33.
53. *HA*, 29 August 1921; *Hawaiian Buddhist Annual* (Honolulu, 1932), p. 216.
54. *50th Anniversary of the Beginning of Mission Work in Hawaii*, p. 4.
55. Takie and Umetarō Okumura, *Hawaii's American-Japanese Problem, A Campaign to Remove Causes of Friction Between The American People and Japanese* (Honolulu, 1921), p. 6.
56. Quoted in the *HA*, editorial column, 20 June 1921.
57. Gulick, *Hawaii's American-Japanese Problem*, p. 24.
58. *HA*, 5 October 1922.
59. *Friend*, May 1902; U. S. Commissioner of Labor *Report* for 1902, quoted (in part) in the *Planters' Monthly*, 15 July 1903, p. 298; Henry B. Restarick, 'Americanizing Hawaii,' *PCA*, 17 May 1907; *PCA*, 17 November 1907; Imamura, 'The Propaganda of the

Island Buddhists'; *HA*, 20 September 1917; *Hawaiian Almanac and Annual for 1918*, p. 165; Mesick, 'Buddhists Build New Temple in Hawaii'; Imamura, *History of the Hongwanji Mission in Hawaii*, p. 19; *Golden Anniversary Edition, 1900–1951*, YBA of Honolulu, HMCS.

60. *Friend*, May 1913; *HA*, 20 May 1923.
61. *Friend*, January 1922; *HA*, 2 March, 25 July 1924; Albert W. Palmer, *Orientals in American Life* (New York, 1934), p. 63; *HSB*, 18 October 1930.
62. *Friend*, November 1928.
63. *HA*, 6 October 1922; 23 April 1926; *Hawaii Honpa Hongwanji Kyōdan Enkakushi*, p. 20; Imamura, *Hawaii Kaikyōshi*, p. 118; Sōga, *Gojūnenkan*, p. 277.
64. *Hawaii Honpa Hongwanji Kyōdan Enkakushi*, p. 31.
65. *HSB*, 6 August 1918.
66. Imamura, *Hawaii Kaikyōshi*, pp. 547–549; *HA*, 4 June 1920.
67. *HA*, 16 August 1918.
68. Imamura, *A Short History*, p. 14; *HSB*, 19 November 1921; *Hawaii Honpa Hongwanji Kyōdan Enkakushi*, p. 29.
69. *HA*, 2 March 1924.
70. *Friend*, January 1922.
71. *Friend*, April 1922.
72. *Official Minutes*, Hawaiian Mission of the Methodist-Episcopal Church, 1922, p. 33.
73. *Ibid.*
74. *HA*, 26 October, 13 December 1922; *Friend*, November 1922.
75. *Labor Problems in Hawaii*, serial 7, part I (Washington, 1921), pp. 214–215, 232, and part II, pp. 667, 688; *Report* of the Governor of Hawaii to the Secretary of the Interior, 1921, p. 6.
76. *Labor Problems in Hawaii*, serial 7, part I (Washington, 1921), p. 381, and part II, pp. 631, 655, 659, 679, 688.
77. Palmer, 'The Task of the Hawaiian Board Today,' p. 81; Minutes of the Japanese Committee, HEA, 7 June 1920.
78. 'Japanese Method of Evangelism,' Okumura Papers.
79. See T. and U. Okumura, *Hawaii's American-Japanese Problem*, pp. 6, 11, 12, 19; and T. Okumura, *Seventy Years*, pp. 132–133.
80. T. Okumura, *Seventy Years*, pp. 52, 81, 130–131.
81. T. and U. Okumura, *op. cit.*, pp. 1–2, 8, 9, 13, 15, 21; T. Okumura, *Seventy Years*, pp. 127–129; 'Work Among Plantation Japanese For the Year 1941,' Okumura Papers; 'The Kona Wind,' *Annual Report*, HEA, 1921, p. 28.
82. 'Educational Campaign Among Plantation Japanese For the Year 1934,' Okumura Papers; *The New Americans* 5 (July–September 1921), Okumura Papers.
83. See 'The Kona Wind,' *Annual Report*, HEA, 1921, p. 27; John P. Erdman to Rev. K. Higuchi, 7 September 1926, HMCS; and *Friend*, June 1922.
84. 'Memo,' 12 September 1935, Okumura Papers.
85. *HSB*, 12 November, 2 December 1921; Wakukawa, *op. cit.*, pp. 275–276; *Report of Sub-Committee No. 7 on Foreign Language*

Schools, Governor's Advisory Committee on Education (Honolulu, 1930), p. 1.

86. *HSB,* 29 July 1922; *Friend,* August 1920; *HA,* 30 July, 13 September 1922; *A Brief Survey of the Foreign Language School Question* (Honolulu: Japanese Educational Association of Hawaii, 1923) pp. 10, 17, 18.

87. Also see *A Brief Survey of the Foreign Language School Question,* pp. 2, 3, 7.

88. *Ibid.,* pp. 4, 7.

89. *Hawaii Hōchi,* 29 March 1926.

90. Quoted in the *HSB,* 8 August 1922.

91. Quoted in the *HA,* 9 August 1922.

92. *HSB,* 11 August 1922.

93. *HA,* 4 July 1922.

94. T. Okumura, *Seventy Years,* p. 156; Tasuku Harada, *The Social Status of the Japanese in Hawaii: Some of the Problems Confronting the Second Generation* (Institute of Pacific Relations, preliminary paper prepared for Second General Session, 15–29 July 1927), pp. 7–8; *Friend,* December 1923.

95. *HA,* 11 August 1922.

96. *A Brief Survey of the Foreign Language School Question,* p. 19; *HA,* 23 August 1922.

97. *HA,* 29 August 1922.

98. *HA,* 30 July 1922; *HSB,* 26 August 1922.

99. *HA,* 9 August 1922.

100. *HA,* 19 August 1922; *A Brief Survey of the Foreign Language School Question,* pp. 14–16.

101. *HSB,* 17 August 1922.

102. *HA,* 19 August 1922.

103. *HA,* 24 August 1922.

104. *HA,* 27 August 1922; *HSB,* 26 August 1922; *A Brief Survey of the Foreign Language School Question,* p. 21.

105. *HA,* 11 September 1922.

106. *HA,* 14 January 1923; *A Brief Survey of the Foreign Language School Question,* p. 13.

107. Lorrin A. Thurston, 'The Language School Problem,' *HA,* 13 September 1922.

108. *HA,* 24 September 1922, 9 January 1923.

109. *HA,* 10 August 1922.

110. Wallace R. Farrington, address of Governor Farrington to the graduating class of Normal School, 2 August 1923; *Message of Hon. W. R. Farrington to the Legislature, Feb. 18, 1925* (Honolulu, 1925), p. 14.

111. *A Brief Survey of the Foreign Language School Question,* p. 25.

112. *HA,* 21 September 1922; *A Brief Survey of the Foreign Language School Question,* pp. 22, 25.

113. *HA,* 11 December 1922.

114. *HA,* 31 December 1922.

115. *HA,* 6 January 1923; *A Brief Survey of the Foreign Language School Question,* p. 6.

116. *HA*, 4 February 1923.
117. *House Journal*, Hawaii Legislature (Honolulu, 1923), pp. 170, 350, 1167, 1346–1347.
118. *Report* of the Governor of Hawaii to the Secretary of the Interior, 1923, p. 6; Albert W. Palmer, *The Human Side of Hawaii: Race Problems in the Mid-Pacific* (Boston, 1924), p. 109.
119. *HA*, 5 May 1923; *Report* of the Governor of Hawaii to the Secretary of the Interior, 1923, p. 7.
120. *HA*, 5 June 1923.
121. *HA*, 29 July, 2 August 1923.
122. *Message of Hon. W. R. Farrington to the Legislature, Feb. 21, 1923*, p. 12; address of Governor Farrington to the graduating class of Normal School, 2 August 1923.
123. Makino to Crawford, *HA*, 9 August 1925; *Report* of the Governor of Hawaii to the Secretary of the Interior, 1923, p. 8; *HA*, 9 July 1925.
124. *HA*, 1, 3 July 1925.
125. *HA*, 2, 3, 9 August 1925.
126. *HA*, 19 January 1927.
127. *HA*, 5 August 1923.
128. *HSB*, 23 November 1921, 17 May 1924, 9 January 1926; Albert Wray, 'The Menace of Dual Citizenship,' *Paradise of the Pacific*, May 1940, p. 9; Barber, *Hawaii: Restless Rampart*, pp. 140–141.
129. Umetarō Okumura to B. D. Baldwin, 19 March 1927, Okumura Papers.
130. *Ibid.*
131. 'Duties of Umetarō Okumura . . . Extra HSPA Community Activities,' manuscript, Okumura Papers; 'Educational Campaign Among Japanese Labor on Various Plantations . . . Report for the Year 1930,' Okumura Papers.
132. Takie Okumura to Dr. Gulick, 20 October 1934, Okumura Papers.
133. Okumura Papers.
134. 'Educational Campaign Among the Japanese . . . Report for the Year 1927,' Okumura Papers; *HA*, 7 August 1928.
135. 'Memo,' 7 December 1934, signed by Takie Okumura, Okumura Papers.
136. *HA*, 13 August 1927; 'Educational Campaign . . . Report for the Year 1929,' Okumura Papers; *Hawaii Hōchi*, 21 June 1934.
137. Palmer, *op. cit.*, pp. xiii, 71.
138. *HSB*, 31 March 1924, 23 July 1925, 5 February, 26 May 1926; *Nippu Jiji*, 2 May 1925; Minutes of the Japanese Committee, HEA, 7 July 1926; *Hawaii Honpa Hongwanji Kyōdan Enkakushi*, p. 145.
139. *Yōjō no Hikari*, p. 6; *HA*, 22 June 1927, 30 August 1928; Kihara, *op. cit.*, p. 221; Mesick, 'The 88 Holy Places on Hawaii's Garden Isle,' p. 93; *Nippu Jiji*, 2 May 1925.
140. *HSB*, 25 June 1924; *Nippu Jiji*, 2 May 1925; 'Buddhist Associations in Hawaii,' *Pan-Pacific*, April–June 1937, p. 30.
141. *HSB*, 21, 25, 27 June 1927; *HA*, 21–25 June 1927.

142. *HA*, 5 August 1927.
143. *HA*, 23 December 1922, 14 October 1923, 7 December 1924, 4, 11 April 1926.
144. *HA*, 2 March 1924.
145. Statement of Ernest Hunt to Louise Hunter, 4 November 1965; *Hawaii Honpa Hongwanji Kyōdan Enkakushi*, p. 32; *Dōbō*, February 1929, private papers of Ernest Hunt, Honolulu, Hawaii.
146. *British Buddhist* 4 (October 1929), private papers of Ernest Hunt.
147. Imamura, *A Short History*, p. 13; *HA*, 2 March 1924; *Hawaiian Buddhist Annual* (Honolulu, 1930), p. 134.
148. *HSB*, 12 August 1924; *HA*, 12 August 1924.
149. *Hawaiian Buddhist Annual* (Honolulu, 1932), p. 257; *HA*, 25 July 1925; *Hilo Tribune*, 8 January 1927; program of scheduled lectures, Society for the Promotion of Buddhist Knowledge, April 1925, private papers of Ernest Hunt.
150. *Hawaiian Buddhist Annual* (Honolulu, 1930), p. 135; *Hawaii Honpa Hongwanji Kyōdan Enkakushi*, p. 32.
151. *Hawaiian Buddhist Annual* (Honolulu, 1930), p. 135; Ernest Hunt, comp., *Vade Mecum* (Honolulu, 1932), p. 1; *HA*, 7 August 1927.
152. *HA* and *HSB*, 9 July 1928.
153. *HSB*, 16 July 1928.
154. *HA*, 15 August 1927.
155. *HA*, 14 September 1915, 20 June 1921.
156. *Friend*, May 1924.
157. *HA*, 1 August 1921.
158. *HA*, 29 May 1916.
159. See *Friend*, August 1921, *HA*, 25 July, 1 August 1921.
160. *HSB*, 2 October 1928.
161. *HA*, 26 June 1921, 30 July 1923.
162. 'Christianity's Attitude Toward Buddhism,' *Room! Supplement to the Friend*, 7, no. 1 (January 1929).
163. See *New Age*, December 1929, and *British Buddhist* 3 (September 1929); *Nation*, 14 August 1929; private papers of Ernest Hunt.
164. The episode was confirmed by Hunt in a private conversation.

CHAPTER 10

1. *Hawaii Hōchi*, 21 June 1934.
2. *Friend*, August 1934.
3. *Dōbō*, English section, February 1929, private papers of Ernest Hunt; Statehood for Hawaii, *Hearings* Before the Subcommittee on the Territories, House of Representatives, 74th Cong., 1st sess., 1936, p. 205; private conversation between Louise Hunter and Mr. Masuo Ogoshi, long-time member of the Makiki Christian Church and acquaintance of the Okumuras.
4. *Dōbō*, March 1928, private papers of Ernest Hunt.
5. *Hawaiian Buddhist Annual* (Honolulu, 1930), p. 1.
6. Denzel Carr, 'Is Buddhism An Obstacle to Americanization?' *Hawaiian Buddhist Annual* (Honolulu, 1934), pp. 1, 2, 4.

7. Manuscript, Okumura Papers; Embree, *Acculturation*, p. 128.
8. Souno Inouye, 'Buddhism in Hawaii: Its Social Aspects,' *HA*, 9 July 1924; Shirō Sokabe, 'Buddhism,' *Friend*, March 1938.
9. *Hawaii Hōchi*, 21 July 1930.
10. Embree, *Acculturation*, pp. 23, 110, 127; *HSB*, 22 July 1931.
11. *Dōbō*, March 1928, private papers of Ernest Hunt.
12. Henry Butler Schwartz, Report of the Japanese Field Secretary, *Official Minutes*, Hawaiian Mission of the Methodist-Episcopal Church, 1922; *HA*, 24 May 1920.
13. *HA*, 29 May 1916, 18 May 1920, 20 July 1925.
14. *Friend*, November 1923.
15. *Room! Supplement to the Friend*, 7, no. 1 (January 1929).
16. Andrew W. Lind, 'Religious Trends in Hawaii,' *Friend*, November 1928.
17. Katsumi C. Yamasaki, 'Thoughts of a Hawaiian-born Buddhist,' Okumura Papers.
18. Imamura, *Hawaii Kaikyōshi*, p. 549; *HA*, 15 August 1918, 26 June, 10 August 1927, 7 July 1928; *Hawaii Honpa Hongwanji Kyōdan Enkakushi*, p. 32; *HSB*, 7, 24 July 1928, 18 November 1931.
19. *HA*, 12 May 1927; Hunt, *Vade Mecum*, p. 14; *Dōbō*, July 1930, private papers of Ernest Hunt.
20. *HA*, 5, 7 April 1929.
21. *Dōbō*, March 1928, private papers of Ernest Hunt; *HA*, 16 July 1930.
22. Imamura, *A Short History*, pp. 15, 17; *Hawaii Hōchi*, 12 April 1929; *HSB*, 18 October 1930, 15 February 1933.
23. *Maha Bodhi*, November 1932, p. 536, private papers of Ernest Hunt; *Hawaiian Buddhist Annual* (Honolulu, 1934).
24. *HA*, 15 May 1930, 6, 24, 25 April 1931, 6 December 1931; *Dōbō*, July 1930, private papers of Ernest Hunt; *HSB*, 5 July 1931; *Hawaiian Buddhist Annual* (Honolulu, 1934).
25. See *HA*, 9 July 1929, 2 April 1931; *HSB*, 18 October 1930; *Hilo Tribune Herald*, 13, 24 February 1930; 'The Report of the Year, 1926,' 10 January 1927, Okumura Papers; *Hawaiian Buddhist Annual* (Honolulu, 1930); *Dōbō*, July 1930, private papers of Ernest Hunt.
26. *Hawaiian Buddhist Annual* (Honolulu, 1930), p. 135; *HA*, 14 September 1963.
27. *Maha Bodhi Journal* (August 1932), private papers of Ernest Hunt; Imamura, *A Short History*, pp. 16, 17.
28. *HA*, 10 July 1929.
29. *Hawaii Hōchi*, 19 July 1930; *Nippu Jiji*, 19, 21, 23 July 1930; *HA*, 17, 20, 24 July 1930; *HSB*, 23 September 1930.
30. *HSB*, 17, 20 September 1930; *HA*, 20 August 1931.
31. Ernest Hunt to Rev. Henry P. Judd, 11 May 1930, HMCS.
32: *HA*, 16 July 1930; *HSB*, 4 November 1932.
33. Sidney L. Gulick, *Mixing the Races in Hawaii: A Study of the Coming Neo-Hawaiian American Race* (Honolulu, 1937), pp. 181, 185.

34. *Hawaiian Buddhist Annual* (Honolulu, 1930), p. 135; *Hawaii Hōchi*, 21 July 1930; *HA*, 16, 19 July 1930.

35. *HSB*, 18 October 1930; C. P. Goto to Umetarō Okumura, [n.d.], Okumura Papers; Shirō Sokabe, 'Buddhism,' *Friend*, March 1938.

36. *HSB*, 25 October 1930.

37. *HSB*, 29 October 1930; *Dōbō*, October 1930, private papers of Ernest Hunt.

38. *Friend*, December 1931; 'Japanese Method of Evangelism,' Okumura Papers; T. Okumura, *Seventy Years*, p. 169.

39. 'Japanese Language Education or "Chain Schools," ' Okumura Papers; Minutes of the Japanese Committee, HEA, 8 May 1929; F. C. Atherton to Umetarō Okumura, 1 December 1930, Okumura Papers.

40. Takie Okumura, 'The Chain School,' *New Americans*, June 1933, Okumura Papers.

41. *Dōbō*, July 1930.

42. *New Americans*, June 1931, Okumura Papers.

43. 'Educational Campaign Among Plantation Japanese for the Year 1934,' Okumura Papers; Minutes of the Japanese Committee, HEA, 11 March 1931; statement of O. W. Robinson, supervising principal of rural Oahu schools; Statehood for Hawaii, *Hearings* Before the Subcommittee on the Territories, House of Representatives, 74th Cong., 1st sess., 1936, p. 83; J. P. Erdman to H. B. Penhallow, 15 April 1931, HMCS; *Nippu Jiji,* 25 January 1933.

44. *New Americans,* June 1933; manuscript, 26 August 1940, Okumura Papers.

45. *Hawaii Hōchi*, 8 August 1933; *Nippu Jiji*, 3 August 1933.

46. Manuscript, 26 August 1940, Okumura Papers.

47. *HSB*, 15, 22, 23 December 1932; *Nippu Jiji*, 22, 23, 24, 27–29 December 1932; *Hawaii Hōchi*, 28 December 1932; *Weekly Hawaii Shimpo*, 14 January 1933, private papers of Ernest Hunt; *HA*, 'History From Our Files,' 24 February 1943.

48. *HSB*, 15 February 1933; *Hawaii Hōchi*, 6 November 1933; personal interview with Ernest Hunt, 4 November 1965.

49. *Hawaii Times* (formerly the *Nippu Jiji*), 24 October 1945; Takie Okumura, 'For General Wells—August 5, 1938,' Okumura Papers.

50. *Buddhist Child* 4, no. 9, September 1936, private papers of Ernest Hunt.

51. Katsumi Onishi, 'The Second Generation Japanese and the Hongwanji,' *Social Process in Hawaii* 5, no. 3 (May 1937), pp. 44, 45; *Golden Anniversary Edition, YBA, 1900–1951*; 'Religious Trends in Hawaii,' *Friend*, July 1937; testimony of Romanzo Adams, Statehood for Hawaii, *Hearings* Before the Joint Committee on Hawaii, 75th Cong., 2nd sess., 1938, pp. 432, 433.

52. K. Onishi, *op. cit.,* pp. 45, 46; idem, ' "Bon" and "Bon-odori" in Hawaii,' *Social Process in Hawaii* 5, no. 4 (May 1938), pp. 50–52, 56; *Nippu Jiji,* 11 August 1934; *HA*, 11, 13 July, 1 August 1935; Embree, *Acculturation*, p. 126; Yukuo Uyehara, 'Bon Festival,' *Paradise of the Pacific,* August 1937, p. 31; *HSB*, 15 July 1967.

53. Testimony of Masao Aizawa, Statehood for Hawaii, *Hearings* Before the Subcommittee on the Territories, 74th Cong., 1st sess., 1936, p. 230–231; Katsumi Onishi, ' "Bon" and "Bon-odori" in Hawaii,' *Social Process in Hawaii* 5, no. 4 (May 1938), pp. 51–56; *Nippu Jiji*, 11 August 1934.

54. *HA*, 5 August 1923; *HSB*, 11 March 1924.

55. *Message of Hon. Wallace R. Farrington to the Legislature, Feb. 20, 1929* (Honolulu, 1929), pp. 17, 18.

56. *HA*, 28 February 1927.

57. *Report of the Sub-Committee No. 7*, Governor's Advisory Committee on Education (Honolulu, 1930), pp. 8, 142.

58. See testimony of Oren E. Long, Superintendent of Public Instruction, Statehood for Hawaii, *Hearings* Before the Subcommittee on the Territories, House of Representatives, 74th Cong., 1st sess., 1936, pp. 81–84.

59. *HA*, 8 May 1936.

60. Latourette, *A Short History of the Far East*, p. 596; T. R. G. Lyell, *Case History of Japan* (New York, 1948), p. 129.

61. Willis Lamott, *Nippon: The Crime and Punishment of Japan* (New York, 1944), p. 210.

62. Daniel C. Holtom, *Modern Japan and Shinto Nationalism: A Study of Present-Day Trends in Japanese Religions* (Chicago, 1947), pp. 138–139.

63. *Ibid.*, pp. 132–133, 137.

64. Kihachi Imai and Motosaburō Matsutani, *The Ideals of the Shinran-Followers* (Tokyo, 1918), pp. 38, 40.

65. W. A. Kinney, *Hawaii's Capacity for Self-Government All But Destroyed* (Salt Lake City, 1927), p. 193.

66. *HA*, 10, 14 November 1928.

67. *HA*, 27 June 1927.

68. *Nippu Jiji*, 27 March 1934.

69. *HA*, 13 October 1935; Statehood for Hawaii, *Hearings* Before the Joint Committee on Hawaii, 75th Cong., 2nd sess., 1938, p. 449.

70. Statehood for Hawaii, *Hearings* Before the Joint Committee on Hawaii, 75th Cong., 2nd sess., 1938, p. 457.

71. *Maha Bodhi* 73, no. 10, October 1965, p. 261; statement of Ernest Hunt, 15 April 1965.

72. Statement of Ernest Hunt, 15 April 1965.

73. 'Assignment Sheet,' CIP, 4 November 1933, Okumura Papers.

74. *HA*, 16 January 1934; *Nippu Jiji*, 13 February 1934; Barber, *Hawaii: Restless Rampart*, p. 148.

75. *HA*, 15 October 1937.

76. Embree, *Acculturation*, pp. 35, 42; Yukiko Kimura, 'A Sociological Analysis of Types of Social Adjustment of Alien Japanese in Hawaii Since the War,' (master's thesis, University of Hawaii, 1947), p. 149 (hereafter cited as 'A Sociological Analysis').

77. *Nippu Jiji*, 24 April 1934; Kihara, *Hawaii Nihonjin Shi*, p. 215; Edwin G. Burrows, *Chinese and Japanese in Hawaii During the Sino-Japanese Conflict* (Honolulu, 1939), pp. 25, 26.

78. *Yōjō no Hikari*, pp. 33, 37, 43; *HA*, 3 July 1932.

79. *HA*, 13 October 1935.
80. *HSB*, 30 September 1937.
81. *Friend*, August 1940.
82. 'For General Wells—August 5, 1938,' Okumura Papers.
83. Umetarō Okumura to Dr. Gulick, 25 November 1935, Okumura Papers; *HA*, 13 October 1935.
84. Statehood for Hawaii, *Hearings* Before the Subcommittee on the Territories, 74th Cong., 1st sess., 1936, p. 152; Statehood for Hawaii, *Hearings* Before the Joint Committee on Hawaii, 75th Cong., 2nd sess., 1938, p. 470.
85. *HA*, 9, 11, 13 October 1935.
86. *HA*, 10, 16, 20 October 1935.
87. See editorial, *HA*, 20 August 1928.
88. *Nippu Jiji*, 9, 10 October 1935.
89. *HSB*, 4 July, 23 August 1928; 23, 25 September 1930; *HA*, 15 October 1937; letter from the Chairman of the Joint Committee on Hawaii, Statehood for Hawaii, *Senate Documents*, No. 151, 75th Cong., 3rd sess., 1938, p. 41.
90. Memo from Takie Okumura to Dr. Gulick, 20 October 1934, Okumura Papers; *New Americans*, June 1933, p. 3.
91. Umetarō Okumura to Dr. Gulick, 25 November 1933, Okumura Papers; *New Americans*, June 1933, p. 3; *HA*, 15 July 1936; Umetarō Okumura to Rev. John P. Erdman, 12 August 1935, HMCS.
92. 'Educational Campaign Among Plantation Japanese For the Year 1934,' Okumura Papers; Takie Okumura, 'Responsibility Of The American Citizens of Japanese Ancestry,' *Paradise Times*, February 1938, Okumura Papers.
93. Manuscript, Okumura Papers; Takie Okumura, 'Responsibility Of The American Citizens of Japanese Ancestry,' *Paradise Times*, February 1938, Okumura Papers.
94. *Ibid.*; *Friend*, March 1940; *HSB*, 15 July 1940.
95. *Hawaiian Buddhist Annual* (Honolulu, 1932), pp. 150, 216; *Hawaii Honpa Hongwanji Kyōdan Enkakushi*, p. 72; Japanese consulate statistics, Statehood for Hawaii, *Hearings* Before the Joint Committee on Hawaii, 75th Cong., 2nd sess., 1938, p. 656; Kenju Ohtomo, ' "Birth," Life of Buddhism in Hawaii Traced by Ohtomo,' *Dōbō*, May 1941.
96. *Hawaii Hōchi*, 21 June 1934.
97. *HA*, 19 October 1937; letter from the Chairman of the Joint Committee on Hawaii, Statehood for Hawaii, *Senate Documents*, no. 151, 75th Cong., 3rd sess., 1938, pp. 41, 45, 46.
98. *HSB*, 15, 19 July 1940; *The Fourteenth New Americans Conference*, 15 to 21 July 1941, p. 65.
99. *HSB*, 15 July 1940.
100. 'Memo—Strictly Confidential,' Okumura Papers; *HSB*, 15 July 1940.
101. *HA*, 12, 18 January, 28 August 1941.
102. *Hilo Tribune*, 14 February 1930; Imamura, *A Short History*, p. 10; Katsumi Onishi, 'The Second Generation and the Hongwanji,'

Social Process in Hawaii 5, no. 3 (May 1937), p. 44; Toshimi Yoshinaga, 'Japanese Buddhist Temples in Honolulu,' *Social Process in Hawaii* 5, no. 3 (May 1937), p. 37.

103. Testimony of Seth Richardson, *Hearings* Before the Subcommittee on the Territories and Insular Affairs of the Committee of Public Lands, 80th Cong., 2nd sess., 1948, p. 465; *HSB*, 15 July 1940.

104. Bernard K. Yamamoto, 'The Assimilation of the Japanese and Juvenile Delinquency,' *Social Process in Hawaii* 5, no. 5 (June 1939), pp. 51–54.

105. Testimony of Miss Edith Field, Statehood for Hawaii, *Hearings* Before the Joint Committee on Hawaii, 75th Cong., 2nd sess., 1938, p. 543.

106. *HSB*, 17 August 1931, 12 August 1933; *Proceedings of the Second General Conference of Pan-Pacific Young Buddhists' Associations* (Tokyo, 1935).

107. *HA*, 25 June 1941; *Dōbō*, September 1941.

108. *Dōbō*, October, November 1941.

CHAPTER II

1. *HSB*, 24 September 1944, 27 April 1946, 28 July 1967; Gwenfread Allen, *Hawaii's War Years* (Honolulu, 1950), p. 10; Mrs. K. Culver, interview with Rev. Ernest Hunt, File 60.06, HWRD; *Hawaii Honpa Hongwanji Kyōdan Enkakushi*, p. 149; *Paradise of the Pacific*, February 1950, p. 5; Matsunami, *A Glimpse of Hawaii Buddhism*, pp. 4, 5.

2. *HSB*, 13 May 1946, 10 March 1947; Thomas D. Murphy, *Ambassadors in Arms* (Honolulu, 1955), p. 111.

3. *HSB*, 27 April 1946; *PCA*, 15 April 1915, quoting the *Nippu Jiji*.

4. Hiro Higuchi to Larry Tajiri, 20 June 1951, Hiro Higuchi Papers, Honolulu, Hawaii; private papers of Ernest Hunt.

5. Mrs. K. Culver, interview with Rev. Ernest Hunt, HWRD.

6. *Chaplain's Section, Central Pacific Base Command*, p. 12, HWRD; Hiro Higuchi to Larry Tajiri, 20 June 1951, Hiro Higuchi Papers.

7. *Yamato Shimbun*, 31 July 1905.

8. Monroe Sweetland, 'Our 49th State—Hawaii?', *Asia and the Americans* 44 (September 1944): 411.

9. Murphy, *Ambassadors in Arms*, p. 47.

10. Yasutarō Sōga, *Tessaku Seikatsu* [Life Behind Barbed Wires] (Hawaii, 1948), pp. 22, 31, 35, 40 (hereafter cited as *Tessaku Seikatsu*).

11. Statement of Hiseki Miyazaki in *Garden Island War Daily*, 18 December 1941; Gwenfread Allen, *op. cit.*, p. 136.

12. See Bradford Smith, *Americans from Japan*, p. 118.

13. Sōga, *Tessaku Seikatsu*, pp. 25, 135, 334–335; interviews with Dr. Kazuo Miyamoto, 21 January 1965 and Rev. Yoshio Hino, 25 January 1965.

14. *Ibid.*, pp. 131–133, 345–346, 349.

15. American Friends Service Committee, Hawaii Branch, *Bulletin* No. 2, 9 February 1944, HSPA Public Relations File, 1939–1946.
16. *Investigation of Un-American Propaganda Activities in the U.S., Report* of the Special Sub-Committee on Un-American Activities, 78th Cong., 2nd sess., 1944, p. 4.
17. Sōga, *Tessaku Seikatsu*, pp. 132, 255; Kazuo Miyamoto, *Hawaii: End of the Rainbow* (Bridgeway Press, 1964), p. 363.
18. Personal interview with Ernest Hunt, 11 November 1965.
19. Stenciled copy of form letter dated 12 January 1943, signed by Takie and Umetarō Okumura, Okumura Papers.
20. *Revised Laws of Hawaii, 1945*, Sec. 1871–1876, p. 281; *Session Laws*, Territory of Hawaii, Reg. Sess., 1943, p. 38.
21. Umetarō Okumura to David Y. K. Akana, 20 February 1943, Okumura Papers.
22. 'Memo,' Okumura Papers.
23. Kenneth B. Carney, 'A Public Relations Plan for the HSPA,' 24 March 1943, HSPA Public Relations File, 1939–1946.
24. Takie Okumura, 'Memo on Campaign Among Japanese,' 1 May 1944, Makiki Christian Church File, HMCS.
25. 'First Draft of a Report Prepared by Dr. Adeline Babbitt for UNESCO,' manuscript, HWRD; Mrs. K. Culver, interview with Ernest Hunt, File 60.05, HWRD; author's interview with Ernest Hunt, 4 November 1965; *Friend*, July 1943; Arleen Pritchard Duncan, 'Some Effects of the War on the Christian Churches in Hawaii,' *Social Process in Hawaii* 8 (1943): 49–54; author's interview with Elder Robert Nomi, 29 July 1963.
26. Kimura, 'A Sociological Analysis,' p. 21.
27. *Ibid.*, p. 3; author's interview with Rev. Yoshiaki Fujitani, 9 July 1963; Nancy M. Horikawa, 'The Transition from Japanese Hospital to Kuakini Hospital,' *Social Process in Hawaii* 21 (1957): 56, 64; Duncan, 'Some Effects of the War on the Christian Churches in Hawaii,' p. 51; *Annual Report,* HEA, 1942, p. 9; Andrew W. Lind, *Hawaii's Japanese: An Experiment in Democracy* (Princeton, 1946), p. 106 (hereafter cited as *Hawaii's Japanese*).
28. 'First Draft of a Report Prepared by Dr. Adeline Babbitt for UNESCO,' manuscript, HWRD.
29. Margaret M. L. Catton, *Social Service in Hawaii* (Palo Alto, 1959), pp. 269–270.
30. Author's interview with Ernest Hunt, 4 November 1965; Mrs. K. Culver, interview with Ernest Hunt, File 60.05, HWRD.
31. *HSB*, 9 March 1946.
32. C. B. Offner and H. Van Straelen, *Modern Japanese Religions: With Special Emphasis Upon Their Doctrines of Healing* (Tokyo, 1963), pp. 43–46; Harry Thomsen, *The New Religions of Japan* (Rutland, 1963), p. 38ff.
33. Dick Gima, 'Isle Tenrikyo sect grows, is building new temple,' *HSB*, 15 July 1965.
34. Offner and Van Straelen, *op. cit.*, p. 51.
35. Burrows, *Hawaiian Americans*, pp. 161–162; Gima, *op. cit.*
36. Offner and Van Straelen, *op. cit.*, pp. 71, 73.

37. Kimura, 'A Sociological Analysis,' pp. 61, 64, 65–66.
38. Tetsusho Hirai, *Todaiji of Hawaii* (Honolulu, n.d.), p. 5.
39. Author's interview with Ernest Hunt, 4 November 1965.
40. Author's interview with Bishop Hirai, 1 November 1962; Barbara B. Robinson, 'Todaiji of Honolulu, Survey of a Regressive Religious Group,' 1962, pp. 64, 65, Hawaiian and Pacific Collection, Sinclair Library, University of Hawaii.
41. *HA*, 2 November 1963.
42. Offner and Van Straelen, *op. cit.*, pp. 76, 77, 79.
43. *HA*, 26 October, 2 November 1963.
44. *The Prophet of Tabuse* (Yamaguchi, 1954), p. 177; *HSB*, 20 October 1962; *Ten Sei* [Voice from Heaven], 2, no. 4 (June 1964).
45. *The Prophet of Tabuse*, pp. 167–168.
46. *Ibid.*, p. 76.
47. Millard E. Jabbour, 'Tensho-Kotai-Jingu-Kyo: The Emergence and Career of a Religious Movement,' (master's thesis, University of Hawaii, 1958) pp. 45–49, 69–70, 85, 120–121; *HSB*, 3 January 1968.
48. *Seikyo News*, no. 40, 26 August 1963 (English-language organ of the Sōka Gakkai); Offner and Van Straelen, *op. cit.*, pp. 103, 106, 107; *HA*, 9 March 1968; *HSB*, 14 March 1968.
49. Sōga, *Tessaku Seikatsu*, p. 384; *Hawaii Honpa Hongwanji Kyōdan Enkakushi*, pp. 45, 72.
50. *HA*, 3 January 1946.
51. *HA*, 18 January, 23, 27 March 1946.
52. *HA*, 26, 31 March 1946.
53. *HA*, 25 March 1946.
54. *HA*, 2, 4 March 1946; Lind, *Hawaii's Japanese*, p. 213.
55. *HA*, 10 April 1946, 4 May 1947.
56. Lind, *Hawaii's Japanese*, p. 215.
57. Kimura, 'A Sociological Analysis,' pp. 45, 96, 126.
58. *HSB*, 9 March 1946.
59. *HA*, 26 March 1946.
60. *HSB*, 3 May 1946; *HA*, 2 May 1946.
61. *HSB*, 25 May 1946.
62. *Report* of the Hawaii Federation of Young Buddhist Associations, 1960.
63. *HA*, 4 November, 19 December 1948, 16 February 1952, 8 April 1965; *HSB*, 2 October 1948, 15 July 1967; *Report* of the 15th Territorial YBA Convention, 1948, pp. 3, 84, 85; *Report* of the 24th Territorial YBA Convention, 1957, p. 39; *Report* of the Hawaii Federation of Young Buddhist Associations, 1960.
64. Hidefumi Akahoshi, 'Hongwanji in Rural Japan and Cosmopolitan Hawaii,' *Social Process in Hawaii* 26 (1963): 81; *Manual for Sunday School Teachers* (Hongwanji, 1951), p. 3; *HA*, 3 January 1946.
65. Yukiko Kimura, 'Sociological Significance of Japanese Language School Campaign in Hawaii,' *Social Process in Hawaii* 20 (1956): 47, 50; *HA*, 29 July 1967; *HSB*, 28 July 1967.
66. *Friend*, July 1949; *HA*, 11 February 1951.

67. Okumura Papers and statement of Mr. Masuo Ogoshi, 16 January 1965.
68. T. Okumura, *Seventy Years*, pp. 7, 9.
69. Res. 1, United Young Buddhists of Hawaii, *30th State YBA Convention*, 21 August 1963; *HSB*, 2 March 1963.
70. *HA*, 28 March 1963.
71. *HSB*, 16 January, 2 March 1963.
72. *HSB*, 2 March 1963.
73. *HA*, 2 March, 30 April 1963.
74. *HSB*, 24 December 1965.
75. *HSB*, 26 November 1960, 19, 24 January 1966.
76. *HSB*, 26 August 1967.
77. Charles Hasegawa, 'The Hongwanji Buddhist Minister in Hawaii,' *Social Process in Hawaii* 26 (1963): 78.
78. *Sunday Star-Bulletin and Advertiser*, 24 January 1965; Bernhard L. Hormann, 'The Problem of the Religion of Hawaii's Japanese,' *Social Process in Hawaii* 22 (1958): 6.
79. Margaret Miki, 'Mother and Her Temple,' *Social Process in Hawaii* 12 (1948): 22.
80. *Sunday Star-Bulletin and Advertiser*, 22 August 1965.
81. F. Blanning-Pooley, 'Buddhism for All,' *Hawaiian Buddhist Annual* (Honolulu, 1931), p. 3; Okusa, *Principal Teachings of the True Sect of Pure Land*, pp. 8, 10.
82. *HSB*, 21 August 1965.
83. A. K. Reischauer, *Studies in Japanese Buddhism*, p. 321.
84. *Bodhi Day Service* (leaflet), 9 December 1951, HMCS.
85. *HSB*, 19, 22 August 1946; John F. Mulholland, *Religion in Hawaii* (Honolulu, 1961), p. 48.
86. *HA*, 11, 12 August 1967; *HSB*, 14 August 1967.
87. Bernhard L. Hormann, 'The Revival of Buddhism in Hawaii,' p. 2, UH Library.
88. A. K. Reischauer, *op. cit.*, p. 212.
89. Kanmo Imamura to Louise Hunter, 8 April 1964.
90. *HA*, 19 August 1948; *Report* of the 15th Territorial YBA Convention (Hilo, 1948), p. 19.

Selected Bibliography

KEY SOURCES IN ENGLISH ON BUDDHISM AND
THE RELIGIONS OF THE ORIENT

Anesaki, Masaharu. *Religious Life of the Japanese People.* Rev. ed. Tokyo: Kokusai Bunka Shinkokai, 1961.

Bellah, Robert N. *Tokugawa Religion.* Illinois: Glencoe Free Press, 1957.

Eliot, Sir Charles. *Japanese Buddhism.* New York: Barnes and Noble, 1959.

Hearn, Lafcadio. *Glimpses of Unfamiliar Japan, II.* Boston: Houghton, Mifflin & Co., 1894.

Holmes, Edmund. *The Creed of Buddha.* London: The Bodley Head Ltd., 1957.

Humphreys, Christmas. *Buddhism.* Great Britain: Penguin Books, Ltd., 1954.

Hunt, Ernest. *Essentials and Symbols of the Buddhist Faith.* Honolulu, 1955.

Holtom, Daniel. *Modern Japan and Shinto Nationalism: A Study of Present-Day Trends in Japanese Religion.* Chicago: University of Chicago Press, 1943.

Morgan, Harry T. *Chinese Symbols and Superstitions.* P. D. and Ione Perkins. California, 1942.

Offner, Clark B. and Van Straelen, Henry. *Modern Japanese Religions With Special Emphasis Upon Their Doctrines of Healing.* Tokyo: Rupert Enderle, 1963.

Oldenberg, Hermann. *Buddha: His Life, His Doctrine, His Order.* Translated from the German by William Hoey. London: Williams & Norgate, 1882.

Prophet of Tabuse. Tabuse: Tensho-Kotai-Jingu-Kyo, 1954.

Rahula, Walpola. *What the Buddha Taught.* New York: Grove Press, Inc., 1962.

Reischauer, August Karl. *Studies in Japanese Buddhism*. New York: The Macmillan Co., 1917.

Reischauer, Edwin Oldfather. *Japan Past and Present*. New York: Knopf, 1956.

Soothill, W. E. *The Lotus of the Wonderful Law or The Lotus Gospel*. Oxford: Clarendon Press, 1930.

Suzuki, Beatrice Lane, 'Jiriki and Tariki: Two Aspects of Mahayana Buddhism,' *Hawaiian Buddhist Annual*. Honolulu, 1934.

Suzuki, Daisetz T. *Buddhist Philosophy and Its Effects on the Life and Thought of the Japanese People*. Japan: Kokusai Bunka Shinkokai, 1936.

———. *Outlines of Mahayana Buddhism*. New York: Schocken Books, Inc., 1963.

Tachibana, S. *The Ethics of Buddhism*. London: Oxford University Press, 1926.

Takakusu, Junjirō and Moore, Charles A., eds., *The Essentials of Buddhist Philosophy*. Honolulu: Office Appliance Co., Ltd., 1956.

Tsunoda, Ryusaku; de Bary, William; and Keene, Donald, comps. *Sources of Japanese Tradition*. New York: Columbia University Press, 1959.

Utsuki, Nishu. *The Shin Sect: A School of Mahayana Buddhism*. Kyoto: Honpa Hongwanji, Publication Bureau of Buddhist Books, 1937.

Warren, Henry Clarke. *Buddhism in Translations*. New York: Atheneum, 1963.

Wright, Arthur F. *Buddhism in Chinese History*. Stanford: Stanford University Press, 1959.

Yang, C. K. *Religion in Chinese Society*. Berkeley: University of California Press, 1961.

KEY SOURCES IN JAPANESE ON
THE JAPANESE AND JAPANESE BUDDHISM IN HAWAII

Fujii, Hidegorō. *Shin Hawaii* [New Hawaii]. Tokyo: Bunken-sha, 1902.

Gomonshu Gojunkyō Kinen Hawaii Honpa Hongwanji Kyōdan Enkakushi [A History of the Hawaii Honpa Hongwanji Mission]. Honolulu: Honpa Hongwanji, 1954.

Imamura, Yemyō. *Beikoku no seishin o ronzu* [In Criticism of the American Spirit]. Tokyo: Honpa Hongwanji, 1921. Bound together with this work is an essay in English, *Democracy According to the Buddhist Viewpoint*. Honolulu: Honpa Hongwanji, 1918.

———. *Chōshōin Kaikoroku* [Recollections of Chōshōin]. Honolulu: Honpa Hongwanji, 1937.

———. *Honpa Hongwanji Hawaii Kaikyōshi* [A History of the Missionary Work of the Honpa Hongwanji in Hawaii]. Honolulu: Honpa Hongwanji, 1918.

Kihara, Ryūkichi. *Hawaii Nihonjin Shi* [A History of the Japanese in Hawaii]. Tokyo: Bunsei-sha, 1935.

Morita, Sakae. *Hawaii Gojūnenshi* [A Fifty Year History of Hawaii]. Honolulu: Shineikan, 1919.

———. *Hawaii Nipponjin Hattenshi* [History of the Japanese in Hawaii]. Honolulu: Shineikan, 1915.

Nakagawa, Zenkyō. *Beifu ni Shishite* [Mission to America and Hawaii]. Kōyasan, Wakayama: 1954.

Nichiren-shū Rikkyō Kaisō Nanahyakunen Hawaii Kaikyō Gojūshūnen Kinen Dai Keisan-e; Kinen Shashin Narabini Hosshu Godairi Junkyō Kiroku [Great Commemorative Celebration of the 700th Anniversary of the Establishment and the 50th Anniversary of the Beginning of Mission Work in Hawaii of the Nichiren Sect; Commemorative Photographs and Records of the Propagation of the Teachings by Representatives of the Lord Abbot]. Nichiren Mission of Hawaii.

Okumura, Takie. *Taiheiyō no Rakuen* [A Paradise in the Pacific]. Honolulu: Saneido, 1922.

Sōga, Yasutarō. *Gojūnenkan no Hawaii Kaiko* [Reflections on Fifty Years in Hawaii]. Osaka, 1953.

————. *Tessaku Seikatsu* [Life Behind Barbed Wires]. Honolulu: United Japanese Society of Hawaii, 1948.

Tsutsumi, Takashi. *Senkyūhyaku-nijū Nendo Hawaii Satō Kōchi Rōdō Undō Shi* [An Account of the Labor Movement on Sugar Plantations in Hawaii in 1920]. Vol. 1. Honolulu, 1921.

Shingonshū Hawaii Betsuin Sōritsu Man-jisshunen-ni Saishite [On the Occasion of the Tenth Anniversary of the Founding of the Shingon Sect Mission in Hawaii]. Honolulu: Hawaii Daigoin Temple, 1927.

Yōjō no Hikari, Dendo Kinen [Mid-Ocean Illumination, Commemorating Missionary Work]. Honolulu: Jōdō Mission of Hawaii, 1934.

Yagisawa, Zenji. 'Hawaii ni okeru Nihon imin shi no issetsu.' ['A chapter in the history of Japanese emigration to Hawaii']. *Shakai Keizai Shigaku* [Studies in Social and Economic History] 4, no. 5 (August 1934).

Additional Recommended Readings on the Japanese and Japanese Buddhism in Hawaii

Andō Tarō. *Andō Tarō Bunshu* [Collected Essays of Andō Tarō]. Honolulu: Hilo Times, 1929.

Fujihana, Kyōdō. *Hawaii Jōdoshu Enkaku Gaiyō* [An Outline History of the Jōdo Sect in Hawaii]. Honolulu: Jōdo Mission of Hawaii, 1964.

Ishimura, Ichigorō. *Yonjūichinen Mae Hawaii Tokōsha Ishimura Ichigorō Kisshin Dan* [An Account of the Life of Ishimura Ichigorō Who Came to Hawaii 41 Years Ago]. 1908.

Katoda, Tetsuei. *Hawaii Shingonshū Kaikyō Enkaku Sōritsu Gojisshūnen Kinen* [The 50th Anniversary of the Establishment of the Shingon Sect Mission of Hawaii]. Honolulu: Shingon Mission of Hawaii, 1966.

Kikuchi, Shigeo, ed. *Kikuchi Chikyoku Ikō Shū* [Posthumous Works of Kikuchi Chikyoku]. Honolulu, 1966.

Komagata, Zenkyō. 'Hawaii Sōtōshū Enkaku Shi' [A History of the Sōtō Sect in Hawaii]. Honolulu: Sōtō Mission of Hawaii, 1950.

Kotani, Tokusaui. *Kaikyō No Reimeiki* [The Early Periods of the Mission]. Honolulu: Kapaa Hongwanji, 1914.

Matsuda, Mitsugu. *The Japanese in Hawaii, 1868–1967: A Bibliography of the First Hundred Years.* Honolulu: Social Science Research Institute, University of Hawaii, 1968.

Watanabe, Jirō. *Hawaii dendō no kaiko to tenbō-gojū nen no shinkō seikatsu o tsuranuita ichi shinto no shuki* [Reflections on the Hawaiian Mission, Memorandum of a Fifty Year Devotee]. Tokyo, 1959.

KEY SOURCES IN ENGLISH ON
LOCAL (HAWAIIAN) HISTORY AND BUDDHISM IN HAWAII

A Brief Survey of the Foreign Language School Question. Honolulu: Japanese Educational Association, 1923.

Anderson, Rufus. *History of the Mission of the American Board of Commissioners for Foreign Missions to the Sandwich Islands.* Boston: Congregational Publishing Society, 1870.

Barber, Joseph, Jr. *Hawaii: Restless Rampart.* New York: The Bobbs-Merrill Co., 1941.

Burrows, Edwin G. *Hawaiian Americans.* New Haven: Yale University Press, 1947.

Conroy, Hilary. *The Japanese Frontier in Hawaii, 1868–1898.* Berkeley: University of California Press, 1953.

Centennial Book: One Hundred Years of Christian Civilization in Hawaii 1820–1920. Honolulu: Central Committee of the Hawaiian Mission Centennial, 1920.

Controversy Between Japanese Labor and the Sugar Planters of Hawaii. Honolulu: Federation of Japanese Labor, 1920.

Dōbō (nos. 320–438). Honolulu: Bukkyō Seinen-kai (Young Buddhist Association of Hawaii).

Dole, Sanford B. *Memoirs of the Hawaiian Revolution.* Honolulu: Advertiser Publishing Co., Ltd., 1936.

Education of the Japanese in Hawaii in Their Own Language. Honolulu: Japanese Educational Association, 1919.

Embree, John F. 'Acculturation Among the Japanese of Kona, Hawaii.' *Memoirs of the American Anthropological Association* No. 59, 1941.

Gowen, Herbert H. *The Paradise of the Pacific: Sketches of Hawaiian Scenery and Life.* London: Skeffington & Son, 1892.

Gulick, Sidney L. *Hawaii's American-Japanese Problem: A Description of the Conditions, A Statement of the Problems and Suggestions for Their Solution.* Honolulu: Star-Bulletin, 1915.

Hawaiian Buddhist Annual (1931–1934). Honolulu: Honpa Hongwanji.

Hawaiian Historical Society Annual Reports (on file at the HMCS Library).

Jarves, James J. *Scenes and Scenery in the Sandwich Islands.* London: Edward Moxon, 1844.

Johannessen, Edward. *The Hawaiian Labor Movement: A Brief History.* Boston: Bruce Humphries, 1956.

Kuykendall, Ralph S. 'The Earliest Japanese Labor Immigration to Hawaii.' University of Hawaii *Occasional Papers,* 25 (1935).

———. *The Hawaiian Kingdom, 1778–1854, Vol. I.* Honolulu: University of Hawaii Press, 1947.

———. *The Hawaiian Kingdom, 1854–1874, Vol. II.* Honolulu: University of Hawaii Press, 1953.

———. *The Hawaiian Kingdom, 1874–1893, Vol. III.* Honolulu: University of Hawaii Press, 1967.

Kuykendall, Ralph S. and Day, A. Grove. *Hawaii: A History*. Englewood Cliffs, N.J.: Prentice-Hall, Inc., 1961.

Mesick, Lillian S. 'Buddhist Propaganda in Hawaii.' *Paradise of the Pacific*, March 1903.

———. 'Buddhists Build New Temple in Hawaii.' *Paradise of the Pacific*, December 1926.

———. 'The 88 Holy Places on Hawaii's Garden Isle.' *Paradise of the Pacific*, December 1926.

———. 'Ancient Faith Lives in the Hills Near Lawaii [*sic*].' *Honolulu Star-Bulletin*, 25 July 1925.

Okumura, Takie. *Seventy Years of Divine Blessings*. Honolulu: Takie Okumura, 1939.

———, ed. *Thirty Years of Christian Mission Work Among the Japanese in Hawaii*. Honolulu: Takie Okumura, 1917. Text is in Japanese with the first part in English.

Okumura, Takie and Okumura, Umetarō, eds. *Hawaii's American-Japanese Problem, A Campaign to Remove Causes of Friction Between the American People and Japanese: Report of the First Year's Campaign, Jan. to Dec., 1921*. Honolulu: Takie and Umetarō Okumura, 1923.

Palmer, Albert W. *The Human Side of Hawaii: Race Problems in the Mid-Pacific*. Boston: The Pilgrim Press, 1924.

Paradise of the Pacific. January 1888 to December 1962.

Short History of the Honpa Hongwanji Mission. Honolulu: Honpa Hongwanji of Honolulu, 1931.

Social Process in Hawaii. Joint annual publication by the Romanzo Adams Social Research Laboratory and the Sociology Club of the University of Hawaii, Honolulu.

Survey of Education in Hawaii, Bulletin No. 16. Washington, D.C.: Bureau of Education, Dept. of the Interior, 1920.

Taylor, Albert P. *Under Hawaiian Skies*. Honolulu: Advertiser Publishing Co., Ltd., 1922.

Thurston, Lorrin A. *Memoirs of the Hawaiian Revolution*. Honolulu: Advertiser Publishing Co., Ltd., 1936.

Wakukawa, Ernest K. *A History of the Japanese People in Hawaii*. Honolulu: The Toyo Shoin, 1938.

Credits for Illustrations

Sōryū Kagahi, Honpa Hongwanji of Hawaii
Lorrin A. Thurston, Public Archives of Hawaii
Hilo Honpa Hongwanji, Bishop Kanmo Imamura
Takie Okumura, Ruth Okumura Neville
Hōji Satomi, Honpa Hongwanji of Hawaii
Yemyō Imamura, Honpa Hongwanji of Hawaii
Kanmo Imamura, Photo Hawaii
Fred Higginbotham Makino, *Hawaii Hōchi*
Edward P. Irwin, Public Archives of Hawaii
George Wright, J. Stowell Wright
Ernest Shinkaku Hunt, Takiko Ichinose
Replica of Kamakura Buddha at Lahaina, Young Buddhist
    Association of Honolulu

Index

68; restriction of immigration of, 71; first generation and faith-healing cults, 186, 193–197; internment of, 187; delinquency statistics, 184–185. *See also* Nisei Japanese Education(al) Association, 97, 98, 114, 139, 180, 183

Japanese Federation of Labor, 119, 119n, 120, 121, 123, 124

Japanese Society of Hawaii, 119, 142, 144

Jōdo-Shin-shū (True Pure Land Sect): origin, 14; struggle for survival in Japan, 17; arrival of first priest in Hawaii, 33–36; arrival of other priests, 79. *See also* Honpa Hongwanji

Jōdo-shū (Pure Land Sect): origin, 14; in Hawaii, 59–60, 74, 94, 150, 178, 181, 187

Joint Committee for the Revision of Textbooks, 138–143

Jones-Costigan Sugar Act, 174, 179n

Judd, Albert F., 108–109, 112–113

Judd, Henry P., 129–130, 156, 157, 166

Kagahi, Sōryū: in Honolulu, 33–36, 38, 40, 41; on the Big Island, 42–44; returns to Japan, 44–45

Kalakaua, King: and reciprocity, 28; trip around the world, 29, 29n; welcomes Gannen Mono, 30; character and scandalous reign of, 36–38; spendthrift policies of, 53; death of, 52

Kameyama, Kōō, 103

Kamikaze, 12, 12n

Kanayasu, Sanju, 62, 86

Kanda, Shigehide, 51, 71, 121

Karma, 9, 10–11, 85, 156

Kashiwa, Ryūten, 189

Kawahara, Senyei, 70, 83

Kegon, School of Buddhism, 195, 195n

Ken-Hokkekyō. *See* Nichiren-shū

Kimura, Saiji, 42, 48, 52, 62, 64, 87

Kinney, Henry W., 112n

Kirby, M. T., 132, 133–134, 151–152, 153, 208

Kitamura, Mrs. Sayo (Ōgamisama), 196–197

Kōbō Daishi, 13, 101, 102n

Komagata, Zenkyō, 130, 189

Kondo, Ryōshō, 204, 205, 205n

Kubokawa, Kyokujo, 189

Kuchiba, Gikyō: as bishop of Honpa Hongwanji, 171–172; intense nationalism of, 178–179, 190; encourages patriotism of Nisei, 185; interned, 189; returns to Japan, 198

Kūkai. *See* Kōbō Daishi

Kwan-Ti, 40, 41

Kwan-Yin (Kwannon-sama; Avalokitesvara), 41

Labor: shortage of, 21, 29, 69; strikes, 69, 72–73, 75, 90–92, 117–124 passim, 134–135; problems attributed to agitators, 120, 121, 122

Lahaina Buddhist Cultural Park, 202

Language schools: early Christian, 86–87; early Buddhist, 87–90 passim; American opposition to, 89–90, 99–100, 124–125; rivalry between Buddhist and Christian (or Christian-sponsored) schools, 95–100 passim, 168–170; revision of textbooks and curriculum, 98–99, 138–143 passim; litigation battle, genesis of, 107–108; bills and acts to regulate, 108–110, 124, 127–129, 145; crisis viewed as religious issue, 112–114; findings and recommendations of Federal Survey Commission, 125–127; testing constitutionality of statutes, 143–147; Supreme Court decision on, 147; revived in 1930s, 174, 179–184; defended by Japanese press, 181–182; and heroism of Nisei, 188; attempts to abolish during World War II, 191–192; revived after World War II, 202

Liliuokalani, Queen, 43, 52–53, 54

McCarthy, Charles J., 107, 128

MacCaughey, Vaughan: opposition to language schools, 108, 141, 142; denounces Buddhism, 111–112

McNally, R. A., 122, 125

Mahāyāna: meaning and historical evolution of, 10–11; schools of, in Japan, 14–16

Makino, Fred H.: as a friend of labor, 90, 92, 117, 118; favors maintenance of schools, 110, 139, 146–147, 183

Massie rape and murder case, 174, 179n

Matheson, Roderick O.: on language school crisis, 114; defends planters, 118, 119

Mead, Royal D., 120, 121, 121n

Meiji Emperor, 22, 22n, 29, 44

Meshiya-kyō, 196

Middle Way. *See* Path, Noble Eight-fold

Ministers. *See* Protestant clergy

Missionaries, earliest Christian, 25–26. *See also* Priests, Buddhist

Miyama, Kanichi, 48–49, 50–51

Miyamoto, Ejun, 60, 61, 62

Miyazaki, Hiseki, 81, 82, 86, 189

Morality, Buddhist view of, 85

Moroi, Rokurō: praises Buddhist work in Islands, 85, 106; advocates revision of language school text-books, 98; animosity toward Shin-gon sect, 102–103; refused member-ship in YMCA, 104; blames Japanese Christians for language school crisis, 112; praises new bonus system, 117

Myōnyo, Abbot, 33, 44, 45

Nakayama, Miki, 194

Nationalism, American: aggravates anti-language school sentiments, 93–94, 107–108, 114, 124; and re-ligion, 111–112, 185, 207

Nationalism, Japanese: displayed by immigrants, 54–55, 75; taught in Buddhist schools, 88, 89, 126; re-surgence of, in 1930s, 174–176, 178; displayed by Buddhist priests, 177, 190, 199

Naturalization of aliens, 110–111

Navayana, 165

New Americans Campaign and Con-ferences, 149–150, 182–183, 184

New religions of Japan (*shin-shūkyō*), 194–197

Nichiren, 15–16, 175

Nichiren-shū: in Japan, 15; in Hawaii, 70, 130, 178, 181

Nippu-Jiji, 140

Nirvana: potential for in all men, 5; impediments to realization of, 6; meaning of, 7–8; ways to realization of, 9–10, 11, 13–14, 167

Nisei (second-generation Japanese): Buddhist work among, 132–133, 151–154 passim, 158, 164–165, 171–172; expatriation of, 148, 185; drift away from Buddhism and Oriental heritage, 148, 158, 160–161, 171–172, 176–177, 184, 186, 192, 193, 206; and dual citizenship problem, 148, 180; pro-Buddhist tendencies, 155, 161–162, 185, 200, 206–207; toward language schools, 172–173; delinquency statistics for, 184–185; in World War II, 187–188; opposi-tion to Shinto, 198. *See* Educational Campaigns; New Americans Cam-paigns and Conferences

Nishi Hongwanji. *See* Honpa Hon-gwanji

Nishizawa, Dōrin, 47, 52

Noble Eightfold Path. *See* Path, Noble Eightfold

Nottingham, Elizabeth K., 31n

Nunome, Chōsei, 122

Ōgamisama. *See* Kitamura, Mrs. Sayo

Ogino, Gyōun, 47

Okabe, Gakuō, 60, 66

Okabe, Jirō, 43–44, 47, 51, 52, 55–56, 71

Okada, Mokichi, 196

Okumura, Takie: arrival in Hawaii, 56–57; assists victims of fire and plague, 64; opposition to Buddhist priests, 66; and first language school of importance, 86, 87, 95; intervenes in 1909 strike, 92; advocates revision of language school textbooks, 97–99 passim; background, 106–107; op-position to Buddhism and Buddhist institutions, 108, 116, 130, 134, 136–137, 138, 140, 149–150, 159, 167, 177, 178–184 passim, 191–192; opposes strike of 1920, 121, 123–124; Chain School program of, 168–170, 180; advocates closing of Shinto temples, 198; death of, 202; last ambition of, 203

Okumura, Umetarō (son of Takie),

263

worship, 44–45, 111; State Shinto (Imperial Cult), 44–45, 174–175, 176, 198; in Hawaii, 103–104, 178; myth of divine favor, 174–175

Shiraishi, Gyōkai, 59

Short, Walter C., 187

Shūshin, 86, 88, 98

Siddhārtha. *See* Gautama

Sit Moon, 40

Sōga, Yasutarō: praises Japan's rise to power, 75; advocates maintenance of language schools, 107, 180; opposes establishment of Hongwanji English Department, 132, 133; on Joint Committee for textbook revision, 138; criticism of interned priests, 189, 190

Sokabe, Shirō, 51, 87, 95, 121, 202

Sōka Gakkai, 197, 206

Sōtō, School of Zen: origin in Japan, 16; origin and growth in Hawaii, 70, 101, 130, 150–151, 155, 181; and 1920 protest march, 123; and Japanese nationalism, 175, 199; YBAS, 201

Statehood and statehood hearings, 177, 179, 179n, 182

Stevens, John L., 53, 54

Stevenson, Robert Louis, 38, 57n

Suffering, Cause of. *See* Four Noble Truths

Sugar industry: beginnings, 20–21; effects of reciprocity on, 28–29; boom after annexation, 68; Jones-Costigan Act, 174

Sunday schools, Buddhist: established on plantations, 83, 84, 131; in Honolulu and other urban areas, 96, 131; growth of, 129; and Nisei criticism of, 162; revitalized by Ernest Hunt, 165; decline in enrollment of, 184; revival of, after World War II, 202

Supreme Court, decisions on foreign language school statutes, 145, 147

Tai Hsü, 164, 167

Takaki, Gyōun, 70, 100

Taniguchi, Masaharu, 194–195

Taoism, 11, 12

Tariki-kyō, 14, 15, 206

Teachings of the Buddha: 7–10, 207, 209; on moral progress, 85; on just wages, 122–123; subordinated to Japanese ethnocentrism, 175–176

Temperance organizations, 24, 35, 50, 57

Temples: early, 42, 43, 60, 64–65, 66, 70, 83–84; outnumber Christian churches, 178, 181; evacuated after Pearl Harbor attack, 187; attempt to abolish during World War II, 192; closing of, 193; restored, 198

Tenney, E. D., 68, 118

Tenrikyō, 194

Tenshō-Kōtai-Jingū-kyō, 196–197

Terakoya: in Japan, 17; in Hawaii, 86

Territory of Hawaii, establishment of, 66–67

Theravāda (Doctrine of the Elders), 10, 65

Thurston, Lorrin A.: role in Revolution of 1893, 37–38, 53; on nationalism, 108; and strike of 1920, 123–124; on language schools, 128, 143, 144

T'ien-t'ai (Tendai) sect, 13

Tōdaiji of Hawaii, 195–196

Tokugawa shogunate, 17–19

Trishnā, 9, 85

True Pure Land sect. *See* Jōdo-Shin-shū

Tsunoda, Ryūsaku, 96, 98

Ullambana Sūtra, 77

Umehara, Shinryū, 176–177

Urabon, season of, 77

Vade Mecum, 154, 162

Van Reed, Eugene, 19, 21–22, 27, 29

Vaughan, Horace, 110, 111, 111n

Wadman, John, 73, 74

Whaling, 20, 21

Wright, George: union leader, 134, 135; as a Buddhist, 154, 208

Yada, Chōnosuke, 103, 138, 143

Yamada, Shōi, 62, 64, 81, 86

Yamasaki, Katsumi C., 162–163

Yamazaki, Jisho, 199, 200, 207

Yempuku, Jōsho, 81, 82

Young Buddhist Association. *See* Young Men's Buddhist Association
Young Men's Buddhist Association: first organized, 65; on plantations, 83, 84; and Honpa Hongwanji's Americanization program, 105; and 1920 strike, 119, 120; growth in membership, 129, 131, 142, 151; Inter-Island Conventions, 151, 166, 172, 176, 185, 200, 206; Inter-Island Federation, 151, 172; Pan-Pacific Conferences, 165–166, 167, 172; Pan-Pacific YMBA, Hawaii Branch, 172; held suspect, 177; decline in membership, 184; reactivated and expanded after World War II, 200–201; "Rainbow" YBA, 201; organization of Young Buddhist Association, 200, 201

Yujiri, Hōgen, 101, 102

Yzendoorn, Reginald, 57n

Zen (Ch'an) sect, 16. *See also* Sōtō and Rinzai